A
Comprehensive
Annotated
Bibliography
of
American
Black
English

A
Comprehensive
Annotated
Bibliography
of
American
Black
English

ILA WALES BRASCH
and
WALTER MILTON BRASCH

LOUISIANA STATE UNIVERSITY PRESS / BATON ROUGE

for

*Milton and Helen Brasch, who have sacrificed so much of
their own lives for others, and in so doing have helped make
this life just a little better—but most of all,
because of their love and guidance*

and for

*Mabel Wales and the memory of Ray Wales for their love
and encouragement through the years*

ISBN 0–8071–0069–2
Library of Congress Catalog Card Number 73–83908
Copyright © 1974 by Louisiana State University Press
Manufactured in the United States of America
Printed by Heritage Printers, Inc., Charlotte, North Carolina
Designed by Albert R. Crochet

Preface

WHAT BEGAN in the spring of 1971 as a simple attempt to classify some of the more significant studies in American Black English scholarship changed direction a few months later as we began to realize the necessity for a comprehensive bibliography that would serve the linguist, educator, social worker, anthropologist, psychologist, sociologist, audiologist, speech pathologist, and journalist, as well as the lay public.

In the early stages of preparing this bibliography, we realized that although there was much duplication of research and review studies—much of it seemingly unnecessary—there were also several gaps in the study of American Black English. These are gaps that, we hope, will be recognized and filled in response to this bibliography.

During our preliminary research, we became increasingly aware of the almost limitless number of errors of resource information—everything from incorrect dates on catalogue cards to incorrect—and, on occasion, false—citations in journals and books. We therefore decided that there would be only two ways in which an article, book, or professional paper would be included in this bibliography. In almost 95 percent of the cases, we used what we called the "direct method"—one of the compilers actually had to *see* the article, book, or professional paper for it to be included. By actually having the material, we solved two major problems. First, we were able to record all bibliographic information accurately. Second, we didn't have to rely upon abstracts, other authors' comments, or hearsay in order to properly annotate the citation. One of us—more often, both of us —actually read or thoroughly skimmed virtually every item that appears in this bibliography. This, obviously, increased our work tremendously, but we believe that this diligence will benefit the reader.

To secure these materials, we used the full resources of the Ohio University and Ohio State University libraries and, through the interlibrary loan system, university, public, and private libraries throughout the country. Tracking down these materials demanded our best journalistic skills— skills that might, on occasion, have rivaled even those of the immortal Mr. Holmes. More than four hundred letters were written, and almost two hundred telephone calls were made, in pursuit of the original material.

However, sometimes it was humanly impossible to secure a copy of the material. It was either extremely rare, of limited circulation, or owned by and for use only in one particular library. Therefore, we used the "double-check method." In slightly more than 5 percent of all entries, we accepted a work as existing if it was referred to in at least two separate articles, if it was listed in a reputable index and confirmed by another source, or if the author or a professional librarian verified its existence by sight. No possibilities were left unchecked. If, with all the resources at our command, we were unable to verify the authenticity of a citation, we then reasoned that it would be unfair to send our readers on what might be a wild book-chase. During the course of compiling and editing this bibliography of about two thousand entries, we accumulated a "No" pile of more than four hundred citations—references that were either irrelevant to the study of Black English but had to be checked out anyway, or were of doubtful existence.

However, it would be a miracle indeed if this bibliography were totally free of error. Dealing with so many entries almost makes it impossible not to have a few errors. A computer analysis indicates that, for such a work, the number of potential errors is comprehensible only to another computer. Our goal has been to reduce error to the absolute minimum; should mistakes occur, we hope they will be insignificant, causing few problems or delays to the reader.

It is also possible that, dealing with a topic as broad as Black English, we may have accidentally overlooked a few references. In fact, we would be surprised if *any* bibliographer could include all possible references to any given topic. If there are omissions, they are entirely unintentional.

More than 80 percent of our entries are annotated. Those that are not annotated should not be considered inferior to those that are. In some instances, the title explains the work better than an annotation could.

After considerable discussion, it was decided that our annotations would be a "modified proposal/summary." We decided against using critical judgments for several reasons, the most important being that we honestly felt that every article had some value in it. We believe that the reader must decide for himself, within his own research framework, whether an article has any value. In our own research, we admit that we found numerous articles and books that we were tempted to dismiss as "Worthless trash. Of little use except to impress the author's tenure committee." But what we think worthless may provide the information to help fill the gap in someone else's research. We also found numerous articles and books that, in our opinions, were well written and had strong insight into the field of Black English study, making a strong contribution to the understanding of a very difficult language. But again we are judging only on the basis of our own experiences, our own world-view. To another, perhaps, the same articles and books would be dull, insignificant, and meaningless.

The function of a bibliography is not to do the work of the researcher, but to provide a valuable reference tool so that the researcher-writer can find information more easily. For that reason, we decided that there was little necessity for doing extensive summaries of each article, book, or professional paper. The annotations are short, crisp, and serve to advise the reader that such an item exists and what its basic content is, thus preventing a lot of wasted searching. As any journalist knows, we found it more difficult to edit a ten-thousand-word article into a couple of sentences than into a couple of paragraphs. Within that couple of sentences—few of the annotations exceed one hundred words—we had to condense the author's material and intention into a meaningful brief statement.

For this first edition, we decided against cross-referencing by topics. Our problem of locating, compiling, and annotating the material was task enough for a first edition. However, the reader should be aware that there are ten classes of entries contained within this bibliography—none of the classes is more important than any other, and the order of their listing is by no means any indication of their importance.

1. Research Studies into American Black English—Included within this class are field surveys, linguistic analyses, and experimental tests of hypotheses. Most master's theses and doctoral dissertations fall within this area.

2. General Studies—Included are the nonquantitative analyses of American Black English. Most historical analyses, including arguments on creolization and African origins, fall within this area.

3. Pedagogy—Citations within this area are usually nonquantitative and have application—either direct or indirect—to the educational system. These articles often suggest ways to teach English—both Black and standard—or express theories on the role of Black English in the classroom.

4. General Interest—Less technical in presentation, these articles survey either a part or the entire field of Black English, and are usually directed to the lay public. Many of the articles on Black English which appear in popular magazines and newspapers are included within this class.

5. Reviews—There are few reviews included within this bibliography, because to include all reviews of every book or major article would have been impossible. Those reviews that are included generally add to the knowledge of American Black English, rather than confine themselves to value judgments or a rehashing of the material.

6. Folklore—To the language scholar, folklore provides one of the richest sources of primary evidence available. But to include all Black folklore within this bibliography would have been a monumental task,

one that would have necessitated a separate bibliography. What is represented, therefore, are the more significant studies in Black folklore, as well as a few minor studies for historical and comparative purposes. There are actually two kinds of folklore represented—primary recording of folktales, and secondary research into Black folklore.

7. Slave Narratives—During the first half of the nineteenth century, slave narratives by the thousands flooded the northern markets. Some narratives sold only a few copies; some went into as many as a dozen editions. One of the problems faced by the journalist and the linguist is to separate those narratives that have been extensively edited (or, in some cases, written by Whites) from those written by Blacks and largely unedited.

8. Literature—We have been able to analyze dialect and trace language origins and development from literature. Several articles, short stories, and books from both the nineteenth and twentieth centuries are included. Both Black and White writers are represented in this section.

9. Related Materials—In elementary mathematics, two points are needed to make a line. The same applies in American Black English studies. The study of American Black English in isolation may be valuable, but it is not complete. It is important to be able to compare and contrast American Black English with other Black English languages. Within the related-materials class are studies of Creoles and Pidgins within several geographic areas—their linguistic descriptions, as well as the folklore of the area. In addition to the Black English studies from other geographical areas, we have included a few studies in Negro-French.

10. "Disadvantaged" Approach—At various times, Blacks have been euphemistically referred to as "culturally disadvantaged," "culturally deprived," "culturally handicapped," or "culturally underprivileged." Many of the articles that use these terms often refer to Blacks. However, many articles actually do refer to the socio-economic class of people—Black, Red, Yellow, *and* White—rather than specifically to race. During our research, we became increasingly aware that being Black and speaking Black English does not make someone "culturally disadvantaged." Because of the many implications within these studies they, too, have been included.

Sometimes it isn't possible to put a label on an article or book. Like people, written materials often defy labeling. Some of the items in this bibliography don't fit into any of the ten classes, but we felt they were of such importance to Black English study that they had to be included. It's highly possible that some people will find these items useful, while others may wonder why we kept such material. We felt that it was better to include the material for possible reference rather than omit it.

Persons working in Black English are well aware that they're operating within a highly controversial field, one in which a major problem is to distinguish myth from fact. Often the Black English scholar finds that he's spending as much time demythologizing attitudes about the language, as he's spending searching out new facts, or making better descriptions, or investigating practical applications. Essentially, there are three main areas of discussion about Black English.

The linguistic Creole position points to certain types of rules and to historical development to justify its claims that Black English is, or has been, a separate language. An additional claim of this position is that Black English is becoming decreolized. The Creolists believe that although surface structures of some Black English varieties and other dialects may be the same, the deep structures are different, and that there are some rules that apply only to Black English speech. The Creolist often makes comparative studies with African and Caribbean languages.

The dialect geographers, representing another position, argue that the rules identified by the Creolists also exist in other dialects of English, as well as in Black English. The speech of Blacks, they maintain, may be closer to the speech of the region they live in, rather than universal. The dialect geographers also note that the language of the Black reflects his own culture, and that it is not possible to assume that all Blacks share a common language.

A third position is that of the deficit theorists. The deficit theory, which is sometimes advanced by educators and social scientists, essentially notes that that there may, in fact, be definite rules that are present in Black English. However, deficit theorists aren't as concerned with the status of rules as they are with the possibility that Black English does not have the potential for success in American society. The deficit theorists often claim that, because of cultural deprivation, the Black English speaker has not only linguistic but cognitive deficiencies.

There are many questions about Black English that cannot be answered at present, only posed. It is hoped that this bibliography will enable the researcher to begin where others have left off in finding answers to these vitally important questions. To the best of our abilities, we have attempted to remain thoroughly objective about these positions in the preparation of the bibliography. We have deliberately avoided making value judgments of these relative positions. But the reader must be aware that controversy exists and that, as yet, there are no definitive answers. Writing *A Comprehensive Annotated Bibliography of American Black English* has been both a pleasant and frustrating experience. It is our hope that the reader will get as much out of this bibliography as we have put into it.

Ila Wales Brasch
Walter Milton Brasch

Athens, Ohio
January, 1974

Acknowledgments

ANYONE WRITING a book is faced with many moments—or, in our case, sometimes days—of utter despair. Nothing is going right. For every error corrected, two more pop up. For every article located, two more remain missing. Sometimes it seemed as if the entire project should never have been begun; the problems generated far exceeded any meaningful solutions. On occasion, we felt like closeting ourselves in our offices and throwing all our articles, books, papers, and records out the window—to be picked up by any wandering person with a sudden masochistic urge.

Through it all, however, we received quite a lot of valuable assistance and comfort which made the struggle worthwhile. Our appreciation and respect go to Richard Brook and Gerald Udell. Dr. Brook, currently associate dean of instruction at Plymouth State College and former director of the linguistics program at the University of Northern Iowa, first initiated us into the study of Black English. It was Dr. Udell, associate professor of English at Ohio University, who provided the impetus for the development of a publishable bibliography. His advice and suggestions were greatly appreciated and most helpful, and his friendship is truly valued.

To Gilbert D. Schneider, former chairman of the department of linguistics at Ohio University, we owe a debt that can never be paid. No greater friend, colleague, or employer have any two people ever had. He kept our spirits up and helped us in more ways than can ever be counted. For his advice, guidance, and encouragement, we are truly thankful.

Norman H. Dohn, professor of journalism at Ohio University and John H. Timmis III, associate professor of interpersonal communications at Ohio University, provided some new insights into historiography and bibliographic writing which added significantly to the base from which we worked. We also appreciate the assistance of librarians Ann T. Johnson and Theodore S. Foster who helped us overcome a number of bibliographic problems.

Thanks are also due John Frederick, the research assistant who aided us during the final stages of the project. Roberta Milligan and Lynne Lysiak assisted in tying together the final loose ends.

Very special thanks are extended to Roger D. Abrahams, professor of English and Anthropology and director of the African and Afro-American Research Institute of the University of Texas; Richard W. Bailey, assistant professor of English at the University of Michigan; William A. Stewart, president of the Education Study Center; Walter A. Wolfram, professor in the Graduate Division of Communication Sciences at Federal City College; and J. L. Dillard, director of the Language and Behavior Program at Yeshiva University. They have generously shared their time and knowledge with us.

Leslie Phillabaum and his staff at the Louisiana State University Press merit special consideration for having ably guided the book to publication.

Our thanks also go to the scores of professional linguists, language specialists, educators, social scientists, speech audiologists and pathologists, and librarians who have assisted us during the course of our research.

Finally, we are indebted to the Ohio University Department of Linguistics, the Research Institute, and the Graduate College for their assistance.

A
Comprehensive
Annotated
Bibliography
of
American
Black
English

A

Aarons, Alfred C., Barbara Y. Gordon, and William A. Stewart, eds. *Linguistic-Cultural Differences and American Education*, special issue of *Florida FL Reporter*, VII (Spring/Summer, 1969). 175 pp.

Teacher-oriented anthology of forty-three articles on culture and dialect, presented in four sections: the role of the school; cultural pluralism; theoretical considerations; and curriculum development. Includes both original and reprinted articles, approximately half of which deal with Black English.

Abbot, Francis H. *Eight Negro Songs*. Edited by Alfred J. Swan. New York: Enoch & Sons, 1923. 47 pp.

An introduction accompanies the lyrics.

Abel, James Walden. "A Study of the Speech of Six Freshmen from Southern University (Negro)." Doctoral dissertation, Louisiana State University, Baton Rouge, 1949. 961 pp.

A general dialect study which includes phonetic transcriptions of question-and-answer sessions. The data suggests that standard English is more prevalent than nonstandard English, but that there is a significant number of nonstandard English patterns.

Abrahams, Roger D. "The Advantages of Black English." *Florida FL Reporter*, VIII (Spring/Fall, 1970), 27–30, 51. [Also in Johanna S. DeStefano, ed., *Language, Society, and Education: A Profile of Black English*. Worthington, Ohio: Charles A. Jones, 1973. Pp. 97–106.]

Discusses ways in which teachers can utilize Black English as a positive factor in classroom situations.

———. *Afro-American Language and Culture in the Classroom*. ERIC document ED 049 203. Washington, D.C., 1970. 23 pp.

Discusses the importance of the child's home-life culture to speech

1

and education. Notes that the schools should try to recognize, then understand, the reasons for linguistic differences. Points out that to understand Black English one must also understand the culture and social status of the speaker.

―――. "Black Talk and Black Education," in Alfred C. Aarons, Barbara Y. Gordon, and William A. Stewart, eds., *Linguistic-Cultural Differences and American Education*, special issue of *Florida FL Reporter*, VII (Spring/Summer, 1969). Pp. 10–12.

Analysis of Black-White culture problems in the schools—stereotypes and misunderstandings fostered by a lack of knowledge of the culture of the student.

―――. "The Black Uses of Black English." Paper presented at the Conference on Continuities and Discontinuities in Afro-American Societies and Cultures, April 2–4, 1970, at Mona, Jamaica.

―――. "The 'Catch' in Negro Philadelphia." *Keystone Folklore Quarterly*, VIII (1963), 107–11.

―――. "The Changing Concept of the Negro Hero," in *The Golden Log*. Publication of the Texas Folklore Society, No. 31. Dallas, 1962. Pp. 119–34. [Reprinted in Bobbs-Merrill Reprint Series in Black Studies, New York.]

Includes a description of signifying.

―――. *Deep Down in the Jungle: Negro Narrative Folklore from the Streets of Philadelphia*. Hatboro, Pa.: Folklore Associates, 1964. Rev. ed., Chicago: Aldine Publishing Co., 1970. 278 pp.

Major pioneering study of the life and language in the urban Black ghetto of Philadelphia. Includes a look at jokes, toasts (Black narrative verse), and the dozens (the Black verbal-insult game). Non-linguistic narrative based upon two years of fieldwork. Glossary.

―――. Foreword to Dorothy Scarborough, *On the Trail of the Negro Folksong*. Reprint edition. Hatboro, Pa.: Folklore Associates, 1963. Pp. i–ix.

―――. Foreword to Howard W. Odum and Guy B. Johnson, *The Negro and His Songs*. Reprint edition. Hatboro, Pa.: Folklore Associates, 1964. Pp. iii–xix.

―――. "Joking: The Training of the Man of Words in Talking Broad," in Thomas Kochman, ed., *Rappin' and Stylin' Out: Communication in Urban Black America*. Champaign: University of Illinois Press, 1972. Pp. 215–20.

Discussion of joking and its relation to the language and culture of Black life. Includes several dozens rhymes and stories.

———. "Playing the Dozens." *Journal of American Folklore*, LXXV (July–September, 1962), 209–20. [Reprinted in Bobbs-Merrill Reprint Series in Black Studies, New York, 1970.] [Also in Alan Dundes, ed., *Mother Wit from the Laughing Barrel*. Englewood Cliffs, N.J.: Prentice-Hall, 1972. Pp. 295–309.]

Examines and analyzes the dozens, citing several examples.

———. *Positively Black*. Englewood Cliffs, N.J.: Prentice-Hall, 1970. 177 pp.

Presents several toasts and folktales. Includes discussion on Black language, pp. 15–24.

———. "Public Drama and Common Values in Two Caribbean Islands." *Trans-action*, VI (July–August, 1968), 62–71. [Also in Norman E. Whitten, Jr., and John F. Szwed, eds., *Afro-American Anthropology: Contemporary Perspectives*. New York: The Free Press, 1970. Pp. 163–78.]

Examines styles of expression common to Black communities in the United States and the British West Indies. Shows how differences in traditional patterns of performance on two Carribbean islands are related to the social structures of the communities.

———. "Rapping and Capping: Black Talk as Art," in John F. Szwed, ed., *Black Americans*. New York: Basic Books, 1970. Pp. 143–53.

———. "The Shaping of Folklore Traditions in the British West Indies." *Journal of Inter-American Studies*, XIII, (July, 1967), 456–80.

———. "Some Jump-Rope Rhymes from South Philadelphia." *Keystone Folklore Quarterly*, VIII (1963), 3–15.

———. "Some Riddles from the Negro of Philadelphia." *Keystone Folklore Quarterly*, VII (1962), 10–17.

———. "Speech Mas' on Tobago," in Wilson Mathes Hudson, ed., *Tire Shrinker to Dragster*. Publication of the Texas Folklore Society, Vol. 34. Dallas, 1968. Pp. 125–44.

Description of Speech Mas' (speech band, speech masquerade), a feature of the West Indies carnival celebration.

———. "Stereotyping and Beyond," in Roger D. Abrahams and Rudolph C. Troike, eds., *Language and Cultural Diversity in American Education*. Englewood Cliffs, N. J.: Prentice-Hall, 1972. Pp. 19–29.

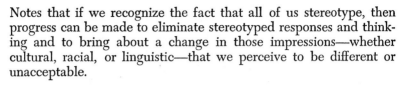

Notes that if we recognize the fact that all of us stereotype, then progress can be made to eliminate stereotyped responses and thinking and to bring about a change in those impressions—whether cultural, racial, or linguistic—that we perceive to be different or unacceptable.

———. " 'Talking My Talk': Black English and Social Segmentation in Black Communities." *Florida FL Reporter*, X (Spring/Fall, 1972), 29–38, 58. [Also in Dell H. Hymes, ed., *Language in Society and Culture*. 2nd ed. New York: Harper & Row, 1974.]

Outlines an approach to Black English which emphasizes the range of varieties of Black English. Also discusses the influence of a strong cultural focus on language.

———. "The Toast," in Horace P. Beck, ed., *Folklore in Action: Essays for Discussion in Honor of MacEdward Leach*. Philadelphia: American Folklore Society, 1962.

———. "Traditions of Eloquence in Afro-American Communities." *Journal of Inter-American Studies and World Affairs*, XII (1970), 505–27.

Discusses the tradition of eloquent speechmaking as observed in Black communities in the West Indies.

———. "The Training of the Man of Words in Talking Sweet." *Language in Society*, I (Spring, 1972), 15–29.

Discussion of social stratification of language in Black English. Distinguishes between "talking sweet" (house talk) and "talking bad" (away from home).

———. "Trickster, The Outrageous Hero," in Tristram Potter Coffin, ed., *Our Living Traditions*. New York: Basic Books, 1968. Pp. 170–78.

———. "A True and Exact Survey of Talking Black." Paper presented at the Conference on Ethnography of Speaking, April 20–22, 1972, at Austin, Texas. 106 pp.

Discussion of the ethnography of communication, especially woofing, jiving, signifying, badmouthing, the dozens, and rapping. Gives examples of Black conversations of many types, but concentrates on house talk and street talk, noting that house talk is primarily between the "Momma" and the children, while street talk is between male peers. Also discusses man-woman talk and situational constraints of speech as the result of physical environment. Appendices on gossip, the checkerboard, and three woofing scenes.

———."The White Community and Black Culture." Paper presented at the Workshop on Issues of Community and Research Group Relationships of the National Institute of Child Health and Human Development, March 8–10, 1970, at New Orleans. 13 pp.

States that the recognition of Black and White cultures is a prerequisite to meaningful study of Black culture.

Abrahams, Roger D., and Geneva Gay. "Black Culture in the Classroom," in Roger D. Abrahams and Rudolph C. Troike, eds., *Language and Cultural Diversity in American Education*. Englewood Cliffs, N.J.: Prentice-Hall, 1972. Pp. 67–84.

Points out anthropological and linguistic distinctions between Black and White American culture.

————. "Talking Black in the Classroom," in Roger D. Abrahams and Rudolph C. Troike, eds., *Language and Cultural Diversity in American Education*. Englewood Cliffs., N.J.: Prentice-Hall, 1972. 200–207.

Deals with Black English implications in the classroom and points to a few biases surrounding Black English.

Abrahams, Roger D., and John F. Szwed. *Afro-American Folklore—An Annotated Bibliography*. Austin: American Folklore Society and University of Texas Press, forthcoming.

Major annotated bibliography of Black folklore. Includes all media.

Abrahams, Roger D., and Rudolph C. Troike, eds. *Language and Cultural Diversity in American Education*. Englewood Cliffs, N.J.: Prentice-Hall, 1972. 339 pp.

A cross-section of articles with the focus on both explaining and demythologizing language and dialects. Divided into six sections: The Problem, Culture in Education, Language, Sociolinguistics, Black English, and Applications. Among the original articles are "Stereotyping and Beyond" by Roger D. Abrahams; and "Black Culture in the Classroom" and "Talking Black in the Classroom" by Roger D. Abrahams and Geneva Gay. Among the reprinted articles are "The Relationship of the Speech of American Negroes to the Speech of Whites" by Raven I. McDavid, Jr., and Virginia Glenn McDavid; "Sociolinguistic Factors in the History of American Negro Dialects" and "On the Use of Negro Dialect in the Teaching of Reading" by William A. Stewart; "The Logic of Nonstandard English" and "Some Sources of Reading Problems for Negro Speakers of Nonstandard English" by William Labov; "Interrelatedness of Certain Deviant Grammatical Structures in Negro Nonstandard Dialect" by Riley B. Smith; "A Second Dialect Is Not a Foreign Language" by Virginia French Allen; and "On Language Arts and Minority-Group Children" by Richard L. Light.

Adams, Anthony. *The Language of Failure*. Urbana, Ill.: National Council of Teachers of English, 1970. 98 pp.

Adams, Edward C. L. *Congaree Sketches*. Chapel Hill: University of North Carolina Press, 1927. 116 pp.
Fifty-four sketches of the lower Carolina Blacks, written in script form. Includes word list.

———. *Nigger to Nigger*. New York: Charles Scribner's Sons, 1928. 270 pp.
Several sketches about Blacks in South Carolina, written in an approximation of the Black language of the area—includes poems, dramatic dialogue, sermons, and a glossary of about 250 words.

Adams, James. *The Pronunciation of the English Language Vindicated from Imputed Anomaly and Caprice*. Edinburgh, Scotland: J. Moin, 1799. 164 pp. [Reprinted by Scholar Press, New York, 1968.]
Includes brief mentions of Black dialect.

Adams, Phoebe. Review of J. L. Dillard, *Black English: Its History and Usage in the United States*. *Atlantic Monthly*, XXIII (September, 1972), 110.
Brief review.

Aderman, Ralph M. See Kerr, Elizabeth M., and Ralph M. Aderman.

Adkins, Dorothy C. *Preliminary Evaluation of a Language Curriculum for Pre-School Children. Final Report*. Education Research and Development Center, University of Hawaii, Honolulu, 1967. 23 pp.
Use of Bereiter-Engelmann teaching strategy in an applied test case.

Adler, Sol. "Dialectal Differences and Learning Disorders." *Journal of Learning Disabilities*, V (June–July, 1972), 344–50.

———. "Dialectical Differences: Professional and Clinical Implications." *Journal of Speech and Hearing Disorders*, XXXVI (February, 1971), 90–100.
Describes several fundamentals of Black English, suggesting that speech clinicians must first learn Black English patterns in order to teach standard English to nonstandard English speakers. Advises teaching standard English as a "school language."

Aiken, Johnnye. "The Speech of Hynesville, Louisiana, at Three Age Levels." Doctoral dissertation, Louisiana State University, Baton Rouge, 1938.

Alatis, James E., ed. *Report of the Twentieth Annual Roundtable Meeting on Linguistics and Language Studies: Linguistics and the Teaching of Standard English to Speakers of Other Languages or Dialects.* Monograph Series on Languages and Linguistics. Washington, D.C.: Georgetown University Press, 1970. 267 pp.

Proceedings and papers of the November 22, 1969, conference. Those presenting papers were William Labov, Raven I. McDavid, Jr., Rudolph C. Troike, Charles T. Scott, David W. Reed, Harold B. Allen, Peter S. Rosenbaum, Betty W. Robinett, Eugène J. Brière, Bernard Spolsky, David DeCamp, Roger W. Shuy, Virginia French Allen, Frederic G. Cassidy, William A. Stewart, Albert H. Marckwardt, Ralph W. Fasold, Walter A. Wolfram, and Joseph R. Applegate.

Alberts, Frank. See Riesman, Frank, and Frank Alberts.

Allen, Anne. See Smith, Arthur L., Deluvina Hernandez, and Anne Allen.

Allen, Harold B., comp. *Linguistics and English Linguistics.* New York: Appleton-Century-Crofts, 1966. 117 pp.

Bibliography.

Allen, Harold B., and Gary N. Underwood, eds. *Readings in American Dialectology.* New York: Appleton-Century Crofts, 1971. 584 pp.

Forty-one articles in dialectology. The seven articles dealing with Black English were written by Lee A. Pederson, Beryl Loftman Bailey, Marvin D. Loflin, William A. Stewart (two articles), Raven I. McDavid, Jr., and William Labov.

Allen, Virginia French. "Preparing Teachers to Teach Across Dialects." Paper presented at Third Annual Conference of Teaching English to Speakers of Other Languages (TESOL), March 5–8, 1969, at Chicago. 10 pp. [Also in *TESOL Quarterly*, III (September, 1969), 251–56.]

Basic discussion for TESOL teachers. Urges cross-disciplinary approach in TESOL.

————. "A Second Dialect Is Not a Foreign Language," in James E. Alatis, ed., *Report of the Twentieth Annual Roundtable Meeting on Linguistics and Language Studies: Linguistics and the Teaching of Standard English to Speakers of Other Languages or Dialects.* Monograph Series on Languages and Linguistics. Washington, D.C.: Georgetown University Press, 1970. Pp. 189–202. [Also in Roger D. Abrahams and Rudolph C. Troike, eds., *Language and Cultural*

Diversity in American Education. Englewood Cliffs, N.J.: Prentice-Hall, 1972.]

Discusses differences between a second language and a second dialect. Describes procedures for second-dialect teaching.

————. "Teaching Standard English as a Second Dialect." *Teachers College Record*, LXVIII (February, 1967), 355–70. [Also in Alfred C. Aarons, Barbara Y. Gordon, and William A. Stewart, eds., *Linguistic-Cultural Differences and American Education*, special issue of *Florida FL Reporter*, VII (Spring/Summer, 1969), 123–29; and David L. Shores, ed., *Contemporary English: Change and Variation.* Philadelphia: J. B. Lippincott, 1972. Pp. 237–55.]

Discusses definitions of standard English, kinds of English, linguistic versatility, instructional strategy, additional *vs.* correctional attitudes of teacher. Evaluates several methods of instruction: drills, roleplaying, reading, writing.

Allen, William Francis [Marcel]. "The Negro Dialect." *Nation,* I (December 14, 1865), 744–45. [Also in Bruce Jackson, ed., *The Negro and His Folklore in Nineteenth-Century Periodicals.* Austin: University of Texas Press, 1967.]

Comments on speech pattern of Gullah, describing differences from standard English as "phonetic decay." Includes some verse.

Allen, William Francis, Charles Pickard Ware, and Lucy McKim Garrison. *Slave Songs of the United States.* New York: A. Simpson, 1867. 115 pp. [Reprinted by Peter Smith Publishers, New York, 1929.]

Includes thirty-eight-page introduction to the music and language of the nineteenth-century Blacks, as recorded "from the lips of the colored people themselves." Also includes some linguistic insight into Black language.

Allsopp, S. R. R. "Expression of State and Action in the Dialect of English Used in the Georgetown Area of British Guiana." Doctoral dissertation, University of London, 1962.

Altiery, Mason. "At Peace with Pidgin." *American Education,* VII (October, 1971), 32–36.

Description of a special language/dialect program at the University of Hawaii.

"America's Language Barrier." *Dayton* (Ohio) *Daily News,* December 7, 1970, p. 28.

Editorial supporting the views of Marvin Loflin, who maintains that Black English is not deficit, but different.

Ames, V. S. "Effects of Nonstandard Dialect on the Oral Reading Behavior of Fourth Grade Black Children." *International Reading Association Conference Papers (Language, Reading, and the Communication Process)*, XV (1971), 63–70.

Ammon, Ulrich. "Dialekt als Sprachliche Barrier: Eine Pilotstudie über Schwierigkeiten Dialektsprechen im Schulaufsatz." *Mutterspache*, LXXXII (July–August, 1972), 224–37.

Advocates mastery of standard language, claiming that regional dialects are inferior.

Anastasi, Anne, and Rita D'Angelo. "A Comparison of Negro and White Preschool Children in Language Development and Goodenough Draw-a-Man I.Q." *Journal of Genetic Psychology*, LXXXI (December, 1952), 147–65.

In this study of a hundred children, no statistically significant race differences were found for mean sentence length, although more "mature" sentence types were reportedly found among White children as compared with Negro children. Girls excelled in White groups; boys excelled in Black groups.

Anastasiow, Nicholas J. "Cognition and Language: Some Observations," in James L. Laffey and Roger W. Shuy, eds., *Language Differences —Do They Interfere?* Newark, Del.: International Reading Association, 1973. Pp. 17–26.

———. "Educating the Culturally Different Children." *Viewpoints*, XLVIII (March, 1972), 21–41.

Argues for allowing dialect differences within the classroom.

Anderson, C. Arnold. See Halsey, A. H., Jean Floud, and C. Arnold Anderson, eds.

Anderson, Edmund A. *A Grammatical Overview of Baltimore Non-Standard English.* Center for the Study of Social Organization of Schools, The Johns Hopkins University, Baltimore, May, 1970. 108 pp.

Describes speech of ten- to twelve-year-olds from lower class in three speech situations—playing games with peers, talking to an older White interviewer, and telling stories. Deals with the copula, possessive markers, noun plural formation, and past tense formation.

Anderson, Jay. "How Can You Do in Street Talk?." *Milwaukee (Wisc.) Journal*, September 17, 1972.

Twenty-four-question quiz on "street talk."

Anderson, Jervis. "Black Writing: The Other Side." *Dissent*, XV (May–June, 1968), 233–42.

Views of Black writers on Black writing—both social and political.

Anderson, John Q. "The New Orleans Voodoo Ritual Dance and Its Twentieth-Century Survivals." *Southern Folklore Quarterly*, XXIV (June, 1960), 135–43.

Historical overview with discussion of the impact of voodoo ritual on American social dances.

Anderson, Larry M., Irving E. Sigel, and Howard Shapiro. "Categorization Behavior of Lower- and Middle-Class Negro Preschool Children: Differences in Dealing with Representation of Familiar Objects." *Journal of Negro Education*, XXXV (Summer, 1966), 218–29.

Anderson, Wallace L., and Norman C. Stageberg, eds., *Introductory Readings on Language*. New York: Holt, Rinehart, & Winston, 1962.

Andreacchi, Joseph. "Listening Comprehension and Reading Comprehension of Negro Dialect Speakers in Negro Dialect and in Standard English." Doctoral dissertation, Columbia University, New York City, 1973. 150 pp.

Experimental testing suggests possibilities of presenting reading material in Black English to Blacks.

Anshen, Frank. "Creoles and Copulas." Paper presented at Creole Symposium, American Anthropological Association, November 2, 1970, at San Diego, Calif.

Notes that Black English has more affinities with Creole than with standard English.

———. "A Sociolinguistic Analysis of a Sound Change." *Language Sciences*, No. 9 (February, 1970), 20–21.

Study of rapid sound change (postvocalic *r*) in Hillsborough, N.C. Establishes the date of change as being between 1927–1937, with evidence of sound change found in a span of one-year age difference of informants.

———. "Some Statistical Bases for the Existence of Black English." *Florida FL Reporter*, X (Spring/Fall, 1972), 19–20.

Offers statistical "proof" of the existence of Black English in refuting arguments by Raven I. McDavid, Jr., Hans Kurath, and Juanita Williamson.

———. "Speech Variation Among Negroes in a Small Southern Community." Doctoral dissertation, New York University, 1969. 104 pp.

Experimental field study to determine sociolinguistic relationships within the Black community of Hillsborough, N.C. Compares and contrasts the relationships to fieldwork conducted by Lewis Levine and Harry J. Crockett, Jr., on the White section of Hillsborough. Study noted that whenever a linguistic variable was shown to be male-female oriented, Black women used more standard English than men. Also noted that the older, more educated persons used more standard English construction than nonstandard English in their own speech.

Appelgate, Joseph R. "Urban Speech Analysis," in James E. Alatis, ed., *Report of the Twentieth Annual Roundtable Meeting on Linguistics and Language Studies: Linguistics and the Teaching of Standard English to Speakers of Other Languages or Dialects.* Monograph Series on Languages and Linguistics. Washington, D.C.: Georgetown University Press, 1970. Pp. 259–61.

Urges methods for sound linguistic description be used in a serious study of speech of people in a Black urban community.

Armstrong, Orland Kay. *Old Massa's People: The Old Slaves Tell Their Story.* Indianapolis, Ind.: Bobbs-Merrill, 1931. 357 pp.

Biographical sketches of former slaves, their lives, customs, and language.

Arthur, Bradford. "Interaction of Dialect and Style in Urban American Education." *Workpapers: Teaching English as a Second Language,* V (June, 1971), 1–10. [Also in *Language Learning,* XXI (December, 1971), 161–73.]

Presents five assumptions with implications for bidialectism in inner-city schools.

Asbury, Charles A. "Some Effects of Training on Verbal Mental Functioning in Negro Pre-School Children: A Research Note." *Journal of Negro Education,* XXXIX (Winter, 1970), 100–103.

Investigation of the effects of a training program and verbal development of Black preschool children as measured by standardized tests. No effect found; further research suggested.

Atkinson, Harold W. "Mauritian Creole." *Modern Quarterly of Language and Literature* [London], Vol. 1 (1897).

Atlanta Public Schools. *Atlanta Model: A Program for Improving Basic Skills.* Communication Skills Laboratories, Atlanta Public Schools, Atlanta, 1967. 12 pp.

Describes program and results in overcoming racial and social differences in speech patterns, reading ability, and social behavior.

Atwood, E. Bagby. *A Survey of Verb Forms in the Eastern United States.* Ann Arbor: University of Michigan Press, 1953. 53 pp.

Auerbach, Irma T. See Coleman, Morris, Albert J. Harris, and Irma T. Auerbach.

Austin, William M. "Nonverbal Communication," in A. L. Davis, William M. Austin, William Card, Raven I. McDavid, Jr., and Virginia Glenn McDavid, eds., *Culture, Class, and Language Variety: A Resource Book for Teachers.* Urbana, Ill.: National Council of Teachers of English, 1972. Pp. 140–69.

————. See Davis, A. L., William M. Austin, William Card, Raven I. McDavid, Jr., and Virginia Glenn McDavid, eds.

————. See McDavid, Raven I., Jr., and William M. Austin, eds.

Axelrod, Judith. See Bartel, Nettie R., and Judith Axelrod.

Ayoub, Millicent R., and Stephen A. Barnett. "Ritualized Verbal Insult in White High School Culture." *Journal of American Folklore,* LXXVIII (October–December, 1965), 337–44.

Description of the Black verbal-insult game, playing the dozens, as practiced by both Blacks and Whites in a high school setting. [See also Jackson, Bruce, Reply; Barnett, Stephen A., Rejoinder to reply.]

Ayres, B. Drummond, Jr. "Negro Defends Uncle Tom as Powerful Character." New York *Times,* February 25, 1968, p. 58.

Discusses Black lexical use of the term "Uncle Tom."

B

Babcock, C. Merton. "A Word List from Zora Neale Hurston." *Publications of the American Dialect Society,* No. 40 (November, 1963), 1–11.

Study of the vocabulary of the Black woman who became one of the outstanding writers of Black folklore and fiction.

Bach, Emmon. "*Have* and *Be* in English Syntax." *Language,* XLIII (June, 1967), 462–85.

Reexamination of *have* and *be* in standard English syntax with their use as main verbs eliminated from the base and reintroduced by transformational rules.

Bachmann, James Kevin. "A Comparison of Nonstandard Grammatical

Usage in Some Negro and White Working-Class Families in Alexandria, Virginia." Doctoral dissertation, Georgetown University, Washington, D.C., 1970. 120 pp.

Field analysis of twenty-four subjects—one kindergarten child and one adult from each of six White and Black families. Noted that Blacks had greater usage than Whites of the zero copula and uninflected third-person-singular verbs.

—————. "Field Technique in an Urban Language Study." Paper presented at annual TESOL conference, March 18–21, 1970, at San Francisco. 8 pp.

Data suggests that language differences between races decreases with age.

Backus, Emma M. "Animal Tales from North Carolina." *Journal of American Folk-Lore*, XI (October–December, 1898), 284–92.

Seven folktales in Black dialect.

—————. "Cradle Songs of Negroes in North Carolina." *Journal of American Folk-Lore*, VII (October–December, 1894), 310.

—————. "Negro Ghost Stories." *Journal of American Folk-Lore*, IX (July–September, 1896), 228–30.

Stories in Black English.

—————. "Negro Hymns from Georgia." *Journal of American Folk-Lore*, XI (January–March, 1898), 22.

Culture study in dialect.

—————. "Negro Songs from North Carolina." *Journal of American Folk-Lore*, XI (January–March, 1898), 60.

Bailey, Beryl Loftman. "Creole Languages of the Caribbean." Master's thesis, Columbia University, New York City, 1953.

—————. *Jamaican Creole Syntax: A Transformational Approach.* Cambridge, England: Cambridge University Press, 1966. 164 pp.

Linguistic analysis of Jamaican Creole by a native speaker. Written with a desire to explode the "non-language" myth, provide a basis for the production of Creole language books, and establish a model for other Creole languages.

—————. "Language and Communicative Styles of Afro-American Children in the U.S." Paper presented at the annual convention of the American Educational Research Association, February 8–10, 1968, at Chicago. [Also in Alfred C. Aarons, Barbara Y. Gordon, and William A. Stewart, eds., *Linguistic-Cultural Differences and American Education*, special issue of the *Florida FL Reporter*, VII (Spring/ Summer, 1969). Pp. 46, 153.]

Discussion of social organization and syntactic features of Black English in children.

————. "Language and Learning Styles of Minority Group Children in the United States." Paper presented at the annual meeting of the American Educational Research Association, February 8, 1968, at Chicago.

General background information, with emphasis on the predictability of nonstandard English.

————. *A Language Guide to Jamaica*. Research Institute for the Study of Man, University of the West Indies, Mona, Jamaica, 1962. 74 pp.

Includes differences between standard and nonstandard Jamaican Creoles, with implications for study of American Black English.

————. "Linguistics in Nonstandard Language Patterns." Unpublished paper, National Council of Teachers of English, Urbana, Ill., 1965.

————. "A Proposal for the Study of the Grammar of Negro English in New York City." *Project Literacy Reports, No. 2,* Cornell University, Ithaca, N.Y., 1964. Pp. 19–22.

————. "Some Arguments Against the Use of Dialect Readers in the Teaching of Initial Reading." *Florida FL Reporter*, VIII (Spring/ Fall, 1970), 8, 47.

Warns against premature introduction of dialect readers. Notes that there are too many unknown variables, including social tension, training of teachers, publishing integrity, and the need to compare reading backgrounds of White children and lower-class Black children.

————. "Some Aspects of the Impact of Linguistics on Language Teaching in Disadvantaged Communities." *Elementary English*, XIV (May, 1968), 570–78, 626. [Also in A. L. Davis, ed., *On the Dialects of Children*. Champaign, Ill.: National Council of Teachers of English, 1968. Pp. 15–24.]

Report of some of the findings of linguistic research in teaching English to nonstandard dialect speakers, with emphasis on speakers of Black English.

————. "Toward a New Perspective in American Negro Dialectology." *American Speech*, XL (October, 1965), 171–77. [Also in Harold B. Allen and Gary N. Underwood, eds., *Readings in American Dialec-*

tology. New York: Appleton-Century-Crofts, 1971. Pp. 421–27; Walt Wolfram and Nona H. Clarke, eds., *Black-White Speech Relationships*. Washington, D.C.: Center for Applied Linguistics, 1971. Pp. 41–50.]

Argues that "blind ethnocentrism" has caused structuralists to believe that Black English is an inferior variety of standard English. Points to differences between standard and Black English. Includes description of Black English by analyzing the speech of Duke in Warren Miller's *The Cool World*.

Bailey, Beryl Loftman, and Joan Gussow, eds. *Summary of the Proceedings of the Working Conference on Language Development in Disadvantaged Children, October 20–22, 1965.* Graduate School of Education, Yeshiva University, New York, 1965. 21 pp.

Bailey, Charles-James N. "Black English." *Working Papers in Linguistics,* Department of Linguistics, University of Hawaii, Honolulu, II (July, 1970). 22 pp.

Discussion of the origins and present state of Black English. Includes reviews of early studies in the Gullah dialect. Argues against assumptions of Carl Bereiter.

———. "The Patterning of Language Variation," in Richard W. Bailey and Jay L. Robinson, eds., *Varieties of Present-Day English.* New York: Macmillan, 1973. Pp. 156–89.

Outlines the requirements of an explanatory theory of language differences in relation to social and psychological factors.

Bailey, Charles-James N., and Roger W. Shuy, eds. *New Ways of Analyzing Variation in English.* Washington, D.C.: Georgetown University Press, 1973.

Bailey, E. B. "The Negro in East Tennessee." Master's thesis, New York University, 1947.

Bailey, Richard W. "Write Off vs. Write On: Dialects and the Teaching of Composition," in Richard W. Bailey and Jay L. Robinson, eds., *Varieties of Present-Day English.* New York: Macmillan, 1973. Pp. 384–412.

Suggests that a set of priorities drawn from past successes and failures must be devised by English teachers who want to respond to the demands of society.

Bailey, Richard W., and Jay L. Robinson, eds. *Varieties of Present-Day English.* New York: Macmillan, 1973. 461 pp.

General reader in language and dialects. The book is divided into three major sections—English in the Modern World, English in America, and English in the Classroom. Following each article is a set of study-questions. The original articles are "The Patterning of Language Variation" by Charles-James N. Bailey; "Go Slow in Ethnic Attributions: Geographic Mobility and Dialect Prejudice" by Raven I. McDavid, Jr.; "Write Off vs. Write On: Dialects and the Teaching of Composition" by Richard W. Bailey; "The Wall of Babel; Or, Up Against the Language Barrier" by Jay L. Robinson; "Standard Average Foreign in Puerto Rico" by J. L. Dillard; and "Some Characteristics of English in Hawaii" by Gloria Glissmeyer. Among the articles that are reprinted are "Pidgin Languages" by Robert A. Hall, Jr.; "The Language of the Master?" by Kenneth Ramchand; "Some Aspects of Bilingualism in San Antonio, Texas" by Janet B. Sawyer; "Some Features of the English of Black Americans," "General Attitudes Towards the Speech of New York City," and "The Logic of Nonstandard English" by William Labov; "White and Negro Listeners' Reactions to Various American-English Dialects" by G. Richard Tucker and Wallace E. Lambert; "Language and Success: Who Are the Judges?" by Roger W. Shuy; and "Doublespeak: Dialectology in the Service of Big Brother" by James Sledd.

Baldwin, James. *Blues for Mr. Charlie*. New York: Dial Press, 1964.

A drama which uses Black English in its study of relationships between the Black and White cultures.

————. *Going to Meet the Man*. New York: Dial Press, 1965. 249 pp.

An anthology of several of Baldwin's writings.

————. *Go Tell It on the Mountain*. New York: Alfred A. Knopf, 1953. 303 pp.

Baldwin's first book, a study of Black people torn by identification problems and inner conflict.

————. *Notes of a Native Son*. Boston: Beacon Press, 1955. 175 pp.

Autobiographical collection of essays about modern life.

Baldwin, Thelma L. See Garvey, Catherine, and Thelma L. Baldwin.

Ballanta, Nickolas George Julius. *Saint Helena Island Spirituals*. New York: G. Schirmer, 1925. 93 pp.

Introduction, with discussion of African as well as American Black music. Includes about one hundred spirituals.

Ballard, James Moses. "The Effect of Syntactical Transformation on the Performance of a Conservation of Meaning Task by Urban Blacks

17

and White Nonstandard Language Students." Doctoral dissertation, University of Minnesota, Minneapolis, 1972. 102 pp.

Ballard, Lou Ellen. "Folktales of Southeast Alabama: An Original Collection." *Louisiana Folklore Miscellany*, II (January, 1961), 50–68.

Several folktales from three southeastern Alabama communities. Author claims that original tales for some of those presented probably date from the Middle Ages. Black-White orientation.

Ballowe, Hewitt L. *The Lawd Sayin' the Same: Negro Folk Tales of the Creole Country*. Baton Rouge: Louisiana State University Press, 1947. 254 pp.

Bambara, Toni Cade. "Black English: What It Is and What It Ain't." *Confrontation*, No. 7 (Winter, 1973–74).

Maintains that bidialectism is essentially a "game," and that Black English is not approached as a language. Also discusses social, historical, grammatical, political, and aesthetic aspects of Black English.

———. Review of J. L. Dillard, *Black English: Its History and Usage in the United States. New York Times Book Review*, September 3, 1972, pp. 3, 16.

Bancroft, Frederic. *Slave Trading in the Old South*. Baltimore: J. H. Furst, 1931. 415 pp.

Study of early slave-trading practices.

Bank, Frank D. "Plantation Courtships." *Journal of American Folklore*, VII (April–June, 1894), 147–49.

Includes a conversation in Black English.

Banks, James A. See Joyce, William W., and James A. Banks, eds.

Banks, Ruth. "Idioms of the Present-Day American Negro." *American Speech*, XIII (December, 1938), 313–14.

Lists about thirty phrases and expressions.

Baratz, Joan C. *Acquisitions of the Plural in Middle Class and Headstart Preschoolers*. Washington, D.C.: Center for Applied Linguistics, 1966.

———. "Ain't Ain't No Error." *Florida FL Reporter*, IX (Spring/Fall, 1971), 39–40, 54.

Several examples of Black English, including negation and zero copula. Claims that most English teachers—brought up thinking about "right" and "wrong" rules of grammar—have difficulty accepting nonstandard English as a legitimite language and not just a bad dialect.

————. "The Application of Dialect Research in the Context of the Classroom—It Ain't Easy." *Acta-Symbolica*, II (Spring, 1971), 3–7.

Notes that the teacher must first accept and understand the Black English language before it is possible to teach a standard English. Calls for dialect readers.

————. "Beginning Readers for Speakers of Divergent Dialects." Paper presented at annual convention of the International Reading Association, May 1, 1969, at Kansas City, Missouri. 9 pp. [Also in J. Allen Figurel, *Reading Goals for the Disadvantaged.* Newark, Del.: International Reading Association, 1970. Pp. 77–83.]

Initial proposal for the development of dialect readers for nonstandard speakers in the elementary grades. Suggests that orthography be in standard English.

————. *A Bi-Dialectical Task for Determining Language Proficiency in Economically Disadvantaged Negro Children.* ERIC document ED 020 519. Washington, D.C., June, 1968, 20 pp. [Also in *Child Development*, XL (September, 1969), 889–901.]

Verbal-recall test of standard and nonstandard English sentences. Noted that Blacks were better able to repeat nonstandard English sentences than Whites were able to repeat standard English sentences. About three fourths of all third-graders tested—both Black and White—stated that nonstandard English was spoken by Blacks, whereas standard English was spoken by Whites. About four fifths of the fifth-graders and nine tenths of the sixth-graders stated the same thing. Author outlines three major theories concerning the language abilities of economically disadvantaged Blacks.

————. "A Cultural Model for Understanding Afro-Americans," in Bernice E. Cullinan, ed., *Black Dialects and Reading.* Urbana, Ill.: ERIC, 1974.

Language model. Following the article are the responses of Martin Deutsch, Vivian Horner, and Dorothy Strickland.

————. "Educational Considerations for Teaching Standard English to Negro Children," in Ralph W. Fasold and Roger W. Shuy, eds., *Teaching Standard English in the Inner City.* Washington, D.C.: Center for Applied Linguistics, 1970. Pp. 20–41.

A slight modification of her article, "Who Should Do What to Whom . . . and Why?"

————. "Expressive and Receptive Control of Plural Inflectional Endings in Middle Class and Culturally Deprived Pre-School Children." Pa-

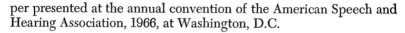

per presented at the annual convention of the American Speech and Hearing Association, 1966, at Washington, D.C.

―――. "Language Abilities of Black Americans: Review of Research, 1966–1970," in Kent Miller and Ralph Dreger, eds., *Comparative Studies of Negroes and Whites in the United States.* New York: Basic Books, 1972. Pp. 125–83.

Linguistic and anthropological data for questioning the validity of using only standardized testing procedures for the purpose of assessing language development of Black children.

―――. "Language and Cognitive Assessment of Negro Children: Descriptions and Research." *ASHA*, XI (March, 1969), 87–91. [Also in *Florida FL Reporter*, VII (Fall, 1969), 11–14.]

Discusses the need for psychologists and speech pathologists to take into account the socio-economic conditions of the Black child when assessing his language and cognitive development. Also discusses some of the features of Black English.

―――. "Language in the Economically Disadvantaged Child: A Perspective." *ASHA*, X (April, 1968), 143–45.

Notes that the disadvantaged have learned a language, but that the language learned is not standard English.

―――. "The Language of the Ghetto Child." *The Center Magazine*, II (January, 1969), 32–33. [Also in Robert H. Bentley and Samuel D. Crawford, eds., *Black Language Reader*. Glencoe, Ill.: Scott, Foresman, 1973. Pp. 77–79.]

A very brief argument for acceptance of nonstandard English dialects as languages.

―――. "The Language Teacher and the Disadvantaged: Testing and the Negro Speaker of Nonstandard English." Paper presented at the Southern Conference on Language Teaching, February, 1969, at Atlanta.

―――. "Linguistic and Cultural Factors in Teaching Reading to Ghetto Children." *Elementary English*, XLVI (February, 1969), 199–203.

Discusses language difficulties which interfere with the disadvantaged Black child's ability to learn to read standard English. Presents a system using Black dialect in beginning readers.

―――. "Relationship of Black English to Reading: A Review of Research," in James L. Laffey and Roger Shuy, eds., *Language Differences—Do They Interfere?* Newark, Del.: International Reading Association, 1973. Pp. 101–13.

————. *Relationship of Negro Nonstandard English Dialect Speech to Reading Achievement.* Washington, D.C.: Education Study Center, 1970.

————. "Reply to Dr. Raph's Article on Speech and Language Deficiencies of Culturally Disadvantaged Children." *Journal of Speech and Hearing Disorders,* XXXIII (August, 1968), 299–300.

Rebuttal to Jane Beasley Raph's argument in *Journal of Speech and Hearing Disabilities,* XXXII (August, 1967), 203–14. The deficit position of a previous article on the language of the disadvantaged children is rejected and replaced by a position of recognizing language variations.

————. "A Review of Research on the Relationship of Black English to Reading." Paper presented at annual conference of the International Reading Association, April 19–21, 1971, at Atlantic City, N.J.

Discusses written research on relationship of oral language skills and acquisition of reading skills. Discusses controversy and use of Black dialect readers.

————. "Should Black Children Learn White Dialect?" *ASHA,* XII (September, 1970), 415–17. [Also in Arthur L. Smith, ed., *Language, Communication, and Rhetoric in Black America.* New York: Harper & Row, 1972. Pp. 3–11.]

Argues that standardization is a sociolinguistic fact of life and urges that students should learn standard English.

————. "Teaching Reading in an Urban Negro School System," in Joan C. Baratz and Roger W. Shuy, eds., *Teaching Black Children to Read.* Washington, D.C.: Center for Applied Linguistics, 1969. Pp. 92–116. [Also in Robert H. Bentley and Samuel D. Crawford, eds., *Black Language Reader.* Glencoe, Ill.: Scott, Foresman, 1973. Pp. 154–71.]

Discusses the necessity for teachers to understand that the inner-city child speaks a language that is well ordered but different, in many respects, from standard English. Also describes some of the differences between Black English and standard English.

————. "Teaching Reading in an Urban Negro School System," in Frederick Williams, ed., *Language and Poverty: Perspectives on a Theme.* Chicago: Markham, 1970. Pp. 11–24.

Less technical version of the article which appears in Joan C. Baratz and Roger W. Shuy, eds., *Teaching Black Children to Read.*

————. "Who Should Do What to Whom . . . and Why?" in Alfred C. Aarons, Barbara Y. Gordon, and William A. Stewart, eds., *Linguis-*

tic-Cultural Differences and American Education, special issue of *Florida FL Reporter,* VII (Spring/Summer, 1969), 75–77, 158–59.
Discusses the need to teach standard English in a quasi-foreign language situation. Rejects the deficit theory and proposes that the language of Black children is different from standard English, but not inferior to it.

————. See Baratz, Stephen S., and Joan C. Baratz. "Negro Ghetto Children and Urban Education: A Cultural Solution."

————. See Baratz, Stephen S., and Joan C. Baratz. "The Social Pathology Model: Historical Basis for Psychology's Denial of the Existence of the Negro Culture."

————. See Baratz, Stephen S., and Joan C. Baratz. "Urban Education: A Cultural Solution."

————. See Stewart, William A., and Joan C. Baratz.

Baratz, Joan C., and Stephen S. Baratz. "Black Culture on Black Terms: A Rejection of the Social Pathology Model," in Thomas Kochman, ed., *Rappin' and Stylin' Out: Communication in Urban Black America.* Champaign, Ill.: University of Illinois Press, 1972.

Baratz, Joan C., and Edna A. Povich. *A Discussion of the Language Studies of the Economically Disadvantaged Child.* Washington, D.C.: Center for Applied Linguistics, 1967. 29 pp.

————. *Grammatical Constructions in the Language of the Negro Preschool Child.* Washington, D.C.: American Speech and Hearing Association, 1967. 30 pp.
Data of Washington, D.C., sample suggests that Black English students have learned a linguistically acceptable language.

Baratz, Joan C., and Roger W. Shuy, eds. *Teaching Black Children to Read.* Washington, D.C.: Center for Applied Linguistics, 1969. 219 pp.
Discusses relationship of language to reading, and language which is appropriate to the context of the experience of the child. Authors are Joan C. Baratz, Ralph Fasold, Kenneth Goodman, William Labov, Raven I. McDavid, Jr., Roger W. Shuy, William A. Stewart, and Walter Wolfram.

Baratz, Joan C., Roger W. Shuy, and Walter A. Wolfram. *Sociolinguistic Factors in Speech Identification. Final Report.* Research Project No. MH 15048-01. National Institute of Mental Health, Washington, D.C., 1969.

Baratz, Stephen S. "The Effects of Race of the Experimenter: Instruction and Comparison of Populations upon the Level of Reported Anxiety in Negro Subjects." *Journal of Personality and Social Psychology,* VII (1967), 194–96.

———. "Social Science Strategy for Research on the Afro-American," in Norman E. Whitten, Jr., and John F. Szwed, eds., *Afro-American Anthropology: Contemporary Perspectives.* New York: Free Press, 1970.

———. See Baratz, Joan C., and Stephen S. Baratz.

Baratz, Stephen S., and Joan C. Baratz. "Negro Ghetto Children and Urban Education: A Cultural Solution." *Bulletin of the Minnesota Council for the Social Studies,* Fall, 1968, pp. 1–4. [Also in *Social Education* (April, 1969); Alfred C. Aarons, Barbara Y. Gordon, and William A. Stewart, eds., *Linguistic-Cultural Differences and American Education,* special issue of *Florida FL Reporter,* VII (Spring/Summer, 1969. Pp. 13–14, 151.]

Asserts that educational solutions to ghetto schools will not work unless dialect is recognized as legitimate in the classroom, especially in the teaching of reading.

———. "The Social Pathology Model: Historical Basis for Psychology's Denial of the Existence of the Negro Culture." Paper presented at the annual meeting of the American Psychology Association, 1969, at Washington, D.C. 22 pp. [Also published as "Black Culture on Black Terms: A Rejection of the Social Pathology Model," in Thomas Kochman, ed., *Rappin' and Stylin' Out: Communication in Urban Black America.* Champaign: University of Illinois Press, 1972.]

Describes ethnocentrism within social sciences in research studies dealing with Afro-Americans. Concentrates on ignorance and denial of Black culture. Also cites a few instances of ignorance on the part of researchers. Suggests that reevaluation within the social sciences will enable better bias-free research, and calls for an understanding of Black culture.

———. "Urban Education: A Cultural Solution." *Bulletin of the Minnesota Council for the Social Studies,* Fall, 1966, pp. 1–4.

Barnes, Ambrose. "Four Goals Set in Teaching English to Those Speaking Black Dialect." Washington *Post,* March 4, 1972, pp. E1, E5.

Brief review of Black dialect programs at national TESOL convention.

Barnett, Stephen A. Rejoinder to reply to "Ritualized Verbal Insult in

White High School Culture." *Journal of American Folklore*, LXXX (January–March, 1967), 89–90.

———. See Ayoub, Millicent R., and Stephen A. Barnett.

Baron, Dennis E. "Non-Standard English, Composition, and the Academic Establishment." Paper presented at the Midwestern Regional Meeting of the American Dialect Society, August 2, 1973, at Ann Arbor, Mich.

Examines the positions of eradicationism and bidialectalism within the school systems. Distinguishes between nonstandard English in writing and nonstandard English in speech.

———. "Reactions to Written Non-Standard English: Toward a Formal Description of the Written Code of Non-Standard English." Paper presented at the Northeast Regional Meeting of the American Dialect Society, April 4–6, 1974, at University Park, Pa.

Barrett, Madie Ward. "A Phonology of Southeast Alabama." Doctoral dissertation, University of North Carolina, Chapel Hill, 1948.

Barritt, Loren S. *The Auditory Memory of Children from Different Socio-Economic Backgrounds.* Center for Research on Language and Language Behavior, University of Michigan, Ann Arbor, 1968. 16 pp.

Test results and analysis pertaining to verbal recall.

———. *The Changes in Psycholinguistic Functioning After One Year in an 'Integrated' School.* ERIC document ED 015 217. Washington, D.C., 1967. 16 pp.

———. *A Comparison of the Auditory Memory Performances of Negro and White Children from Different Socio-Economic Backgrounds.* Center for Research on Language and Language Behavior and School of Education, University of Michigan, Ann Arbor, February 1, 1969. 29 pp.

Barritt, Loren S., Melvyn I. Semmel, and Paul D. Weener. *A Comparison of the Psycholinguistic Function of "Educationally-Deprived" and "Educationally-Advantaged" Children.* Center for Research on Language and Language Behavior, University of Michigan, Ann Arbor, 1965. 16 pp.

Barta, Gary T. "Implementing the Dialects Course," in Robert B. Bentley and Samuel D. Crawford, eds., *Black Language Reader.* Glencoe, Ill.: Scott, Foresman, 1973. Pp. 125–27.

Bartel, Nettie R., and Judith Axelrod. "Nonstandard English Usage in

Reading Ability in Black Junior High Students." *Exceptional Children*, XXXIX (May, 1973), 653–54.

Brief report on experimental study of reading interference.

Barth, Ernest A. T. "The Language Behavior of Negroes and Whites." *Pacific Sociological Review*, IV (Fall, 1961), 69–72.

Asserts that social distance is reinforced by language behavior. Indicates that words have a more personalized meaning for Blacks.

Bartley, Diane E. See Politzer, Robert L., and Diane E. Bartley.

Bartley, Diane E., and Carl James. "Teacher Training in Adult Basic Education—TESOL: A Step to Eradicating Illiteracy in Standard English." *Modern Language Journal*, LVI (October, 1972), 374–77.

Bascomb, William R. "Acculturation among Gullah Negroes." Paper presented to Central Section, American Anthropological Association, April 26, 1940, at Indianapolis. [Also in *American Anthropology*, n.s., XLIII (January–March, 1941), 43–50; J. L. Dillard, ed., *Perspectives on Black English*. The Hague: Mouton, forthcoming.]

Argues that explanation of European influence *only* is methodologically unsound; he would use African influence in the explanation.

Bass, Robert Duncan. "Negro Songs from the Pedee Country." *Journal of American Folk-Lore*, XLIV (October–December, 1931), 418–36.

Lyrics of sixty-four songs, with a brief introduction and comments by the compiler.

Baumkel, Marilyn. "Some Pertinent Comments on *Teaching Black Children to Read*." *Elementary English*, XLVIII (January, 1970), 90–94. Review of Joan C. Baratz and Roger W. Shuy, eds., *Teaching Black Children to Read*.

Reviewer agrees with the main premise of the book, but criticizes the "ivory tower" approach.

Bayliss, John F. *Black Slave Narratives*. London: Macmillan and Company 1970. 150 pp.

Beadle, J. H. *Western Wilds and the Men Who Redeem Them*. Cincinnati: Jones Brothers, 1877. 624 pp.

A few references to Black language, including a discussion of the influences of Black language on American English.

Bear, R. M., Robert D. Hess, Virginia C. Shipman, and G. Brophy. *The Cognitive Environments of Urban Preschool Negro Children*. Report to the Children's Bureau, School Administration, Department of Health, Education, and Welfare, Washington, D.C., 1968.

Beck, Horace P., ed. *Folklore in Action: Essays for Discussion in Honor of MacEdward Leach*. Philadelphia: American Folklore Society, 1962. 210 pp.

Beck, Robert [Iceberg Slim]. *Pimp: The Story of My Life*. Los Angeles: Holloway House, 1969. 317 pp. [Foreword also published in Thomas Kochman, ed., *Rappin' and Stylin' Out: Communication in Urban Black America*. Champaign: University of Illinois Press, 1972. Pp. 386–89.]

Narrative about the life of a former Black pimp. Includes a discussion of the function of language in hustling and rapping. Glossary.

Bell, Bernard W., ed. *Modern and Contemporary Afro-American Poetry*. Boston: Allyn & Bacon, 1972. 193 pp.

An anthology of Black poetry which includes the works of Claude McKay, Jean Toomer, Melvin B. Tolson, Sterling A. Brown, Langston Hughes, Arna Bontemps, Countee Cullen, Frank Marshall Davis, Robert Hayden, Dudley Randall, Margaret Walker, Gwendolyn Brooks, Margaret Danner, Naomi Long Madgett, Gloria C. Oden, Ted Joans, Conrad Kent Rivers, Etheridge Knight, LeRoi Jones, Audre Lorde, A. B. Spellman, Bob Kaufman, Sonia Sanchez, Lucille Clifton, Clarence Major, Keorapestse Kgositsile, Julia Fields, Don L. Lee, and Nikki Giovanni.

Benedict, Helen Dymond. *Belair Plantation Melodies*. Cincinnati: Willis Music, 1924. 17 pp.

Recording of original lyrics of Black folksongs.

Bennett, John. "The 'Comedie Humaine' of the Gullah Darkey." New York *Evening Post*, December 9, 1922, Literary Review section.

Review of Ambrose E. Gonzales, *The Black Border: Gullah Stories of the Carolina Coast*.

————. "Gullah: A Negro Patois." *South Atlantic Quarterly*, VII (1908), 332–47; VIII (1909), 39–52.

Description of Gullah by a writer well acquainted with the language. Includes numerous interesting observations, and cites several examples and anecdotes. Notes similarity of Gullah to Elizabethan English.

Bennett, Louise. *Anancy Stories and Dialect Verse*. Kingston, Jamaica: Pioneer Press, 1957. 94 pp.

Folktales recorded in dialect as well as standard English. Anancy, a folk character, always wins out and, in the process, begins a new tradition. Also includes poetry in dialect.

Bentler, P. M., and M. S. Marshall. "IQ Increases of Disadvantaged Minority-Group Children Following Innovated Enrichment Program." *Psychological Reports*, XXIX (June, 1971), 805–806.

Nine-month enrichment program involving eleven Black four-year-olds. Following participation in an enrichment program involving language skills, the children gained an average of 23.5 points on the Peabody Picture Vocabulary Test (Form A).

Bentley, Robert H. "On Black Dialects, White Linguistics, and the Teaching of English," in Charlton Laird and Robert M. Gorrell, eds., *Readings About Language*. New York: Harcourt Brace Jovanovich, 1971. Pp. 275–77.

A response to James Sledd's charges that English teachers disregard dialects when teaching standard English to students. Bentley contends that teachers must recognize dialects as legitimate, but must also teach standard English as the "language of the marketplace" in American society.

Bentley, Robert H., and Samuel D. Crawford, eds. *Black Language Reader*. Glencoe, Ill.: Scott, Foresman, 1973. 256 pp.

Twenty-eight articles, plus an introduction. Divided into seven parts. Part I ("What Is a Dialect?") includes articles by Jean Malmstrom and Raven I. McDavid, Jr. Part II ("The Origins: English in Africa and Early America") includes articles by Gilbert D. Schneider and William A. Stewart. Part III ("Black Language Today") includes articles by Ossie Davis, Joan C. Baratz, Samuel Crawford, J. L. Dillard, Riley B. Smith, and William Labov. Part IV ("Down Where It's At: Reports from Five Teachers") includes articles by Larry Bowers, Joan Gayle Wilson, H. James Anding, Gary T. Barta, and Mary T. LaBute. Part V ("Where Do We Go from Here? Language and Education") includes articles by Thomas Kochman, Kenneth R. Johnson, Anita E. Dunn, Joan C. Baratz, Walter A. Wolfram and Ralph Fasold, Wayne O'Neil, and James Sledd. Part VI ("And the 'Others'") includes articles written by Murray Wax, Armando Rodriguez, Terry Link, and Chief Joseph. Part VII ("The End") includes an article by Janice Gilmore and a cartoon by G. B. Trudeau.

Berdan, Robert. Have/got *in the Speech of Anglo and Black Children*. Southwest Regional Laboratory, Los Alamitos, California, 1973. 15 pp.

Berdan, Robert, and Carol W. Pfaff. *Sociolinguistic Variation in the Speech of Young Children: An Experimental Study*. Southwestern Regional Laboratory, Los Alamitos, California, October, 1972. 19 pp.

Investigation of seven syntactical and phonological variations of thirty Black and White kindergarten children. Among the conclusions were that income level and linguistic usage were not significantly correlated; that Black English usage is more prevalent by Blacks in core urban areas; that only among Black English-speakers is there no agreement in syntactical presentation of *have* and *do* phrases.

Berdie, Robert F. "Playing the Dozens." *Journal of Abnormal and Social Psychology*, VLII (January, 1947), 120–21.

Brief description of the dozens.

Bereiter, Carl. "Academic Instruction and Preschool Children," in Richard Corbin and Muriel Crosby, eds., *Language Programs for the Disadvantaged: The Report of the NCTE Task Force on Teaching English to the Disadvantaged.* Champaign, Ill.: National Council of Teachers of English, 1965. Pp. 195–203.

Description of a preschool experiment directed by Bereiter at the University of Illinois.

Bereiter, Carl, and Siegfried Engelman. *Language Learning Activities for the Disadvantaged Child.* New York: B'nai B'rith Anti-Defamation League, 1965. 34 pp.

A book of game-like activities to facilitate language development.

———. *Teaching Disadvantaged Children in the Preschool.* Englewood Cliffs, N.J.: Prentice-Hall, 1966. 312 pp.

Discussion and analysis of teaching procedures for preschool disadvantaged children.

Bereiter, Carl, Siegfried Engelman, Jean Osborn, and Philip A. Reidford. "An Academically Oriented Pre-School for Culturally Deprived Children," in Fred M. Hechinger, ed., *Pre-School Education Today: New Approaches to Teaching Three-, Four-, and Five-Year-Olds.* Garden City, N.Y.: Doubleday, 1966. Pp. 105–37.

Discussion of a preschool grammar program to facilitate language education of Blacks.

Berg, Paul Conrad. "Language Barriers of the Culturally Different." Paper presented at the annual meeting of the College Reading Association, March 13–15, 1969, at Boston. 14 pp.

Discussion of the effects of language on the individual and the interdependence on language.

Bernal, Ernest M., Jr. "Concept Learning among Anglo, Black, and Mexican-American Children Using Facilitation Strategy and Bilingual

Teaching." Doctoral dissertation, University of Texas, Austin, 1971. 112 pp.

Bernstein, Basil. "Elaborate and Restricted Codes: Their Social Origins and Some Consequences," in John Gumperz and Dell H. Hymes, eds., *The Ethnography of Communication*, special issue of *American Anthropologist*, LXVI (1964). Pp. 55–69.

———. "Language and Social Class." *British Journal of Sociology*, XI (September, 1960), 271–76.

Claims that language of the lower classes discourages verbal elaboration of subject intent, and limits them to descriptive rather than abstract thought.

———. "Linguistic Codes, Hesitation Phenomena and Intelligence." *Language and Speech*, V (1962), 31–46.

Comparative social-racial class studies involving language.

———. "Social Class and Linguistic Development: A Theory of Social Learning," in A. H. Halsey, Jean Floud, and C. Arnold Anderson, eds., *Education, Economy and Society: A Reader in the Sociology of Education*. New York: Free Press of Glencoe, Inc., 1961. Pp. 288–314.

Compares middle-class and lower-working-class values and parent-child linguistic relationships. Emphasizes apparent predominant use of public (impersonal) language in lower-class relationships.

———. "Social Class, Linguistic Codes, and Grammatical Elements." *Language and Speech*, V (1962), 221–40.

Elaboration on an earlier article.

———. "A Sociolinguistic Approach to Socialization: With Some References to Educability," in Frederick Williams, ed., *Language and Poverty: Perspectives on a Theme*. Chicago: Markham, 1970. Pp. 25–61. [Also in John J. Gumperz and Dell H. Hymes, eds., *Directions in Sociolinguistics*. New York: Holt, Rinehart, & Winston, 1972. Pp. 465–97.]

Describes the social origin of linguistic codes and nonspecific relations between family-role systems and linguistic codes. Speculates on consequences of attempts to change the linguistic codes of groups.

Berry, Jack. "English Loanwords and Adaptations in Sierra Leone Krio." *Creole Language Studies*, II (1961), 1–16.

Beynon, Erdmann Doane. "The Voodoo Cult among Negro Migrants in Detroit." *American Journal of Sociology*, XLIII (May, 1938), 894–907.

Claims that the voodoo cult arose from the disillusionment and race-consciousness of Blacks recently migrating to the North. Includes several references to names.

Bezark, Mary Jane. "Pull Your Coattails to This: Webster Has a Black Glossary." Washington *Post*, January 2, 1972, p. F6.

Discusses Black lexicon, and the thousand-word glossary compiled by Hermese Roberts for the *Living Webster Encyclopedic Dictionary of the English Language.*

A *Bibliography of American English Dialects: Their Nature and Social Consequences.* Washington, D.C.: Center for Applied Linguistics, 1969. 42 pp.

Bickerton, Derek. "The Nature of a Creole Continuum." *Language*, XLIX (September, 1973), 640–69.

Attempts to describe Creole continuums with a single dynamic model which incorporates not only the polar extremes, but intermediate variations as well. Claims that his model is applicable to all language rather than just Creole languages.

Biddle, B. See Loflin, Marvin, T. Guzette, and B. Biddle.

Bienvenu, Charles Joseph. "The Negro-French Dialect of St. Martin Parish." Master's thesis, Louisiana State University, Baton Rouge, 1933.

Compilation and phonetic transcription of about five hundred medical formulas.

Bills, Garland, and Walter S. Stoltz. An *Investigation of the Standard-Nonstandard Dimensions of Central Texas English.* Child Development Evaluation and Research Center, University of Texas, Austin, August, 1968.

Comparative study of twenty-three people, mostly White—but with implications for Black dialect study.

Bing, Elizabeth. "The Effect of Child-Rearing Practices on Development of Differential Cognitive Abilities." *Child Development*, XXXIV (September, 1963), 631–48.

Bins, Carolyn Fitchett. "Toward an Ethnography of Contemporary African-American Oral Poetry," in William K. Riley and David M. Smith, eds., *Languages and Linguistics: Working Papers, Number 5: Sociolinguistics.* Washington, D.C.: Georgetown University Press, 1972. Pp. 79–94.

Presents a stylistic analysis of a poem as a communicative event. Develops a model of a typology of Afro-American oral poetry.

Blackburn, Ruth M. "Dialects in Eugene O'Neill's Plays," in Juanita V. Williamson and Virginia M. Burke, eds., *A Various Language: Perspectives on American Dialects.* New York: Holt, Rinehart, & Winston, 1971, Pp. 230–41.

> Edited version of her doctoral dissertation.

————. "Representation of Negro English Rustic Dialect in the Plays of Eugene O'Neill." Doctoral dissertation, New York University, New York City, 1967.

> Includes O'Neill's treatment of Black English in his plays, with transcription and analysis.

"Black Dialect and History: NCTE Warns of Overreacting." *Library Journal*, XCIV (April 15, 1969), 1,708. [Also in *School Library Journal*, XVI (April 15, 1969), 40.]

> News report about the controversies surrounding bidialectism.

"Black English." *Time*, C (August 7, 1972), 46.

> Brief discussion-review of J. L. Dillard's *Black English.* Includes a few sentences from *Ollie*, an experimental dialect reader developed by William A. Stewart and Joan C. Baratz.

Black, Joe. Letter to the editor. *Louisiana Weekly*, July 10, 1971.

> Expresses opposition to Black English studies.

"Black Names." *Newsweek*, LXXII (July 29, 1968), 80.

> Discusses trend by American Blacks to disregard White American Christian naming practices in preference for African and Islamic names.

"Black Nonsense." *Crisis*, LXXVIII (April–May, 1971), 78.

> Sharp editorial attack against Black English study programs—especially the one at Brooklyn College—which are described as a "cruel hoax" to Blacks.

Blackwell, Edward H. "2 Little Words Can Mean a Lot." *Milwaukee* (Wis.) *Journal*, November 1, 1970.

> A Black journalist discusses a powerful two-word phrase used by Blacks. Also notes that Black English is a legitimate dialect.

Blades, William C. *Negro Poems, Melodies, Plantation Pieces, Camp Meeting Songs, etc.* Boston: R. C. Badger, 1921. 168 pp.

Blair, Louise H. *The Prosperity of the South, Dependent upon the Elevation of the Negro.* N.p., 1889.

Blank, Marion. *Cognitive Gains in "Deprived" Children through Individual Teaching of Language for Abstract Thinking.* ERIC document ED 019 346. Washington, D.C., 1967. 4 pp.

A proposal and experimental study for the creation of an abstract language program.

Blok, H. P. "Annotations to Mr. L. D. Turner's *Africanisms in the Gullah Dialect.*" *Lingua,* VIII (September, 1959), 306–21.

Review and criticisms of Lorenzo Dow Turner's pioneer work.

Bloomfield, Leonard. *Language.* New York: Henry Holt, 1933/1950. 564 pp.

General language discussion, with brief references to Negro dialects and their historical connection to Creoles (pp. 474–75).

————. "Literate and Illiterate Speech." *American Speech,* II (July, 1927), 432–39. [Also in Dell H. Hymes, ed., *Language in Culture and Society: A Reader in Linguistics and Anthropology.* New York: Harper & Row, 1964. Pp. 391–96.]

Discusses misconceptions about "good" and "bad" language. Says that references should be made to "standard language with dialect features."

Blotner, Joseph L. See Gwynn, Frederick L., and Joseph L. Blotner.

Boag, Mrs. E. T. "De Secon' Flood, Story of a Negro Nurse." *Journal of American Folk-Lore,* XI (July–September, 1898), 237–38.

Dialect folktale.

Board of Education, City of Chicago. See Davis, Olga, Mildred R. Gladney, Lloyd Leaverton, Melvin J. Hoffman, and Zorenda P. Patterson.

Bock, Philip K. "Social Structure and Language Structure," in Joshua Fishman, ed., *Readings in the Sociology of Language.* The Hague: Mouton, 1968. Pp. 212–22.

Suggests several analogies between language structure and social structure; formulates statements on the structural units of a community and the relationship between the units.

Bolton, James Albert. "Verbal Behavior of White Teachers in Black, White, and Integrated Classrooms." Doctoral dissertation, Claremont Graduate School, Claremont, California, 1972. 133 pp.

Notes significant differences in verbal behavior of teachers in different racial situations.

Bondurant, Slettie Vera. "Black English: Detention Camps without Walls." *Freedomways*, XIII (Spring, 1973), 157–59.

Essential opposition to linguistic concepts of Black English.

Bontemps, Arna. See Hughes, Langston, and Arna Bontemps, eds.

Bordie, John G. "When Should Instruction in a Second Language or Dialect Begin?" *Elementary English*, XLVIII (May, 1971), 551–58. [Also in Thomas D. Horn, ed., *Research Bases for Oral Language Instruction*. Urbana, Ill.: National Council of Teachers of English, 1971. Pp. 21–28.]

General discussion which advises beginnings in kindgergarten or nursery school if pronunciation is of social importance.

Bosmajian, Haig A. "The Language of White Racism." *College English*, XXXI (December, 1969), 263–72.

Causes and effects of racist vocabulary. Includes symbolism of colors, black as well as white.

Boswell, John J. See Marwitt, Samuel J., Karen L. Marwitt, and John J. Boswell.

Botkin, B. A. *Folk-Say: A Regional Miscellany*. Norman: University of Oklahoma Press, 1930.

Anthology which includes studies of Black speech.

————. *Lay My Burden Down: A Folk History of Slavery*. Chicago: University of Chicago Press, 1945/1968. 297 pp.

Approximately 250 narratives by former slaves.

————, ed. *A Treasury of Mississippi River Folklore: Stories, Ballads, Traditions, and Folkways of the Mid-American River Country*. New York: Crown Publishers, 1955. 620 pp.

————, ed. *A Treasury of Southern Folklore: Stories, Ballads, Traditions of the People of the South*. New York: Crown Publishers, 1949. 776 pp.

Includes Black worksongs and folklore.

Bouchard, Ellen L. *Psycholinguistic Attitude Study*. Center for Research on Language and Language Behavior, University of Michigan, Ann Arbor, 1969. 14 pp.

Experimental test of hypothesis that children are conscious of racial differences in language.

Bourgeois, Eugene O. "Creole Dialect." Master's thesis, Louisiana State University, Baton Rouge, 1927. 86 pp.

Discusses features of American Black Creole. Includes phonetic transcription.

Bousquet, Robert J. "Black-White Speech Differences as Depicted in Selected Prose Works of William Gilmore Simms." Paper presented at the annual meeting of the American Dialect Society, December 26–27, 1973, at Chicago. 9 pp.

Analysis of literary dialect used by Simms. Notes that the Gullah was accurately portrayed. Points out that the true origin of Black English is probably a combination of African and English sources.

————. "Loss of Inflections in Black English: A Phonological or Morphological Phenomenon?" Paper presented at the annual conference of the International Linguistic Association, March 9–10, 1974, at Philadelphia.

Bowdre, Paul H. "Eye Dialect as a Literary Device in the Works of Sidney Lanier." *South Atlantic Bulletin*, XXX (January, 1965), 3.

Brackenridge, Hugh Henry. *Modern Chivalry*. Philadelphia: John M. M'Culloch, 1792.

Includes lengthy speech by a Black.

Braddock, Clayton. "Where Standard English Seems Foreign and Is Taught as If It Were." *Southern Education Report*, IV (January–February, 1969), 18–21. [Also in *Education Digest*, XXXIV (April, 1969), 52–53. Condensed.]

Description of a language program for teaching standard English as a foreign language. Discusses program in Wakulla County, Fla.

Bradford, Roark. *Ol' Man Adam an' His Chillun: Being Tales They Tell About the Time When the Lord Walked the Earth Like a Natural Man*. New York: Harper & Bros., 1928. 254 pp. Illustrated by A. B. Walker.

A novel in Black English that tells the stories of the Bible as viewed by Blacks. Provided inspiration for Marc Connelly's *The Green Pastures*.

Brasch, Ila Wales. "Opinion: A Rebuttal to Bayard Rustin." *Afro-American Affairs*, October 12, 1971, p. 6.

Opposition to eradicationist argument of Bayard Rustin. Argues for acceptance of Black English as a legitimate dialect rather than "poor" English.

————. "The Origin of Black English and Its Relationship to Standard English." Unpublished paper, Department of English, University of Northern Iowa, Cedar Falls, 1971. 17 pp.

Discusses various theories on origin of Black English and the question of dialect language. Concludes existence of separate language base. Both synchronic and diachronic analysis used.

Brasch, Ila Wales, and Walter Milton Brasch. "A Review of Black English Research, and Discussion of the Development of the Black English Bibliography." Paper presented at the Linguistics Colloquium on Black English, January 23, 1973, at Ohio University, Athens.

General discussion of the methodology and approaches, as well as problems, in developing *A Comprehensive Annotated Bibliography of American Black English*. Also reviews the field of Black English research and related studies. Discusses the availability and the use of primary data in Black English analysis.

Brasch, Walter Milton. "Black English and the Mass Media." Paper presented at the Midwestern Regional Meeting of the American Dialect Society, August 2, 1973, at Ann Arbor, Mich. 60 pp.

————. "Black English and the Mass Media." Doctoral dissertation, Ohio University, Athens, 1974.

Expansion of his paper presented to the members of the American Dialect Society. Discussion of the integration and interrelationships of Black English and the mass media. Discusses the field from two general directions—what is being reported in the mass media about Black English, and the use of the mass media as vital sources of primary data. Approaches the discussion from historical as well as contemporary perspectives. Concludes that Black English sources fall within five cycles—Colonial-Reconstruction, Antebellum, Reconstruction, Negro Renaissance, and Civil Rights.

————. See Brasch, Ila Wales, and Walter Milton Brasch.

Brasch, Walter Milton, and Gilbert D. Schneider. "Zim, *The Judge*, and the Negro Stereotype: A Study of the Grotesque Distortion in Illustrated Journalism." Department of Linguistics, Ohio University, Athens, 1974.

Historical review of the late nineteenth- and early twentieth-century socio-satirical cartoons of Eugene Zimmerman, believed to be one of the first cartoonists to develop the grotesque distortion—both physical as well as verbal—in the treatment of the Black. Presents linguistic analysis of the language, with comparisons to the present. Discusses the use of both the drawing and the caption as primary source information for Black English research.

Brengelman, F. H. "Dialect and the Teaching of Spelling." *Research in Teaching of English*, IV (Fall, 1970), 129–38.

Outlines the relevance of dialect studies to the teaching of English.

Brewer, Jeutone. "Possible Relationships between African Languages and Black English Dialects: Implications for Teaching Standard English as an Alternate Dialect." Paper presented at the fifty-sixth annual meeting of the Speech Communications Association, December, 1970, at Atlanta, Georgia.

Concerned with the historical aspects of Black English in view of recent descriptive studies. Overview of the Niger-Congo language family. Urges that coursework for the study of history of the English language include study of Afro-American language tradition.

Brewer, John. See Cohen, Rosalie, Gerd Fraenkel, and John Brewer.

Brewer, John M. "Ghetto Children Know What They're Talking About." *New York Times Magazine*, December 25, 1966, pp. 32–35.

Discusses the "hidden language" of Blacks in urban ghetto schools. Cites numerous examples of the language and discusses an informal language program.

Brewer, John Mason. "Afro-American Folklore." *Journal of American Folklore*, LX (October–December, 1947), 377–83.

Discussion of compilation of folklore.

———. *American Negro Folklore*. Chicago: Quadrangle Books, 1968. 386 pp.

Stories of Black folklore across the United States. Describes customs, habits, beliefs, philosophies, life-styles, and reactions to incidents and pressures within the environment. Much of the book is transcribed from Black English.

———. *Aunt Dicy Tales: Snuff-Dipping Tales of the Texas Negro*. Austin: University of Texas Press, 1956. 80 pp.

———. *Dog Ghosts and Other Texas Negro Folk Tales*. Austin: University of Texas Press, 1958. 124 pp.

Introduction includes discussion of language.

———. "Juneteenth," in J. F. Dobie, ed., *Tone the Bell Easy*. Austin: Texas Folklore Society, 1932. Pp. 9–54.

Study of George Washington Carver, including his language.

———. *Negrito: Negro Dialect Poems of the Southwest*. San Antonio,

Tex.: Naylor Printing Co., 1933. 97 pp. [Reprinted by Books for Libraries Press, Freeport, N. Y., 1972.]

Study of Black life in Texas. Part IV (pp. 89–97) is a study of Black proverbs in epigrams.

————. *The Word on the Brazos: Negro Preacher Tales from the Brazos Bottoms of Texas.* Austin: University of Texas Press, 1953. 109 pp.

————. *Worser Days and Better Times: The Folklore of the North Carolina Negro.* Chicago: Quadrangle Books, 1965. 192 pp.

Includes folktales and anecdotes, folktalk, superstitions, folk rhymes, and verse. Explanations and introduction in the preface.

Briggs, Delores Griffin. "Deviations from Standard English in Papers of Selected High School Students." Doctoral dissertation, University of Alabama, University, Ala., 1968. 322 pp.

Analysis and field experimentation. Notes that only in spelling and vocabulary was there a regular decrease by year of deviations per thousand words. Subjects were thirty high-school students.

Briggs, Olin Dewitt. "A Study of Deviations from Standard English in Papers of Negro Freshmen at an Alabama College." Doctoral dissertation, University of Alabama, University, Ala., 1968. 256 pp.

Notes some dialect shifting. Data suggests average deviation of twenty-five units per five-hundred-word essay.

Bright, William, ed. *Sociolinguistics: Proceedings of the UCLA Sociolinguistics Conference, 1964.* The Hague: Mouton, 1966. 324 pp.

Thirteen papers, with discussion, from a 1964 conference in Los Angeles sponsored by the University of California at Los Angeles. Includes papers by Henry H. Hoeningswald, Raven I. McDavid, Jr., William Labov, and William J. Samarin. All involve nonstandard English.

Bronstein, Arthur J. "A Sociolinguistic Comment on the Changing Attitudes Toward the Use of Black English and an Experimental Study to Measure Some of These Attitudes." Paper presented at the annual convention of the Speech Communications Association, December, 1970, at New Orleans. 19 pp.

Bronstein, Arthur J., Lawrence J. Raphael, and Elsa M. Bronstein. "The Swinging Sociolinguistic Pendulum." *Illinois Schools Journal,* LII (1972), 2–6.

Examines the role of Black language in a linguistic setting. Discusses changes of attitudes about Black English with respect to the deficit-different theories. Advises classroom language development for each student in that student's own dialect.

Bronstein, Elsa M. See Bronstein, Arthur J., Lawrence J. Raphael, and Elsa M. Bronstein.

Brookins, Melvin S. "Aspiration." *Liberator*, VII (December, 1967). [Also in Thomas Kochman, ed. *Rappin' and Stylin' Out: Communication in Urban Black America.* Champaign: University of Illinois Press, 1972. Pp. 381–85.]

A story about a hustler, his language and idioms.

Brooks, Charlotte E. "The Culturally Deprived Reader," in Leonard Courtney, ed., *Highlights of the 1965 Pre-Convention Institutes.* Vol. 1. Newark, Del.: International Reading Association, 1966.

————. "Motivating Students for Second-Language and Second-Dialect Learning." Paper presented at the annual TESOL convention, March 3–5, 1969, at Chicago. 14 pp.

Presents the idea that teachers must be motivated to accept their students' first languages.

————. "Opportunities for Research in Urban Social Dialects," in Roger W. Shuy, ed., *Social Dialects and Language Learning: Proceedings of the Bloomington, Indiana, Conference, 1964.* Champaign, Ill.: National Council of Teachers of English, 1965. Pp. 140–42.

Emphasizes that Black English does not apply to all Blacks. Presents brief overview of racial and language problems within the formerly segregated Washington, D.C., school system.

Brooks, Cleanth. "The English Language of the South," in *A Treasury of Southern Life and Literature*, New York: C. Scribner's Sons, 1937. [Also in *A Vanderbilt Miscellany.* Nashville: Vanderbilt University Press, 1944; Juanita V. Williamson and Virginia M. Burke, eds. *A Various Language: Perspectives on American Dialects.* 1971. Pp. 136–42.]

Suggests that southern speech—White and Black—is derived from seventeenth-century British standard speech and the provincial dialects of Devon, Dorset, Somerset, and Wiltshire. Also notes that modern speech still contains these older forms. Compares dialects in Uncle Remus tales to dialects of southern and southwestern England.

————. *The Relation of the Alabama-Georgia Dialect to the Provincial Dialects of Great Britain.* Baton Rouge: Lousiana State University Press, 1935. 91 pp.

Uses word lists from Uncle Remus tales and Leonida W. Payne's "A Word List from East Alabama" to compare provincial dialects in eighteenth-century England.

Broussard, James F. *Louisiana Creole Dialect*. Baton Rouge: Louisiana State University Press, 1942. 134 pp.

The first third of this book deals with the folklore of French-speaking Blacks in southern Louisiana, recorded in Creole dialect. Supplies a phonetic transcription for most dialects; the remainder are in orthographic transcription. Includes translation of thirteen fables of LaFontaine from French into Creole. Includes Creole Negro phonetics and idioms, an eight-page glossary.

Brown, Bert A., Martin Whiteman, and Martin Deutsch. *Some Effects of Social Class and Race on Children's Language and Intellectual Abilities*. New York Institute for Developmental Studies, New York University, 1965. 31 pp. [Revised from "Some Effects of Social Class and Race on Children's Language and Intelligence Abilities." Paper presented at biannual meeting of Society for Research in Child Development, March, 1965, at Minneapolis.]

Cross-comparative analysis of environmental and performance test scores.

Brown, Claude. "The Language of Soul." *Esquire*, LXIX (April, 1968), 88. [Also in Thomas Kochman, ed., *Rappin' and Stylin' Out: Communication in Urban Black America*. Champaign: University of Illinois Press, 1972. Pp. 134–39.]

Discusses tone and semantic meanings of *nigger* and other soul words. Claims that pronunciation stress and intonation form basis of Black ethnic speech.

———. *Manchild in the Promised Land*. New York: Macmillan, 1965.

Novel. Includes Black English.

Brown, Dwight. See Politzer, Robert L., Mary Rhodes Hoover, and Dwight Brown. *An Experiment in Teaching Reading to Bidialectal Children*.

———. See Politzer, Robert L., Mary Rhodes Hoover, and Dwight Brown. *A Test of Proficiency in Black Speech and Nonstandard Speech*.

Brown, H. Rap. *Die, Nigger, Die!* New York: Dial Press, 1969. 145 pp. [Section on street talk also in Thomas Kochman, ed., *Rappin' and Stylin' Out: Communication in Urban Black America*. Champaign: University of Illinois Press, 1972. Pp. 205–208.]

Autobiography. Includes discussion of Black street language, with reference to the dozens and signifying.

Brown, John Mason. "Songs of the Slave." *Lippincott's Magazine*, II (December, 1868), 617–23.

Brown, John Pairman. "Black English." Letter to the editor in *New Republic*, CLXIV (January 16, 1971), 34–35.

Suggests program of urban dialect enrichment for suburban Whites.

Brown, Lillian Lollar. "A Comparative Descriptive Study of the Syntactic Structures in the Language of Low-Income Black and White Preschool Children." Doctoral dissertation, Southern Illinois University, Carbondale, 1972. 90 pp.

Concludes from experimental testing that there is no significant difference in the number of structures used on any of three grammatical levels. However, author points out that Black English is a syntactically developed language. Uses Noam Chomsky's generative theory for basis of linguistic analysis.

Brown, Sterling. "Negro Folk Expression: Spirituals, Seculars, Ballads, and Worksongs." *Phylon*, XIV (Spring, 1953), 45–61.

Discusses Black spirituals and folk music. Includes several lyrics.

Brown, Warren, comp. *Checklist of Negro Newspapers in the United States, 1827–1946*. School of Journalism, Lincoln University, Jefferson City, Mo., 1946.

Complete list.

Broz, James J., Jr. *Trends and Implications of Current Research in Dialectology*. ERIC document ED 010 690. Washington, D.C., July, 1967. 29 pp.

Review of linguistic studies in five metropolitan cities.

Bruce, Beverlee. "The Sociological and Psychological Implications of Language Change." *American Behavioral Scientist*, XII (March–April, 1969), 34–37.

Brief overview of Black English, with implications for language within a racial-identification setting.

Bruder, Mary Newton, and Luddy Hayden. "Teaching Composition: A Report on a Bidialectal Approach." Paper presented at the convention of the Teachers of English to Speakers of other Languages, February 27–March 1, 1972, at Washington, D.C. [Also in *Language Learning*, XXIII (June, 1973), 1–15.]

Bryden, James Davenport, Jr. "An Acoustic and Social Dialect Analysis of Perceptual Variables in Listener Identification and Rating of Negro Speakers." Doctoral dissertation, University of Virginia, Charlottesville, 1968. [Also published as *Final Report*. Washington, D.C. Department of Health, Education and Welfare, Project contract 7–C–00C.; Department of Speech Pathology and Audiology Research Laboratory, University of Virginia, Charlottesville.]

Study of social and acoustic variables which function significantly in racial identification and the rating of Black and White speakers by both Black and White listeners. Concludes that identification is phonological.

Buchanan, O. Lee. See North, George E., and O. Lee Buchanan.

Buck, Joyce F. "The Effects of Negro and White Dialectical Variation upon Attitudes of College Students." *Speech Monographs*, XXXV (June, 1968), 181–86.

Experimental test suggests that female college students prefer standard English to nonstandard English, and did not express preferences between White or Black speakers when both spoke standard English. However, standard English was associated with Whites. On tests of trustworthiness, Black and White standard English speakers were perceived as being more trustworthy than Whites speaking nonstandard English, but Blacks speaking Black English were not judged to be less trustworthy than Whites or Blacks speaking standard English.

————. "Sociolinguistic Implications of the Phonological Variation of Black and White Speakers." Doctoral dissertation, City University of New York, 1972. 285 pp.

Extensive, in-depth elaboration of her article "The Effects of Negro and White Dialectical Variation upon Attitudes of College Students."

Buckley, Richard Dale. "Negro Periodicals: Historical Notes and Suggestions for Use." *Social Education*, XXXIII (April, 1969), 426–28.

List of contemporary Black periodicals.

Burke, Carolyn. "Dialect and the Reading Process," in James L. Laffey and Roger Shuy, eds., *Language Differences—Do They Interfere?* Newark, Del.: International Reading Association, 1973. Pp. 91–100.

Burke, John Philip. "The Performance of Five-Year-Old Children on Oregon Language Profile: A Study of Language Patterns in an Urban Black Population." Doctoral dissertation, University of Oregon, Eugene, 1972. 123 pp.

Notes that there are no significant differences among the fifty children sampled. Indicates that test findings show that Black children have language patterns closely paralleling those of White children, as far as the Oregon test is concerned. Concludes that the Oregon test is a valid test of language ability for both the Black and the White child.

Burke, Virginia M. See Williamson, Juanita V., and Virginia M. Burke, eds.

Burks, Ann, and Polly Guilford. "Wakulla County Oral Language Project." *Elementary English*, XLVI (May, 1969), 606–11.

Includes list of phonological variations between standard and nonstandard English. Primary focus is on audio-lingual language methods.

Burley, Dan. *Dan Burley's Original Handbook of Harlem Jive*. New York: n.p., 1944. 158 pp. Illustrated by Melvin Tapley.

Burling, Robbins. *English in Black and White*. New York: Holt, Rinehart, & Winston, 1973. 168 pp.

Description and brief analysis of Black English, with emphasis on educational implications.

————. *Man's Many Voices: Language in Its Cultural Context*. New York: Holt, Rinehart, & Winston, 1970. 222 pp.

General language and culture text, with concentration on the effects of culture upon language. Chapter 9 ("Black English") discusses origin of diversity, a stigmatized dialect, phonological contrasts, loss of suffixes, grammatical changes, and ghetto education.

————. "Standard Colloquial and Standard Written English: Some Implications for Teaching Literacy to Nonstandard Speakers." *Florida FL Reporter*, VIII (Spring/Fall, 1970), 9–15, 47.

Emphasizes the importance of distinguishing between standard speech and standard writing skills.

————. "Talking to Teachers about Social Dialects." *Language Learning*, XXI (December, 1971), 221–34.

Underlines differences between teachers and linguists in dialect beliefs and orientation. Urges that prospective teachers take linguistics courses.

Burns, Augustus M. See Otto, John Solomon, and Augustus M. Burns.

Burroughs, Evelyn. "The Berlin Wall of Language." *Missouri English Bulletin*, XXVI (January, 1969), 1–5.

Points out a number of barriers to Black English and nonstandard English speakers. Discusses teaching techniques for facility of code-switching and language recognition.

42

Bush, Douglas. "Does Anybody Here Speak English?" Washington *Evening Star*, March 19, 1972, pp. B3–B4.

Bush, Terri, and June Jordan, eds. *The Voice of the Children.* New York: Holt, Rinehart, & Winston, 1970. 101 pp.

Butcher, Margaret J. *The Negro in American Culture: Based on Materials Left by Alain Locke.* New York: Alfred A. Knopf, 1956/1971. 294 pp.

Butler, Melvin Arthur. "African Linguistic Remnants in the Speech of Black Louisianans." *Black Experience: A Southern University Journal*, LV (June, 1969), 45–52.

Brief historical overview on African origins of Black English and Gullah. Includes brief studies of several African-originated Gullah words.

––––––. "Lexical Usage of Negroes in Northeast Louisiana." Doctoral dissertation, University of Michigan, Ann Arbor, 1968. 182 pp.

Notes low frequency of French usage. Analyzes ethnic terms and remnants. Makes no conclusions on validity of a Black English distinct and separate from standard English.

Butterfield, Stephen Thomas. "Black Autobiography: The Development of Identification, Language and Viewpoint from Douglass to Jackson." Doctoral dissertation, University of Massachusetts, Amherst, 1972. 517 pp.

Discusses social context and impact of narratives. Notes that although slave narrative language is modeled after White styles, it is distinctive. Traces Black rhetoric, noting that the language of the narrative is "ironic, concrete, full of double meaning, a weapon of struggle, a way of redefining the human image." Places the language into social and historical context.

Butters, R. Ronald. "A Linguistic View of Negro Intelligence." *Clearing House*, XLVI (January, 1972), 259–63.

Buttitta, Anthony J. "Negro Folklore in North Carolina," in Nancy Cunard, ed., *Negro Anthology*. London: privately published, 1934. Pp. 62–66.

A few proverbial sayings.

Butts, David P. "Context and Teachers in Oral Language Aquisition— Means or Ends?" *Elementary English*, XLVIII (March, 1971), 290–97. [Also in Thomas D. Horn, ed., *Research Bases for Oral Language Instruction*. Urbana, Ill.: National Council of Teachers of English, 1971. Pp. 52–62.]

Suggests that a main problem in oral language development is the failure to teach children to discriminate between ideas in their own language.

Byers, Jim. "Using Poetry to Help Educationally Deprived Children Learn Inductively." *Elementary English*, XLII (March, 1965), 275–79. [Also in Eldonna Evertts, ed., *Dimensions of Dialect*. Champaign, Ill.: National Council of Teachers of English, 1967. Pp. 47–51.]

Asserts that choral verse work may help children who speak a nonstandard dialect learn inductively to read.

Byrne, Margaret C. *Head Start Evaluation and Research Center, University of Kansas, Report No. III—Effect of a Language Program on Children in a Head Start Nursery.* Department of Human Development, University of Kansas, Lawrence, 1967. 33 pp.

Experimental study involving a compensatory language program with twenty-five students, three to six years old.

C

Cable, George Washington. "Creole Slave Songs." *Century Magazine*, XXXI (April, 1887), 807–28. [Also in Bruce Jackson, ed., *The Negro and His Folklore in Nineteenth-Century Periodicals*. Austin: University of Texas Press, 1967. Pp. 211–42.]

A few observations, including dialect-switching by slaves.

———. "The Dance in the Place Congo." *Century Magazine*, XXXI (February, 1886), 517–32.

Description of slaves dancing in New Orleans. Includes music and lyrics of several songs.

———. *Old Creole Days: A Story of Creole Life.* New York: C. Scribner's Sons, 1879. 229 pp.

Primarily a discussion of the French Creole.

Cade, John B. "Out of the Mouths of Ex-Slaves." *Journal of Negro History*, XX (July, 1935), 294–337.

Recordings of several passages regarding slavery, told by former slaves.

Caffee, Nathaniel M. "Transcriptions of a Phonograph Record of the Speech of a Negro between 70 and 75 Years Old and a Life-Long Resident of Charlottesville, Va." *American Speech*, X (December, 1935), 298–99.

Cairns, Charles E. See Williams, Frederick, Charles E. Cairns, and Helen S. Cairns.

Cairns, Helen S. See Williams, Frederick, Charles E. Cairns, and Helen S. Cairns.

Caliver, Ambrose, comp. *Bibliography on Education of the Negro, Comprising Publications from January, 1928, to December, 1930.* Washington, D.C.: U.S. Government Printing Office, 1931. 34 pp.

————. *A Personal Study of Negro College Students: A Study of the Relations between Certain Background Factors of Negro College Students and Their Subsequent Careers in College.* Westport, Conn.: Negro University Press, 1970. 146 pp.

Campbell, G. L. "Comments on Broken Speech in American Colonies." *London Magazine,* XV (July, 1746), 321–30.

Several observations on nonstandard English.

Campbell, Killis. "Poe's Treatment of the Negro and Negro Dialect." *University of Texas Bulletin: Studies in English,* No. 16 (July 8, 1936), 106–14.

Evaluation of the political-racial beliefs of Poe, based upon his literary treatment of Blacks. Says that the dialect is stiff and inaccurate.

Cannon, Garland. "Multidialects: The Student's Right to His Own Language." *College Composition and Communication,* XXIV (December, 1973), 382–85.

Cansler, Charles W. *Three Generations: The Story of a Colored Family of Eastern Tennessee.* Kingsport, Tenn.: Kingsport Press, 1939. 173 pp.

Carawan, Candie. See Carawan, Guy, and Candie Carawan.

Carawan, Guy, and Candie Carawan. *Ain't You Got a Right to the Tree of Life? The People of Johns Island, S.C.—Their Faces, Their Words and Their Songs.* New York: Simon & Schuster, 1966. 190 pp.

Brief study of the Black folk-traditions on Johns Island. Includes photos by Robert Yellin.

Card, William. See Davis, A. L., William M. Austin, William Card, Raven I. McDavid, Jr., and Virginia Glenn McDavid, eds.

Card, William, and Virginia Glenn McDavid. "Problem Areas in Grammar," in A. L. Davis, William M. Austin, William Card, Raven I. McDavid, Jr., and Virginia Glenn McDavid, eds., *Culture, Class, and Language Variety: A Resource Book for Teachers.* Urbana, Ill.: National Council of Teachers of English, 1972. Pp. 89–132.

Lists important differences between standard and nonstandard English languages.

Caroline, Lawrence. See Lane, Harlan, Lawrence Caroline, and Charles Curran.

Carroll, John B. "Language and Cognition: Current Perspectives from Linguistics and Psychology," in James L. Laffey and Roger Shuy, eds., *Language Differences—Do They Interfere?* Newark, Del.: International Reading Association, 1973.

Carroll, William S. "A Phonology of Washington Negro Speech." Doctoral dissertation, Georgetown University, Washington, D.C., 1971. 107 pp.

Preliminary investigation of segmental phonology of Washington, D.C., Black English of the lower socio-economic segment of the Black community. Principal subject was an eight-year-old Black boy.

———. "A Teaching Experiment." *TESOL Quarterly*, I (September, 1967), 31–36.

Basic discussion of Black English features.

Carroll, William S., and Irwin Feigenbaum. *Oral Language Teaching Materials*. Washington, D.C.: Center for Applied Linguistics, 1966.

———. "Teaching a Second Dialect and Some Implications for TESOL." *TESOL Quarterly*, I (September, 1967), 31–39.

Two articles with one title and individual subtitles. Authors summarize major differences between standard and nonstandard English in Washington, D.C., and describe the development of educational plans for teaching standard English along foreign-language methodological lines.

Carson, A. S., and A. I. Rabin. "Verbal Comprehension and Communication in Negro and White Children." *Journal of Educational Psychology*, LI (April, 1960), 47–51.

Carter, John L. *The Long Range Effects of a Language Stimulation Program upon Negro Educationally Disadvantaged First Grade Children*. Houston: University of Houston, May, 1967. 33 pp.

Carter, Thomas P. "Cultural Context for Linguistically Different Learners." *Elementary English*, XLVIII (February, 1971), 162–75. [Also in Thomas Horn, ed., *Research Bases for Oral Language Instruction*. Urbana, Ill.: National Council of Teachers of English, 1971. Pp. 36–49.]

Discusses the extent to which cultures, curriculum, and cross-cultural schooling should be included in English programs. Suggests some approaches.

Carton, Aaron S. *Basic Speech Improvement Program for Disadvantaged Pupils in Non-Public Schools—Regular Day Schools.* Center for Urban Education, New York University, August, 1966. 49 pp.

Caselli, Ron. "Keys to Standard English." *Elementary School Journal,* LXXI (November, 1970), 86–89.

General discussion of nonstandard English. Emphasizes teacher acceptance.

Caskei, P. G. "Predictability of the Position of the Deleted Auxiliary Verb in the Speech of Black and White Children at Two Age Levels." Paper presented at the Southeastern Conference on Linguistics, October 16–17, 1970, at Atlanta.

Predictability allows the writing of specific rules.

Cassidy, Frederic G. *Jamaica Talk: Three Hundred Years of the English Language in Jamaica.* New York: St. Martin's Press, 1961. 468 pp.

Detailed study of Jamaican English and Creole. Several implications for American Black English study.

———. "Teaching Standard English to Speakers of Creole in Jamaica, West Indies," in James E. Alatis, ed., *Report of the Twentieth Annual Roundtable Meeting on Linguistics and Language Studies: Linguistics and the Teaching of Standard English to Speakers of Other Languages or Dialects.* Monograph Series on Languages and Linguistics. Washington, D.C.: Georgetown University Press, 1970. Pp. 203–14.

Discusses social and educational barriers to effective teaching in Jamaica.

———. "Toward a Recovery of Early English-African Pidgin." Paper presented at the Symposium on Multilingualism, 1962, at Brazzaville, The Congo Republic.

Cassidy, Frederic G., and Robert B. LePage. *Dictionary of Jamaican English.* London: Cambridge University Press, 1967. 484 pp.

Cattell, Raymond Bernard. "Are IQ Tests Intelligent?" *Psychology Today,* I (March, 1968), 56–62.

Includes discussion and description of non–culture bound, non-verbal language items.

Cazden, Courtney B. "The Neglected Situation in Child Language Research and Education," in Frederick Williams, ed., *Language and*

Poverty: Perspectives on a Theme. Chicago: Markham, 1970. Pp. 81–101.

Warns against accepting totally either the deficit-language theory or the different-language hypothesis. Points to inadequacies in both.

————. "Speech: A Social Matter?" *Contemporary Psychology,* XIII (June, 1968), 320–22.

Review of William Labov, *The Social Stratification of English in New York City.*

————. "Some Implications of Research on Language Development for Preschool Education." Paper presented at Social Science Research Council Conference on Preschool Education, February 2–7, 1966, at Chicago. 31 pp.

————. "Subcultural Differences in Child Language—An Interdisciplinary Review." *Merrill-Palmer Quarterly of Behavior and Development,* XII (July, 1966), 185–219.

Describes language usage by children, including nonstandard English.

————. "Sociolinguistic Views of the Language and Speech of Lower-Class Children—with Special Attention to the Work of Basil Bernstein." *Developmental Medicine and Child Neurology,* X (October, 1968), 600–12.

Cazden, Courtney B., Vera P. John, and Dell H. Hymes, eds. *Functions of Language in the Classroom.* New York: Teachers College Press, Columbia University, 1972. 394 pp.

General reader, with only two of the fourteen articles being reprints. Among the articles are "What Has the Sociology of Language to Say to the Teacher? On Teaching the Standard Variety to Speakers of Dialectal or Sociolectal Varieties" by Joshua A. Fishman and Erika Lueders-Salmon; "Bilingualism, Bidialectism, and Classroom Interaction" by John J. Gumperz and Eduardo Hernandez-Chavez; "John and Mary: A Pilot Study in Linguistic Ecology" by Vivian M. Horner and Joan D. Gussow; "On the Status of Black English for Native Speakers: An Assessment of Attitudes and Values" by Claudia Mitchell-Kernan; and "Black American Speech Events and a Language Program for the Classroom" by Thomas Kochman. Includes forty-seven-page introduction by Dell Hymes.

"CBE Interviews: Kenneth B. Clark." *Bulletin of the Council for Basic Education,* XIV (1969), 8–18.

Defense of a proposal for a "reading and arithmetic mobilization

48

year" to bring every normal ghetto child, White and Black, to his proper grade level in reading, language, and arithmetic skills.

Center for Applied Linguistics. *Current Social Dialect Research at American Higher Institutions. Report 2.* Center for Applied Linguistics, Washington, D.C., and the National Council of Teachers of English, Urbana, Illinois, November 15, 1966. 38 pp.

"Certain Beliefs and Superstitions of the Negro." *Atlantic Monthly*, LXVIII (August, 1891), 286–88.

Several reflections by nineteenth-century Blacks on philosophical questions. Recorded in their language.

Chall, Jeanne. "Research in Linguistics and Reading Instruction: Implications for Further Research and Practice." Paper presented at the International Reading Association conference, April 24–27, 1968, at Boston. 23 pp.

Chall, Jeanne, and Shirley C. Feldmann. *A Study in Depth of First-Grade Reading: An Analysis of the Interactions of Professional Methods, Teacher Implementation, and Child Background.* New York: College of the City of New York, 1966.

Chamberlain, A. F. "Goober, a Negro Word for Peanuts." *American Notes and Queries*, II (January 5, 1889), 120.

————. "Negro Dialect." *Science*, XII (July 13, 1888), 23–24.

Letter to the editor; discusses derivation of terms in Black English.

Chan, Shui Hon. "Should Black English Be Considered as a Dialect of English?" Unpublished paper, Department of English, University of Northern Iowa, Cedar Falls, 1971. 11 pp.

Examination of the question of dialect or separate language by using a discussion of Black English phonology. Concludes that Black English is a dialect of English.

Chandler, B. J., and Frederick D. Erickson. *Sounds of Society: A Demonstration Program in Group Inquiry.* ERIC document ED 018 522. Washington, D.C., January, 1968. 108 pp.

Discusses cultural differences and their influence on behavior in relation to language styles of the lower-class Negro and middle-class White.

Chapman, Abraham. *The Negro in American Literature and a Bibliography of Literature by and about Negro Americans.* Oshkosh, Wis.: Wisconsin Council of Teachers of English, 1966. 135 pp.

Chapman, Robert L. "They Were Speaking Prose All the Time." *Nation,* CCXV (October 2, 1972), 278–79.

> Review of J. L. Dillard's *Black English: Its History and Usage in the United States.* Discusses the failure of orthodox education to deal with Black English.

Charters, Samuel Barclay. *The Poetry of the Blues.* New York: Oak Publications, 1963. 111 pp.

> American poetry by Black writers.

Chavanachat, Ponsawan. "Gullah Dialect: The Origin of Black English." Unpublished paper, Department of English, University of Northern Iowa, Cedar Falls, 1971, 13 pp.

> Discusses the development of Gullah on the Sea Islands. Also discusses the question of whether Black languages have a common origin in Gullah.

Chesnutt, Charles Waddell. *The Conjure Woman.* Boston: Houghton Mifflin, 1899. 229 pp.

> Series of dialect tales about slavery, as recollected by a Black gardener.

———. *The Marrow of Tradition.* Boston: Houghton Mifflin, 1901. 329 pp.

> Novel. Includes dialect.

———. *The Wife of His Youth, and Other Stories of the Color Line.* Boston: Houghton Mifflin, 1901. 323 pp. Illustrated by Clyde O. De Land.

Cheyney, Arnold B. *Teaching Culturally Disadvantaged in the Elementary School.* Columbus, Ohio: Charles E. Merrill, 1967. 164 pp.

> Includes two basic sections: potentialities and problems faced by children and teachers in disadvantaged areas; and language development, with a discussion of methodology.

Chicago Board of Education. See Davis, Olga, Mildred R. Gladney, and Lloyd Leaverton.

Child, Lydia M. *Fact and Fiction.* New York: C. S. Francis and Sons, 1847. 282 pp.

> Several tales.

Choppin, Jules. "Entretien sur les 12 Mois de l'Année par un Vieux Nègre St. Jacquois Nommé 'Pa Guitin'." *Comptes Rendus,* XIV (January, 1897), 17–20; (March, 1897), 57–61.

A one-year case study of an old Black, including his language, written in the Creole language of the Louisiana area.

———. "Les Singes et le Léopard." *Comptes Rendus*, XVII (July, 1900), 114.

A short fable, written in French, then translated into American Black Creole.

Christensen, Mrs. A. M. H. *Afro-American Folk Lore, Told Round Cabin Fires on the Sea Islands of South Carolina.* Boston: J. G. Cupples, 1892. 116 pp. [Reprinted by Negro Universities Press, Westport, Conn., 1969.]

Eighteen animal folk tales, written in Gullah. Shows influence of African thought.

Christophersen, Paul. "A Note on the Words *Dash* and *Ju-Ju* in West African English." *English Studies*, XL (1959), 115–18. [Also in J. L. Dillard, ed., *Perspectives on Black English*. The Hague: Mouton, forthcoming.]

Concludes that both words have European origins, rather than West African as previously believed.

———. "Some Special West African Words." *English Studies*, XXXIV (1953), 282–91. [Also in J. L. Dillard, ed., *Perspectives on Black English*. The Hague: Mouton, forthcoming.]

General discussion of West African English, with several words and phrases of interest to American dialectologists.

Cifuentes, Maria Antonia. "The Teaching of Standard English to Negro Students." Unpublished paper, Department of English, University of Northern Iowa, Cedar Falls, 1971. 22 pp.

Discusses teaching standard English to Black students. Evaluates experimental texts developed by the psycholinguistics staff of the Chicago Board of Education.

Claerbant, David. *Black Jargon in White America.* Grand Rapids, Mich.: Eerdmans, 1972. 89 pp.

Report of a teaching program to introduce Black jargon to students.

Clapp, O. H. "Why Color It White?" *Instructor*, LXXX (October, 1970), 74–75.

Clark, Dennis, Abraham Wolf, Henry Goehl, and Donald Ecroyd. *Dialect Remediation Program.* Temple University, Philadelphia, Pa., n.d.

Report on an experimental study involving 160 students.

Clark, Virginia P., Paul A. Eschholz, and Alfred A. Rosa, eds. *Language: Introductory Readings.* New York: St. Martin's Press, 1972. 558 pp.

General introduction to language and linguistics. Among the fifty-six articles are "The English Language Is My Enemy" by Ossie Davis; "Speech Communities" by Paul Roberts; "The Reasons for Dialect Differences" by Roger W. Shuy; "Standard English" by Charles C. Fries; "Sense and Nonsense about American Dialects" by Raven I. McDavid, Jr.; "The Study of Nonstandard English" by William Labov; "Sociolinguistic Factors in the History of American Negro Dialects" by William A. Stewart; "Should Ghettoese Be Accepted?" by William Raspberry; "Bi-Dialectism: The Linguistics of White Supremacy" by James Sledd; and "Some Aspects of Bilingualism in San Antonio, Texas" by Janet B. Sawyer.

Clarke, Nona H. See Wolfram, Walter A., and Nona H. Clarke eds.

Claudel, Calvin. "Four Tales from the French Folklore of Louisiana." *Southern Folklore Quarterly,* IX (December, 1945), 191–208.

Includes a few Creole phrases.

―――. "Three Tales from the French Folklore of Louisiana." *Journal of American Folklore,* LVI (January, 1943), 38–44.

Clearinghouse for Social Dialect Studies. See Center for Applied Linguistics.

Clemens, Samuel Langhorne [Mark Twain]. *The Adventures of Huckleberry Finn.* London: Chatto & Windus, 1884.

Cloud, Virginia Woodward. *From an Old Garden.* Baltimore: Norman, Remington, 1922. 30 pp.

Coady, James M. Review of Ralph W. Fasold and Roger W. Shuy, eds., *Teaching Standard English in the Inner City. Language Sciences,* No. 16 (August, 1971), 41–43.

Points out that there is no evidence to support claims that foreign-language teaching methods would help teach standard English to speakers of Black English.

―――. Review of Walter A. Wolfram and Nona H. Clarke, eds., *Black-White Speech Relationships. Language Sciences,* XXVIII (December, 1973), 27–28.

Essentially notes that there is no definitive evidence to support either the Creolist or the dialect-geographer positions on Black English.

Cobb, Henry E. "The African Background of the American Negro: Myth and Reality." *Bulletin of the Southern University and A&M College,* LV (June, 1969), 9–19.

Cockrell, Wilma, and Kenneth R. Johnson. *Standard Oral English, Tenth Grade: Instructional Guide C.* Los Angeles: Los Angeles City School System, 1967. 161 pp.

Report of the ESEA Title I project, administered by the Los Angeles City School System, which had as its purpose the elimination of nonstandard pronunciation among tenth-grade Blacks.

Coffin, Tristram Potter, ed. *Our Living Traditions.* New York: Basic Books, 1968. 301 pp.

Includes toasts and Black narrative verse.

Cohen, Inez Lopez. *Our Darktown Press.* New York: D. Appleton, 1932. 79 pp.

Discusses several aspects of Black language.

Cohen, Irvin S., and Rayford W. Logan. *The American Negro: Old World Background and New World Experience.* Boston: Houghton Mifflin, 1970. 325 pp.

Cohen, Karen M., and Flo Gryn Kimmerling. "Attitudes Based on English Dialect Differences: An Analysis of Current Research." *Language Research Report Number 4*, Language Research Foundation, Cambridge, Mass., July, 1971. 54 pp.

Analysis and critique of eighteen separate studies involving attitudes toward dialects.

Cohen, Lily Young. *Lost Spirituals.* New York: W. Neale, 1928. 143 pp.

Music and lyrics composed by Charlestown, Va., Blacks.

Cohen, Octavus Roy. *Florian Slappey Goes Abroad.* Boston: Little, Brown, 1928. 310 pp.

A dialect novel from the Florian Slappey series.

———. *Polished Ebony.* New York: Dodd, Mead, 1919. 309 pp.

Dialect tales.

Cohen, Paul. "Creativity, Grading, and Standards of Excellence." Paper presented at the Conference on English—Black and White, March 4–6, 1971, at Purdue University, West Lafayette, Ind.

———. "Some Methods in Sociolinguistic Research." Paper presented at Research Planning Conference on Language Development in Disadvantaged Children, June 7–8, 1966, at the Graduate College of Education, Yeshiva University, New York.

Discusses ways in which the Labov team resolved problems of social situation and its controlling effect on interviewing; patterns of leadership and prestige of the group and their range of repertoire.

———. See Labov, William, and Paul Cohen. *Some Suggestions for Teaching Standard English to Speakers of Nonstandard Dialects.*

———. See Labov, William, and Paul Cohen. "Systematic Relations of Standard and Nonstandard Rules in the Grammars of Negro Speakers."

———. See Labov, William, Paul Cohen, and Clarence Robins.

———. See Labov, William, Paul Cohen, Clarence Robins, and John Lewis. "Classroom Correction Tests."

———. See Labov, William, Paul Cohen, Clarence Robins, and John Lewis. *A Study of the Non-Standard English of Negro and Puerto Rican Speakers in New York City.*

Cohen, Rosalie, Gerd Fraenkel, and John Brewer. "Implications for 'Culture Conflict' from a Semantic Feature Analysis of the Lexicon of the Hard-Core Poor." *Linguistics,* XLIV (1968), 11–21.

Develops a taxonomy of the language of the hard-core poor, with intention of generating testable hypothesis. About five thousand lexical items.

Cohen, S. Alan. "A Curriculum Demonstration Project for Teaching Literacy Skills to Disadvantaged 7th and 8th Graders." Paper presented at the Research Planning Conference on Language Development in Disadvantaged Children, June 7–8, 1966, at the Graduate College of Education, Yeshiva University, New York.

Discusses principles of education and learning.

———. "Some Learning Disabilities of Socially Disadvantaged Puerto Rican and Negro Children." *Academic Therapy Quarterly,* II (Fall, 1966), 37–41, 52.

Examines perceptual dysfunction as a factor causing reading and learning problems in disadvantaged children.

Cohen, S. Alan, and Gita S. Kornfeld. "Oral Vocabulary and Beginning Reading in Disadvantaged Black Children." *Reading Teacher,* XXIV (October, 1970), 33–38.

Notes that Black children can handle most of the conceptual vocabulary in beginning readers. Based on Detroit study, then generalized for all urban areas.

Cohen, S. Alan, and Steven Reinstein. "Skill Centers: A Systems Approach to Reading Instruction." Paper presented at College Reading Association Conference, March 13–15, 1969, at Boston. 10 pp.

Outlines the Yeshiva University program which emphasises self-directing and self-correcting techniques for teaching of basic reading skills. Implications for nonstandard English speakers.

Cohn, Werner. "On the Language of Lower-Class Children." *School Review*, LXVII (Winter, 1959), 435–40.

Discusses basic differences between the rules of standard and nonstandard English. Urges a "morally neutral consideration of the two types of language"—Black English and standard English—by inquiring into the function of each language.

Cole, David W. "An Ephraimite Perspective on Bidialectism." *College Composition and Communication*, XXIII (December, 1972), 371–72.

An updated version of how a linguist–English teacher might handle the problems that the Ephraimites had when they tried to pass through the land of the Gileads. From Judges 12:5–6. Several implications for students of bidialectism and Black English.

Coleman, Morris, Albert J. Harris, and Irma T. Auerbach. "The Reading Performances of Disadvantaged Early and Non-Early Readers from Grades 1 Through 3." *Journal of Educational Research*, LXV (September, 1971), 23–26.

Data suggests early reading is not detrimental to language range achievement.

Collier, Eugenia W. "James Weldon Johnson: Mirror of Change." *Phylon*, XXI (Winter, 1960), 351–59.

Discussion of Black dialect in poetry, with emphasis on the works of James Weldon Johnson in comparison to Paul Laurence Dunbar.

Combs, J. H. "A Word-List from Georgia," *Dialect Notes*, V (1922), 183–84.

A word-list from Uncle Remus stories.

Comhaire-Sylvain, Suzanne. *Le Créole Haitien: Morphologie et Syntaxe.* Port-au-Prince, Haiti: De Meester Publishing, 1936. 180 pp.

Notes that Black languages have African origins.

Committee on Negro Studies, American Council of Learned Societies. See *Negro Newspapers on Microfilm.*

Cone, James H. *The Spirituals and the Blues: An Interpretation.* New York: Seabury Press, 1972. 152 pp.

Conference of Negro Writers. *The American Negro Writer and His Roots: Selected Papers.* New York: American Society of African Culture, 1959. 70 pp.

Among the papers are those by Langston Hughes, Saunders Redding, Samuel Allen, John Henrik Clarke, Julian Mayfield, Arthur Davis, William Branch, Arna Bontemps, and Loften Mitchell.

Conklin, Nancy. Review of Harold B. Allen and Gary N. Underwood, eds., *Readings in American Dialectology. Language Learning,* XXI (December, 1971), 269–74.

Connelly, Marc. *The Green Pastures.* New York: Farrar and Rinehart, 1929.

Pulitzer Prize–winning drama. A humorous study of how Blacks in the Deep South, within their own world-view, might see the stories of the Bible. All-Black cast, with dialogue in Black English. First presented in 1930 at the Mansfield Theater, New York.

Connors, C. Keith, and Leon Eisenberg. *The Effect of Teacher Behavior on Verbal Intelligence in Operation Head Start Children.* Baltimore: The Johns Hopkins University School of Medicine, 1966. 26 pp.

Conrad, Earl. "The Philology of Negro Dialect." *Journal of Negro Education,* XIII (Spring, 1944), 150–54.

Points to the literary prejudice in reproducing Black dialects and White standard English. Also notes that not all Blacks speak Black English. Discusses code-switching.

Conroy, Pat. "Conrock, You're Crazy." *Life,* LXXII (June 2, 1972), 55–72.

Abridged from *The Water Is Wide,* 1972.

———. *The Water Is Wide.* Boston: Houghton Mifflin Co., 1972.

Narrative of a young male teacher's determination to help the Gullah-speaking Blacks of the Sea Islands, his successes and frustrations. Powerful indictment against inferior teaching methods and indifference to problems of nonstandard English speakers.

Cooke, Benjamin G. "An Initial Classification on Nonverbal Communication among Afro-Americans." Master's thesis, Northeastern Illinois State College, Chicago, 1968.

———. "Non-Verbal Communication among Afro-Americans: An Initial Classification," in Thomas Kochman, ed., *Rappin' and Stylin' Out:*

Communication in Urban Black America. Champaign: University of Illinois Press, 1972; Pp. 32–64.

Identification, classification, and explanation of nonverbal language in the Black community. Includes discussion of "giving skin," stances, rapping styles, use of eyes, walking, and the Black Power handshake.

Cooley, Ralph E. Review of Juanita V. Williamson and Virginia M. Burke, eds., *A Various Language: Perspectives on American Dialects. Language Learning,* XXI (December, 1971), 263–68.

Cooper, James Fenimore. *Satanstoe: Or, The Littlepage Manuscripts.* New York: Burgess, Stringer, 1845. 2 vols.

Novel. Note language of Jaap.

Corbin, Richard, and Muriel Crosby, eds. *Language Problems for the Disadvantaged: The Report of the NCTE Task Force on Teaching English to the Disadvantaged.* Champaign, Ill.: National Council of Teachers of English, 1965. 327 pp.

Presents the problems, programs, theories, and commentaries of Task Force members, as well as the general recommendations.

Correll, Charles. See Gosden, Freeman, and Charles Correll.

Couch, W. T., ed. *Culture in the South.* Chapel Hill: University of North Carolina Press, 1934.

Courlander, Harold. *Negro Folk Music, USA.* New York: Columbia University Press, 1963. 324 pp.

Comprehensive study of Black folk music.

Courtney, Leonard, ed. *Highlights of the 1965 Pre-Convention Institutes.* Newark, Del.: International Reading Association, 1966. 6 vols.

Several studies pertinent to Black English students.

Covington, Ann Juanita. "A Study of Teachers' Attitudes toward Black English: Effects on the Standard Achievement." Doctoral dissertation, University of Pittsburgh, 1972. 93 pp.

Notes that teacher attitudes are only "mildly positive." Uses twenty-seven third-grade Black children for survey.

Cowart, Harry. See Rystrom, Richard, and Harry Cowart.

Cowles, Milly, ed. *Perspectives in the Education of Disadvantaged Children.* Cleveland: World Publishing, 1967. 314 pp.

Collection of writings concerning poverty, children of poverty, and the educational implications for the social sciences and language.

Cox, Adrienne F. "The Receptiveness of Black Students to Dialects Sometimes Different from Their Own." Doctoral dissertation, Wayne State University, Detroit, 1971. 156 pp.

Test of identification of Black language on tapes. Inner-city students identify Black language better than outer-city students.

Cox, Oliver C. *Caste, Class, and Race: A Study in Social Dynamics*. Garden City, N.Y.: Doubleday, 1948. 624 pp.

Background information. Part 3 (pp. 317–603) focuses on race.

Craig, Myrtle. "Reading and Writing Standard English." Paper presented at the annual meeting of the National Council of Teachers of English, November 23–25, 1967, at Honolulu. 7 pp.

Argues that the teacher must accept the standards of English spoken by the child at home, and that, in writing, communication should be of greater value than mechanical skills.

Cramer, Ronald L. "Dialectology—A Behavior to be Considered in Teaching Children to Read." Paper presented at the Conference of the International Reading Association, May 6–9, 1970, at Anaheim, California.

Discusses how to match child's dialect with reading material. Suggests a "talk written down" approach.

———. "Dialectology: A Case for Language Experience." *Reading Teacher*, XXV (October, 1971), 33–39.

Discusses interrelationship between language and reading. Presents three alternate theories for the teaching of reading to nonstandard English speakers.

———. "When Children Speak a Dialect." *Instructor*, LXXXI (March, 1972), 60–61.

Brief comments showing that nonstandard and Black English are languages. Urges toleration and suggests teaching Black English, but with the use of recorders for individual speech and later transcription.

Crawford, Samuel D. See Bentley, Robert H., and Samuel D. Crawford, eds.

Creber, J. W. Patrick. "English as a Foreign Language: Reflections on a Novel Aspect." *English in Education*, IV (Autumn, 1970), 96, 98.

Contends that schools routinely teach English as a foreign language.

Crews, Ruthellen. "An Experiment in Dialect Study." *English Education*, IV (Fall, 1972), 27–32.

Describes a twelve-hour special program in dialect study for elementary education students at the University of Florida. Notes that the program generally followed the recommendations of Roger W. Shuy in nonstandard dialects.

————. "Nonstandard Dialects and the Language Classroom." *Educational Horizons*, L (Spring, 1972), 112–15.

Classroom suggestions. Notes that the system of education requires both the standard-dialect-speaking teacher and the nonstandard-dialect-speaking student to understand each other's dialects.

Criswell, Robert. *Uncle Tom's Cabin Contrasted with Buckingham Hall: Planter's Home, Or, a Fair View of Both Sides of the Slavery Question.* New York: D. Fanshaw, 1852. 152 pp.

Crockett, Harry J., Jr. Review of William Labov, *The Social Stratification of English in New York City. American Sociological Review*, XXXIII (October, 1968), 819–20.

————. See Levine, Lewis, and Harry J. Crockett, Jr.

Cromack, Robert E. "The Functional Nature of Social Dialects: Social Change and the Teaching of Black English." *English Record*, XXI (April, 1971), 74–82.

Argues that teachers must be socially aware that Black English is a reality.

Cromer, Ward. See Wiener, Morton, and Ward Cromer.

Cronise, Florence M., and Henry W. Ward. *Cunnie Rabbit, Mr. Spider, and Other Beef: West African Folk Tales.* London: Swan Sonnenschein, 1903. 330 pp.

Folklore of Sierra Leone, believed to be where some of the Gullah originated.

Cronnell, Bruce. *The Applicability of Rules of Correspondence for Speakers of Black English.* Inglewood, Calif.: Southwest Regional Laboratory, February 6, 1970.

————. See Kligman, Donna Schwab, Bruce A. Cronnell, and Gary B. Verna.

Crosby, Muriel. "Future Research: Implications Growing Out of the Wilmington Study," in Roger W. Shuy, ed., *Social Dialects and Language Learning: Proceedings of the Bloomington, Indiana, Conference, 1964.* Champaign, Ill.: National Council of Teachers of English, 1965. Pp. 135–39.

Presents four proposals. Developed from the Wilmington, Del., study.

―――――. "New Dimensions and New Demands," in Eldonna L. Evertts, ed., *Dimensions of Dialect*. Champaign, Ill.: National Council of Teachers of English, 1967. Pp. 1–6.

―――――. See Corbin, Richard, and Muriel Crosby, eds.

Crowell, Sheila, and Ellen Kolba. "Contrastive Analysis in the Junior High School," in Bernice E. Cullinan, ed., *Black Dialects and Reading*. Urbana, Ill.: ERIC, 1973.

Crown, Phyllis Jo. "The Effects of Race of Examiner and Standard vs. Nonstandard Administration of the Wechsler Preschool and Primary Scale of Intelligence on the Performance of Negro and White Children." Doctoral dissertation, Florida State University, Tallahassee, 1970. 65 pp.

Fifty-six-subject study in Wakulla County, Fla. Concludes that there is no significant difference between standard English and nonstandard English in Blacks and Whites and no significant difference in Black and White performance as a function of the race of the examiner. However, a Black examiner produced better verbal results with both Black and White children.

Crum, Mason. *Gullah: Negro Life in the Carolina Sea Islands*. Durham, N. C.: Duke University Press, 1940. 351 pp.

Social history of the Gullah Blacks, from the antebellum era to 1940. Includes description of the Sea Islanders—cultural, historical, religious, linguistic. Chapter 6, "The Gullah Dialect," outlines the language; Chapter 7, "Spiritual of the Sea Islanders," includes lyrics and discussion.

Crystal, Daisy. "Dialect Mixture and Sorting Out the Concept of Freshman English Remediation," *Florida FL Reporter*, X (Spring/Fall 1972), 43–46.

Argues that Freshman English remediation should not repeat the mistakes of the high schools, and should teach the ability to use a second dialect or language.

―――――. "On Beryl L. Bailey on Negro Dialect Readers." *Florida FL Reporter*, IX (Spring/Fall, 1971), 44, 56.

Rebuttal to Bailey's article opposing dialect readers, *Florida FL Reporter*, VIII (Spring/Fall, 1970), 8.

Cullinan, Bernice E., ed. *Black Dialects and Reading*. Urbana, Ill.: ERIC, 1974.

Among the articles (all but one original) are "Issues in Research in Black Dialects" by Bernice E. Cullinan; "Relating Oral Language to Reading" by Angela M. Jaggar and Bernice E. Cullinan; "Evaluating Children's Language" by Estelle Fryburg; "Comparison of Black Children's Language and the Language of Selected Reading Materials" by Beatrice K. Levy; "Expanding Children's Language in the Primary Grades" by Bernice E. Cullinan, Angela M. Jaggar, and Dorothy Strickland; "Strategies for Language Programs in the Intermediate Grades" by Arlene Mantell; "Contrastive Analysis in the Junior High School" by Sheila Crowell and Ellen Kolba; "Beginning Reading—Let's Make It a Language Experience" by Angela M. Jaggar; "Teaching Reading Skills to Dialect Speakers" by Beatrice K. Levy; "A Cultural Model for Understanding Afro-Americans" by Joan C. Baratz (with responses from Martin Deutsch, Vivian Horner, and Dorothy Strickland); "On the Use of Dialect Readers" by Dorothy Strickland and William A. Stewart; "A Descriptive Guide to Features Characteristic of Black English" by Estelle Fryburg; and a bibliography by Margaret Kocher.

————. "Issues in Research in Black Dialects," in Bernice E. Cullinan, ed., *Black Dialects and Reading*. Urbana, Ill.: ERIC, 1974.

————. See Jaggar, Angela M., and Bernice E. Cullinan.

Cullinan, Bernice E., and Angela M. Jaggar. "Relating Oral Language to Reading," in Bernice E. Cullinan, ed., *Black Dialects and Reading*. Urbana, Ill.: ERIC, 1974.

Cullinan, Bernice E., Angela M. Jaggar, and Dorothy Strickland. "Expanding Children's Language in the Primary Grades," in Bernice E. Cullinan, ed., *Black Dialects and Reading*. Urbana, Ill.: ERIC, 1974.

————. "A Language Expansion Program for Primary Grades: A Research Report." *Young Children*, XXIX (January, 1974), 98–112.

Test of five hundred children in kindergarten through third grade in New York City. Concludes that with controlled program students are able to distinguish standard English forms.

Cunard, Nancy, ed. *Negro Anthology*. London: privately published, 1934. 855 pp. [Reprinted by Negro Universities Press, Westport, Conn., 1969.]

Approximately 150 articles covering many aspects of Black life, including a few articles of interest to linguists and educators.

Curran, Charles. See Lane, Harlan, Lawrence Caroline, and Charles Curran.

Curry, Julia, See Wood, Barbara Sundene, and Julia Curry.

Cushman, Dan. *Stay Away, Joe.* New York: Viking Press, 1953. 249 pp.
Novel which includes Black dialect.

D

Dalby, David. "The African Element in Black American English," in
Thomas Kochman, ed., *Rappin' and Stylin' Out: Communication in
Urban Black America.* Champaign: University of Illinois Press, 1972.
Pp. 170–86.
Documents the lexical impact of African languages on American Eng-
lish. Includes annotated list of Africanisms and probable Africanisms
in English.

————. "Americanisms That May Once Have Been Africanisms." London
Times, July 19, 1969, p. 9.
Discusses a few lexical parallels.

————. "Black Through White: Patterns of Communication in Africa and
the New World." Hans Wolfe Memorial Lecture delivered at Indiana University, Bloomington, 1969. [Also in Walt Wolfram and
Nona H. Clarke, eds., *Black-White Speech Relationships.* Washington, D.C.: Center for Applied Linguistics, 1971. Pp. 99–138.]
Discusses deviation of African Creoles, including American Black
English, Black Portuguese, Black Dutch, and Black French. Points
to existence of Creoles on West Coast of Africa and subsequent
occurences in American Black English.

————. "Reflections on the Historical Development of Afro-American
Languages: A Discussion of Mervyn C. Alleyne's Paper 'The Linguistic Continuity of Africa in the Caribbean'." Paper presented at
the Symposium on Continuities and Discontinuities in Afro-American Societies and Cultures, April 25, 1970, at Mona, Jamaica.
Discusses use of Wolof in the American colonies.

Dale, Edgar. "Vocabulary Deprivation of the Underprivileged Child."
Elementary English, XLII (November, 1965), 778–86. [Also in
Eldonna L. Evertts, ed., *Dimensions of Dialect.* Champaign, Ill.: Na-
tional Council of Teachers of English, 1967. Pp. 30–38.]
Examines the sources of vocabulary limitations in the underprivi-
leged child.

D'Angelo, Rita. See Anastasi, Anne, and Rita D'Angelo.

———. See Walsh, John F., Rita D'Angelo, and Louis Lomangino.

Daniel, Artie A., and Douglas E. Giles. *A Comparison of the Oral Language Development of Head Start Pupils With Non–Head Start Pupils.* ERIC document ED 010 848. Washington, D.C., August, 1966. 54 pp.

Daniel, J. L. "Black Folk and Speech Education." *Speech Teacher,* XIX (March, 1970), 123–29.

Defines "relevant speech for Blacks" as speech education that results in economic, psychological, and political benefits.

Darrow, Anne E. *Phonetic Studies in Folk Speech and Broken English: For Use on Stage, Screen, Radio, Platform and in School and College.* Boston: Expression, 1937. 113 pp.

Naïve, nonlinguistic treatment of Black English by a New York City principal. See especially Chapter 4, "American Negro English."

Daves, J. H. *A Sociological Study of the Colored Population of Knoxville, Tenn.* Knoxville, Tenn.: Free Colored Library, 1926.

Davino, Antoinette C. "The Reading Program for the Afro-American." Paper presented at the International Reading Association Conference, May 6–9, 1970, at Anaheim, California. 12 pp.

Rationale for an ethnic reading program for Blacks. Only implied references to Black English.

Davis, A. L. "Culture, Class, and the Disadvantaged," in A. L. Davis, William M. Austin, William Card, Raven I. McDavid, Jr., and Virginia Glenn McDavid, eds., *Culture, Class, and Language Variety: A Resource Book for Teachers.* Urbana, Ill.: National Council of Teachers of English, 1972. Pp. 21–60.

Pulls together culture and class structure in urban society, with attention to the effects on members of specific groups. Includes semifictional accounts of a middle-class White boy, a hillbilly, a Puerto Rican boy, and a Black boy, all living in urban areas.

———. "Dialect Research and the Needs of the Schools." *Elementary English,* XLV (May, 1968), 558–60, 608. [Also in A. L. Davis, ed., *On the Dialects of Children.* Champaign, Ill.: National Council of Teachers of English, 1968. Pp. 1–4.]

Discusses research in dialectology, including nonstandard and Black English. Also discusses relationship of Black English to other dialects.

————. *Language Resource Information for Teachers of the Culturally Disadvantaged.* Chicago: Center for American English, Illinois Institute of Technology, 1969. 269 pp.

————, ed. *On the Dialects of Children.* Champaign, Ill.: National Council of Teachers of English, 1968. 29 pp. [Reprinted from *Elementary English*, XLV (May, 1968).]

Five articles by Davis, Raven I. McDavid, Jr., Roger W. Shuy, Beryl Loftman Bailey, and Gaston Saint-Pierre.

————. "Social Dialects and Social Change: Negro Dialect." *Instructor*, LXXV (March, 1966), 93, 100.

A brief look at Black English.

————, ed. *Studies in Linguistics in Honor of Raven I. McDavid, Jr.* University, Ala.: University of Alabama Press, 1972. 461 pp.

Collection of original articles in honor of one of the nation's outstanding dialectologists. Included in the collection are "Black Speech–White Speech and the Al Smith Syndrome" by Lee A. Pederson, and "A Look at the Direct Question" by Juanita V. Williamson.

————. "Teaching Language and Reading to Disadvantaged Negro Children." *Elementary English*, XL (November, 1965), 791–97.

Describes problems faced by teachers in teaching language skills to lower-class Blacks. Presents several suggestions.

Davis, A. L., William M. Austin, William Card, Raven I. McDavid, Jr., and Virginia Glenn McDavid, eds. *Culture, Class, and Language Variety: A Resource Book for Teachers.* Urbana, Ill.: National Council of Teachers of English, 1972. 222 pp.

Among the twelve articles included within the book are "Historical, Regional, and Social Variation" by Raven I. McDavid, Jr.; "Culture, Class, and the Disadvantaged" by A. L. Davis; "Problem Areas in Grammar" by William Card and Virginia Glenn McDavid; "A Checklist of Significant Features for Discriminating Social Dialects" by Raven I. McDavid, Jr.; "Nonverbal Communication" by William M. Austin; and "Transcriptions" by Dagna Simpson, Emily Pettigrew Morris, and N. Louanna Furbee. "Transcriptions" includes audio casette of three conversations.

Davis, A. L., Raven I. McDavid, Jr., and Virginia Glenn McDavid. *A Compilation of the Work Sheets of the* Linguistic Atlas of the United States and Canada *and Associated Projects.* 2nd ed. Chicago: University of Chicago Press, 1969.

Provides information on worksheet solicitation of pronunciation, grammar, vocabulary, and semantics, based on forthcoming *Linguistic Atlas of the United States and Canada.*

Davis, Allison. "Teaching Language and Reading to Disadvantaged Negro Children." *Elementary English,* XLII (November, 1965), 791–97. [Also in Eldonna L. Evertts, ed., *Dimensions of Dialect.* Champaign, Ill.: National Council of Teachers of English, 1967. Pp. 57–63.]

Suggests methods for beginning teachers in the inner-city schools. Charges that stereotyped attitudes of teachers toward Black English need to be changed. Several observations about schools in the Black community.

————. See Eells, Kenneth, Allison Davis, Robert J. Havinghurst, Vergil E. Herrick, and Ralph W. Tyler.

Davis, Edwin Adams. See Hogan, William Ransom, and Edwin Adams Davis, eds.

Davis, Henry C. "Negro Folk-Lore in South Carolina." *Journal of American Folk-Lore,* XXVII (July–September, 1914), 241–54.

Collection of South Carolina folklore. Not restricted to Gullah. Several observations about folklore from the South.

Davis, Lawrence. "Dialect Research: Mythology vs. Reality." *Orbis,* XVIII (1969), 332–37.

Argument opposing theories of creolization stage in American Black English.

————. "Social Dialectology in America: A Critical Survey." *Journal of English Linguistics,* IV (March, 1970), 46–56.

Discusses history of the *Linguistic Atlas.* Also presents aspects of the controversy between relationship of Black English to standard English.

————. "Some Aspects of the Speech of Bluegrass Kentucky." *Orbis,* XIX (Summer, 1970), 336–41.

Includes data from one Black informant. Claims that only five or six words pronounced by the Black differed from those of the Whites of his social and educational classes.

Davis, Olga, Mildred R. Gladney, and Lloyd Leaverton. *All About Me* (52 pp.); *All About Me and My Family* (57 pp.); *In My House and in My School* (69 pp.); *Yesterday* (two books, written in "Everyday Talk" and "School Talk," 22 pp.); *At School* (two books, written in "Everyday Talk" and "School Talk," 31 pp.); *Working and Playing* (two books, written in "Everyday Talk" and "School Talk," 31 pp.);

I Am Scared When. . . (two books, written in "Everyday Talk" and "School Talk," 22 pp.); *Afro-Americans* (16 pp.). Psycholinguistics Reading Series, Board of Education, City of Chicago, 1968.

A series of dialect readers developed for bidialect education training in the Chicago public schools. Series includes teacher's manual.

————. *The Psycholinguistics Reading Series: Teacher's Manual; A Bi-Dialectal Approach.* Board of Education, City of Chicago, 1969. 185 pp.

Guidelines and texts of the eight-step series. Includes worksheets and evaluation techniques.

Davis, Olga, Mildred R. Gladney, Melvin J. Hoffman, Lloyd Leaverton, and Zorenda P. Patterson. *Psycholinguistics Oral Language Program; A Bi-Dialectal Approach.* Experimental edition. Board of Education, City of Chicago, 1968. 181 pp.

Lessons on verbs and endings, including /-s/ and /-es/; *am, is,* and *are; was* and *were; do* and *does; have* and *has.* Includes pronunciation practices.

Davis, Ossie. "The English Language Is My Enemy." *American Teacher,* LI (April, 1967), 13, 18. [Also in *Negro History Bulletin,* XXX (April, 1967), 18 (abridged); Neil Postman, Charles Weingartner, and Terrence Moran, eds., *Language in America.* New York: Pegasus, 1969. Pp. 73–79; Arthur L. Smith, ed., *Language, Communication, and Rhetoric in Black America.* New York: Harper & Row, 1972. Pp. 49–57; Virginia P. Clark, Paul A. Eschholz, and Alfred A. Rosa, eds. *Language: Introductory Readings.* New York: St. Martin's Press, 1972; Robert H. Bentley and Samuel D. Crawford, eds., *Black Language Reader,* Glencoe, Ill.: Scott, Foresman, 1973. Pp. 71–77.]

The noted Black writer-actor lashes out against the racist overtones of the English language.

————. *Purlie Victorious.* New York: French, 1961. 90 pp.

Three-act comedy about a Black minister and his congregation in the South. Extensive use of Black dialect.

Day, Charles William. *Five Years Residence in the West Indies.* London: Colburn, 1852. 2 vols.

A few passages on beliefs about language, including the conviction that Creole is merely broken English.

Day, David E. "The Effects of Different Language Instruction on the Use of Attributes of Prekindergarten Disadvantaged Children." Paper presented at the annual meeting of the American Educational Research Association, February, 1968, at Chicago.

Day, E. M. "Philological Curiosities." Letter to the editor, *North American Review,* CXLVI (June, 1888), 709.

A brief inquiry into the meaning of the word *brottus* (a bonus given to a child or a Black shopper during the early nineteenth century).

Dean, Leonard F., Walker Gibson, and Kenneth G. Wilson, eds. *The Play of Language.* 3rd ed. New York: Oxford University Press, 1971. 404 pp.

DeCamp, David. "Introduction: The Study of Pidgin and Creole Languages," in Dell Hymes, ed., *Pidginization and Creolization of Languages: Proceedings of a Conference Held at the University of the West Indies, Mona, Jamaica, April, 1968.* Cambridge, England: Cambridge University Press, 1971. Pp. 13–39.

Discusses characteristics and historical background of Pidgin and Creole languages.

———. "Mock Bidding in Jamaica" in Wilson Mathes Hudson, ed., *Tire Shrinker to Dragster.* Austin, Tex.: Encino Press, 1968. Pp. 145–53.

Describes the custom of "mock bidding" on Jamaica. Defines language and characteristics.

DeCoy, Robert H. *The Nigger Bible.* Los Angeles: Holloway House, 1967. 304 pp.

Nonfiction narrative. Not written in Black English, but includes within the text Black English phrases. Also includes a brief glossary.

Delia, Jesse G. "Dialects and the Effects of Stereotypes on Interpersonal Attraction and Cognitive Processes in Impression Formation." *Quarterly Journal of Speech,* LVIII (October, 1972), 285–97.

Dendrick, S. A. "Verbal Ability: An Obsolete Measure!" *Council Journal,* VI (March, 1968), 8–12.

A strong argument for colleges to reevaluate entrance examinations, particularly sections dealing with verbal skills.

Dennis, Leah. "A Word-List from Alabama and Some Other Southern States." *Publication of the American Dialect Society,* No. 2 (1944), 6–16.

Dentler, Robert A., Bernard Mackler, and Mary Ellen Warshauer, eds. *The Urban R's: Race Relations and the Problem in Urban Education.* New York: Praeger, 1967. 304 pp.

Useful for sociological background.

Denton, Herbert H. "Negro Dialect: Should the Schools Fight It?" Washington *Post*, December 22, 1968, pp. C1–C2.

DeStefano, Johanna S. "Black Attitudes Toward Black English: A Pilot Study." *Florida FL Reporter*, IX (Spring/Fall, 1971), 23–27.

Original proposal and experimental study in California to determine Black English acceptance, the result of a four-respondent, four-question survey. Also presents a brief review of literature that discusses Black objections to the study of Black English.

———. "Black English" in Johanna S. DeStefano, ed., *Language, Society, and Education: A Profile of Black English.* Worthington, Ohio: Charles A. Jones, 1973. Pp. 4–9.

Discusses research being conducted in Black English and assumptions on which most linguists are in agreement.

———, ed. *Language, Society, and Education: A Profile of Black English.* Worthington, Ohio: Charles A. Jones, 1973. 326 pp.

General reader with introductory comments by Johanna S. DeStefano. The included articles are "Black English" by Johanna S. DeStefano; "The Logic of Nonstandard English" by William Labov; "The Setting" by Ulf Hannerz; "The Social and Economic Status of the Negro in the United States" by St. Clair Drake; "The Advantages of Black English" by Roger D. Abrahams; "Modes of Mitigation and Politeness" by William Labov; "Some Linguistic Features of Negro Dialect" by Ralph W. Fasold and Walter A. Wolfram; "Systematic Relations of Standard and Nonstandard Rules in the Grammars of Negro Speakers" by William Labov and Paul Cohen; "Urban Negro Speech: Sociolinguistic Factors Affecting English Teaching" by William A. Stewart; "Language in the Classroom: Studies of the Pygmalion Effect" by Frederick Williams and Jack L. Whitehead; "Teacher's Attitude Toward the Nonstandard Negro Dialect— Let's Change It" by Kenneth R. Johnson; "Register: A Concept to Combat Negative Teacher Attitudes Toward Black English" by Johanna S. DeStefano; "The Linguistic Problems of Teachers" and "Language Variation in the Training of Teachers" by Roger W. Shuy; "Social Factors in the Consideration of Teaching Standard English" by Thomas Kochman; "Some Suggestions for Teaching Standard English to Speakers of Nonstandard and Urban Dialects" by William Labov and Paul Cohen; "Problems in Applying Foreign Language Teaching Methods to the Teaching of Standard English as a Second Dialect" by Robert L. Politzer; "Sociolinguistic Implications for Educational Sequencing" by Walter A. Wolfram; "Dialect Barriers to Reading Comprehension" by Kenneth S. Goodman; "On the

Use of Negro Dialect in the Teaching of Reading" by William A. Stewart; "Sociolinguistic Alternatives in Teaching Reading to Non-standard Speakers" by Walter A. Wolfram; and "A Note on the Relation of Reading Failure to Peer-Group Status in Urban Ghettos" by William Labov and Clarence Robins.

————. "Productive Language Differences in Fifth Grade Black Students' Syntactic Forms." *Elementary English*, XLIX (April, 1972), 552–58.

Experimental field study in Philadelphia. Data suggests that non-standard verb forms account for about three fourths of all speech differences and about three fifths of all written differences.

————. "Register: A Concept to Combat Negative Teacher Attitudes Toward Black English," in Johanna S. DeStefano, ed., *Language, Society, and Education: A Profile of Black English*. Worthington, Ohio: Charles A. Jones, 1973. Pp. 189–95.

Slightly revised version of "Register: Social Variation in Language Use: Implications for Teaching Reading to Ghetto Children." Discusses society's prescriptivist view of language and its conflict with descriptivist evidence. Her study reveals that Black children produce more standard English forms than Black English forms in school settings.

————. "Register: Social Variation in Language: Implications for Teaching Reading to Ghetto Children." Paper presented at the annual convention of the International Reading Association, April 19–23, 1971, at Atlantic City.

————. "Register: Social Variation in Language Use." *Elementary School Journal*, LXXII (January, 1972), 189–94.

Discusses code-switching.

Deutsch, Cynthia. "Auditory Discrimination and Learning Social Factors." Paper presented at the Arden House Conference on Preschool Enrichment of Socially Disadvantaged Children, December, 1962, at Harriman, N.Y. [Also in *Merrill-Palmer Quarterly*, X (July, 1964), 274–96.]

Deutsch, Martin, Irwin Katz, and Arthur Jensen, eds. *Social Class, Race, and Psychological Development*. New York: Holt, Rinehart, & Winston, 1968. 423 pp.

Environment studies, not specifically related to Black English.

Deutsch, Martin, and Martin Whiteman. "Social Disadvantaged as Related to Intellective and Language Development" in Martin Deutsch, Irwin Katz, and Arthur Jensen, eds., *Social Class, Race, and Psy-*

chological Development. New York: Holt, Rinehart, & Winston, 1968.

DeVere, Louise A. "Black English: Problematic But Systematic." *South Atlantic Bulletin,* XXXVI (1971), 38–46.

Dickens, Milton, and Granville M. Sawyer. "An Experimental Comparison of Vocal Quality Among Mixed Groups of Whites and Negroes." *Southern Speech Journal,* XVII (March, 1952), 178–85.

Study to investigate perceptual differences in vocal quality. Blacks and Whites were used as both judges and speakers.

Different But Equal: A Special Report. University of California, Berkeley, May, 1967. 20 pp.

Special report on improvement of educational status of California's disadvantaged students. Includes description of dialect differences.

Dil, Anwar S., ed. *Language Acquisition and Communicative Choice: Essays by Susan M. Ervin-Tripp.* Stanford, Calif.: Stanford University Press, 1973. 383 pp.

Dillard, J. L. *Afro-American and Other Vehicle Names.* Special study No. 1, Institute of Caribbean Studies, University of Puerto Rico, Rio Piedras, Puerto Rico, March, 1963.

———. "Afro-American, Spanglish, and Something Else: St. Cruzan Naming Practices." *Names,* XX (December, 1972), 225–30.

Examines Black naming practices. Concludes that there is a separate naming tradition from the mainstream American-European practices. Sees many West African survivals.

———. "Black English in New York." *The English Record,* XXI (April, 1971), 114–20.

Discusses social history of Black English in the North, with references to the Dutch Creole. Includes several brief anecdotes, as well as references to literature.

———. *Black English: Its History and Usage in the United States.* New York: Random House, 1972. 361 pp.

Thorough analysis and description of Black English, written for the nonlinguist, but also of value to the linguist, educator, social worker, speech pathologist, and speech teacher. Chapters are "Black English and the Academic Establishment"; "On the Structure of Black English"; "A Sketch of the History of Black English" (historical analysis and predictions of the future; includes naming practices and the "African Question"); "Pidgin English in the United States—

Black, Red, and Yellow" (includes discussion of American Indian
and Chinese Pidgins); "The Negro Dialect and the Southern Dialect" (similarities and contrasts, as well as the influence of each
upon the other; includes several literary passages for emphasis);
"Who Speaks Black English?" (includes a discussion of "Fancy
Talk," "Elegant Behavior," and use of the language); "Black English
and Problems" (theories and problems). Book includes glossary of
linguistic phrases.

————. "The Creolist and the Study of Negro Nonstandard Dialects in
the Continental United States" in Dell Hymes, ed., *Pidginization
and Creolization of Languages: Proceedings of a Conference Held
at the University of the West Indies, Mona, Jamaica, April, 1968.*
Cambridge, England: Cambridge University Press, 1971. Pp. 393–
408.

Several observations about American Black English, with discussion
of several of the problems of the dialectologist. Includes comparative studies of non-American Black English languages.

————. "The English Teacher and the Language of the Newly Integrated
Student." *Teachers College Record,* LXIX (November, 1967), 115–
20.

Includes sections on "Mapping the Negro Dialect," "The Influence
of the English-Based Creoles on Black English," "The Core of the
Language," and "Teaching a Second Language."

————. "How to Tell the Bandits from the Good Guys, or What Dialect
to Teach?" in Alfred C. Aarons, Barbara Y. Gordon, and William A.
Stewart, eds., *Linguistic-Cultural Differences and American Education,* special issue of *Florida FL Reporter,* VII (Spring/Summer,
1969). Pp. 84–85, 162. [Also in David L. Shores, ed., *Contemporary
English: Change and Variation.* Philadelphia: J. B. Lippincott, 1972.
Pp. 289–93.]

Argues that because dialect adequacy varies, some students need to
learn a second dialect in order to function well within society, nota-
bly within educational and economic situations.

————. Letter to the editor, New York *Times,* August 14, 1971, p. 24.
Brief rebuttal to eradicationist arguments by Bayard Rustin. Notes that
linguists don't make up the language, only describe it.

————. "Negro Children's Dialect in the Inner City." *Florida FL Re-
porter,* V (Fall, 1967), 7–8, 10. [Also in Robert H. Bentley and
Samuel D. Crawford, eds., *Black Language Reader.* Glencoe, Ill.:
Scott, Foresman, 1973. Pp. 84–89.]

Notes that the speech of Black children is more independent of White standard English than the speech of Black adults. Concludes that it is far more advantageous, therefore, to study Black speech of children.

————. "Non-Standard Negro Dialects—Convergence or Divergence?" *Florida FL Reporter*, VI (Fall, 1968), 9–10, 12. [Also in Norman E. Whitten, Jr., and John F. Szwed, eds., *Afro-American Anthropology: Contemporary Perspectives.* New York: The Free Press, 1970. Pp. 119–29.]

Discusses the question of whether Black English represents a dialect which has branched off from English or whether it is African-oriented and now becoming more like White standard English. Outlines the theories of Raven I. McDavid, Jr., (divergence) and William A. Stewart (convergence).

————. "Observations on the Dictionary of Jamaican English." *Caribbean Studies*, X (July, 1970), 118–24.

Review of Frederic G. Cassidy and Robert B. LePage, *Dictionary of Jamaican English.*

————. "On a Context for Dialect Data: The Case of Black English." *Florida FL Reporter*, X (Spring/Fall, 1972), 17–18, 53–54.

Defends Creolist position in Black English theory.

————. "On the Grammar of Afro-American Naming Practices." *Names*, XVI (September, 1968), 230–37.

Examination of names of Black store-front churches, with relationships to linguistic grammar. Compares names of Black churches to those of White churches.

————, ed. *Perspectives on Black English.* The Hague: Mouton, forthcoming.

General reader. Section I (Black English and Dialectology) includes "American Linguistic Geography: A Sociological Appraisal" by Glenna Ruth Pickford; "Observations (1966) on the Problems of Defining Negro Dialect" by William A. Stewart; "Black American English and Syntactic Dialectology" by Marvin D. Loflin; "Dialectology in Generative Grammar" by Philip A. Luelsdorff; and "*Ain't, Not,* and *Don't* in Black English" by Joan G. Fickett. Section II (The History of Black English) includes "Das Neger-Englisch an der Westküste von Afrika" by P. Grade; "Negro-English" by James A. Harrison; "A Word List from East Alabama" by Leonida W. Payne; "A Note on the Words *Dash* and *Ju-Ju* in West African English" and "Some Special West African Words" by Paul Christophersen; "Negro Dialect" by C. M. Wise; "Sociolinguistic Factors in the History of American Negro Dialects" and "Continuity and Change in American Negro Dialects" by William A. Stewart; and "Some Aspects of English in Liberia" by Ian F. Hancock. Section III (Black English and the Acculturation Process) includes "Acculturation among Gullah Negroes" by William R. Bascomb; "The Writings of Herskovitz and the Study of New World Negro Language" by J. L. Dillard; and "Black Kinesics—Some Non-Verbal Communication Patterns in the Black Culture" by Kenneth R. Johnson. Section IV (Black English and Psycholinguistics) includes "Classroom Correction Tests" by William Labov, Clarence Robins, Paul Cohen, and John Lewis; "The Learning of Black English by Puerto Ricans in New York City" by Stuart Silverman; "A Sociolinguistic Consideration of the Black English of Children in Northern Florida" by Susan H. Houston; and "White and Negro Listeners' Reactions to Various American-English Dialects" by G. Richard Tucker and Wallace E. Lambert.

————. "Principles in the History of American English—Paradox, Virginity, and Cafeteria." *Florida FL Reporter*, VIII (Spring/Fall, 1970), 32–33.

Discusses the three principles: Paradox—no dialects existed, except Gullah on the Sea Islands and pseudo-Gullah in literature; Virginity—only the first time a vocabulary item is found (the earliest use) counts, and that item cannot become a true part of another language; and Cafeteria—speakers "pick and choose" specific features from a variety of true languages.

————. Review of Frederick Williams, ed., *Language and Poverty: Perspectives on a Theme. Language*, XLVIII (June, 1972), 479–87.

Sharp rebuttal to the deficit theory. Sharply attacks what he believes to be the basic premise of the book—the correlation between poverty and language deficiency.

————. Review of Joan C. Baratz and Roger W. Shuy, eds., *Teaching Black Children to Read. College English*, XXXI (April, 1970), 733–36.

————. "Standard Average Foreign in Puerto Rico," in Richard W. Bailey and Jay L. Robinson, eds., *Varieties of Present-Day English*. New York: Macmillan, 1973. Pp. 77–88.

————. "Toward a Bibliography of Works Dealing with the Creole Languages of the Caribbean Area, Louisiana, and the Guianas." *Caribbean Studies*, III (April, 1963), 84–95.

A list of citations on Creoles to supplement those presented by another author in the January, 1963, issue.

―――. "The Urban Language Study of the Center for Applied Linguistics." *Linguistics Reporter*, VIII (October, 1965), 1–2.

Examination of the center's program and nonstandard English.

―――. "The West African Day-Names in Nova Scotia." *Names*, XIX (December, 1971), 257–61.

Discusses the practice of naming slaves for the days of the week, or some close variant.

―――. "The Writings of Herskovitz and the Study of New World Negro Language." *Caribbean Studies*, IV (July, 1964), 35–43.

Discusses the changing views of Black English, with reference to the foundation studies of Melville Herskovitz and Lorenzo Dow Turner.

DiLorenzo, Louis T., Ruth Salter, and Robert Hayden. "Empirical Bases for a Pre-Kindergarten Curriculum for Disadvantaged Children." Paper presented at the annual convention of the Educational Research Association of New York State, November 11, 1968. 15 pp.

Dobie, J. Frank, ed. *Follow de Drinkin' Gou'd*. Austin: Texas Folklore Society, 1928. 201 pp.

Study of Black folklore.

―――, ed. *Tone the Bell Easy*. Austin: Texas Folklore Society, 1932. 190 pp.

[Dodge, N. S.] "Negro Patois and Its Humor." *Appleton's Journal of Literature, Science, and Art*, III (February 5, 1870), 161–62.

Brief discussion of the Black language. Includes several examples with focus on Black humor.

Dollard, John. "The Dozens: The Dialect of Insult." *American Imago*, I (November, 1939), 3–25.

Pioneer study on the Black insult game, with psychoanalytic focus on the language.

Donaldson, Patricia L. See Forfeit, Karen G., and Patricia L. Donaldson.

Donelson, Kenneth L. "Teaching Standard English as an Alternate Dialect." *Arizona English Bulletin*, XII (October, 1969), 11–16.

Presents several suggestions for teachers faced with Black English problems. Gives examples of Black English features.

Donicie, A. See Pée, Willem, W. Gs. Hellinga, and A. Donicie.

74

Donovan, Gail M. "Summary of *Teaching Black Children to Read.*" Memorandum, School District of Philadelphia, Board of Education, Office of the Superintendent of Schools, Philadelphia, July 31, 1969.

Explanatory memo regarding the use of Black English readers at the elementary level.

Dooley, Mrs. James H. *Dem Good Ole Times.* New York: Doubleday, Page, 1906. 150 pp. Illustrated by Suzanne Gutherz.

Includes transcriptions of Black English.

Dorne, William P. "The Comprehensibility of the Speech of Representative Sixth-Grade Negro Children in Lee County Schools, Alabama." Doctoral dissertation, University of Florida, Gainesville, 1959. 131 pp.

Panels of White southern judges rated Negro children's speech more comprehensible than did panels of northern or Negro judges. Data also suggests that Black judges were more critical of speech patterns than were White panels.

Dorr, Anita, ed. *Problems and Practices in New York City Schools.* New York: New York Society for the Experimental Study of Education, 1965.

See especially William A. Labov, "Linguistic Research on the Non-Standard English of Negro Children," pp. 110–17.

Dorson, Richard M., ed. *Negro Folktales from Pine Bluff, Arkansas, and Calvin, Michigan.* Indiana University Folklore Series, No. 23, Bloomington, 1958. 292 pp.

———, ed. *Negro Folktales in Michigan.* Cambridge: Harvard University Press, 1956. 245 pp. [Reprinted by Fawcett Publications, Greenwich, Conn., 1967.]

About 250 folktales, many in Black English.

———, ed. "Negro Tales from Boliver County, Mississippi." *Southern Folklore Quarterly*, XIX (June, 1955), 104–16.

Douglass, Frederick. *My Bondage and Freedom.* New York: Miller, Orton, & Mulligan, 1855. 464 pp.

Autobiographical slave narrative written in standard English, but including several Black English phrases.

Dove, Adrian. "Soul Story." *New York Times Magazine*, December 8, 1968, pp. 82 ff. Includes a brief case-study of a White culture-bound job test. Presents glossary of about twenty-five Black words.

Dover, Cedric. *Half-Caste*. London: M. Secker and Warburgh, 1937. 324 pp.

Downing, Gertrude L. "The Effects of Systematic Phonics Instruction on the Reading Achievement of Adolescent Retarded Readers with Problems of Dialect Speech: A Study of Relative Effectiveness of Systematic Phonics Instruction and Incidental Phonics Instruction on the Improvement in Phonics Knowledge, Word Knowledge, and Silent Reading Achievement of 7th and 8th Grade Retarded Readers in a Community Characterized by American Negro Dialects." Doctoral dissertation, New York University, New York City, 1965. 79 pp.

Concludes that systematic phonics instruction was more effective than incidental phonics instruction in increasing phonics knowledge. Notes lack of correlation between gains in phonics knowledge and word knowledge or reading abilities.

Drake, St. Clair. "The Social and Economic Status of the Negro in the United States," in Johanna S. DeStefano, ed., *Language, Society, and Education: A Profile of Black English*. Worthington, Ohio: Charles A. Jones, 1973. Pp. 66–94.

Dreger, Ralph. See Miller, Kent, and Ralph Dreger, eds.

Drehsler, Alex. "Black Dialect: Check It Out, Man." *Arizona Daily Star*, December 3, 1972, p. D-3.

News feature on Black English. Discusses Black Dialect course at a Sierra Vista, Arizona, high school.

Drennan, Margaret, and Halvor P. Hansen. "The Children Who Don't Speak Standard English." *Acta Symbolica*, I (Fall, 1970), 3–15.

Uses phonetics, grammatical analysis, and syntactic structure to show that Black English is an organized language system.

Dreyfuss, Joel. "Black English: Whose to Say." Washington *Post*, July 1, 1973, pp. L–1, L–6.

General review of Black English controversies. Quotes William A. Stewart, J. L. Dillard, Walter A. Wolfram, June Jordan, and Nick Aaron Ford.

Drzick, Kathleen, John Murphy, and Constance Weaver. *Annotated Bibliography of Works Relating to the Negro in Literature and to Negro Dialects*. Kalamazoo, Mich.: n.p., 1969.

Short bibliography with emphasis on literature.

Dubner, Frances S. "Nonverbal Aspects of Black English." *Southern Speech Communications Journal*, XXXVII (Summer, 1972), 361–74.

States that the lack of understanding between Blacks and Whites is often a matter of problems in understanding the nonverbal language. Points to a need for further research in Black kinesics.

DuBois, W. E. B. *The Souls of Black Folks: Essays and Sketches.* Chicago: A. L. McClurg, 1903. 264 pp. [Reprinted by Blue Heron Press, New York, 1953.] [21 subsequent editions.]

Duffy, Edward. "Off My Turf!" *Grosbeak*, I (March, 1972), 7.

Discussion of argot and names associated with urban Black and Puerto Rican gangs.

Dunbar, Paul Laurence. *The Best Stories of Paul Laurence Dunbar.* New York: Dodd, Mead, 1938. 258 pp.

Anthology of some of the best short stories of one of the nation's outstanding Black writers. Many of the stories include passages in Black English.

————. *Candle-Lightin' Time.* New York: Dodd, Mead, 1901. 127 pp.

————. *Chris'mus Is a Comin', and Other Poems.* New York: Dodd, Mead, 1905. 48 pp.

————. *The Complete Poems of Paul Laurence Dunbar.* New York: Dodd, Mead, 1913. 312 pp.

Complete collection of more than four hundred poems, many written entirely in Black English; others include Black English syntax or phonology.

————. *The Fanatics.* New York: Dodd, Mead, 1901. 312 pp.

————. *Folks from Dixie.* New York: Dodd, Mead, 1898. 263 pp. Illustrated by E. W. Kembel.
Short sketches.

————. *The Heart of Happy Hollow.* New York: Dodd, Mead, 1904. 309 pp. Illustrated by E. W. Kembel.

————. *Howdy Honey Howdy.* New York: Dodd, Mead, 1905.
Twenty-one poems in Black verse.

————. *In Old Plantation Days.* New York: Dodd, Mead, 1903. 307 pp.

————. *Joggin' Erlong.* New York: Dodd, Mead, 1906. 119 pp.

————. *The Life and Works of Paul Laurence Dunbar.* Nashville, Tenn.: J. L. Nichols, 1907.
Includes all poems, plus a few sketches and short stories.

———. *Li'l Gal.* New York: Dodd, Mead, 1904. 123 pp.
Anthology of twenty-two poems in Black verse. Includes photos by Leigh Richmond Miner.

———. *Little Brown Baby.* New York: Dodd, Mead, 1913. 106 pp.
Collection of Black verse poems.

———. *The Love of Landry.* New York: Dodd, Mead, 1900. 200 pp.
Novel.

———. *Lyrics of Love and Laughter.* New York: Dodd, Mead, 1903. 180 pp.

———. *Lyrics of Lowly Life.* New York: Dodd, Mead, 1896. 208 pp.
First major collection of Dunbar's poetry, much of it in Black verse.

———. *Lyrics of Sunshine and Shadow.* New York: Dodd, Mead, 1914. 109 pp.
Poetry collection.

———. *Lyrics of the Hearthside.* New York: Dodd, Mead, 1899. 227 pp.
Poetry collection.

———. *Majors and Minors.* Toledo, Ohio: Hadley and Hadley, 1895. 148 pp.
Poetry collection representing his first poems.

———. *Oak and Ivy.* Elgin, Ill.: Press of the United Brethren Publishing House, 1893. 62 pp.

———. *A Plantation Portrait.* New York: Dodd, Mead, 1905. 50 pp.

———. *Speaking of Christmas.* New York: Dodd, Mead, 1914. 96 pp.

———. *The Strength of Gideon.* New York: Dodd, Mead, 1900. 362 pp.
Illustrated by E. W. Kembel.

———. *The Uncalled.* New York: Dodd, Mead, 1898. 225 pp.
Believed to be the first novel Dunbar wrote, this book contains many Black English passages.

———. *Uncle Eph's Christmas.* N.p., 1900. 11 pp.
One-act Black musical sketch, entirely in Black English, with music by Will Marion Cook.

———. *When Malindy Sings.* New York: Dodd, Mead, 1903. 144 pp.
Poetry collection.

78

Dundes, Alan. "African Tales Among the North Carolina Indians." *Southern Folklore Quarterly*, XXIX (1966), 208–19.

———. *Mother Wit from the Laughing Barrel.* Englewood Cliffs, N.J.: Prentice-Hall, 1972.

Dunlap, Howard. " 'Be' in the Speech of One Hundred Atlanta Fifth-Grade Students." Doctoral dissertation, Emory University, Atlanta, 1972.

Dunn, Anita E. "Reading and the Disadvantaged," in Robert H. Bentley and Samuel D. Crawford, eds., *Black Language Reader.* Glencoe, Ill.: Scott, Foresman, 1973.

Dunn, Lloyd M. *The Effectiveness of the Peabody Language Development Kits and the Initial Teaching Alphabet with Disadvantaged Children in the Primary Grades: After Two Years.* Institute on Mental Retardation and Intellectual Development, George Peabody College for Teachers, Nashville, Tenn., 1967. 140 pp.

Concludes that the Initial Teaching Alphabet (ITA) and the Peabody Language Development Kit (PLDK) have some promise for the inner-city disadvantaged or Black child with reduced verbal abilities, restricted or nonstandard English.

Durand, Sidney Joseph. "A Phonetic Study of the Creole Dialect." Master's thesis, Louisiana State University, Baton Rouge, 1930. 48 pp.

Notes that consonant sounds in Creole do not differ very much from the French, but that a difference in articulation exists.

Durham, Frank, ed. See Peterkin, Julia. *Collected Short Stories of Julia Peterkin.*

Durrell, Gerald M. *The Overloaded Ark.* New York: Viking Press, 1958. 272 pp. Illustrated by Sabine Bauer.

Narrative of a trapping safari by Whites in the Cameroun area. Includes West African Pidgin English.

Dwyer, David, and David Smith. *An Introduction to West African Pidgin English.* African Studies Center, Michigan State University, East Lansing, n.d.

Produced for the Peace Corps to be used as a training manual.

E

Eastman, Mary Henderson. *Aunt Phillis's Cabin, or, So Life As It Is.* Philadelphia: Lippincott, Grambo, 1852. 280pp. [Reprinted by Negro Universities Press, New York, 1968.]

A novel about the antebellum South and its slaves. Includes Black language.

Echtold, Johannes Julius Marius. *The English Words in Sranan (Negro-English of Surinam).* Groningen, Netherlands: J. B. Wolters, 1962. 219 pp.

Investigation of the extent to which English has contributed to the vocabulary and word-structure of Sranan.

Ecroyd, Donald. "Negro Children and Language Arts." *Reading Teacher,* II (April, 1968), 624–29.

Argument for the understanding and acceptance of Black English as a structural language with definite rules and forms.

———. See Clark, Dennis, Abraham Wolf, Henry Goehl, and Donald Ecroyd.

Eddy, Kathryn. "Black English and Generative Grammar: A Harder Look at the Issue." Unpublished paper, Department of English, University of Northern Iowa, Cedar Falls, 1971. 12 pp.

Offers criticism of theories of Susan Houston, Walter A. Wolfram, Marvin Loflin, and Beryl Bailey. Discusses viewpoints and positions of William A. Stewart, Ralph W. Fasold, and Riley B. Smith.

Eells, Kenneth, Allison Davis, Robert J. Havinghurst, Vergil E. Herrick, and Ralph W. Tyler. *Intellectual and Cultural Differences: A Study of Cultural Learning and Problem-Solving.* Chicago: University of Chicago Press, 1951. 388 pp.

Includes studies of Black verbal response to selected IQ tests.

Elam, William Cecil. "Lingo in Literature." *McBride's Magazine,* LV (1895), 286–88.

Opposes concept of Black English as a dialect. Claims it is also "the lingo of the wholly uneducated and socially degraded white."

Elder, Jacob Delworth. "Evolution of the Traditional Calypso of Trinidad and Tobago: A Socio-Historical Analysis of Sound Change." Doctoral dissertation, University of Pennsylvania, Philadelphia, 1967. 410 pp.

Eliason, Norman E. "Some Negro Terms." *American Speech*, XIII (April, 1938), 151–52.

A brief list of words used by Blacks in college. List originally researched by Nathaniel Louis Sayles.

————. *Tarheel Talk: An Historical Study of the English Language in North Carolina to 1860.* Chapel Hill: University of North Carolina Press, 1956. 324 pp.

History of language/dialects of North Carolina. Includes description of Black languages and Gullah. Also includes five-hundred-word glossary.

Elkind, David. "Black English." *Instructor*, LXXXIII (December, 1973), 26.

Elkins, Deborah. See Taba, Hilda, and Deborah Elkins.

Elliot, Dale. See Legum, Stanley E., Dale Elliot, and Sandra A. Thompson.

Ellis, Herbert G. See Newman, Stanley M., and Herbert G. Ellis.

Ellison, Ralph. *Invisible Man.* New York: Random House, 1952. 439 pp.

A powerful study of the Black in America. Implications for sociolinguistic study of Black language.

————. "Tell It Like It Is, Baby." *Nation*, CCI (September 21, 1965), 129–36.

Elton, William. "Playing the Dozens." *American Speech*, XXV (October, 1950), 230–33.

Describes and expands upon studies by John Dollard.

Emans, Robert. "The Effect of Verb Simplification on the Reading Comprehension of Culturally Different High School Students." Paper presented at the annual conference of the American Educational Research Association, February 4–7, 1972, at New York City. 11 pp.

Concludes that verb simplification presentation is of greater benefit to Blacks than to Whites.

————. See Mattleman, Marcene S., and Robert L. Emans.

Emmett, Dan. *Dixie.* 1859.

The rallying song of the South was originally written for a minstrel show and was meant to be sung by Blacks.

Engelman, Siegfried. See Bereiter, Carl, and Siegfried Engelman. *Language Learning Activities for the Disadvantaged Child.*

——. See Bereiter, Carl, and Siegfried Engelman. *Teaching Disadvantaged Children in the Preschool.*

——. See Bereiter, Carl, Siegfried Engelman, Jean Osborn, and Philip A. Reidford.

English, Thomas Dunn. "Caesar Rowan." *Scribner's Magazine*, II (July, 1871), 300.

One of the first Black verse poems printed in the northern media during Reconstruction.

——. *Fairy Stories and Wonder Tales.* New York: Frederick A. Stokes, 1897. 303 pp.

A collection of some of English's better works, a significant number which were written extensively in Black English.

——. "Leonard Grimleigh's Shadow." *Lippincott's Magazine*, VIII (September, 1871), 256–59.

Major poem in Black verse.

——. "Mahs' Lewis's Ride." *Appleton's*, V (May 6, 1871), 519–20.

Black verse.

——. "Momma Phoebe." *Scribner's Magazine*, III (November, 1871), 62–63.

Black verse.

——. *The Selected Poems of Dr. Thomas Dunn English.* Edited by Alice English. N.p., 1894. 694 pp.

Extensive collection of English's poetry which appeared in leading magazines and in collected anthologies between 1870–90. Most of the poetry was either written in Black dialect or included significant passages in Black dialect.

"English as a Second Language." *Time*, LXXXVII (February 18, 1966), 60.

Brief news feature on second-language teaching programs for Blacks in several urban school systems.

Entwisle, Doris R. "Developmental Sociolinguistics: Inner City Children." *American Journal of Sociology*, LXXIV (July, 1968), 37–49.

Experimental data suggests that some inner-city youths are more advanced on certain language skills than suburban children.

82

————. Review of Ralph W. Fasold and Roger W. Shuy, *Teaching Standard English in the Inner City. American Journal of Sociology,* LXXVII (September, 1971), 396–98.

————. "Semantic Systems of Children: Some Assumptions of Social Class and Ethnic Differences," in Frederick Williams, ed., *Language and Poverty: Perspectives on a Theme.* Chicago: Markham, 1970. Pp. 123–39.

Discusses research on semantic structure characteristics of Black and White speakers, both middle- and lower-class.

————. *Semantic Systems of Minority Groups.* Center for the Study of Social Organization of Schools, The Johns Hopkins University, Baltimore, June, 1969. 49 pp.

Supplies evidence that widening gaps exist between the lower class and the middle class in language development from the first grade onward. Suggests that more integration of students is needed.

————. "Subcultural Differences in Children's Language Development." *International Journal of Psychology,* III (1968), 13–22.

Field survey and experimental analysis. Results indicate that rural Maryland children fell behind suburban Maryland children in most aspects of language. First-grade white children in the Baltimore slums performed better than first-grade White suburban children; first-grade Negro slum children equaled the performance of White suburban children.

————. *Word Associations of Disadvantaged Children,* Center for the Study of Social Organization of Schools, The Johns Hopkins University, Baltimore, n.d.

Entwisle, Doris R., and Catherine Garvey. *Adjective Usage.* Center for the Study of Social Organization of Schools, The Johns Hopkins University, Baltimore, 1969. 33 pp.

Outlines arguments for distinction between language and cognition. Experimental field study using both Black and White children.

Entwisle, Doris R., and Ellen Greenberger. *Differences in the Language of the Negro and White Grade School Children.* Report No. 19, Center for the Study of Social Organization of Schools, The Johns Hopkins University, Baltimore, 1968. 59 pp.

Study of children in Baltimore, Md.

EPDA Institute in Standard English as a Second Dialect. Director's Report, (June 23–August 1, 1969). South Florida University, Tampa, 1969. 33 pp.

Report of a six-week institute for thirty-eight teachers (kindergarten through third grade) to give teachers an awareness of linguistics, a knowledge of differences and similarities between Black and standard English, and a background in the role of the Black American history.

ERIC Clearinghouse for Urban Disadvantaged, Yeshiva University, New York. *Language Development in Disadvantaged Children: An Annotated Bibliography.* ERIC document ED 026 414. Washington, D.C., 1968. 86 pp.

A few references of interest to dialectologists and sociolinguists.

Erickson, Frederick David. "'F'Get You Honky!': A New Look at Black Dialect and the School." *Elementary English,* XLVI (April, 1969), 495–99, 517. [Also in William W. Joyce and James A. Banks, eds., *Teaching the Language Arts to Culturally Different Children.* Reading, Mass.: Addison-Wesley, 1971. Pp. 96–102; Arthur L. Smith, ed., *Language, Communication, and Rhetoric in Black America.* New York: Harper & Row, 1972. Pp. 18–27.]

Reports of research project involving Basil Bernstein's theories of restricted and elaborated language codes. Notes that data supports counterhypothesis that inner-city Blacks and suburban Whites are not bound exclusively to either "high" or "low" context. Data supports hypothesis that language of Blacks is adequate for abstract communication. Suggests use of bidialectal readers to produce greater productive communication situations. Article draws upon research project, *Sounds of Society.*

Erickson, Frederick David, and B. J. Chandler. *Sounds of Society: A Demonstration Program in Group Inquiry.* Northwestern University, Evanston, Ill., January, 1968. 108 pp.

Research analysis involving cultural differences and their influence in language behavior of lower-class Blacks and middle-class Whites.

Ervin-Tripp, Susan M. "Children's Sociolinguistic Competence and Dialect Diversity," in Herman G. Richey, ed., *Early Childhood Education: The Seventy-first Yearbook of the National Society for the Study of Education, Part 2.* Chicago: National Society for the Study of Education, 1972. Pp. 123–160. [Also in Anwar S. Dil, ed., *Language Acquisition and Communicative Choice: Essays by Susan M. Ervin-Tripp.* Stanford, Calif.: Stanford University Press, 1973. Pp. 262–301.]

Comparative studies of language development. Includes discussion of need for additional research in area of dialects of children.

84

Ervin-Tripp, Susan M., and Wick R. Miller. "Language Development," in Joshua A. Fishman, ed., *Readings in the Sociology of Language.* The Hague: Mouton, 1968. Pp. 68–98.

Suggests that a way to evaluate a child's development is to determine that child's sound system and rules for formulating of sentences, as well as his own progress in the mastery of the adult's linguistic system.

Eschholz, Paul A. See Clark, Virginia P., Paul A. Eschholz, and Alfred A. Rosa, eds.

Eustis, Celestine. *Cooking in the Old Creole Days.* New York: R. H. Russell, 1903. 129 pp.

In addition to recipes, this book includes the lyrics and music of eight Creole songs, as well as two pages of proverbs.

Evans, Mari. "Creative Writing and the Black Idiom." Paper presented at the Conference on English—Black and White, March 4–6, 1971, at Purdue University, West Lafayette, Ind.

Discussion by a Black poet of the use of Black phrases and idioms in creative writing.

Everett, Russell I. "The Speech of the Tri-Racial Group Composing the Community of Clinton, La." Doctoral dissertation, Louisiana State University, Baton Rouge, 1958.

Evertts, Eldonna L., ed. *Dimensions of Dialect.* Champaign, Ill.: National Council of Teachers of English, 1967. 78 pp.

Anthology of articles. Included are "New Dimensions and New Demands" by Muriel Crosby; "A Checklist of Significant Features for Discriminating Social Dialects" by Raven I. McDavid, Jr.; "Understanding the Language of the Culturally Disadvantaged Child" by Eddie Ponder; "Vocabulary Deprivation of the Underprivileged Child" by Edgar Dale; "Dialect Barriers to Reading Comprehension" by Kenneth S. Goodman; "Talk Written Down" by Lila Sheppard; "Teaching Language and Reading to Disadvantaged Negro Children" by Allison Davis.

"Exploring the Racial Gap." *Time,* XCIII (May 9, 1969), 75–76.

Discussion of the sociolinguistic basis of Black English, both verbal and nonverbal language.

F

Faber, A. Dilworth. "Negro American Vocabulary: Cleveland, Ohio, 1936." *Writer*, XLVI (July, 1937), 239.

A list of about seventy words and idioms of Cleveland Blacks in 1936. Claims that "much of the urban Negro slang is of White origin."

Fabio, Sarah Webster. "What Is Black?" *College Composition and Communication*, XIX (December, 1968), 286–87.

Short discussion of Black lexicon.

Fagan, Edward R., ed. *English and the Disadvantaged*. Scranton, Pa.: International Textbook, 1967. 128 pp.

Faine, Jules. *Philologie Créole: Etudes Historiques et Etymologiques sur la Langue Créole d'Haiti*. Port-au-Prince, Haiti: Imprimatieur, 1936. 303 pp.

Linguistic analysis of the Haitian Creole.

Fanon, Frantz. *Black Skin, White Masks*. Translated from the French by Charles Lam Markmann. New York: Grove Press, 1967. 232 pp.

Includes a chapter on "The Negro and His Language" (pp. 17–40).

Farmer, Marjorie. See Horowitz, David A., I. Ezra Staples, and Marjorie Farmer.

Farr, Helen Louise Kuster. "Cultural Change in the English Classroom: An Anthropological Approach to the Education of Culturally Disadvantaged Students." Doctoral dissertation, University of Illinois, Urbana, 1966. 270 pp.

Suggests use of anthropological goals in English language instruction, particularly among nonstandard speakers.

Farrison, W. Edward. "Dialectology Versus Negro Dialect." *CLA Journal*, XIII (September, 1969), 21–26. [Also in Juanita V. Williamson and Virginia M. Burke, eds., *A Various Language: Perspectives on American Dialects*. New York: Holt, Rinehart, & Winston, 1971. Pp. 187–92.]

Defines the term *dialect* and discusses what he calls the "myth of Negro dialect." Uses literary passages for his evidence. Also discusses misconceptions regarding Black English.

————. "The Phonology of the Illiterate Negro Dialect of Guilford County, North Carolina." Doctoral dissertation, Ohio State University, Columbus, 1937. 88 pp.

Study of elderly illiterate Blacks. Includes transcription.

Fasold, Ralph W. "Decreolization and Autonomous Language Change." *Florida FL Reporter*, X (Spring/Fall, 1972), 9–12, 51.

Discusses the stages of decreolization which are shown in the history of vernacular Black English.

————. "A Dilemma in Sociolinguistic Theory." Paper presented at annual meeting of the Linguistic Society of America, July 1, 1969, at Champaign, Ill.

————. "Distinctive Linguistic Characteristics of Black English," in James E. Alatis, ed., *Report of the Twentieth Annual Roundtable Meeting on Linguistics and Language Studies: Linguistics and the Teaching of Standard English to Speakers of Other Languages or Dialects.* Monograph Series on Languages and Linguistics. Washington, D.C.: Georgetown University Press, 1970. Pp. 233–38.

Discusses linguistic characteristics of Black English as presented by various linguists.

————. "Isn't English the First Language, Too?" Paper presented at annual meeting of National Council of Teachers of English, November, 1968, at Milwaukee, Wis.

————. "A Look at the Form *be* in Standard English," in William K. Riley and David M. Smith, eds., *Languages and Linguistics: Working Papers, Number 5: Sociolinguistics.* Washington, D.C.: Georgetown University Press, 1972. Pp. 95–101.

Linguistic analysis developed from major study.

————. "Orthography in Reading Materials for Black English Speaking Children," in Joan C. Baratz and Roger W. Shuy, eds., *Teaching Black Children to Read.* Washington, D.C.: Center for Applied Linguistics, 1969. Pp. 68–91.

Outlines the necessity for teachers to be familiar with Black English pronunciation according to the rules not of standard English but of Black English itself. Notes that if pronunciations are consistent with Black English phonology in reading, one of the problems of teaching English to Blacks will be alleviated.

————. *Report on the Uses of a Dialect Bible Translation with YDI Teenagers.* Washington, D.C.: Center for Applied Linguistics, 1971.

87

Project developed from Bible translation developed by Fasold and Walter Wolfram.

————. *A Sociolinguistic Study of the Pronunciation of Three Vowels in Detroit Speech.* Washington, D.C.: Center for Applied Linguistics, 1968.

————. "A Strategy for Teaching for Nonuse of Black English Distributive 'be.'" Unpublished paper, Center for Applied Linguistics, Washington, D.C., 1969. 13 pp.

————. "Tense and the Form *Be* in Black English." *Language,* XLV (December, 1969), 763–76.

Discusses use of the word *be* in Black English as a main verb expressing iteration rather than instantaneous or constant state. Argues that the best analysis is one which recognizes only one verb *to be,* which can occur without tense in Black English.

————. *Tense Marking in Black English: A Linguistic and Social Analysis.* Arlington, Va.: Center for Applied Linguistics, 1973. 254 pp.

Major sociolinguistic study of Washington, D.C., Black English, concentrating on the verb forms. Includes both syntactical and phonological analysis. Includes a chapter by Carolyn Kessler on noun plural absence.

————. "Three Models for Dealing with Socially Significant Language." Unpublished paper, Washington, D.C.: Center for Applied Linguistics, July, 1969.

————. *Two Fricatives in Black English: A Generative Phonology Approach.* Washington, D.C.: Center for Applied Linguistics, 1967. 5 pp.

————. "What Can an English Teacher Do About Non-Standard Dialects?" *The English Record,* XXI (April, 1971), 82–91.

Urges that objectives in hearing, speaking, reading, and writing should be based upon individual needs; should be related to the language spoken by the individual, rather than to standard English.

————. See Shuy, Roger W., and Ralph W. Fasold, eds.

————. See Wolfram, Walter A., and Ralph W. Fasold. "A Black English Translation of John 3:1–21, with Grammatical Annotations."

————. See Wolfram, Walter A., and Ralph W. Fasold. *Social Dialects in the United States.*

————. See Wolfram, Walter A., and Ralph W. Fasold. "Toward Reading

Materials for Speakers of Black English: Three Linguistically Appropriate Passages."

Fasold, Ralph W., and Roger W. Shuy, eds. *Teaching Standard English in the Inner City*. Washington, D.C.: Center for Applied Linguistics, 1970. 141 pp.

Contains six articles by William A. Stewart, Joan C. Baratz, Irwin Feigenbaum, Walter A. Wolfram, Roger W. Shuy, and Ralph W. Fasold. Part of the Center for Applied Linguistics Urban Language Series.

Fasold, Ralph W., and Walter A. Wolfram. "Some Linguistic Features of Negro Dialect." *Language, Speech, and Hearing Services in Schools*, III (1972), 16–49, 72. [Also in Ralph W. Fasold and Roger W. Shuy, eds., *Teaching Standard English in the Inner City*. Washington, D.C.: Center for Applied Linguistics, 1970. Pp. 41–86; David L. Shores, ed., *Contemporary English: Change and Variation*. Philadelphia: J. B. Lippincott, 1972. Pp. 53–85; Johanna S. DeStefano, ed., *Language, Society, and Education: A Profile of Black English*. Worthington, Ohio: Charles A. Jones, 1973. Pp. 116–48.]

Mildly technical presentation of many of the features of Black English, putting the language into proper sociological and linguistic perspective.

Faulk, John Henry. "Quickened by de Spurit: Ten Negro Sermons." Master's thesis, University of Texas, Austin, 1940.

Faulkner, William. *Absalom, Absalom!* New York: Random House, 1936. 384 pp.

Novel. Includes Black English.

———. *As I Lay Dying*. New York: Cape and Smith, 1930. 254 pp.

Novel. Includes Black English.

———. *Go Down, Moses, and Other Stories*. New York: Random House, 1942. 383 pp.

Several short stories which include Black English.

———. *Intruder in the Dust*. New York: Random House, 1948. 247 pp.

Novel. Includes Black English.

———. *Light in August*. New York: Harrison Smith and Robert Haas, 1932. 480 pp.

Novel. Includes Black English.

———. *Sanctuary*. New York: Cape and Smith, 1931. 380 pp.

Novel. Includes Black English.

————. *Sartoris.* New York: Harcourt, Brace, 1929. 380 pp.

Novel. Includes Black English.

————. *The Sound and the Fury.* New York: Jonathan Cape and Harrison Smith, 1929. 401 pp.

Novel. Includes Black English.

Fedder, Ruth, and Jacqueline Gabaldon. *No Longer Deprived: The Use of Minority Cultures and Languages in the Education of Disadvantaged Children and Their Teachers.* New York: Columbia University Teacher's College Press, 1970. 211 pp.

Federal Writers Project. *Slave Narratives: A Folk History of Slaves in the United States, From Interviews With Former Slaves.* Washington, D.C.: U.S. Government Printing Office, 1941.

About two thousand autobiographical narratives of former slaves, compiled in seventeen states during the years 1936–1938. Most of the narratives are verbatim transcripts.

Fehderau, Harold U. See Nida, Eugene A., and Harold U. Fehderau.

Feigenbaum, Irwin. "The Concept of Appropriateness and Developing Materials for TESOL." *TESOL Quarterly,* I (September, 1967), 36–39. [Part 2 of "Teaching a Second Dialect and Some Implications for TESOL" by Irwin Feigenbaum and William S. Carroll, *TESOL Quarterly,* I (September, 1967), 33–39.]

Advises teachers to add standard English to the student's language and not to replace or eliminate Black English.

————. "Developing Fluency in Standard Oral English." *Elementary English,* XLVII (December, 1970), 1,053–59. [Also in Thomas D. Horn, ed., *Research Bases for Oral Language Instruction.* Urbana, Ill.: National Council of Teachers of English, 1971. Pp. 91–97.]

Questions the use of second-language methodology for second-dialect education. Urges more rigorous research.

————. *English Now: A Self-Correcting Workbook with "Write and See."* New York: Meredith, 1970. 158 pp.

This workbook consists of fourteen programmed lessons, each with an audio tape, with stress on both formal and informal language. Designed for seventh through twelfth grades.

————. Introduction to "Standard and Nonstandard English: Learning and Teaching Problems," in David L. Shores, ed., *Contemporary English: Change and Variation.* Philadelphia: J. B. Lippincott, 1972. Pp. 219–24.

Presents some issues and theories within study of Black English.

————. Review of William Labov, *The Study of Nonstandard English.* *TESOL Quarterly*, IV (December, 1970), 371–72.

————. "The Use of Nonstandard English in Teaching Standard: Contrast and Comparison," in Ralph W. Fasold and Roger W. Shuy, eds., *Teaching Standard English in the Inner City.* Washington, D.C.: Center for Applied Linguistics, 1970. Pp. 87–104.

Presents general observations regarding classroom situations.

————. "Using Foreign Language Methodology to Teach Standard English: Evaluation and Adaptation," in Alfred C. Aarons, Barbara Y. Gordon, and William A. Stewart, eds., *Linguistic-Cultural Differences and American Education,* special issue of the *Florida FL Reporter*, VII (Spring/Summer, 1969). Pp. 116–22, 156–57. [Also in David L. Shores, ed., *Contemporary English: Change and Variation.* Philadelphia: J. B. Lippincott, 1972. Pp. 256–77.]

Discussion of early work and classroom innovation in the area, drills, concept of appropriateness, response activities, use of writing. Emphasizes the need for adaptation of foreign language materials to second dialect teaching.

Feigenbaum, Irwin. See Carroll, William S., and Irwin Feigenbaum.

Feldmann, Shirley C. See Chall, Jeanne, and Shirley C. Feldmann.

Ferguson, Charles A. "Absence of Copula and the Notion of Simplicity: A Study of Normal Speech, Baby Talk, Foreigner Talk and Pidgins." Paper presented at Conference on Pidginization and Creolization of Languages, April, 1968, at Kingston, Jamaica. 17 pp.

Presents several observations about grammatical simplicity, with implications for American Black English and nonstandard English.

————. "Diglossia." *Word*, XV (August, 1959), 325–40. [Also in Pier Paolo Giglioli, ed., *Language and Social Context.* Harmondsworth, England: Penguin Books, 1972. Pp. 232–51.]

Some theoretical interpretations involving language varieties.

————. "Teaching Standard Languages to Dialect Speakers," in Roger W. Shuy, ed., *Social Dialects and Language Learning: Proceedings of the Bloomington, Indiana, Conference, 1964.* Champaign, Ill.: National Council of Teachers of English, 1965. Pp. 112–17.

A brief discussion with implications on the controversy between forces urging eradication and forces advocating bidialectism.

Ferris, William R., Jr. "Black Prose Narrative in the Mississippi Delta." *Journal of American Folklore*, LXXXV (April–June, 1972), 140–51.

Cross-sectional study of Blacks of the Mississippi Delta region. Discusses the dozens, personalized tales, conte fables, trickster tales, sacred and profane, and high pro.

Fickett, Joan. "*Ain't, Not*, and *Don't* in Black English," in J. L. Dillard, ed., *Perspectives on Black English*. The Hague: Mouton, forthcoming.

Discusses *ain't, not*, and *don't* in relation to the seven possible tenses in Black English. Says that the use of these negatives of Black English only partially supports optional tense system, but does distinguish between time-limited negatives and general negatives.

———. "Aspects of Morphemics, Syntax, and Semology of an Inner-City Dialect (Merican)." Doctoral dissertation, State University of New York, Buffalo, 1970. 139 pp. [Reprinted by Meadowood Publishers, New York, 1972; Department of Anthropology, Southern Illinois University, Carbondale, 1974.]

Linguistic analysis of Black English. Concludes that Black English is a separate language with its own well-defined rules. Coins the name "Merican" to describe this different language.

———. "Reading, Writing, and Reality." Unpublished paper, Department of Social Sciences, Fairleigh-Dickinson University, Rutherford, N.J., April 20, 1972. 5 pp.

Advocates undistorted teaching practices in teaching English to dialect speakers by showing distinction between oral and written language.

———. *Tense and Aspect in Black English*. Paper presented at the annual meeting of the American Anthropological Association, November, 1971, at New York. 5 pp. [Also in *Journal of English Linguistics*, VI (March, 1972), 17–19.]

Discussion of the six degrees of tense, or "phrases," varying from the present tense. Points out that Black English does not have an obligatory past tense. Also discusses the function of the five aspects.

———. "Why O. J. Had Did It Again." Unpublished paper, Department of Social Sciences, Fairleigh-Dickinson University, 1973. 4 pp.

Discusses differences between English and Black English (Merican) production of past tenses. Points out need for teachers to know how English lexical items fit into the structure of each language.

Fiege-Kollmann, Laila. See Key, Mary Ritchie, Laila Fiege-Kollmann, and Ernie Smith.

Figueroa, John J. *Creole Studies.* University of the West Indies, Mona, Jamaica, 1968. 45 pp.

Includes bibliography of Creole studies and English teaching.

Figurel, J. Allen, ed. *Reading Goals for the Disadvantaged.* Newark, Del.: International Reading Association, 1970. 339 pp.

Fillmer, H. T., and Mary Hayman Hurt. "Language Patterns of Disadvantaged Pupils." *Education,* XCIII (November–December, 1972), 184–88.

Basic research into Black English. Suggests bidialectal approach.

Finocchiaro, Mary. "Teaching English to Speakers of Other Languages: Problems and Priorities." Presidential address, New York TESOL Affiliate, November 11, 1970, at New York. [Also in *English Record,* XXI (April, 1971), 39–46.]

Personalizes and demythologizes several aspects of bilingual and bidialectal study, with focus on the classroom.

Fishbin, Justin M. "A Nonstandard Publisher's Problems" in James L. Laffey and Roger Shuy, eds., *Language Differences—Do They Intefere?* Newark, Del.: International Reading Association, 1973.

Fisher, John C. "Generating Standard Sentence Patterns—and Beyond." *College Composition and Communication,* XXI (December, 1970), 364–68.

Discusses reasons why there are no widely adopted methods of teaching nonstandard English speakers to generate standard speech.

Fisher, Mary L., comp. *The Negro in America: A Bibliography.* 2nd ed. Cambridge: Harvard University Press, 1970. 350 pp. [Original edition compiled by Elizabeth W. Miller.]

Fisher, Miles Mark. *Negro Slave Songs of the United States.* Ithaca, N.Y.: Cornell University Press, 1953. 223 pp.

Includes language (nonphonetic transcription) and history of the music.

Fishman, Joshua, ed. *Readings in the Sociology of Language.* The Hague: Mouton, 1968, 808 pp.

Collection of articles (many original) dealing with sociolinguistics. Includes articles on the sociology of language.

———. Review of P. E. Vernon, *Intelligence and Cultural Environments,* and Joan C. Baratz and Roger W. Shuy, eds., *Teaching Black Children to Read. Science,* CLXV (September 12, 1969), 1,108–1,109.

The two books are reviewed together to contrast the differing schools of thought.

————. *Sociolinguistics: A Brief Introduction*. Rowley, Mass.: Newbury House, 1970. 127 pp.

Introductory text. Includes review and study of bilingualism.

Fishman, Joshua A., and Erika Lueders-Salmon. "What Has the Sociology of Language to Say to the Teacher? On Teaching the Standard Variety to Speakers of Dialectal or Sociolectal Varieties," in Courtney B. Cazden, Vera P. John, and Dell H. Hymes, eds., *Functions of Language in the Classroom*. New York: Teachers College Press, Columbia University, 1972. Pp. 67–83.

Comparative study of the German Swabian dialect of Stuttgart to High German dialect, and of American Black English to American standard English. Points out subtle differences between attempts by German educators to require the people to be able to read and write High German while permitting them to retain dialectal speech. Compares and contrasts to bidialectism and eradication theories in America.

Fleming, Elizabeth McClellan, "William Gilmore Simms's Portrayal of the Negro." Master's thesis, Duke University, Durham, N.C., 1965.

Fleming, James T. "Childrens' Perception of Social Significant Speech Variants." Paper presented at annual convention of American Education Research Association, 1968, at Chicago. [Also in *Education and Urban Society*, III (May, 1971), 323–32.]

Speech identification exercise.

Floud, Jean. See Halsey, A. H., Jean Floud, and C. Arnold Anderson, eds.

Flowers, Paul. "Picturesque Speech." *Tennessee Folklore Society Bulletin*, X (March, 1944), 9–10.

Discusses use of word *bo-dollar* (silver dollar) by Blacks.

Focke, H. C. *Neger-Englisch Woorden-Boek*. Leiden, The Netherlands: P. H. Van Den Heuvell, 1855. 160 pp.

Folb, Edith A. *Black Vernacular Vocabulary: A Study of Intercultural Concerns and Usage*. Center for Afro-American Studies, University of California at Los Angeles, Westwood, Calif., 1973.

Includes seven-hundred-word lexicon, with description and analysis.

————. *A Comparative Study of Urban Black Argot*. San Francisco, United States Office of Education, March, 1972. 162 pp.

Study of the argot among Blacks in south central Los Angeles. Includes glossary of 138 terms or phrases. Tends to confirm hypothesis of existence of separate Black argot language. Author notes that Blacks in a wide geographical area of Los Angeles recognized and understood the argot, while lower-class Whites within close proximity of the Black population did not. Several charts and graphs included. Author claims that being a female aided in her interviewing process.

Foley, Lawrence N. *A Phonological and Lexical Study of the Speech of Tuscaloosa County, Alabama*. Arlington, Va.: Publication of the American Dialect Society, forthcoming.

An analysis of the speech of twenty-seven native respondents of an Alabama county that is near the proposed boundaries of Southern and South Midland speech areas. Uses methodology of the *Linguistic Atlas of the United States*. Concludes that there is a mixed influence from several areas, including Inland South, South Midland, and coastal features. Notes that Black speech of that area includes some aspects of the speech of socially prominent White respondents.

"Folk-Lore From St. Helena, South Carolina." *Journal of American Folk-Lore*, XXXVIII (April–June, 1925), 217–38.

Several Gullah tales and spirituals, mostly edited into standard English.

"Folk-Tales From Students in Tuskegee Institute, Alabama." *Journal of American Folk-Lore*, XXXII (July–September, 1919), 397–401.

Forbes, Jack D. *Afro-Americans in the Far West: A Handbook for Educators*. Berkeley, Calif.: Far West Laboratory for Educational Research and Development, 1967. 112 pp.

First five chapters are an overview of Black heritage. Useful for understanding sociocultural base of Black English.

Forfeit, Karen G., and Patricia L. Donaldson. "Dialect, Race, and Language Proficiency: Another Dead Heat on the Merry-Go-Round." *Child Development*, XLII (November, 1971), 1,572–74.

Authors claim methodological flaws in Joan C. Baratz, "A Bi-Dialectical Task for Determining Language Proficiency in Economically Disadvantaged Negro Children, *Child Development*, XL (1969), 889–901.

Formanek, R. See Greenberg, S., and R. Formanek.

Fortier, Alcée. "The French Language in Louisiana and the Negro-French

Dialect." *Transactions of the Modern Language Association,* I (1884–85), 96–111.

Historical examination of Louisiana Creole and Negro-French. Includes description of phonetics of Negro-French, as well as parts of speech analysis.

————. *Louisiana Folk-Tales in French Dialect and English Translation.* New York: American Folk-Lore Society, 1895. 122 pp.

Forty-one fables, stories, and fairy tales recorded in Black Creole, then translated into standard English.

————. *Louisiana Studies.* New Orleans: F. F. Hansell & Bro., 1894. 307 pp.

Includes description of phonetics and grammar of Creole.

Foster, Charles W. *The Phonology of the Conjure Tales of Charles W. Chesnutt.* Arlington, Va.: Publication of the American Dialect Society, No. 55, forthcoming.

Concludes that Chesnutt was remarkably accurate in his representation of Black dialect of the Cape Fear–Peedee River corridor.

————. "The Representation of Negro Dialect in Charles W. Chesnutt's *The Conjure Woman.*" Doctoral dissertation, University of Alabama, University, Ala., 1968. 258 pp.

Analysis of the North Carolina Black dialect presented by Chesnutt in an anthology of dialect tales. Concludes that Chesnutt was substantially accurate in his dialect representation.

Foster, Herbert Lawrence. "Dialect-Lexicon and Listening Comprehension." Doctoral dissertation, Columbia University, 1969. 159 pp.

Study to determine the effects of introducing Black English into the classroom. Recommends judicious use of Black English instruction by teachers, but also suggests that students be allowed not only to speak Black English, but to write in the language if they so desire.

————. "A Pilot Study of the Cant of the Disadvantaged, Socially Maladjusted Secondary School Child." *Urban Education,* II (July, 1967), 99–114.

Based on his dissertation, "Dialect-Lexicon and Listening Comprehension."

Fox, Sister Anthony Mary. "Standard English vs. the Black Dialect." *Clearing House,* XLVII (December, 1972), 204–208.

Brief overview of Black English.

Fox, George Thomas, Jr. "The Effect of Black Dialect and Standard English on 10-12-Year-Olds' Willingness to State Apparent Contradictions: A Language Comparison Between Black Dialect and Standard English That Tests the Whorf Hypothesis and the Bernstein Thesis." Doctoral dissertation, University of Wisconsin, Milwaukee, 1972. 273 pp.

Fraenkel, Gerd. See Cohen, Rosalie, Gerd Fraenkel, and John Brewer.

Francis, W. Nelson. "Opportunities for Research in Dialectology and Applied Linguistics in the Brown University-Tougaloo College Co-Operative Program," in Roger W. Shuy, ed., *Social Dialects and Language Learning: Proceedings of the Bloomington, Indiana, Conference, 1964.* Champaign, Ill.: National Council of Teachers of English, 1965. Pp. 147–48.

Brief description of a program that involves dialect research as well as language improvement in a predominantly Black Mississippi college.

———. *The Structure of American English.* New York: Ronald Press, 1958. 614 pp.

Includes chapter on dialects written by Raven I. McDavid, Jr. Brief mention of Gullah.

Fraser, Bruce. *Nonstandard English.* Washington, D.C.: Center for Applied Linguistics, April, 1970. 22 pp.

Briefly reviews research in the field of nonstandard English. Outlines four theories for classification of a dialect.

———. "Some 'Unexpected' Reactions to Various American-English Dialects," in Roger W. Shuy and Ralph W. Fasold, eds., *Language Attitudes: Current Trends and Prospects.* Washington, D.C.: Georgetown University Press, 1973. Pp. 29–35.

Study of listener-reaction to taped voice characteristics and speech styles of Blacks and Whites from various geographical areas. Notes presence of stereotypes of nonstandard English speakers.

Fraser, C. Gerald. "Use of Black English to Help Children Fit in at School Is Debated Here." New York *Times*, May 16, 1971, p. 57.

News feature about Black English. Quotes J. L. Dillard and William Labov.

Frazier, Alexander. "Helping Poorly Languaged Children." *Elementary English*, XLI (February, 1964), 149–53.

Not dialect-oriented, but points to problems within the language arts.

————. *New Directions in Elementary English: Papers Collected from the 1966 Spring Institute on the Elementary Language Arts of the National Council of Teachers of English.* Champaign, Ill.: National Council of Teachers of English, 1967. 221 pp.

Anthology of conference papers, with focus on newer teaching methods. Includes implications for the teacher within a Black English–standard English setting.

French, Patrice. "Gestural Effectiveness: Black and White." *Language Sciences*, in press.

An experimental study which concludes that in nonverbal communication the gestures of Blacks are more universally understood than the gestures of Whites.

————. "Kinesics in Communication: Black and White." *Language Sciences*, No. 28 (December, 1973), 13–16.

Experimental study.

————. "White Bias in Black Language Studies." Paper presented at Southeastern Conference on Linguistics, April 20–21, 1973, in Blacksburg, Va.

Study of kinesic abilities shows that lower-class and Black English speakers are "deprived" in kinesic ability only in response to White middle-class materials. Middle-class White children show less ability to decode kinesics than Black and lower-class children.

French, Patrice, and Walburga von Raffler Engel. "Kinesic Dialect? Language and Paralanguage in Black English Speakers." Paper presented at Midwestern Regional Meeting of American Dialect Society August 2, 1973, in Ann Arbor, Mich.

Study of the use of kinesics in experimental situation shows that Black English speakers have a more highly ordered kinesic system than standard English speakers.

Frentz, Thomas Stanley. "Children's Comprehension of Standard and Black English." Doctoral dissertation, University of Wisconsin, Madison, 1970. 98 pp.

Study to determine whether the deep structures of Black English and standard English are the same or different and whether syntactic differences are restricted to surface structures or whether they exist also at the deep-structure level.

————. "Children's Comprehension of Standard and Negro Nonstandard English Sentences." *Speech Monographs*, XXXVIII (March, 1971), 10–16.

Abridged version of his doctoral dissertation.

Freshour, Frank W. "The Effects of Parent Education Program on Reading Readiness and Achievement of Disadvantaged First Grade Negro Children." Doctoral dissertation, University of Florida, Gainesville, 1970. 77 pp.

Notes the existence of a probable, but not significant, difference in favor of experimental group.

Friedlander, George H. *Report on the Articulatory and Intelligibility Status of Socially Disadvantaged Pre-School Children*. Institute of Retarded Children of the Shield of David, New York, December, 1965. 63 pp.

Fries, Charles C. "Standard English," in Virginia P. Clark, Paul A. Eschholz, and Alfred A. Rosa, eds., *Language: Introductory Readings*. New York: St. Martin's Press, 1972. Pp. 349–51.

Fruit, J. P. "Uncle Remus in Phonetic Spelling." *Dialect Notes*, I (1896), 196–98.

Says that the Black was "a great factor in forming our spoken language." Presents a phonetically transcribed folktale.

Fryburg, Estelle. "A Descriptive Guide to Features Characteristic of Black English," in Bernice E. Cullinan, ed., *Black Dialects and Reading*. Urbana, Ill.: ERIC, 1974.

————. "Evaluating Children's Language," in Bernice E. Cullinan, ed., *Black Dialects and Reading*. Urbana, Ill.: ERIC, 1974.

————. "The Relations Among English Syntax, Methods of Instruction, and Reading Achievement of First Grade Disadvantaged Children." Doctoral dissertation, New York University, 1972. 327 pp.

Finds high degree of correlation between oral language and reading ability: standard English speakers have more gains in reading and in arithmetic than nonstandard English speakers.

Funkhouser, James L. "A Various Standard." *College English*, XXXIV (March, 1973), 806–27.

Examines a number of syntactical rules in what he calls Black Vernacular English. Presents 103 sentences illustrating basic rules.

Furbee, N. Louanna. See Simpson, Dagna, Emily Pettigrew Morris, and N. Louanna Furbee.

Furfey, Paul H. "The Sociological Implications of Substandard English." *American Catholic Sociological Review*, V (1944), 3–10.

Recognizes deviations from standard English as being legitimate, but gives a frank appraisal of the social implication of nonstandard usage.

G

Gabaldon, Jacqueline. See Fedder, Ruth, and Jacqueline Gabaldon.

Gaidoz, H., and Paul Sébillot. *Bibliographie des Traditions et de la Litterature Populaire des Frances d'Outre-Mer*. Paris: Maisonneuve Frères et C. Leclerc, 1886.

Bibliography and discussion of French-English Creole dialects and customs, mostly between 1800 and 1850.

Gantt, Walter N., and Robert M. Wilson. "Syntactical Speech Patterns of Black Children from a Depressed Urban Area: Educators Look at Linguistic Findings." ERIC document ED 070 679. Washington D.C., November 29, 1972. 27 pp.

Study of the syntactical speech patterns characteristic of Black children living in a depressed area of an eastern city. It was determined that the patterns were a mixture of standard English and nonstandard English, with more standard patterns produced.

Gardiner, Richard Andrew. "Nonverbal Communication Between Blacks and Whites in a School Setting." Doctoral dissertation, University of Florida, Gainesville, 1972. 71 pp.

Concludes that differences do exist, noting that Blacks may be more attuned to facial than vocal clues.

Garrett, Romeo B. "African Survivals in American Culture." *Journal of Negro History*, LI (October, 1966), 239–45. [Also in Arthur L. Smith, ed., *Language, Communication, and Rhetoric in Black America*. New York: Harper & Row, 1972. Pp. 356–62.]

Overview of Black English. Uses research of Lorenzo Dow Turner as the basis.

Garrison, Lucy McKim. See Allen, William Francis, Charles Pickard Ware, and Lucy McKim Garrison.

Garvey, Catherine. See Entwisle, Doris R., and Catherine Garvey.

Garvey, Catherine, and Thelma L. Baldwin. *A Self-Instructional Program in Standard English Development and Evaluation.* Center for the Study of Social Organization of Schools, The Johns Hopkins University, Baltimore, 1969.

Developed for fifth-grade Black students in Baltimore, Md.

Garvey, Catherine, and Paul T. McFarlane. "A Measurement of Standard English Proficiency of Inner-City Children." *American Educational Research Journal,* VII (January, 1970), 29–40.

Notes that social class and race are important determinants in tests of grammatical structures.

———. *A Preliminary Study of Standard English Speech Patterns in Baltimore City Public Schools.* Center for the Study of Social Organization of Schools, The Johns Hopkins University, Baltimore, March, 1968. 45 pp.

Experimental study.

Gay, Geneva. See Abrahams, Roger D., and Geneva Gay. "Black Culture in the Classroom."

———. See Abrahams, Roger D., and Geneva Gay. "Talking Black in the Classroom."

Gay, William O. See Stephenson, Bobby L., and William O. Gay.

George, Albert Donald. "Some Louisiana Isoglosses, Based on the Work Books of the Louisiana Dialect Atlas." Master's thesis, Louisiana State University, Baton Rouge, 1951. 175 pp.

Georgetown University School of Languages and Linguistics. See Alatis, James E., ed.

Gerber, A. "Uncle Remus Traced to the Old World." *Journal of American Folk-Lore,* VI (October–December, 1893), 245–57.

Discusses African origins of Uncle Remus folktales.

Gester, Friedrich W. "Negro, Afro-American oder Black? Zu Einer Aktuellen Spracheichen Auseinamdersetzung in der Vereinigten Staaten." *Die Neueren Sprachen,* XX (1971), 53–63.

Getze, George. "English of Some Blacks Differs, Gets Defended." Atlanta *Sunday Journal-Constitution,* November 22, 1970, p. 16-c.

Geuder, Patricia A. "A Writing Seminar for Speakers of Black English." *College Composition and Communication,* XXIII (December, 1972), 417–19.

Discusses an elementary English program for Blacks at the University of Nevada at Las Vegas. Program utilizes Black media as texts. Author notes that of twelve Black English interferences, seven were zero markers.

Gibson, Walker. See Dean, Leonard F., Walker Gibson, and Kenneth G. Wilson, eds.

Gifford, Carolyn. "Black English: An Introduction." *Acta Symbolica*, I (Spring, 1970), 24–30.

Review of Black English.

Giglioli, Pier Paolo, ed. *Language and Social Context*. Harmondsworth, England: Penguin Books, 1972. 339 pp.

General reader. Includes articles by Basil Bernstein, Charles A. Ferguson, Joshua A. Fishman, John J. Gumperz, Dell H. Hymes, and William Labov.

Gilbert, Glenn G. Review of William Labov, *The Social Stratification of English in New York City*. *Language*, XLV (June, 1969), 469–76.

Giles, Douglas E. See Daniel, Artie A., and Douglas E. Giles.

Gillespie, Elizabeth. "The Dialect of the Mississippi Negro in Literature." Doctoral dissertation, University of Mississippi, University, Miss., 1939.

Gilman, Richard. "More on Negro Writing." *New Republic*, CLVII (April 13, 1968), 25–28.

Follow-up to his article "White Standards and Negro Writing."

———. "White Standards and Negro Writing." *New Republic*, CLVII (March 9, 1968), 25–30.

Reviews Eldridge Cleaver's *Soul on Ice*. Claims that White writers cannot judge Black writing, which is a different type of writing.

Gladney, Mildred R. "Problems in Teaching Children with Nonstandard Dialects," in James L. Laffey and Roger Shuy, eds., *Language Differences—Do They Interfere?* Newark, Del.: International Reading Association, 1973. Pp. 140–46.

———. See Davis, Olga, Mildred R. Gladney, Melvin J. Hoffman, Lloyd Leaverton, and Zorenda P. Patterson.

———. See Davis, Ogla, Mildred R. Gladney, and Lloyd Leaverton, entries for Psycholinguistic Reading Series text and guidelines.

Gladney, Mildred R., and Lloyd Leaverton. "A Model for Teaching English to Non-Standard English Speakers." *Elementary English*, XLV (October, 1968), 758–63. [Also in William W. Joyce and James A. Banks, eds., *Teaching the Language Arts to Culturally Different Children*. Reading, Mass.: Addison-Wesley, 1971. Pp. 130–38.]

Program of language arts developed to use the child's home language in contrast to school talk. Attempts to elicit "school talk" in informal settings.

Glissmeyer, Gloria. "Some Characteristics of English in Hawaii," in Richard W. Bailey and Jay L. Robinson, eds., *Varieties of Present-Day English*. New York: Macmillan, 1973. Pp. 190–225.

Discusses distinctive features of Hawaiian Pidgin English as well as social conditions which led to its development and continued use.

Goehl, Henry. See Clark, Dennis, Abraham Wolf, Henry Goehl, and Donald Ecroyd.

Goff, Harry. See Murphy, John, and Harry Goff, comps.

Gold, Robert S. *A Jazz Lexicon*. New York: Alfred A. Knopf, 1964. 363 pp.

Dictionary of jazz argot which is believed to have evolved from Black language and slang.

Golden, Ruth I. "Changing Dialects by Using Tapes," in Roger W. Shuy, ed., *Social Dialects and Language Learning: Proceedings of the Bloomington, Indiana, Conference, 1964*. Champaign, Ill.: National Council of Teachers of English, 1965. Pp. 63–66.

Experimental study conducted in Detroit. Focuses on foreign language–dialect teaching.

———. *Learning Standard English by Linguistic Methods*. ERIC document ED 018 783. Washington, D.C., October, 1968. 10 pp.

Believes that the student should learn the sounds (language) of both the school and business worlds.

———. "Speaking the Same Language: Folk Speech of Negroes and Disadvantaged White Migrants." *NEA Journal*, LVI (March, 1967), 40, 53–54, 56, 58.

Discusses theories of standard English language development.

Golden, Ruth I., and Helen A. Martellock. *Teaching Standard English to Urban Primary Children*. Detroit Public Schools, Detroit, Mich., August, 1967. 313 pp.

Report of a project to bring about the standardization of English in a public-school system.

Goldstein, L. S. See John, Vera P., and L. S. Goldstein.

Golub, Lester S. "Reading, Writing, and Black English." *Elementary School Journal*, LXXII (January, 1972), 195–202.

Advocates an approach that accepts and uses the language that the students, Black and White, bring to school. Notes correlation between speech and written language. Emphasizes that English has a variety of dialects. Prefers "experience charts" prepared by student and teacher, rather than dialect readers.

Gonzales, Ambrose E. *The Black Border: Gullah Stories of the Carolina Coast*. Columbia, S.C.: State, 1922. 348 pp.

Collection and transcription of forty-three tales, many with humor and wit. Includes a glossary of about 1,700 Gullah words. Calls Gullah "mangled English," but also notes that the Gullah folktales have African origins.

―――. *The Captain: Stories of the Black Border*. Columbia, S.C.: State, 1924. 384 pp.

―――. *Laguerra: A Gascon of the Black Border*. Columbia, S.C.: State, 1924. 318 pp.

―――. *Two Gullah Tales: "The Turkey Hunter" and "At the Crossroads."* New York: Purdy Press 1926. 29 pp.

―――. *With Aesop Along the Black Border*. Columbia, S.C.: State, 1924. 298 pp. [Reprinted by Negro Universities Press, Westport, Conn., 1969.]

Gullah reaction to the fables of Aesop—adaptations from the original.

Gonzalez, Joseph Frank. "A Comparative Study of the Spontaneous Connected and Orally Read Speech of a Selected Group of Black and White Children With Normal and Defective Articulation." Doctoral dissertation, Florida State University, Tallahassee, 1972. 159 pp.

Notes significant differences. Suggests a need to revise standard methods of testing articulation.

Gonzalez, Laverne. "A New Program." Paper presented at the Conference on English—Black and White, March 4–6, 1971, at Purdue University, West Lafayette, Ind. 6 pp.

Describes first results of an unusual Purdue University freshman English program designed to stimulate the language skills of students inadequately prepared to undertake a college curriculum. The program involves mostly Black students, although non-Blacks were also admitted to the program.

Goodman, Kenneth S. "Dialect Barriers to Reading Comprehension." *Elementary English*, XLII (December, 1965), 853–60. [Also in Eldonna L. Evertts, ed., *Dimensions of Dialect*. Champaign, Ill.: National Council of Teachers of English, 1967. Pp. 39–46; Joan C. Baratz and Roger W. Shuy, eds., *Teaching Black Children to Read*. Washington, D.C.: Center for Applied Linguistics, 1969. Pp. 14–28; David L. Shores, ed., *Contemporary English: Change and Variation*. Philadelphia: J. B. Lippincott, 1972. Pp. 294–305; Johanna S. DeStefano, ed., *Language, Society, and Education: A Profile of Black English*. Worthington, Ohio: Charles A. Jones, 1973. Pp. 265–75.]

Discussion of effects of dialect in urban classrooms. Suggests that teachers who recognize extent of dialect differences are able to teach reading more effectively.

————. "Dialect Rejection and Reading: A Response." *Reading Research Quarterly*, V (Summer, 1970), 601–603.

Reaction to article by Richard Rystrom in *Reading Research Quarterly*, (Summer, 1970), 581–99. Argument in opposition to view that Black children can be treated as deficient and can be "remediated" by eliminating the deficiencies.

————. "Linguistic Differences and the Ethnocentric Researcher." Paper presented at American Educational Research Association meeting, February 8, 1969, at Los Angeles. 9 pp.

Describes a methodology for the sociolinguist who wishes to compare two populations that differ linguistically.

Goodman, Kenneth S., and Catherine Buck. "Dialect Barriers to Reading Comprehension Revisited." *Reading Teacher*, XXVII (October, 1973), 6–12.

Hypothesizes that many of the problems of speakers of "low-status" dialects stem from linguistically ignorant teachers.

————. "Up-Tight Ain't Right!" *Library Journal*, XCVII (October 15, 1972), 3,424–26. [Also in *School Library Journal*, October, 1972, pp. 82–84.]

Discusses a number of concepts about language, noting that a common spelling system transcends dialects. Argues against "purifying, standardizing, or homogenizing language."

Goodman, Paul. "Sub-Language as Social Badge." *Dissent*, XIX (December, 1971), 607–12.

Discusses "small talk" as an identifying badge to specific groups.

Goodman, Yetta M. See Zuck, Louis V., and Yetta M. Goodman. "On Dialects and Reading."

————. See Zuck, Louis V., and Yetta M. Goodman, comps. *Social Class and Regional Dialects: Their Relationship to Reading—an Annotated Bibliography.*

Goodwin, Sarah Hall. "Development and Evaluation of a Sentence-Repetition Test of Dialect For Black Adult Basic Education Students." Doctoral dissertation, North Carolina State University, Raleigh, 1972. 91 pp.

Determination of validity of a sentence-repetition test. Uses subjects from Milwaukee area, and concludes that the test is valid.

Gordon, A. C., and Thomas Nelson Page. *Befo' de War: Echoes in Negro Dialect.* New York: Charles Scribner's Sons, 1888. 131 pp. [Reprinted by Books for Libraries Press, Freeport, N.Y., 1971.]

Thirty-two folktales, told in dialect-poetry.

Gordon, Barbara Y. Review of Joan C. Baratz and Roger W. Shuy, eds., *Teaching Black Children to Read,* in Alfred C. Aarons, Barbara Y. Gordon, and William A. Stewart, eds., *Linguistic-Cultural Differences and American Education,* special issue of *Florida FL Reporter,* VII (Spring/Summer, 1969). Pp. 149–75.

————. See Aarons, Alfred C., Barbara Y. Gordon, and William A. Stewart, eds.

Gordon, Edmund W., ed. *IRCD Bulletin,* I (November, 1965). 8 pp.

Special bulletin of the Ferkauf Graduate School of Humanities and Social Sciences, Yeshiva University, New York. Discusses research related to language development in disadvantaged children.

Gorrell, Robert M., and Charlton Laird. *Readings About Language.* New York: Harcourt Brace Jovanovich, 1971.

Gosden, Freeman, and Charles Correll. *Here They Are: Amos n' Andy.* New York: R. R. Smith, 1931.

Original drama. The hit radio show provides a rich source of sociolinguistic data on Black language. During the 1950s, the comedy series became a television hit.

The Gospels Written in the Negro Patois, With Arabic Characters. N.p., n.d. 12 pp. (Author identified only as "A Mandigo Slave in Georgia.")

Gottesman, Ruth L. "Auditory Discrimination Ability in Standard English

Speaking and Negro Dialect Speaking Children." Doctoral dissertation, Columbia University, New York, 1968. 109 pp.

Discusses problems of Black speakers' use of homonyms.

———. "Auditory Discrimination Ability in Standard English Speaking
and Negro Dialect Speaking Children." *Journal of Learning Disabilities*, V (February, 1972), 94–101.

Abridged version of her dissertation.

Grade, P. "Bemerkungen über das Neger-Englisch an der Westküste von
Afrika." *Archiv für das Studium der Neueren Sprachen*, LXXXIII
(1928), 261–72.

———. "Das Neger-Englisch an der Westküste von Afrika." *Anglia*, XIV
(1892), 362–93. [Also in J. L. Dillard, ed., *Perspectives on Black
English*. The Hague: Mouton, forthcoming.]

Early study of West Coast African Pidgin English. Includes discussions of parts of speech, syntax, and orthography.

Grant, Walter N., and Robert M. Wilson. *Syntactic Speech Patterns of
Black Children from a Depressed Urban Area: Educators Look at
Linguistic Findings*. ERIC document ED 070 079. Washington,
D.C., November 29, 1972. 27 pp.

Replication study of eight patterns first reported by Joan C. Baratz.
Determines that there are more standard dialect patterns in the urban
areas than there are nonstandard patterns, although both are used.
Notes that all eight of Baratz's charactertistics were produced within
their test areas.

Graves, Barbara W. See Ruddell, Robert B., and Barbara W. Graves.

Graves, Richard Layton. "Language Difference Among Upper- and Lower-
Class Negro and White Eighth-Graders in East Central Alabama."
Doctoral dissertation, Florida State University, Tallahassee, 1967.

Several usage findings, including use of *be* in place of *is, are, was,
were*, or *am* among lower-class Blacks. Noted absence of *ain't* among
upper-class Black and White students.

Grayson, William John. *The Hireling and the Slave, Chicora and Other
Poems*. Charleston, S.C.: McCarter, 1856. 169 pp.

Green, Gordon C. "Negro Dialect: The Last Barrier to Integration." *Jour-
nal of Negro Education*, XXXII (Winter, 1963), 81–83. [Also in
Arthur L. Smith, ed., *Language, Communication, and Rhetoric in
Black America*. New York: Harper & Row, 1972. Pp. 12–17.]

Urges abolition of Black English, calling it "substandard" and a hindrance to total integration of the Black within American society.

Green, Margaret Baker. "Improving the Meaning Vocabulary of Inner-City Children." Paper presented at annual conference of International Reading Association, April 30–May 3, 1969, at Kansas City, Mo. 20 pp.

Includes a Black vocabulary list in her discussion of methods for strengthening the educational curriculum to benefit the language needs of the inner-city Blacks.

Green, Robert L., ed. *Racial Crisis in American Education.* Chicago: Follett Educational Corp., 1969. 328 pp.

Includes sections on "The Oppressed Communication," "The Urban School," "The Curriculum," and "Leadership for Change." Chapter II (written by Kenneth R. Johnson) discusses "The Language of Black Children: Instructional Implications."

Green, William D. "Language and the Culturally Different." *The English Journal,* LIV (November, 1965), 724–33.

A description of six programs for the nonstandard English speaker.

Greenberg, S., and R. Formanek. "Social Class Differences in Spontaneous Verbal Interactions." Paper presented at the annual meeting of the American Educational Research Association, February, 1971, at New York.

Greenberger, Ellen. See Entwisle, Doris R., and Ellen Greenberger.

Greenfield, Patricia M. "Oral or Written Language—The Consequences for Cognitive Development in Africa and the United States." Paper presented at Symposium on Cross-Cultural Cognitive Studies, American Educational Research Association, February 9, 1968, at Chicago.

Outlines differences between spoken and written language.

Greet, William Cabell. "Southern Speech," in W. T. Couch, ed., *Culture in the South.* Chapel Hill: University of North Carolina Press, 1934. Pp. 594–615.

General overview, with references to Black speech.

Gregory, Dick (with Robert Lipsyte). *Nigger: An Autobiography.* New York: Dutton, 1964, 224 pp.

An autobiographic account of a Black comedian.

Greibesland, Solveig. "A Comprehension of Uncultivated Black and White

Speech in the Upper South." Master's thesis, University of Chicago, 1970.

Discusses the question of creolization stage in Black English.

Griffin, Junius. "The Last Word from Soul City." *New York Times Magazine*, August 23, 1964, pp. 62, 64.

Discussion of slang in Harlem.

Griffith, Jerry, and Lynn E. Miner, eds. *The First Lincolnland Conference on Dialectology (University Park, Ill.).* University, Ala.: University of Alabama Press, 1970. 188 pp.

Presentation of seven papers dealing with various aspects of dialectology. Includes "Basic Factors Relating to the Development of Dialect" by Charles G. Hurst, Jr.

Grigsby, Eugene III. "The Urban Teacher, His Pupil, and the Language Barrier." *Education and Urban Society*, II (February, 1970), 157–68.

Determines that a common language barrier exists between the White teacher and the Black student. Opposes forced teaching of standard English.

Groper, George, Jerry G. Short, Audrey Holland, and Jacqueline Liebergott. *Development of a Program for Teaching Standard American English to Speakers of Non-Standard Dialects.* Pittsburgh: American Institute for Research, n.d.

Grose, Francis. *Classical Dictionary of the Vulgar Tongue.* London: S. Hooper, 1785. 182 pp.

Attributes several common phrases to "the negroe language."

Gross, Mary Anne. *Ah, Man, You Found Me Again.* Boston: Beacon Press, 1972.

Informal collection of urban Black dialect.

Guest, [Charles] Boyd. "A Survey of the Dialect of the Lee County, Alabama, Negro." Master's thesis, Alabama Polytechnic Institute, Auburn, 1932. 289 pp.

Phonetic field analysis. Pre-Turner views on Black English as a language, but notes that among the influences on Black speech was the language of Methodist, Baptist, and Campbellite preachers. Includes a two-thousand-word vocabulary.

Guest, Kristin E. See Severson, Roger A., and Kristin E. Guest.

Guilford, Polly. See Burks, Ann, and Polly Guilford.

Guiora, Alexander Z. See Hartman, John J., and Alexander Z. Guiora.

Gumperz, John J., and Eduardo Hernandez-Chavez. "Bilingualism, Bidialectism, and Classroom Interaction," in Courtney B. Cazden, Vera P. John, and Dell H. Hymes, eds., *Functions of Language in the Classroom.* New York: Teachers College Press, Columbia University, 1972. Pp. 84–108.

Argues for teacher acceptance of nonstandard American dialects, suggesting that teachers must understand the sociocultural background of their students and of the language they speak.

Gumperz, John J. and Dell H. Hymes, eds. *Directions in Sociolinguistics.* New York: Holt, Rinehart, & Winston, 1972. 598 pp.

———. *The Ethnography of Communication,* special issue of *American Anthropologist,* LXVI (1964). 176 pp.

Anthology of several articles.

Gunderson, Doris V. "An Interdisciplinary Approach to Teaching Reading." *Florida FL Reporter,* VIII (Spring/Summer, 1969), 112–52.

Urges change in teacher attitudes for acceptance of nonstandard English speakers. Says that if attitudes change, reading abilities may increase.

———. See Jewett, Arno, Joseph Mersand, and Doris V. Gunderson.

Gupta, Willa. See Stern, Carolyn, and Willa Gupta.

Gupta, Willa, and Carolyn Stern. "Comparative Effectiveness of Speaking Versus Listening in Improving the Spoken Language of Disadvantaged Young Children." Paper presented at annual conference of American Educational Research Association, February, 1969, at Los Angeles.

Test of hypothesis that oral response is better in Black standard class than just listening. Conclusions tend to support hypothesis.

Guskin, Judith Toby. "The Social Perception of Language Variation: Black and White Teachers' Attitudes Toward Speakers from Different Racial and Social Class Backgrounds." Doctoral dissertation, University of Michigan, Ann Arbor, 1970. 185 pp.

Study to determine whether language variations associated with race and social class produce unfavorable stereotyping in minds of teachers—both Black and White.

Gussow, Joan D. See Horner, Vivian M., and Joan D. Gussow.

Gussow, Joan, and Beryl L. Bailey, eds. *Summary of the Proceedings of the Working Conference on Language Development in Disadvantaged Children.* Graduate School of Education, Yeshiva University, New York, October, 1965. 21 pp.

Guzette, T. See Loflin, Marvin, T. Guzette, and B. Biddle.

Gwynn, Frederick L., and Joseph L. Blotner. "William Faulkner on Dialect." *University of Virginia Magazine,* II (Winter–Spring, 1958), 7–13, 32–37.

H

Hagen, Gunther von. *Kurzes handbuch für Neger-Englisch an der Westküste Afrikas Unter Besonderer Berücksichtigung von Kamerun.* Berlin: Dingleday & Werres, 1908. 68 pp.

Hagerman, Barbara P. *Teaching Standard English as a Second Dialect to Speakers of Non-Standard English in High School Business Education.* ERIC document ED 038 630. Washington, D.C., 1970. 11 pp.

Discusses the results of a two-semester experimental business-speech program.

Haggerty, Sandra. "Doin' the Dozens a Poor Game." Milwaukee *Journal,* January 15, 1973.

Brief news feature on the dozens, which argues for the elimination of this Black verbal-insult game.

———. "Secret Humor in Words." Milwaukee *Journal,* May 15, 1972.

Humor as its relates to the language of the Black experience.

———. "Shades of a Difference." Milwaukee *Journal,* March 26, 1973.

Differences between Black English and standard English phrases.

———. "Words Get a New Meaning." Milwaukee *Journal,* February 28, 1972.

Black redefinition of formerly obscene words.

Hair, P. E. H. "Sierra Leone Items in the Gullah of American English." *African Language Review,* IV (1965), 79–84.

Suggests that of four thousand African-originating words in Gullah cited by Lorenzo Dow Turner, about five hundred represent true vocabulary items, while the rest are names, but most of the five hundred words are from the Sierra Leone region. Casts several other doubts on Turner's data, but agrees with Turner's conclusion that Gullah is an African-based language.

Hale, Horatio. "Race and Language." *Popular Science Monthly*, XXXII (January, 1888), 340–51.

Claims a relationship between race and language, with the argument that race and linguistic stock are synonymous.

Hall, Beatrice. See Hall, R. M. R., and Beatrice L. Hall.

Hall, Beatrice, and R. M. R. Hall. "Editorial: Black English and TESL: A Programmatic Statement." *Journal of English as a Second Language*, IV (Spring, 1969), 1–6.

Urges the application of ESL methodology to teach standard English as a second dialect to Black English speakers.

Hall, Joe Daniel. "A Dialect Study of Langdale, Chambers County, Alabama, Made as a Primary Investigation for the Preparation of Worksheets for the Linguistic Atlas." Master's thesis, Alabama Polytechnical Institute, Auburn, 1941. 394 pp.

Dialect analysis. Includes phonological comparison of thirty-seven words between Lee County and Langdale Blacks. Concludes there are no significant comparisons. Also includes phonetic transcriptions of several interviews. (See also Guest, [Charles] Boyd, "A Survey of the Dialect of the Lee County, Alabama, Negro.")

Hall, R. M. R. See Hall, Beatrice L., and R. M. R. Hall.

Hall, R. M. R., and Beatrice L. Hall. "The 'Double'-Negative: A Non-Problem." *Florida FL Reporter*, VII (Spring, 1969), 113–15.

Discusses problems surrounding the double negative. Suggests drills to provide good passive control of negative structures of standard English.

Hall, Richard W. "A Muddle of Models: The Radicalization of American English." *English Journal*, LXI (May, 1972), 705–10.

Discusses the role of street language within the classroom, and argues for greater flexibility in both classroom speech and writing.

Hall, Robert A., Jr. "African Substratum in Negro English." *American Speech*, XXV (February, 1950), 51–54.

Review of Lorenzo Dow Turner, *Africanisms in the Gullah Dialect*, 1949, and of previous studies in American Black English dialects.

———. "Can Pidgin Be Used for Instruction in New Guinea?" *Pacific Island Monthly*, XXVI (1954), 95, 97, 98.

———. "Creolized Languages and Genetic Relationships." *Word*, XIV (August and December, 1956), 367–73.

Discussion of Creole languages, their origins and development, from a structuralist position.

———. "Expert Urges Extended Use of Pidgin English." *Pacific Islands Monthly*, XXIV (October, 1954), 47, 49–50.

———. "Forms in Pidgin English," in Wallace L. Anderson and Norman C. Stageberg, eds., *Introductory Readings on Language*. New York: Holt, Rinehart, & Winston, 1962. Pp. 400–409.

Review of Pidgins with emphasis on grammatical aspects.

———. "Further English Borrowings in Haitian Creole." *American Speech*, XXV (May, 1950), 150–51.

A few additional Creole words added to the Schwartz listing. (See Schwartz, William Leonard. "American Speech and Haitian Creole.")

———. *Haitian Creole: Grammar, Texts, Vocabulary*. Menasha, Wis.: American Anthropological Association, 1953. 309 pp. [Also in *American Anthropologist*, LV, Part 2 (April–June, 1953); *Memoir No. 43* of the American Folklore Society, Philadelphia.]

———. "Linguistic Structure of Taki-Taki." *Language*, XXIV (January, 1948), 92–116.

Linguistic analysis of the language of Paramaribo and Dutch Guiana.

———. *Melanesian Pidgin English: Grammar, Texts, Vocabulary*. Baltimore: Waverly Press for the Linguistic Society of America, 1943. 159 pp.

Identical to an edition published for the U.S. Armed Forces Institute, Madison, Wis.

———. *Melanesian Pidgin Phrase-Book and Vocabulary*. Special publication of the Linguistic Society of America, Baltimore, 1943.

Designed for use with Robert A. Hall, Jr., *Melanesian Pidgin English: Grammar, Texts, Vocabulary*, at the U.S. Armed Forces Institute. Excellent dictionary of Melanesian terms.

———. *Pidgin and Creole Language*. Ithaca, N.Y.: Cornell University Press, 1966. 189 pp.

Survey of Pidgins and Creoles—nature, origins, and present distribution: General discussion of structure by a well-known student of Pidgins and Creoles.

———. "Pidgin English and Linguistic Change." *Lingua*, III (February, 1952), 138–46.

Sociolinguistic discussion of the origins of Pidgin English.

———. "Pidgin Languages." *Scientific American*, CC (February, 1959), 124–34. [Also in Richard W. Bailey and Jay L. Robinson, eds., *Varieties of Present-Day English*. New York: Macmillan, 1973. Pp. 91–108.]

Basic overview of Pidgin languages. Strong argument for acceptance of Pidgins as legitimate languages. Identifies twenty-three Pidgins and Creoles, including Negro English and Gullah. Includes charts and word-lists showing derivations.

Hall, Robert A., Jr., and Douglas Leechman. "American Indian Pidgin English: Attestations and Grammatical Peculiarities." *American Speech*, XXX (October, 1955), 163–71.

Hall, Vernon C., and Ralph R. Turner. "Comparison of Imitation and Comprehension Scores Between Two Lower-Class Groups and the Effects of Two Warm-Up Conditions on Imitation of the Same Groups." *Child Development*, XLII (December, 1971), 1,735–50.

Test of validity of Osser, Wang, Zaid test which measures speech comprehension. Focuses upon "warm-up" and feedback during "warm-up."

Hall, William S. *Variations in the Structure and Use of Standard English. First Report*. Princeton University, Princeton, N.J., February 28, 1973. 45 pp.

Experimental study leads to conclusion that sex of the respondent is believed to be the least important variable in Black English, while strong correlations exist between race and age of respondents and Black English competence. Claims that Blacks are better able to understand Black English than Whites, and that Whites are better able to understand standard English than Blacks.

Hallman, Clemens L. "Linguistics and the Disadvantaged," in Edward R. Fagan, ed., *English and the Disadvantaged*. Scranton, Pa.: International Textbook, 1967. Pp. 59–65.

Asserts many TEFL methods could be adapted to teaching English to disadvantaged and minority youth groups.

Halsey, A. H., Jean Floud, and C. Arnold Anderson, eds. *Education, Economy and Society: A Reader in the Sociology of Education*. New York: Free Press of Glencoe, Inc., 1961. 625 pp.

See especially Part Four: "Social Factors in Educational Achievement," pp. 269–390.

Hammerschlag, Dorie. "Preparing Composition Teachers for the Inner City." Paper presented at Conference on English—Black and White, March 4–6, 1971, at Purdue University, West Lafayette, Indiana.

Hammond, Boone. See Yancey, William, and Boone Hammond.

Hampton, Bill R. "On Identification and Negro Tricksters." *Southern Folklore Quarterly*, XXXI (March, 1967), 55–65.

Discussion of role of tricksters in Black folklore.

Hancock, Ian F. "A Domestic Origin for the English-Derived Atlantic Creoles." *Florida FL Reporter*, X (Spring/Fall, 1972), 7–8, 52.

Discusses a possible pattern of creolization in West Africa which he terms the "domestic hypothesis." Concludes that this pattern may explain the development of Krio and Crioulo, but that development of the Atlantic group of Creoles is more complex.

———. "A Provisional Comparison of the English-Derived Atlantic Creoles," in Dell H. Hymes, ed., *Pidginization and Creolization of Languages: Proceedings of a Conference Held at the University of the West Indies, Mona, Jamaica, April, 1968.* Cambridge, England: Cambridge University Press, 1971. Pp. 287–91.

A brief comparison of six English-derived Creoles: Gullah, Krio (Sierra Leone), Sranan, Saramaccan (Surinam), Jamaican Creole, and Cameroons Pidgin.

———. "Some Aspects of English in Liberia," in J. L. Dillard, ed., *Perspectives on Black English.* The Hague: Mouton, forthcoming.

———. "A Survey of the Pidgins and Creoles of the World," in Dell H. Hymes, ed., *Pidginization and Creolization of Languages: Proceedings of a Conference Held at the University of the West Indies, Mona, Jamaica, April, 1968.* Cambridge, England: Cambridge University Press, 1971. Pp. 509–23.

Map, list, and brief annotations of eighty Creoles, including seven in the United States. Suggests that Gullah is Sierra Leone–originated.

Handy, W. C. *Blues: An Anthology Tracing the Development of the Most Spontaneous and Appealing Branch of Negro Folk Music from the Folk Blues to Modern Jazz.* New York: A. & C. Boni, 1926. 180 pp.

Includes lyrics and discussion of Black music.

Hannerz, Ulf. "Gossip, Networks and Culture in a Black American Ghetto." *Ethnos*, XXXII (1967), 35–60.

Social and cultural variables affecting gossip as shown in a study of speech and interaction events among Blacks in an urban ghetto.

————. "The Rhetoric of Soul: Identification in Negro Society." *Race,* IX (April, 1968), 453–65. [Also in Arthur L. Smith, ed., *Language, Communication, and Rhetoric in Black America.* New York: Harper & Row, 1972. Pp. 306–22.]

A few insights into "soul" as a part of language as well as of culture.

————. "The Second Language: An Anthropological View." *TESOL Quarterly,* VII (September, 1973), 235–48.

Discusses the relationships of social anthropology to the teaching of second languages and dialects, with emphasis on the use of teaching standard English as a second dialect to speakers of Black English.

————. "The Setting," in Johanna S. DeStefano, ed., *Language, Society, and Education: A Profile of Black English.* Worthington, Ohio: Charles A. Jones, 1973. Pp. 47–65.

————. *Soulside: Inquiries into Ghetto Culture and Community.* New York: Columbia University Press, 1969. 236 pp.

Anthropological approach to ghetto life. No direct references to Black English, but useful in sociolinguistics.

————. "What Negroes Mean by 'Soul'." *Trans-action,* V (July–August, 1968), 58–59.

Notes that the word "soul" expresses the essence of Black pride, an attempt to establish and maintain a self-image.

Hannerz, Ulf, Bengt Loman, and Carolyn Herndon. "Extracts from Free Conversation: I." Unpublished memorandum, Center for Applied Linguistics, Washington, D.C., 1969.

————. "Intonation Papers in a Negro American Dialect." Unpublished paper, Center for Applied Linguistics, Washington, D.C., 1969.

Hansen, Halvor P. See Drennan, Margaret, and Halvor P. Hansen.

Hare, Maud Cuney. "Folk Music of the Creole." *Musical Observer,* XIX (September–October, 1920), 16–18; (November, 1920), 12–14.

Harms, L. S. "Social Dialect and Speech Communication Proficiency." Speech delivered at Tenth International Congress of Linguistics, August 28–September 3, 1967, at Bucharest, Romania.

A progress report of a tutorial program in nonstandard English at the University of Hawaii, which allows students to gradually modify their dialects.

116

————. "Status Cues in Speech: Extra-Race and Extra-Region Identification." *Lingua*, XII (December, 1963), 300–306.

Researchers taped twelve Black speakers in Washington, D.C., retelling Aesop's fable about the lion and the mouse. Tapes were judged by students at eastern and midwestern colleges.

Harris, Albert J. See Coleman, Morris, Albert J. Harris, and Irma T. Auerbach.

Harris, C. "A Study of the Articulation of 5- and 6-year-old Lower-Class Negro Children and Upper-Lower-Class Negro Children and Upper-Lower-Class Caucasian Children in Amory, Mississippi." Master's thesis, University of Tennessee, Knoxville, 1969.

Harris, Joel Chandler. "An Accidental Author." *Lippincott's Magazine*, XXXVII (April, 1886), 417–20.

A brief autobiographical sketch of the journalist who became known as the most successful recorder of American Black English in the nineteenth century.

————. *Balaam and His Master, and Other Sketches and Stories*. Boston: Houghton Mifflin, 1891. 293 pp.

————. *Brer Rabbit: Stories from Uncle Remus*. Adapted by Margaret Wise Brown. New York: Harper & Bros., 1941. 132 pp.

————. *The Chronicles of Aunt Minervy Ann*. New York: Charles Scribner's Sons, 1899. 210 pp. [Reprinted by Garrett Press, New York, 1968, 1969.]

————. *Daddy Jake the Runaway, and Short Stories Told After Dark, by Uncle Remus*. New York: Century, 1889. 145 pp.

————. *Free Joe, and Other Georgian Sketches*. New York: C. Scribner's Sons, 1887. 236 pp.

————. *Gabriel Tolliver: A Story of Reconstruction*. New York: McClure, Phillips, 1902. 448 pp. [Reprinted by Gregg Press, Ridgewood, N.J., 1967.]

————. *Mingo, and Other Sketches in Black and White*. Boston: J. R. Osgood and Company, 1884. 273 pp.

————. *Nights with Uncle Remus: Myths and Legends of the Old Plantation*. Boston: J. R. Osgood, 1883. 416 pp.

In the introduction, Harris identifies Gullah as a mixture of English and African words.

———. *Stories from Uncle Remus.* Edited by Mrs. Joel Chandler Harris. Akron, Ohio: Saalfield Publishing, 1934. 34 pp. Illustrated by A. B. Frost.

———. *Tales from Uncle Remus.* Boston: Houghton Mifflin, 1935. Illustrated by Milo Winter.

———. *The Tar-Baby and Other Rhymes of Uncle Remus.* New York: D. Appleton, 1904. 189 pp. Illustrated by A. B. Frost.

———. *Told by Uncle Remus: New Stories of the Old Plantation.* New York: McClure, Phillips, 1905. 295 pp. Illustrated by A. B. Frost, J. M. Conde, and Frank Verbeck.

———. *Uncle Remus and Br'er Rabbit.* New York: F. A. Stokes, 1907. 63 pp.

———. *Uncle Remus and His Friends: Old Plantation Stories, Songs and Ballads, with Sketches of Negro Character.* Boston: Houghton Mifflin, 1892. 357 pp. Illustrated by A. B. Frost.

———. *Uncle Remus and the Little Boy.* Boston: Small Maynard, 1910. 173 pp. Illustrated by J. M. Conde.

———. *Uncle Remus: Being Legends of the Old Plantation.* Mt. Vernon, N.Y.: Peter Pauper Press, 1937. 135 pp. Illustrated by Fritz Eichenberg.

———. *Uncle Remus, His Songs and His Sayings: The Folklore of the Old Plantation.* New York: D. Appleton, 1881. 231 pp.

———. *Uncle Remus Returns.* Boston: Houghton Mifflin, 1918. Illustrated by A. B. Frost and J. M. Conde.

———. *Uncle Remus Stories.* Edited by Mrs. Joel Chandler Harris. Akron, Ohio: Saalfield, 1934. 12 pp. Illustrated by A. B. Frost.

Harrison, James A. "The Creole Patois of Louisiana." *American Journal of Philology*, III: 11 (1882), 285–96.

Development of the Creole languages in Louisiana. Brief mention of lexical items in works by Joel Chandler Harris and George Washington Cable.

———. "Negro-English." *Modern Language Notes*, VII (February, 1881), 123.

Disputes authenticity in dialect writing of Harriet Beecher Stowe.

———. "Negro-English." *Anglia*, VII (1884), 232–79. [Also in *Proceed-*

ings of the American Philological Association, XVI (July, 1885), 31–33; J. L. Dillard, ed., *Perspectives on Black English.* The Hague: Mouton, forthcoming.]

Includes dictionary of "specimen negroisms."

Harrison, Joseph G. "The Right to Speak Black." *Christian Science Monitor,* August 2, 1972, p. 11.

Review of J. L. Dillard's *Black English: Its History and Usage in the United States.*

Hartman, John J. "Psychological Conflict in Negro American Language Behavior: A Case Study." *American Journal of Orthopsychiatry,* XLI (July, 1971), 627–35.

Study of a Black female graduate student in a northern university who is self-conscious about her Southern Black dialect.

Hartman, John J., and Alexander Z. Guiora. "Talkin' Like the Man: A Case Study in Negro Dialect." *New Directions in Teaching,* I (Fall–Winter, 1968), 16–21.

Explores assumptions underlying attempts to "standardize" American Black English in order to prepare Blacks for the labor market. Uses case-study method to examine psychological implications.

Hartman, Marilyn D. "A Psycholinguistic Study: Contrastive Analysis of Black and Standard Dialects to Junior High Reading Subjects." Doctoral dissertation, University of California at Los Angeles, Westwood, Calif., 1972. 105 pp.

Empirical test study to determine whether Black English–speaking students could effectively learn reading in a standard English environment. Tests indicate that further study should be undertaken.

Haskell, Ann Sullivan. "The Representation of Gullah-Influenced Dialect in Twentieth Century South Carolina Prose: 1922–1930." Doctoral dissertation, University of Pennsylvania, Philadelphia, 1964. 280 pp.

Analysis of the dialect in the writings of six authors who developed characterization of lower-class Blacks of the South Carolina coastal plain.

Haskell, Marion Alexander. "Negro 'Spirituals'." *Century,* XXXVI (August, 1899), 577–81.

Haskins, James. *The Psychology of Black Language.* New York: Barnes & Noble, 1973. 112 pp.

Interrelates the social and psychological history of the Blacks with language development. Includes glossary.

Hasselberg, Joachim. "Die Abhängegkeit des Schulerfolge vom Einfluss des Dialekts." *Muttersprache*, LXXXII (July–August, 1972), 201–23.

Experimental test of hypothesis that dialect interferes with academic learning. Concludes that dialects should be included in an academic program, but only to enable the student to learn and master the standard language.

Hatch, Evelyn. See Hensley, Anne, and Evelyn Hatch.

Haugen, Einar. "Bilingualism and Bidialectism," in Roger W. Shuy, ed., *Social Dialects and Language Learning: Proceedings of the Bloomington, Indiana, Conference, 1964.* Champaign, Ill.: National Council of Teachers of English, 1965. Pp. 124–26.

Argues that persons speaking a nonstandard English should be made aware of standard English.

————. *Bilingualism in the Americas: A Bibliography and Research Guide.* Publication of the American Dialect Society, Gainesville, Fla., November, 1965. 159 pp.

Discusses historical and creolization aspects of Black English. Covers the scope of the problem of bilingualism and related research. Includes index of technical terms and index of languages.

Havinghurst, Robert J. See Eells, Kenneth, Allison Davis, Robert J. Havinghurst, Vergil E. Herrick, and Ralph W. Tyler.

Hayden, Luddy. See Bruder, Mary Newton, and Luddy Hayden.

Hays, Anne DeLacroix. " 'Like' for 'Lack'." *American Speech*, I (March, 1926), 349.

A brief note asking why Blacks "confuse" the words *like* and *lack*.

Haywood, Charles, comp. *A Bibliography of North American Folklore and Song.* 2nd ed. New York: Dover, 1961. 1,292 pp.

Hearn, Lafcadio. *An American Miscellany.* New York: Dodd, Mead, & Co., 1924. 2 vols.

Presents many of Hearn's short stories, including some with Black themes and Black language. Includes seventy-six-page introduction by Albert Mordell, compiler.

————. "The Creole Patois." *Harper's Weekly*, XXIX (January 10, 1885), 27; (January 17, 1885), 43.

Part 1 presents a basic look at Black Creole and includes some history. Part 2 presents some Black Creole verses, with some observations about folk music of Blacks.

————. "Dr. Merciér's Essay on the Creole Patois." New Orleans *Item,* July 10, 1880.

————. *Gombo Zhèbes.* New York: W. H. Coleman, 1885. 42 pp.

Proverbs from six Creole dialects, transcribed into French and English. A few comments on Creoles.

————. "New Orleans Superstitions." *Harper's Weekly,* XXX (December 25, 1886), 843.

Discusses voodoo. Includes a few phrases of Black language.

————. "The Scientific Value of Creole." New Orleans *Times-Democrat,* June 14, 1886.

Discussion of Creole, both American and non-American. Claims that the stories of Creole life would have been lost in history had not the language proved to be of value to the linguists.

————. "A Sketch of Creole Patois." New Orleans *Times-Democrat,* October 17, 1886.

————. "Some Notes on Creole Literature." New Orleans *Times-Democrat,* June 13, 1886.

A few comments about Creole studies of 1800–1875.

Hechinger, Fred M., ed. *Pre-School Education Today: New Approaches to Teaching Three-, Four-, and Five-Year-Olds.* Garden City, N.Y.: Doubleday, 1966. 150 pp.

Hellinga, W. Gs. See Pée, Willem, W. Gs. Hellinga, and A. Donicie.

Hellmuth, Jerome, ed. *Disadvantaged Child.* New York: Bruner/Mazel, 1968. 2 vols.

Includes discussions of language development, with implications for speakers of nonstandard English.

Helm, June, ed. *Essays on the Verbal and Visual Arts: Proceedings of the 1966 Annual Spring Meeting of the American Ethnological Society.* Seattle: University of Washington Press, 1967. 215 pp.

Henderson, Edmund H., and Barbara H. Long. "Predictors of Success in Beginning Reading Among Negroes and Whites," in J. Allen Figurel, ed., *Reading Goals for the Disadvantaged.* Newark, Del.: International Reading Association, 1970. Pp. 34–42.

Experimental study involving reading abilities of Blacks and Whites.

Henderson, Elliott Blaine. *Plantation Echoes: A Collection of Original*

Negro Dialect Poems. Columbus, Ohio: Press of F. J. Heer, 1904. 95 pp.

Several Black dialect poems written by Henderson.

Hendrickson, John R. "Response to CCCC Executive Committee's Resolution 'The Student's Right to His Own Language'." *College Composition and Communication.* XXIII (October, 1972), 300–301.

Argument that students cannot write effectively in dialect. Opposition to executive committee statement of the Conference on College Composition and Communication (1972).

Henrici, Ernst. "Westafrikanisches Negerenglisch." *Anglia,* XX (1898), 397–403.

Claims that the Negro-English of West Africa is a "passing phenomenon."

Henrie, Samuel Nyal, Jr. "A Study of Verb Phrases Used by Five-Year-Old Non-Standard Negro English Speaking Children." Doctoral dissertation, University of California, Berkeley, 1969. 140 pp.

Analysis of verb forms—declarative, yes/no questions, "why" questions, negatives. Subjects were kindergarten children. Data suggests ability of five-year-olds to handle all standard English forms, although about one third of their syntax was in nonstandard forms.

Hensley, Anne. *Black High School Students' Evaluation of Black Speakers.* ERIC document ED 054 663. Washington, D.C., 1970. 54 pp.

Uses a "matched guise" technique to measure high school students' reactions to taped voices using Black and standard English. Concludes that there is an overwhelming preference by Blacks for standard English.

Hensley, Anne, and Evelyn Hatch. "Black High School Students' Reactions to Speakers of Standard and Black English." *Language Learning,* XXII (December, 1972), 253–60.

Revision of *Black High School Students' Evaluations of Black Speakers.*

Herlein, J. D. *Beschryvinge van de Volksplantinge Zuriname.* Leeuwarden: M. Injema, 1718.

Includes transcription of Negro-English speech in Surinam.

Herman, Lewis, and Marguerite Shalett Herman. *American Dialects: A Manual for Actors, Directors, and Writers.* New York: Theater Arts Books, 1959. 328 pp.

Several sections pertaining to Gullah and Creoles.

————. *Manual of American Dialects for Radio, Stage, Screen, and TV.* Chicago: Ziff-Davis, 1947. 326 pp.

Speech mannerisms which identify American dialects to audiences. Chapter 7 (pp. 185–248), "The Negro Dialect," presents some information about Gullah, mostly dated.

Herman, Marguerite Shalett. See Herman, Lewis, and Marguerite Shalett Herman. *American Dialects: A Manual for Actors, Directors, and Writers.*

————. See Herman, Lewis, and Marguerite Shalett Herman. *Manual of American Dialects for Radio, Stage, Screen, and TV.*

Hernandez, Deluvina. See Smith, Arthur L., Deluvina Hernandez, and Anne Allen.

Hernandez, Luis F. *Standard Oral English, Seventh Grade: Instructional Guide B.* Los Angeles City Schools, Los Angeles, 1967. 156 pp.

Guide for teaching "correct" English to Mexican-Americans in the Los Angeles City School system. Similar to *Guide C* for Blacks.

Hernandez, Luis F., and Kenneth R. Johnson. "Teaching Standard Oral English to Mexican-American and Negro Students for Better Vocational Opportunities." *Journal of Secondary Education,* XLII (April, 1967), 151–55.

Survey of equal-opportunity employers reveals they have a distinct preference for persons speaking standard English. Focus of the L.A. school program is for job preparation by teaching standard English.

Hernandez-Chavez, Eduardo. See Gumperz, John J., and Eduardo Hernandez-Chavez.

Herndon, Carolyn. See Hannerz, Ulf, Bengt Loman, and Carolyn Herndon. "Extracts from Free Conversation: I."

————. See Hannerz, Ulf, Bengt Loman, and Carolyn Herndon. "Intonation Papers in a Negro American Dialect."

————. See Loman, Bengt, Ulf Hannerz, and Carolyn Herndon.

Herrick, Vergil E. See Eells, Kenneth, Allison Davis, Robert J. Havinghurst, Vergil E. Herrick, and Ralph W. Tyler.

Herriford, Merle. "Slang Among Nebraska Negroes." *American Speech,* XIII (December, 1938), 316–17.

Slang primarily from Omaha, with some recorded from Lincoln, Nebraska.

Herskovitz, Frances S., ed. *The New World Negro: Selected Papers in Afro-American Studies.* Bloomington: Indiana University Press, 1966. 370 pp.

―――. See Herskovitz, Melville J., and Frances S. Herskovitz. *Suriname Folklore.*

―――. See Herskovitz, Melville J., and Frances S. Herskovitz. "Tales in Pidgin English from Nigeria."

Herskovitz, Melville J. *The Myth of the Negro Past.* New York: Harper & Bros., 1941. 374 pp. [Reprinted by Beacon Press, Boston, Mass., 1958.]

Thirty-page final chapter discusses Blacks and their language, music, and dance. Also discusses studies on Gullah being done by Lorenzo Dow Turner, as well as opposition theories of Guy Johnson, Reed Smith, and Ambrose Gonzales as to the basis of Gullah as a Niger-Congo language in origin. Compares Gullah to other Black languages.

―――. "The Present Status and Needs of Afro-American Research." Paper presented at the annual meeting of the Association for the Study of Negro Life and History, October 28, 1950, at Atlanta. [Also in *Journal of Negro History*, XLVI (April, 1951), 123–47.]

Includes brief discussion of the work of Lorenzo Dow Turner.

―――. "Some Next Steps in the Study of Negro Folklore." *Journal of American Folklore*, LVI (January–March, 1943), 1–7.

Eulogy of Elsie Clews Parsons, and sketch of what needs to be done in collection of Black folklore.

Herskovitz, Melville J., and Frances S. Herskovitz. *Suriname Folklore.* New York: Columbia University Press, 1936. 766 pp.

Major research study of the Paramaribo Negro. Includes stories, tales, and proverbs.

―――. "Tales in Pidgin English from Nigeria." *Journal of American Folklore*, XXXIV (October–December, 1931), 448–66.

Seven tales in Pidgin, each abstracted in standard English for comparative purposes.

Hess, Karen M. "Dialects and Language Learning." *English Education,* V (October/November, 1973), 26–34.

Discusses existing and planned programs in nonstandard dialects for teachers at all levels.

————. "Is Learning a Standard English Important? An Overview." *Florida FL Reporter*, X (Spring/Fall, 1972), 39–42, 54.

Reviews the arguments for and against teaching standard English to nonstandard English speakers. Concludes that because others attach certain values to knowing standard English, the nonstandard speaker should learn the language in order not to be handicapped socially, educationally, and economically.

Hess, Karen, Barbara Long, and John C. Maxwell. *Dialects and Dialect Learning—Inservice Kit for Language Arts Teachers. Programmed Instruction.* Upper Midwest Regional Educational Laboratory, Minneapolis, Minn., 1971.

Hess, Robert D. See Olim, Ellis G., Robert D. Hess, and Virginia C. Shipman.

Hess-Lüttich, Ernest W. B., and Wolfgang Steinig. "Differenz oder Defizit? Überlegungen zu Kontroversen Sprachlichen Socialisationshypothesen." *Wirkendes Wort*, XXIII (September–October, 1973), 327–42.

General discussion of the deficit-*vs.*-difference controversy in dialect.

Hewett, Nancy. "Reactions of Prospective English Teachers Towards Speakers of a Nonstandard Dialect." Paper presented at the fifth annual TESOL meeting, March 7, 1971, at New Orleans. 16 pp. [Also in *Language Learning*, XXI (December, 1971), 205–12.]

Data and conclusions in support of hypothesis that educated Whites react negatively to phonological variations of standard English. The field survey suggests that hypothesis holds true for college students planning to become English teachers. Respondents seemed to be "willing" to judge personality of speaker only from hearing the speech.

Heydenfeldt, S. "Those Queer Words." *North American Review*, CXLVII (September, 1888), 348.

Discusses *brottus*.

Heyward, Dorothy. See Heyward, DuBose. *Porgy.*

Heyward, DuBose. *Mamba's Daughters.* Garden City, N.Y.: Doubleday, Doran, 1929. 311 pp.

Novel of Black life. Later dramatized by DuBose and Dorothy Heyward in 1939.

————. *Porgy.* New York: George H. Doran, 1925. 196 pp. [Reprinted by Modern Library, New York, 1934.]

Classic story of Blacks on the Charleston waterfront. Dramatization in 1926 by DuBose and Dorothy Heyward. Later expanded into a folk opera, *Porgy and Bess,* with music by George Gershwin, lyrics by Ira Gershwin and DuBose Heyward, and book by DuBose Heyward. Black language is less defined in the musical version than in the novel.

Hibbard, Addison. "Aesop in Negro Dialect." *American Speech,* I (June, 1926), 495–99.

Aesop tale about a crab, told in various Black dialects.

Hibler, Madge Beatrice. "A Contemporary Study of Speech Patterns of Selected Negro and White Kindergarten Children." Doctoral dissertation, University of Southern California, Los Angeles, 1960. 113 pp.

Concludes that trained observers can consistently recognize race differences in the speech of young children, but cannot consistently recognize sex differences in the voices of any children except Black males.

Higgins, Cleo Surry. "The Spoken English of Black and White High School Students of Dalatka, Fla.: Implications for Teaching and Curriculum Development." Doctoral dissertation, University of Wisconsin, Madison, 1973. 203 pp.

Higginson, Thomas Wentworth. *Army Life in a Black Regiment.* Boston: Fields & Osgood, 1870. 296 pp.

Numerous references to the language of Black soldiers. Includes references to the features of the language—both Gullah and non-Gullah. Written by a White colonel in charge of a Black Union regiment.

————. "Negro Spirituals." *Atlantic Monthly,* XIX (June, 1867), 685–93.

Hinton, James. See Kohl, Herbert, and James Hinton.

Hobson, Arline. *The Maria Hughes Language Training Model.* Research and Development Center, National Laboratory on Early Childhood Education, Tucson, Arizona, 1968. 27 pp.

Model to aid Mexican-American students to speak "correct" English. Implications for Black English studies may be inferred.

Hockman, Carol H. "Black Dialect Reading Tests in the Urban Elementary School." *The Reading Teacher,* XXVI (March, 1973), 581–83.

Very brief review of an empirical test. Author used 128 Black and White third-, fourth-, and fifth-grade students. Test involves same stories in both Black and standard English. Author concludes that there are no significant differences, based upon test scores.

Hoffman, Judy. See Reinstein, Steven, and Judy Hoffman.

Hoffman, Melvin J. "Bidialectism is Not the Language of White Supremacy: Sense vs. Sensibilities." *English Record*, XXI (April, 1971), 95–102.

Discussion of the intensive, often emotional, beliefs for and against teaching standard English to Blacks as a second dialect. Discusses the problems of the bidialectist in overcoming sensibilities of many persons.

————. "The Harmful Effects of Traditional Language Arts Teaching Methods When Used with Disadvantaged Afro-American Children." *Elementary English*, XLVII (May, 1970), 678–83.

Urges teachers to be linguistically aware of dialects, claiming that much damage has been done to students whose teachers were ignorant of dialects.

————. "Phonology: Its Role in the Second Dialect Classroom." Paper presented at annual TESOL convention, February 29, 1972, at Washington, D.C. 8 pp.

Brief review of literature in the field. Suggests that major differences between Black and White English are in grammatical-syntactical variation.

————. "The Segmental and Suprasegmental Phones, Phonemes, and Morphophones of an Afro-American Dialect." Doctoral dissertation, State University of New York at Buffalo, 1970. 125 pp.

Linguistic analysis of the phonology of Black English in Buffalo, N.Y. Phonological analysis on phonetic, phonemic, and morphophonic levels. Author concludes from phonological analysis and comparison that there is insufficient "diversity from familiar English" to justify Black English in that area being considered to be a separate language.

————. See Davis, Olga, Mildred R. Gladney, Melvin J. Hoffman, Lloyd Leaverton, and Zorenda P. Patterson.

Hogan, William Ransom, and Edwin Adams Davis, eds. *William Johnson's Natchez: The Ante-Bellum Diary of a Free Negro.* Baton Rouge: Louisiana State University Press, 1951.

Holbrook, David. *English for the Rejected.* Cambridge, England: Cambridge University Press, 1964. 291 pp.

Discussion of teaching secondary school students to read. Nonstandard dialect implications.

Holland, Audrey. See Groper, George, Jerry G. Short, Audrey Holland, and Jacqueline Liebergott.

Holt, Grace Sims. "The Changing Frames of Reference in Speech Communication Education for Black Students." *Florida FL Reporter*, IX (Spring/Fall, 1971), 21–22, 52.

The establishment of a Black frame of reference.

————. "The Ethno-Linguistic Application to Speech-Language Learning." *Speech Teacher*, XIX (March, 1970), 98–100. [Also in Arthur L. Smith, ed., *Language, Communication and Rhetoric in Black America*. New York: Harper & Row, 1972. Pp. 43–48.]

Advocates the ethnolinguistic approach as a basis for speech-language implementation, with certain flexibility to account for individual needs. Also discusses the "language destruction process."

————. " 'Inversion' in Black Communication." *Florida FL Reporter*, IX (Spring/Fall, 1971), 41–43, 55. [Also in Thomas Kochman, ed., *Rappin' and Stylin' Out: Communication in Urban Black America*. Champaign: University of Illinois Press, 1972. Pp. 152–59.]

Theoretical assumptions on language inversion by Blacks. Shows how minority groups protect individual and cultural identity against stereotyping definitions imposed by dominant culture.

————. "Stylin' Outta the Black Pulpit," in Thomas Kochman, ed., *Rappin' and Stylin' Out: Communication in Urban Black America*. Champaign: University of Illinois Press, 1972. Pp. 189–204.

Discussion and analysis of sermons and congregational response in the Black church. Includes background on history of American Black religion, role of the preacher, and both verbal and nonverbal messages.

Hooper, Peggy P., and Evan R. Powell. "Note on Oral Comprehension in Standard English and Nonstandard English." *Perceptual and Motor Skills*, XXXIII (August, 1971), 34–44.

Field survey revealed that Black students had difficulty switching from Black to standard English, and that White students had difficulty switching from standard to Black English. Suggests teaching English as a second language or using decoding exercises.

Hoover, Mary Rhodes. See Politzer, Robert L., and Mary Rhodes Hoover. *The Development of Awareness of the Black Standard/Black Nonstandard Dialect Contrast among Primary School Children: A Pilot Study.*

————. See Politzer, Robert L., and Mary Rhodes Hoover. *The Effect of Pattern Practice and Standard/Nonstandard Dialect Contrast on Language Achievement among Black Children.*

————. See Politzer, Robert L., and Mary Rhodes Hoover. *Teaching Standard English as a Second Dialect: Suggested Teaching Procedures and Sample Microlessons.*

————. See Politzer, Robert L., Mary Rhodes Hoover, and Dwight Brown. *An Experiment in Teaching Reading to Bidialectal Children.*

————. See Politzer, Robert L., Mary Rhodes Hoover, and Dwight Brown. *A Test of Proficiency in Black Speech and Nonstandard Speech.*

Horn, Thomas D., ed. *Reading for the Disadvantaged: Problems of Linguistically Different Learners.* New York: Harcourt, Brace & World, 1970. 267 pp.

Articles by twenty-four reading specialists dealing with the disadvantaged and minority-group child in the schools.

————, ed. *Research Bases for Oral Language Instruction.* Urbana, Ill.: National Council of Teachers of English, 1971. 113 pp.

Twelve articles reprinted from two volumes of *Elementary English.* Authors are Walter Wolfram, Muriel R. Saville, John G. Bordie, Ray Past and Jack W. Gibson, Thomas P. Carter, P. David Pearson, David P. Butts, Mark W. Seng, Irwin Feigenbaum, Willie R. Harmes, and Richard L. Venezky.

Horner, Vivian M. "The Verbal World of the Lower Class Three-Year-Old." Doctoral dissertation, University of Rochester, Rochester, N.Y., 1969. 323 pp.

Study of conversation of the lower-class three-year-old Black child. Methodology included sophisticated electronic detection (with permission of the parents of the subjects). Primarily involved in observation of child's sociolinguistic life. Asserts that the standard of language function must move beyond an essentially taxonomic position to one which permits a direct control of environment for the purposes of educational intervention. Basic argument against correcting Black phonology and syntax.

Horner, Vivian M., and Joan D. Gussow. "John and Mary: A Pilot Study in Linguistic Ecology," in Courtney B. Cazden, Vera P. John, and Dell H. Hymes, eds., *Functions of Language in the Classroom.* New York: Teacher's College Press, Columbia University, 1972. Pp. 155–94.

Based on Horner's doctoral dissertation. Less technical presentation, with focus on social and educational aspects.

Horowitz, David A., I. Ezra Staples, and Marjorie Farmer. *A Statement of Position on the Teaching of English in the Philadelphia Schools.* Board of Education, Philadelphia, August 15, 1969.

Position policy paper by three high-ranking educators of the Philadelphia public-school system. Establishes policy that there is no linguistic distinction between Black and White English. Reaction to earlier memorandum by a district administrator suggesting that teachers think about dialect readers.

Horowitz, Floyd R. See Horowitz, Frances Degen, and Floyd R. Horowitz.

Horowitz, Frances Degen, and Floyd R. Horowitz. *Head Start Evaluation and Research Center, University of Kansas, Report No. 9—Verbal Recall Research.* Department of Human Development, University of Kansas, Lawrence, 1967. 19 pp.

Test of children aged three to five to determine language usage and recall. Most of the students were Black or Mexican-American.

Horton, John. "Time and Cool People." *Trans-action,* IV (April, 1967), 5–12. [Also in Thomas Kochman, ed., *Rappin' and Stylin' Out: Communication in Urban Black America.* 1972. Pp. 19–31.]

Discussion of street-corner language and culture based on field interviews. Includes discussion of "hustling" and "colored people's time."

Houston, Susan H. "Black English." *Psychology Today,* VI (March, 1973), 45–48.

Describes the two "registers" of Black English—one for in-class use and one for home or environment. Contends that the school "register" is abbreviated, producing a system that seems to be incomplete. The home "register," she maintains, is complete. She contends that both "registers" of Black English are similar to standard White English, but additional factors (the lack of toys and storytelling) leads to a highly developed verbal ability in Black English speakers.

———. *Child Black English in Northern Florida: A Sociolinguistic Consideration.* Southeastern Educational Laboratory, Atlanta, September, 1969. 57 pp.

Experimental study of her hypothesis that the basic difference between White and Black English is phonological rather than syntactical. Lists the phones, a probable inventory of phonemes, and their
phonological rules. Also found four main morphosyntactical deviations from standard English.

―――. "Competence and Performance in Child Black English." Speech
presented at the University of Wisconsin, Madison, Spring quarter,
1970. [Also in *Language Science*, No. 12 (October, 1970), 9–14.]

Speculative theory of "contingency grammar."

―――. "A Sociolinguistic Consideration of the Black English of Children
in Northern Florida." *Language*, XLV (September, 1969), 599–607.
[Also in J. L. Dillard, ed., *Perspectives in Black English*. The Hague:
Mouton, forthcoming.]

Sociolinguistic examination of the linguistic composition of the
speech of Florida Black children from one rural northeastern
county.

―――. "Systematic Complexity and Information Transmission in First-
Graders: A Cross-Cultural Study." *Journal of Psycholinguistic Research*, II (April, 1973), 99–114.

"How to Talk Black." *Newsweek*, LXXIX (February 21, 1972), 79.

Background on a course in inner-city speech patterns, taught by
Joseph Keller at Indiana University, Indianapolis. Also discusses
thousand-word glossary of Black English words and phrases compiled by Hermese Roberts.

Howren, Robert Ray, Jr. "The Speech of Louisville, Kentucky." Doctoral
dissertation, Indiana University, Bloomington, 1958. 211 pp.

Dialect analysis of fifteen Black and White persons living in Louisville, Ky. Concludes that Louisville speech is one ninth Southern,
one third Northern, and five ninths Midland.

Hubbard, James L., and Leonore T. Zarate. *An Exploratory Study of Oral
Language Development Among Culturally Different Children*. Child
Development Evaluation and Research Center, University of Texas,
Austin, 1967. 105 pp.

Investigation of language program of Austin Head Start. Cites methodological flaws in evaluation.

Hubbell, Allan Forbes. *The Pronunciation of English in New York City:
Consonants and Vowels*. New York: King's Crown Press, 1950.
169 pp.

Dialect analysis of representative populations.

Hudson, Julius. "The Hustling Ethic," in Thomas Kochman, ed., *Rappin'* *and Stylin' Out: Communication in Urban Black America*. Champaign: University of Illinois Press, 1972. Pp. 410–24.

Study of the Black hustler and pimp. Includes discussion of language and idioms.

Hudson, Wilson Mathes, ed. *Tire Shrinker to Dragster*. Austin, Tex.: Encino Press, 1968. 248 pp.

Collection of folklore in Texas—Black and White.

Huey, Edmund Burke. *The Psychology and Pedagogy of Reading*. New York: Macmillan, 1908. 469 pp. [Reprinted by MIT Press, Cambridge, Mass., 1968.]

Includes discussion of dialect interference.

Hughes, Anne E. "An Investigation of Certain Socio-Linguistic Phenomena in the Vocabulary, Pronunciation and Grammar of Disadvantaged Pre-School Children, Their Parents, and Their Teachers in the Detroit Public Schools." Doctoral dissertation, Michigan State University, East Lansing, 1967. 208 pp.

Data suggests that many teachers are naïve about nonstandard English, and Black English in particular.

Hughes, Langston, ed. *The Best Short Stories by Negro Writers: An Anthology from 1899 to the Present*. Boston: Little, Brown, 1967. 508 pp.

Both standard English and Black English dialogue.

———, ed. *The Book of Negro Humor*. New York: Dodd, Mead, 1966. 265 pp.

Includes stories and jokes by several leading Black comedians. Also includes poetry and short stories by and about Blacks.

———. *Simple*. Caedmon Records, TC 1222.

Actor-writer Ossie Davis reads seven of the famous Simple tales.

———. *Simple's Uncle Sam*. New York: Hill & Wang, 1965.

Anthology of forty-six stories about the fictional Black, Jesse B. Simple. Many of the stories are reprinted from newspapers and popular magazines.

———, ed. *Something in Common and Other Stories*. New York: Hill & Wang, 1963.

Anthology of stories by and about Blacks. Some with Black dialogue.

Hughes, Langston, and Arna Bontemps, eds. *The Book of Negro Folklore.*
New York: Dodd, Mead, 1958. 624 pp.

Anthology of more than 450 folktales, including poetry, animal tales
and rhymes, slave narratives, sermons and preachings, ghost stories,
black magic, spirituals and gospel songs, ballads, blues, work songs,
street cries, play songs, jazz, Harlem jive, and short stories.

Hughes, Langston, LeRoi Jones, and John A. Williams. "Problems of the
Negro Writer." *Saturday Review,* XLVI (April 20, 1963), 19–21, 40.

Three short essays about problems faced by Black writers, from
marketing problems to language.

Hughes, Louis. *Thirty Years a Slave: From Bondage to Freedom.* Milwaukee, Wis.: South Side Printing, 1897. 210 pp.

Slave narrative.

Huntsman, Beverly D. "Practical Help for English Dialect Speakers."
Paper presented at the annual meeting of the National Association
for Student Advisors, November, 1971, at Vancouver, British Columbia. [Also in *Viewpoints,* XLVIII (March, 1972), 43–61.]

Discusses a remedial program for students who speak a nonstandard
English, with the purpose of allowing the student to be able to develop skills to write standard English, but not necessarily to speak
it. The goal of the program is to meet college entrance requirements.

Hurst, Charles G., Jr. "Basic Factors Relating to the Development of
Dialect by Disadvantaged Children," in Jerry Griffith and Lynn E.
Miner, eds., *The First Lincolnland Conference on Dialectology.*
University, Ala.: University of Alabama Press, 1970. Pp. 45–61.

States that the nonstandard English of the poor and underprivileged
is rigid in syntax and restricted in verbal organization. Also includes
review of literature in language aquisition.

————. *Psychological Correlates in Dialectolalia.* Communication Science
Research Center, Howard University, Washington, D.C., 1965. 122
pp.

Tests of several hypotheses on language and dialectolalia.

Hurst, Charles G., Jr., and Wallace L. Jones. "Generating Spontaneous
Speech in the Underprivileged Child." *Journal of Negro Education,*
XXXVI (Fall, 1967), 362–67.

Claims many methods to generate spontaneous speech in children
are unsuccessful or of questionable value.

Hurston, Zora Neale. "Characteristics of Negro Expression," in Nancy Cunard, ed., *Negro Anthology*. London: privately published, 1934. Pp. 39–46.

Discusses some of the Black languages and slang. Includes kinesics.

————. "Cudjo's Own Story of the Last African Slaver." *Journal of Negro History*, XII (October, 1927), 648–63.

Feature story–interview with one of the nation's few living former slaves. Numerous quotes.

————. "Hoodoo in America." *Journal of American Folk-Lore*, XLIV (October–December, 1931), 318–417.

In-depth analysis of Hoodoo. Includes sketches of some of the practitioners, their ceremonies and language.

————. *Mules and Men*. Philadelphia: J. B. Lippincott, 1935. 342 pp.

Folktales. Includes study of Hoodoo, lyrics of some Black songs, formulae of Hoodoo doctors, and language expressions.

————. "Story in Harlem Slang." *American Mercury*, LV (July, 1942), 84–89.

Literary sketch of Black life, with emphasis on the language of Harlem. Includes a brief glossary of Harlem slang.

Hurt, H. Thomas. "Negro Dialect and Ethnocentricism: A Study of Social Concepts." Master's thesis, Ohio University, Athens, 1970. 111 pp.

Suggests that Blacks must be socially aware of the relationships between Black English speech and stereotyping by Whites. Data shows that high ethnocentricism results in greater stereotyping of Black English.

————. "Negro Dialect, Ethnocentricism, and the Distortion of Information in the Communicative Process." *Central States Speech Journal*, XXIII (Summer, 1972), 118–25.

Article developed from his master's thesis.

Hurt, Mary Hayman. See Fillmer, H. T., and Mary Hayman Hurt.

Hutchinson, June O'Shields. "Reading Tests and Nonstandard Language: Metropolitan Achievement Tests." *Reading Teacher*, XXV (February, 1972), 430–37.

Challenges use of Word Discrimination Test section of the Metropolitan Achievement Test, saying that it is not appropriate for Blacks. Emphasizes need for dialect-fair test.

134

Hyatt, Harry Middleton. *Hoodoo—Conjuration—Witchcraft—Rootwork: Beliefs According to Many Negroes and White Persons, These Being Orally Recorded among Blacks and Whites.* New York: Memoirs of the Alma Egan Hyatt Foundation, 1970. 2 vols. 1,843 pp.

Field investigation in folklore of Blacks in southeastern United States and along the Atlantic coast. Informants were 1,605 Blacks and one White. Includes extensive transcriptions of Black language, as well as a "potpourri" of Black values, customs, and beliefs.

Hymes, Dell H. "The Ethnography of Speaking," in *Anthropology and Human Behavior,* Anthropological Society of Washington, Washington, D.C. Pp. 13–58. [Also in Joshua Fishman, ed., *Readings in the Sociology of Language.* The Hague: Mouton, 1968. Pp. 99–138.]

Includes discussion of speech in cognitive and expressive behavior. Descriptive analysis of speaking and speech in socialization. Implications for nonstandard language studies.

————, ed. *Language in Culture and Society: A Reader in Linguistics and Anthropology.* New York: Harper & Row, 1964. 764 pp.

Anthology of articles, several with implications for Black English study.

————. "On Communicative Competence," in *Research Planning Conference on Language Development in Disadvantaged Children, June 7–8, 1966.* Graduate School of Education, Yeshiva University, New York, 1966. Pp. 1–16.

Says that theory and practical applications must work together in order to meet the problems of language development in disadvantaged and minority-group children.

————, ed. *Pidginization and Creolization of Languages: Proceedings of a Conference Held at the University of the West Indies, Mona, Jamaica, April, 1968.* Cambridge, England: Cambridge University Press, 1971. 530 pp.

Several studies of Black English—theoretical, applied, and historical. Numerous implications for study of American Black English.

————. See Cazden, Courtney B., Vera P. John, and Dell H. Hymes, eds.

————. See Gumperz, John J., and Dell H. Hymes, eds. *Directions in Sociolinguistics.*

————. See Gumperz, John J., and Dell H. Hymes, eds. *The Ethnography of Communication.*

I

Iceberg Slim. See Beck, Robert [Iceberg Slim].

Imhoof, Maurice. "Extending Language Action." *Language Learning*, XXII (December, 1972), 189–201.

Urges recognition of social environment of the student. Suggests that extension of language abilities of nonstandard speakers can be improved through participation in social actions that place him in "new and sometimes unexpected language producing situations."

————, ed. *Social and Educational Insights into Teaching Standard English to Speakers of Other Dialects.* Special issue of *Viewpoints*, XLVII (March, 1971). 138 pp.

Transcripts of several lectures delivered at Indiana University, Bloomington, in the Spring of 1970 by Roger W. Shuy, Walter A. Wolfram, Joshua Fishman, Helen Johnson, and Peter Rosenbaum. Orientation is toward aceptance of biloquialism.

Index to Periodical Articles by and about Negroes. Boston: G. K. Hall, 1950.

Primarily concerned with literature.

International Reading Association. See Courtney, Leonard, ed.

Irwin, John V. *Head Start Evaluation and Research Center, University of Kansas, Report No. 4—a Comparison of Four Modes of Eliciting Brief Oral Responses from Children.* Department of Human Development, University of Kansas, Lawrence, 1967. 14 pp.

Primarily concerned with the disadvantaged, but has application for teachers of nonstandard English-speaking students.

Iscoe, Ira, and John Pierce-Jones. "Divergent Thinking, Age, and Intelligence in White and Negro Children," *Child Development*, XXXV (September, 1964), 785–97.

Isenbarger, Joan, and Veta Smith. "How Would You Feel If You Had to Change *Your* Dialect?" *English Journal*, LXII (October, 1973), 994–97.

Discusses results and implications of experimental program in which standard English-speaking students were treated as if their language was nonstandard and were required to learn how to communicate in Black English.

Ives, Sumner. "Dialect Differentiation in the Stories of Joel Chandler Harris." *American Literature*, XXVII (March, 1955), 88–96. [Also in Juanita V. Williamson and Virginia M. Burke, eds., *A Various Language: Perspectives on American Dialects*. New York: Holt, Rinehart, & Winston, 1971. Pp. 222–29.]

Discusses the social dialects of the Joel Chandler Harris stories. Notes that the characters are from the same region, but with social dialectal differences.

———. "The Negro Dialect of the Uncle Remus Stories." Doctoral dissertation, University of Texas, Austin, 1952. 199 pp.

A thorough analysis of the orthography in the Uncle Remus tales; reveals a consistent phonology based on accurate observations of a genuine folk speech. Concludes that Joel Chandler Harris recorded the Black language accurately.

———. *The Phonology of the Uncle Remus Stories*. Publications of the American Dialect Society, No. 22, Gainesville, Fla., 1954. 59 pp.

Based upon his dissertation, "The Negro Dialect of the Uncle Remus Stories."

———. "A Theory of Literary Dialect." *Tulane Studies in English*, II (1950), 137–82.

Indicates that literary dictums prescribe that the author, when dealing with dialects, must work out a compromise between what is aesthetically advantageous and what is linguistically correct.

J

Jackson, Bruce. "Circus and Street: Psychosocial Aspects of the Black Toast." *Journal of American Folklore*, LXXXV (April–June, 1972), 123–39.

Discussion of the use of the toast and the dozens by tricksters and badmen. Includes six toasts.

———, ed. *The Negro and His Folklore in Nineteenth-Century Periodicals*. Austin: University of Texas Press, 1967. 374 pp.

Collection of thirty-five articles, letters, reviews, and folktales from leading ninteenth-century periodicals. Includes Creole slave songs, works of scholarship, and anthropological studies, as well as dialect presentation.

————. "Prison Folklore." *Journal of American Folklore*, LXXVIII (October–December, 1965), 317–29.

Section on prose narratives and toasts, slang, and nicknames.

————. Reply to "Ritualized Verbal Insult in White High School Culture." *Journal of American Folklore* LXXIX (April–June, 1966), 374–77.

Jackson, Margaret Y. "Folklore in Slave Narratives Before the Civil War." *New York Folklore Quarterly*, XI (1955), 5–19.

Classifies folklore narratives into eight separate divisions—Dreams and Visions, Fortunetelling, Devil-Lore, Death Lore, Falling Stars, Luck, Witchcraft and Magic, and Folkmusic. Includes song lyrics and Black phrases.

Jacobs, Harriet. *Incidents in the Life of a Slave Girl.* Boston: n.p., 1861.

Slave narrative.

Jacobs, James. "Black English, Never." Letter to the editor, Pasadena *Star News*, December 23, 1972.

A Black speaks out against the use of Black English.

Jacobs, John F. "The Use of Dialect in Reading Materials for Black Inner-City Children." *Negro Educational Review*, XXIII (January, 1972), 13–23.

Jacobson, Rudolpho. "The Bidialectal Student." Paper presented at the annual meeting of TESOL, April 22, 1972, at Grossinger, N.Y. [Also in *English Record*, XXIV (Fall, 1973), 41–51.]

————. "Cultural Linguistic Pluralism and the Problem of Motivation." *TESOL Quarterly*, V (December, 1971), 265–84.

Says that only when speakers of nonstandard languages of English view America as a pluralistic society, which has both a common language as well as numerous other acceptable languages, will it be possible to be properly motivated to accepting the principles of standard English training.

————. "An Inquiry into the Relevancy of Current English Instruction." *Language Learning*, XXII (June, 1972), 79–98.

Discusses descriptive and historical aspects of Black English and current motivational factors regarding English language instruction. Urges formation of more interdisciplinary courses.

————, ed. *Studies in English to Speakers of Other Languages, and Standard English to Speakers of Non-Standard Dialects.* Special anthology issue of the *English Record*, XXI (April, 1971).

Several articles dealing with nonstandard dialects.

Jaffe, Harry Joe. *Black Speech: A Mirror of Social and Cultural Isolation.* Publications of the American Dialect Society, in press.

Jaffee, Cabot L., and Robert Whitacre. "An Unobtrusive Measure of Prejudice Toward Negroes Under Differing Durations of Speech." *Psychology Reports,* XXVII (December, 1970), 823–28.

States that more prejudice is shown toward highly verbal Blacks than toward Blacks who are less verbal.

Jaggar, Angela M. "Beginning Reading—Let's Make It a Language Experience," in Bernice E. Cullinan, ed., *Black Dialects and Reading.* Urbana, Ill.: ERIC, 1974.

———. "The Effect of Native Dialect and Written Language on Reading Comprehension in Negro and White Elementary School Children." Doctoral dissertation, New York University, 1971. 166 pp.

Cloze reading comprehension test indicates a relationship between reading and dialect, but notes that linguistic interference does not appear to cause serious reading problems at the third- and fourth-grade levels.

———. See Cullinan, Bernice E., and Angela M. Jaggar.

———. See Cullinan, Bernice E., Angela M. Jaggar, and Dorothy Strickland. "Expanding Children's Language in the Primary Grades."

———. See Cullinan, Bernice E., Angela M. Jaggar, and Dorothy Strickland. "A Language Expansion Program for Primary Grades: A Research Report."

Jaggar, Angela M., and Bernice E. Cullinan. *A Study of Young Black Children's Receptive and Productive Language and Reading Competence in Standard English Grammatical Forms.* National Institute of Education, Washington, D.C., forthcoming.

Study of oral comprehension, oral production, and oral reading comprehension of elementary-age Black children. Uses twelve grammatical contrasts in twenty-four sentences.

Jahn, Mike. "If You Think It's Groovy to Rap, You're Shucking." *New York Times Magazine,* June 6, 1971, pp. 28–29, 93.

Discussion of "hip" terms and phrases, with brief mention of the "hip black subculture."

James, Carl. See Bartley, Diane E., and Carl James.

James, Willis Laurence. "The Romance of the Negro Folk Cry in America." *Phylon*, XVI (Spring, 1955), 15–30.

Discussion of various cries, including military, sports, river, religious, street and selling, field, mountain, and dance. Defines a "cry" as the most elemental song sound of a language.

Jarreau, Lafayette. "Creole Folklore of Point Coupee Parish." Master's thesis, Louisiana State University, Baton Rouge, 1931. 66 pp.

Notes that Blacks had to forget their native languages and learn French in order to understand their masters. Presents folktales (phonetically transcribed) from about twenty Blacks.

Jensen, Arthur R. "How Much Can We Boost IQ and Scholastic Achievement?" *Harvard Educational Review*, XXXIX (Winter, 1969), 1–123.

Includes discussion (pp. 111–17) on language learning abilities, with references to the Blacks. Presents strong deficit theory argument.

————. See Deutsch, Martin, Irwin Katz, and Arthur Jensen, eds.

Jewett, Arno, Joseph Mersand, and Doris V. Gunderson. *Improving Language Skills in Culturally Different Youth in Large Cities*. Washington, D.C.: U.S. Government Printing Office, 1964. 216 pp.

John, Vera P. "The Intellectual Development of Slum Children: Some Preliminary Findings." *American Journal of Orthopsychiatry*, XXXIII (October, 1963), 813–22.

Discusses patterns of linguistic and cognitive behavior in Blacks, with analysis of labeling, categorization, and relating.

————. See Cazden, Courtney B., Vera P. John, and Dell H. Hymes, eds.

John, Vera P., and L. S. Goldstein. "The Social Context of Language Acquisition." Paper presented at the Arden House Conference on Pre-School Enrichment of Socially Disadvantaged Children, December, 1962, at Harriman, N.Y. [Also in *Merrill-Palmer Quarterly of Behavior and Development*, X (July, 1964), 265–75.]

Discusses the use of "label" words.

John-Steiner, Vera. See John, Vera P.

Johnson, Bruce. "White Dozens and Bad Sociology." *Journal of American Folklore*, LXXIX (April–June, 1966), 374–77.

Reply to assumptions of Millicent R. Ayoub and Stephen A. Barnett, *Journal of American Folklore*, LXXVIII (October–December, 1965), 337–44.

Johnson, Charles S. *The Negro in American Civilization.* New York: Henry Holt, 1930. 538 pp.

Attributes Black English origins to seventeenth-century England.

———. *Shadow of the Plantation.* Chicago: University of Chicago Press, 1934. 214 pp.

Study of about six hundred families of the Macon County, Alabama, area. Description of Black life and customs. Many references to Black English, including Black English dialect, but notes that Black English is a survival of colonial speech.

Johnson, Edwin D. "The Speech of the American Negro Folk." *Opportunity,* V (July, 1927), 195–97.

Equates Black English with poor standard English. Uses phrases from American literature to prove his point.

Johnson, Guion Griffis. *A Social History of the Sea Islands; with Special Reference to St. Helena Island, South Carolina.* Chapel Hill: University of North Carolina Press, 1930. 245 pp. [Reprinted by Negro Universities Press, Westport, Conn., 1969.]

Social history of the Sea Islands to the Reconstruction. Background and discussion of the Gullah-speaking residents.

Johnson, Guy B. *Folk Culture on St. Helena Island, South Carolina.* Chapel Hill: University of North Carolina Press, 1930. 183 pp.

Comprehensive look at the life on St. Helena Island during the late 1920s and early 1930s. Sections on Gullah language characteristics. Discounts African origins in vocabulary, but claims African origins in pronunciation and tonal characteristics.

———. "Folk Values in Recent Literature on the Negro," in B. A. Botkin, ed., *Folk-Say: A Regional Miscellany.* Norman: University of Oklahoma Press, 1930. Pp. 359–72.

Discusses aspects of Black life as treated by White writers E. C. L. Adams, Roark Bradford, DuBose Heyward, Howard C. Odum, Julia Peterkin, and John B. Sale. Urges novelists and folklorists to reproduce the Black speech accurately.

———. "Negro Folk Songs," in W. T. Couch, *Culture in the South.* Chapel Hill: University of North Carolina Press, 1934. Pp. 547–69.

Discusses evolution of Black folksongs. Presents several lyrics.

———. "St. Helena Songs and Stories," in T. J. Woofter, Jr., ed., *Black Yeomanry: Life on St. Helena Island.* New York: H. Holt, 1930. Pp. 48–81.

Describes Gullah as "little more than peasant English" of the eighteenth century.

———. "The Speech of the Negro," in B. A. Botkin, ed., *Folk-Say: A Regional Miscellany*. Norman: University of Oklahoma, Press, 1930. Pp. 346–58.

States that Black dialects have strong Anglo-English bases. Cites several examples to support his hypothesis. Also discusses literary representations of the Black dialects.

Johnson, H. P. "Who Lost the Southern r?" *American Speech*, III (June, 1928), 377–83.

Suggests that Black speech is imitative of White speech and had no influence on White speech.

Johnson, Helen A. "Teacher Attitudes and Ghetto Language," in Maurice Imhoof, ed., *Social and Educational Insights into Teaching Standard English to Speakers of Other Dialects*, special issue of *Viewpoints*, XLVII (March, 1971). Pp. 73–81.

Includes short list of attitudes and competencies needed by teachers.

Johnson, James Weldon. *God's Trombones: Seven Negro Sermons in Verse*. New York: Viking Press, 1927. 56 pp.

Black sermons in standard English. Notable for Johnson's introductory remarks (pp. 7–9) on why he chose to record in standard English rather than Black English.

Johnson, Joseph Carlton II. See Vick, Marian Lee, and Joseph Carlton Johnson II.

Johnson, Kenneth R. "Black Kinesics—Some Non-Verbal Communication Patterns in the Black Culture." *Florida FL Reporter*, IX (Spring/Fall, 1971), 17–20, 57. [Also in J. L. Dillard, ed., *Perspectives on Black English*. The Hague: Mouton, forthcoming.]

A general discussion of nonverbal Black communication, including eye contact, walking, the "rapping stance," and the "soul" handshake.

———. "A Comparison of Traditional Techniques and Second Language Techniques for Teaching Grammatical Structures of Standard Oral English to Tenth Grade Negro Students Who Speak a Non-Standard Dialect." Doctoral dissertation, University of Southern California, Los Angeles, 1969. 155 pp.

Data supports hypothesis that second-language techniques are more effective than traditional techniques. Also suggests nonstandard

142

English speakers be taught standard English as a second dialect and recommends the "total immersion" approach.

―――. "The Influence of Nonstandard Negro Dialect on Reading Achievement." *English Record*, XXI (Summer, 1971), 148–55.

Asserts that Black children who read nonstandard dialect first can be switched to standard English with less conflict, than if forced to read standard English in the beginning.

―――. "The Language Barrier: A Crisis in the Education of Black Children." Unpublished paper, University of Illinois, Chicago, n.d. 9 pp.

Warns that speakers of Black English may not accept standard English in the schools if teachers criticize Black English speech.

―――. "The Language of Black Children: Instructional Implications," in Robert L. Green, ed., *Racial Crisis in American Education*. Chicago: Follett Educational Corp., 1969. Pp. 234–48.

Analyzes Black dialect, historical origins, gives examples of common speech patterns. Proposes a second-language approach to teaching standard English.

―――. "Language Problems of Culturally Disadvantaged Negro Students." *California English Journal*, II (Spring, 1966), 28–33.

―――. "The Language Program for Culturally Disadvantaged Students." Unpublished paper, College of Education, University of Illinois, Chicago, n.d.

―――. "Pedagogical Problems of Using Second Language Techniques for Teaching Standard English to Speakers of Nonstandard Negro Dialect," in Alfred C. Aarons, Barbara Y. Gordon, and William A. Stewart, eds., *Linguistic-Cultural Differences and American Education*, special issue of the *Florida FL Reporter*, VII (Spring/Summer, 1969). Pp. 78–80, 154.

Discusses dialect interference, attitudes toward Black English, motivation, changing dialects which are closely related.

―――. "Should Black Children Learn Standard English?" in Maurice Imhoof, ed., *Social and Educational Insights into Teaching Standard English to Speakers of Other Dialects*, special issue of *Viewpoints*, XLVII (March, 1971), 83–101.

―――. "Social Backgrounds of Specific Groups: Blacks," in Thomas D. Horn, ed., *Reading for the Disadvantaged: Problems of Linguistically Different Learners*. New York: Harcourt, Brace & World, 1970. Pp. 29–38. [Also in Robert H. Bentley and Samuel D. Crawford, eds.,

Black Language Reader. Glencoe, Ill.: Scott, Foresman, 1973. Pp. 137–47.]

Social factors tending to separate backgrounds of White and Black students in urban areas. Includes plan for teachers to accept Black English as a language.

———. "Standard English and Disadvantaged Black Children: Teaching Strategies," in William W. Joyce and James A. Banks, eds., *Teaching the Language Arts to Culturally Different Children*. Reading, Mass.: Addison-Wesley, 1971. Pp. 121–29.

Some observations about Black English and the classroom teacher.

———. "Teachers' Attitude toward the Nonstandard Negro Dialect—Let's Change It." *Elementary English*, XLVIII (February, 1971), 176–84. [Also in *Education Digest*, XXXVI (May, 1971), 45–48; Johanna S. DeStefano, ed., *Language, Society, and Education: A Profile of Black English*. Worthington, Ohio: Charles A. Jones, 1973. Pp. 177–88.]

Discusses effect of attitude on teaching and urges teachers to adopt attitude of standard English as an alternate dialect, not replacement dialect. Discusses several of the negative attitudes that teachers have regarding nonstandard English; claims teachers are not successful in teaching standard English because their efforts are based on false assumptions regarding the dialect.

———. *Teaching Culturally Disadvantaged Pupils (Grades K–12). Unit VII: Improving Language Skills of the Culturally Disadvantaged.* Chicago: Science Research Association, 1967. 44 pp.

Part of an eight-unit series. In this unit, Part I discusses nonstandard vs. standard English; Part II discusses dialects of Black and Appalachian Negro slang; Part III discusses language problems of Mexican-Americans.

———. "The Vocabulary of Race," in Thomas Kochman, ed., *Rappin' and Stylin' Out: Communication in Urban Black America*. Champaign: University of Illinois Press, 1972. Pp. 140–51.

Racial terms and the social situations in which they occur and develop. Points to relationship between vocabulary and culture. Includes description of negative, neutral, and positive terms and phrases to refer to the White man, as well as negative, neutral, and positive terms and phrases Black have for self-reference.

———. "When Should Standard English Be Taught to Speakers of Non-Standard Negro Dialects?" *Language Learning*, LXX (June, 1970), 19–30.

Urges that standard English not be taught to speakers of nonstandard English until adolescence or high school.

————. See Cockrell, Wilma, and Kenneth R. Johnson.

————. See Hernandez, Luis F., and Kenneth R. Johnson.

Johnson, Kenneth R., and Herbert D. Simons. "Black Children and Reading: What Teachers Need to Know." *Phi Delta Kappan*, LIII (January, 1972), 288–90.

Calls for a three-part remedy for teaching Black children: understand Black culture, understand Black dialect, and adapt teaching strategies.

Johnson, Lawrence. "Sound Change in Los Angeles." Paper presented at the annual meeting of the Linguistic Society of America, December 28–30, 1973, at San Diego.

Johnson, Mae Coleman. "An Investigation of the Extent of Standard English and Black English Used by Children from Schools of Varying Racial Compositions." Doctoral dissertation, University of Maryland, College Park, 1971. 166 pp.

Data suggests that Black English speakers should be tested for listening comprehension in both standard English and nonstandard English to determine the extent of receptive bidialectism. Black English is spoken more in Black schools than in White schools, and White students in Black schools speak Black English more than in non-Black schools. Hypotheses are tested in a study of children in the third grade in a predominantly Black school, in a predominantly White school, and in a mixed-composition school.

Johnson, Mrs. William Preston. "Two Negro Tales." *Journal of American Folklore*, IX (July–September, 1896), 194–98.

Jones, Arlynne Lake. "An Investigation of the Response Patterns Which Differentiate the Performances of Selected Negro and White Freshmen on SCAT." Doctoral dissertation, University of Colorado, Boulder, 1960. 128 pp.

Claims that her experimental study indicates that Black English restricts concept formulations and perceptual discriminations, resulting in lower test scores and educational achievement.

Jones, Bessie Washington. "A Descriptive and Analytical Study of the American Negro Folktale." Doctoral dissertation, George Peabody College for Teachers, Nashville, 1967. 188 pp.

Discusses folklore writings of Arna Bontemps, B. A. Botkin, J. Mason Brewer, Richard M. Dorson, Joel Chandler Harris, Langston Hughes,

Zora Neale Hurston, and Philip Sterling. Also examines stylistic features of Negro folklore.

Jones, Beverly Jane. "A Study of Oral Language Comparison of Black and White Middle and Lower Class, Pre-School Children Using Standard English and Black Dialect in Houston, Texas." Doctoral dissertation, University of Houston, 1972. 150 pp.

Notes significant differences between comprehension levels among Black English-speaking persons and those who speak a standard dialect. Uses Carrow Test for Auditory Language.

Jones, Charles C., Jr. *Negro Myths from the Georgia Coast, Told in the Vernacular.* New York: Houghton Mifflin, 1888. 166 pp. [Reprinted by Singing Tree Press, Book Tower, Detroit, Mich., 1969.]

Sixty-one folktales in Gullah. Glossary.

Jones, Charles Colcock, Sr. *A Catechism of Scripture, Doctrine and Practice for Families and Sabbath Schools; Designed Also for the Oral Instruction of Colored Persons.* Philadelphia: Presbyterian Board of Publications, 1852.

Jones, E. D. "Some English Fossils in Krio." *Sierra Leone Studies,* n.s., III (1969), 295–97.

Jones, Gwendelyn Storrs. "Speech and Language Characteristics of Adult Negro Speakers." Doctoral dissertation, Purdue University, West Lafayette, Ind., 1972. 98 pp.

Comparative-contrastive speech analysis. Black subjects rated themselves "average" in speech characteristics (pitch, purity, tone, articulation, pronunciation, etc.). A judging panel of faculty, students, and speech pathologists rated the speakers "below average" to "average" when compared to speakers outside the South. Most mean scores were somewhat "below average."

Jones, J. Ralph. "Portraits of Georgia Slaves." *Georgia Review,* XXI (Spring, 1967), 126–32; (Summer, 1967), 268–73; (Fall, 1967), 407–11; (Winter, 1967), 521–25.

Four-part series of interviews with former slaves, first compiled in the early 1900s.

Jones, LeRoi. *Blues People: Negro Music in White America.* New York: William Morrow, 1963. 244 pp.

————. *Home: Social Essays.* New York: William Morrow, 1966. 252 pp.

The chapter on "Expressive Language" (pp. 166–72) presents some observations about Black definitions and semantics.

146

————. See Hughes, Langston, LeRoi Jones, and John A. Williams.

Jones, Nancy Nell Alsobrook. "'Be' in Dallas Black English." Doctoral dissertation, North Texas State University, Denton, Tex., 1972. 178 pp.

Analysis of the copula from the viewpoint of transformational-generative theory. Reveals significant syntactical and phonological differences between Black English and standard English, with a number of rules restricted to Black English.

Jones, Shirley A. "The Role of the Public School Speech Clinician with the Inner City Child." *Language, Speech, and Hearing Services in the Schools*, III (1972), 20–29.

Jones, Wallace L. See Hurst, Charles G., Jr., and Wallace L. Jones.

Joos, Martin. *The Five Clocks*. New York: Harcourt Brace Jovanovich, 1961. 108 pp.

Although primarily concerned with five major styles of English, does strongly present views for toleration and acceptance of nonstandard dialects.

Jordan, June. "Black English: The Politics of Translation." *Library Journal*, XCVIII (May 15, 1973), 1,631–34. [Also in *School Library Journal* (May, 1973), 21–24.]

A Black professional writer discusses her pride in Black English which she identifies as a separate language. Argues that Black English is a viable, distinguishable separate language that serves the needs of the people.

————. *Dry Victories*. New York: Holt, Rinehart, & Winston, 1972. 80 pp.

Black dialogue between two boys who look at the eras of reconstruction and civil rights.

————. "White English: The Politics of Language." *Black World*, XXII (August, 1973), 4–10.

Jordan, June, and Terri Bush, eds. *The Voice of the Children*. New York: Holt, Rinehart, & Winston, 1970. 101 pp.

Poems by twenty Black and Puerto Rican ghetto children. Provides insight into both the language and the ghetto experience.

Jordon, Winthrop D. *White Over Black: American Attitudes toward the Negro, 1550–1812*. Chapel Hill: University of North Carolina Press, 1968. 651 pp.

Explores attitudes of White toward Blacks. Social background.

Joyce, William W., and James A. Banks, eds. *Teaching the Language Arts to Culturally Different Children*. Reading, Mass.: Addison-Wesley, 1971. 325 pp.

Several articles of interest to the teacher within a Black English situation.

K

Kampf, Louis, and Paul Lauter, eds. *The Politics of Literature*. New York: Pantheon Books, 1972. 429 pp.

Kane, Elisha K. "The Negro Dialects Along the Savannah River." *Dialect Notes*, V (1925), 354–67.

Identifies three geographical Black dialects—Gullah, Swamp Nigger, and one unnamed dialect. Includes phonetic transcriptions of conversations with two Blacks, and sermons of three other Blacks.

Kantrowitz, Joanne S., See Kantrowitz, Nathan, and Joanne S. Kantrowitz.

Kantrowitz, Nathan. "The Vocabulary of Race Relations in a Prison." *Publications of the American Dialect Society*, LI (April, 1969), 23–34.

Revision of his paper, "Stateville Names: A Prison Vocabulary."

Kantrowitz, Nathan, and Joanne S. Kantrowitz. "Stateville Names: A Prison Vocabulary." Paper presented at the annual meeting of the American Dialect Society, December 27–28, 1967, at Chicago.

Analysis of names used by Black and White prisoners to identify each other. Found 1,098 separate names of common vocabulary, and 252 racially unique names.

Kaplan, Arthur M. "A Master of Negro Dialect." *Jewish Tribune*, September 23, 1927, pp. 38, 61.

Feature story about Octavus Roy Cohen, author of the Florian Slappey stories and other humor tales using Black language.

Kaplan, Robert "On a Note of Protest (in a Minor Key): Bidialectism vs. Bidialecticism." Paper presented at the annual meeting of the American Educational Research Association, February 8–10, 1968, at Chicago. [Also in *College English*, V (February, 1969), 368–89; Alfred C. Aarons, Barbara Y. Gordon, and William A. Stewart, eds., *Linguistic-Cultural Differences and American Education*, special issue of the *Florida FL Reporter,* VII (Spring/Summer, 1969). Pp. 86, 165.]

States that dialect deviation is not a racial, but an economic matter. Notes that verbal language must be seen in context of the Black; that to change his language, he must change his world of experiences.

Karnes, Merle B. *Helping Young Children Develop Language Skills: A Book of Activities.* Washington, D.C.: Council for Exceptional Children, 1968. 144 pp.

Developed to improve language skills of the culturally disadvantaged preschool children or those with learning disabilities. Not primarily Black English–oriented, though it has applications to Blacks.

Kasden, Lawrence M. "Language Experience Approach for Children with Non-Standard Dialects." Paper presented at the annual meeting of the National Council of Teachers of English, November 23–25, 1967, at Honolulu. 9 pp.

Urges a total approach to reading, rather than just a method.

Katz, Irwin. See Deutsch, Martin, Irwin Katz, and Arthur Jensen, eds.

Keil, Charles. "Motion and Feeling through Music," in Thomas Kochman, ed., *Rappin' and Stylin' Out: Communication in Urban Black America.* Champaign: University of Illinois Press, 1972.

Keiser, R. Lincoln. *Vice Lords: Warriors of the Streets.* New York: Holt, Rinehart, & Winston, 1969. 83 pp. [Also published as "Roles and Ideologies," in Thomas Kochman, ed., *Rappin' and Stylin' Out: Communication in Urban Black America.* Champaign: University of Illinois Press, 1972. Pp. 349–68.]

Study of an urban Black gang. Includes identification of roles, as well as description of the language.

Keislar, Evan. See Stern, Carolyn, and Evan Keislar. "Comparative Effectiveness of Echoic and Modeling Procedures in Language Instruction with Culturally Disadvantaged Children."

———. See Stern, Carolyn, and Evan Keislar. *An Experimental Investigation of the Use of Dialect vs. Standard English as a Language of Instruction.*

Keislar, Evan, and Carolyn Stern. *The Value of the Spoken Response in Teaching Listening Skills to Young Children through Programmed Instruction.* ERIC document ED 027 973. Washington, D.C., January, 1969. 164 pp.

Description of project to evaluate spoken language by lower-class and Black kindergarten children.

Keller, Suzanne. "The Social World of the Urban Slum Child: Some Early Findings." *American Journal of Orthopsychiatry*, XXXIII (October, 1963), 823–31.

Comparative study of Black and White children in first and fifth grades in New York city schools.

Kelly, William Melvin. "If You're Woke You Dig It." *New York Times Magazine*, May 20, 1962, pp. 45, 50.

Discussion of Black English slang and jargon. Includes glossary of about fifty words.

Kellogg, Theodore H. "English Phonology." *Popular Science Monthly*, XXXII (January, 1888), 387–96.

Some interesting comparisons between British and American English, including studies of the postvocalic /r/. Argues that "all educated persons" should correct their sloppy language and "preserve the purity of the mother-tongue."

Kemble, Frances Anne. *Journal of a Residence on a Georgian Plantation in 1838–1839*. New York: Harper & Bros., 1863. 337 pp.

Study of slavery on one plantation. Some dialect material.

K[ennedy]., A[rthur]. G. Review of George Philip Krapp, *The English Language in America*. *American Speech*, (March, 1925), 340–46.

Several insights into Krapp's book. Includes some information on Black English beyond that presented by Krapp.

Kennedy, R. Emmet, *Black Cameos*. New York: A. & C. Boni, 1924. 210 pp.

Transcriptions of Black English. About twenty-five dialect tales. Includes several songs.

Kenyon, Samuel. *American Pronunciation*. 10th ed. Ann Arbor, Mich.: G. Wahr, 1950. 265 pp.

Kerr, Elizabeth M., and Ralph M. Aderman. *Aspects of American English*. 2nd ed. New York: Harcourt Brace Jovanovich, 1971. 380 pp.

Reader in American language. Includes articles by Raven I. McDavid, William Labov, and Claude Brown.

Kessler, Sister Ann Carolyn. "Noun Plural Absence," in Ralph W. Fasold, *Tense Marking in Black English: A Linguistic and Social Analysis*. Arlington, Va.: Center for Applied Linguistics, 1973. Pp. 223–37.

Revision of her Georgetown University paper. Discusses zero morpheme of noun plural markers.

———. "Noun Plural Realization in Black English." Unpublished paper, Department of Languages and Linguistics, Georgetown University, Washington, D.C., n.d.

Key, Mary Ritchie, Laila Fiege-Kollmann, and Ernie Smith. "Some Linguistic and Stylistic Features of Child Black English." Paper presented at the Conference in Child Language, March 22–24, 1971, at Chicago. 24 pp. [Also in *Preprints of the Conference in Child Language*, 1971, pp. 170–92.]

General discussion of Black English patterns among children. Includes detailed discussion of paralanguage, rhythm, and phonological features. Also includes original transcription. Children were ages nine through twelve and in grades one through three.

Kilham, Elizabeth. "Sketches in Color." *Putnam's Magazine*, n.s., IV (December, 1869), 741–46; V (January, 1870), 31–38; (February, 1870), 205–10; (March, 1870), 304–11.

Four-part series. Early historical recognition by a northern teacher in the South about Black English and its relationship to reading interference. Primary focus is on the teaching of Blacks in the South after the Civil War.

Kimbrough, Mrs. Marvin. "Again 'Black English'." *Crisis*, LXXVIII (November, 1971), 303–304.

Opposition argument to eradicationist position of the National Association for the Advancement of Colored People.

Kimmerling, Flo Gryn. See Cohen, Karen M., and Flo Gryn Kimmerling.

King, Woodie, Jr. *Black Spirits*. New York: Random House, 1972. 252 pp.

Anthology of Black poetry. Included are the poems of Johari Amini, S. E. Anderson, Imamu Amini Baraka, Ed Bullins, Stanley Crouch, Randu Davis, Jackie Earley, Mari Evans, Nikki Giovanni, David Henderson, Mae Johnson, Norman Jordan, Gylan Kain, Kali, Keorapestse Kgositsile, Don Lee, Felipe Luciano, Clarence Major, Amus Mor, Larry Neal, David Nelson, Arthur Pfister, Clara Reed, Carolyn Rodgers, Sovia Sanchez, Welton Smith, Richard Thomas, James W. Thompson, Askria Mohammed Toure, and Quincy Troupe.

———. "The Game," in Thomas Kochman, ed., *Rappin' and Stylin' Out: Communication in Urban Black America*. Champaign: University of Illinois Press, 1972. Pp. 390–98.

Short story about a stud. Written in first-person Black English.

Kinkaid, J. Peter. *Use of Automated Reading Index for Evaluating Peer-Prepared Material for Use in Adult Reading Education.* Statesboro: Georgia Southern University, September, 1972. 62 pp.

Study to determine Black readability levels when materials are written in three different levels using the Automated Reading Index (ARI). Stories prepared were "life-oriented."

Kinsley, William. "Black and White Again." *College English,* XXXI (May, 1970), 862–63.

Discusses Black-White symbolism and racial implications.

Kirwin, William. " 'Black English' in Newfoundland?" *RLS—Regional Language Studies,* IV (1972), 33.

News report of joint lecture by Raven I. McDavid and Harold Paddock, suggesting that many Black English features are present in dialect in Newfoundland.

Klammer, Thomas P. "On the Notion 'Standard English' in Modern American Linguistics and Education." Paper presented at the Midwestern Regional Meeting of the American Dialect Society, August 2, 1973, at Ann Arbor, Michigan.

Kleeman, Richard P. "Washington Tries New Method to Teach Speech to Negroes." Minneapolis *Tribune,* February 12, 1967.

News story about teaching of Black English in Washington, D.C.

Kligman, Donna Schwab, Bruce A. Cronnell, and Gary B. Verna. "Black English Pronunciation and Speech Performance." *Elementary English,* XLIX (December, 1972), 1,247–53.

Research study indicating that Black English affects spelling. But the authors note that it isn't serious enough to justify concern.

Klima, Ursula Bellugi. *Evaluating the Child's Language Competence.* National Laboratory for Early Childhood Education, University of Illinois, Urbana, 1968. 21 pp.

Says that comprehension is based on syntactic cues.

Knobloch, Hilda. See Pasamanick, Benjamin, and Hilda Knobloch.

Kocher, Margaret. "The State of the Art: Black English." Paper presented at the annual conference of the International Linguistic Association, March 9–10, 1974, at Philadelphia.

Kochman, Thomas. "Black American Speech Events and a Language Program for the Classroom," in Courtney B. Cazden, Vera P. John, and Dell H. Hymes, eds., *Functions of Language in the Classroom.*

New York: Teachers College Press, Columbia University, 1972. Pp. 211–61.

Presents strong sociolinguistic analysis of how language functions for the Black child, and the interrelationships between language and action (shucking, jiving, rapping, etc.). Discusses toasts and signifying, and includes a typical conversation. Several pedagogical suggestions to correlate Black English language and actions with effective classroom instruction.

———. "Black English in the Classroom," in Courtney B. Cazden, Vera P. John, and Dell H. Hymes, eds., *Functions of Language in the Classroom*. New York: Teachers College Press, Columbia University, 1972.

Discussion of Black English and the teacher.

———. "Cross-Cultural Communication: Contrasting Perspectives, Conflicting Sensibilities." *Florida FL Reporter*, IX (Spring/Fall, 1971), 3–16, 53–54.

Background for teachers in cross-cultural situations. Discusses cross-cultural interferences as pertaining to noise.

———. "Culture and Communication: Implications for Black English in the Classroom," in Alfred C. Aarons, Barbara Y. Gordon, and William A. Stewart, eds., *Linguistic-Cultural Differences and American Education*, special issue of *Florida FL Reporter*, VII (Spring/Summer, 1969). Pp. 89–92.

Notes that oral ability is more highly prized than writing ability in the Black culture, as well as in Africa. Emphasizes peer-group influence. Explores basic goals and assumptions in developing a language program for Blacks.

———. "The Kinetic Element in Black Idiom." Paper presented at the annual meeting of the American Anthropological Association, November, 1968, at Seattle. [Also in Thomas Kochman, ed., *Rappin' and Stylin' Out: Communication in Urban Black America*. Champaign: University of Illinois Press, 1972. Pp. 160–69.]

Discussion and analysis of Black words denoting motion or action. Notes that these words usually have favorable connotation in Black cultures.

———. *Language Behavior in the Negro Ghetto*. Center for Inner-City Studies, Northeastern Illinois State College, Chicago, 1968.

General discussion with analysis.

————. *The Lexicon of American Negro Slang.* Department of English and Linguistics, Illinois Teachers College, Chicago, n.d.

Etymology and variations of slang by regions. Cities studied were New York, Chicago, Philadelphia, and Pittsburgh.

————, ed. *Rappin' and Stylin' Out: Communication in Urban Black America.* Champaign: University of Illinois Press, 1972. 424 pp.

Anthology of articles and short stories on language and culture—both verbal and nonverbal—in the Black community. Articles in the section on nonverbal communication are "Time and Cool People" by John Horton; "Non-Verbal Communication among Afro-Americans" by Benjamin C. Cooke; "Black Folk Music" by Elkin T. Sithole; "Motion and Feeling through Music" by Charles Keil; and "Dynamics of a Black Audience" by Annette Powell Williams. Articles in the section on vocabulary and culture are "Names, Graffiti, and Culture" by Herbert Kohl and James Hinton; "The Language of Soul" by Claude Brown; "The Vocabulary of Race" by Kenneth R. Johnson; " 'Inversion' in Black Communication" by Grace Sims Holt; "The Kinetic Element in Black Idiom" by Thomas Kochman; and "The African Element in Black American English" by David Dalby. Articles in the section on the expressive uses of language are "Stylin' Outta the Black Pulpit" by Grace Sims Holt; "Street Talk" by H. Rap Brown; "Shoe-shine on 63rd" by James Maryland; "Joking: The Training of the Man of Words in Talking Broad" by Roger D. Abrahams; "Toward an Ethnography of Black American Speech Behavior" by Thomas Kochman; "Rules for Ritual Insults" by William Labov; "Signifying, Loud-Talking, and Marking" by Claudia Mitchell-Kernan; "Black Poetry—Where It's At" by Carolyn Rodgers. Articles in the section on expressive role behavior are "Roles and Ideologies" by R. Lincoln Keiser; "The Greaser Is a 'Bad Ass'; the Gowster Is a 'Muthah': An Analysis of Two Urban Youth Roles" by Stanley M. Newman and Herbert G. Ellis; "Aspiration" by Melvin S. Brookins; the Foreword from *Pimp: The Story of My Life* by Iceberg Slim; "The Game" by Woodie King, Jr.; "Lovers and Exploiters" by Elliot Liebow; and "The Hustling Ethic" by Julius Hudson. An introductory chapter—"Black Culture on Black Terms: A Rejection of the Social Pathology Model"—was written by Joan C. Baratz and Stephen S. Baratz.

————. "Rapping in the Black Ghetto." *Trans-action*, VI (February, 1969), 26–34.

Discussion of rapping, signifying, and language behavior by Blacks. Includes idiomatic phrases.

———. "Social Factors in the Consideration of Teaching Standard English." Paper presented at the third annual meeting of Teachers of English to Speakers of Other Languages (TESOL), March 5–8, 1969, at Chicago. [Also in Alfred C. Aarons, Barbara Y. Gordon, and William A. Stewart, eds., *Linguistic-Cultural Differences and American Education*, special issue of the *Florida FL Reporter*, VII (Spring/Summer, 1969). Pp. 87–88, 157; Johanna S. DeStefano, ed., *Language, Society, and Education: A Profile of Black English*. Worthington, Ohio: Charles A. Jones, 1973. Pp. 211–17; Robert H. Bentley and Samuel D. Crawford, eds., *Black Language Reader*. Glencoe, Ill.: Scott, Foresman, 1973. Pp. 132–37.]

Insights into language usage, with implied references to Black English.

———. "Toward an Ethnography of Black American Speech Behavior." *Trans-action*, VI (February, 1969), 26–34. [Also in Norman E. Whitten, Jr., and John F. Szwed, eds., *Afro-American Anthropology: Contemporary Perspectives*. New York: The Free Press, 1970. Pp. 145–62 (expanded and revised version of original); Thomas Kochman, ed., *Rappin' and Stylin' Out: Communication in Urban Black America*. Champaign: University of Illinois Press, 1972. Pp. 241–64.]

Study of language within a specific context. Explores features of form, style, and function to show how they are used to differentiate between different kinds of Black English speech. Discusses rapping, shucking, jiving, etc.

Kohl, Herbert. "Children Writing: The Story of an Experiment." *New York Review*, November 17, 1966, pp. 26–32.

Teaching dialectal pride through writing. Discussion of a language-arts program developed by the author in a Black urban community.

———. "4 Myths About 'Standard English'." *Teacher*, XC (April, 1973), 36–37.

Brief discussion of four myths commonly identified with language. Written for elementary-education teachers, but has direct implications for Black English study.

———. *Thirty-Six Children*. New York: New American Library, 1967. 227 pp.

Narrative of problems a White teacher faces in a Black school, most of which involve indifference and incompetence by supervisors, administrators, and fellow teachers. Includes serious discussion of role of language in a ghetto school.

Kohl, Herbert, and James Hinton. "Names, Graffiti, and Culture." *Urban Review*, II (April, 1969). [Also in Thomas Kochman, ed., *Rappin' and Stylin' Out: Communication in Urban Black America*. Champaign: University of Illinois Press, 1972. Pp. 109–33.]

Several observations into the roles that names and graffiti play in Black and Puerto Rican cultural situations. Includes case studies.

Kolba, Ellen. See Crowell, Sheila, and Ellen Kolba.

Kornfeld, Gita S. See Cohen, S. Alan, and Gita S. Kornfeld.

Krapp, George Philip. *The English Language in America*. New York: Century, 1925. 2 vols.

Chapter on literary dialects (pp. 225–73) contains several references to Black English. Early recognition that the dialects of the Black are not one singular language, but notes little influence of Black English on standard English, except as a literary dialect. Points to great diversity of regional and social dialects. Notes a British influence on Black English.

———. "The English of the Negro." *American Mercury*, II (June, 1924), 190–95.

Observes that there was little or no influence of African languages upon Black English. Notes no influence either phonologically or syntactically.

———. *The Pronunciation of Standard English in America*. New York: Oxford University Press, 1919. 235 pp.

Analysis and description of standard English as it existed during the second decade of the twentieth century. Useful for comparative purposes in dialect studies in folklore.

———. "The Test of English." *American Mercury*, I (January, 1924), 94–98.

Study of the American English language with its variations.

Krehbiel, Henry Edward. *Afro-American Folksongs: A Study in Racial and National Music*. New York: G. Schirmer, 1914. 176 pp.

Several references to the Black language, especially Chapter 10 (pp. 127–39), "Songs of the Black Creoles." Observes that Blacks use words from the African languages, but have forgotten their original meanings.

Kriger, Albert. "A Study of the Speech of Clinton, Louisiana, at Three Age Levels." Master's thesis, Louisiana State University, Baton Rouge, 1942.

Kurath, Hans. "The Investigation of Urban Speech." *Publications of the American Dialect Society*, XLIX (April, 1968), 1–7.

Discusses the present and future importance of urban language studies.

———. "The Origins of the Dialectal Differences in Spoken American English." *Modern Philology*, XXV (1928), 385–95.

———. *A Word Geography of the Eastern United States.* Ann Arbor: University of Michigan Press, 1949. 88 pp., 163 maps.

Brief reference to Black dialect (see especially p. 6), but no clear separation of Black/White speech.

Kypriotaki, Lyn. "Why Black Johnnie Can't Read." Paper presented at the Southeastern Conference on Linguistics, April 20–21, 1973, at Blacksburg, Va.

L

Labov, William. "Academic Ignorance and Black Intelligence." *Atlantic Monthly*, CCXXIX (June, 1972), 59–67.

———. "Contradiction, Deletion, and Inherent Variability in the English Copula." *Language*, XLV (December, 1969), 715–62. [Also in William Labov, *Language in the Inner City: Studies in the Black English Vernacular*. Philadelphia: University of Pennsylvania Press, 1972. Pp. 65–129.]

Discussion of the copula and auxiliary *be* in Black English. Points out that a phonological rule exists for the deletion of the copula. This is the major statement of those linguists who believe that differences between Black English and other dialects are phonological, not syntactic.

———. "The Effect of Mobility on Linguistic Behavior." *Sociological Inquiry*, XXXVI (Spring, 1969), 186–203. [Also in Stanley Lieberson, ed., *Explorations in Sociolinguistics*. Bloomington: Indiana University Research Center in Anthropology, Folklore, and Linguistics, 1969; *International Journal of American Linguistics*, XXX, No. 3, Part 2 (April, 1967).]

Analysis of sociolinguistic stratification and mobility.

———. "General Attitudes towards the Speech of New York City," in William Labov, *The Social Stratification of English in New York City*.

Washington, D.C.: Center for Applied Linguistics, 1966. Pp. 482–503. [Also in Richard W. Bailey and Jay L. Robinson, eds., *Varieties of Present-Day English*. New York: Macmillan, 1973. Pp. 274–92.]

Discussion of attitudes toward New York speech recorded in his study of speech in New York's lower east side.

————. "Hypercorrection by the Lower Middle Class as a Social Factor in Linguistic Evaluation," in William Bright, ed., *Sociolinguistics: Proceedings of the UCLA Sociolinguistics Conference, 1964*. The Hague: Mouton, 1966. Pp. 84–113.

Examines role of hypercorrection. Says that lower-class Blacks perceive middle-class language and, in trying to compensate, overcorrect.

————. "Language Characteristics of Specific Groups: Blacks," in Thomas D. Horn, ed., *Reading for the Disadvantaged: Problems of Linguistically Different Learners*. New York: Harcourt, Brace & World, 1970. Pp. 139–57. [Also in Robert H. Bentley and Samuel D. Crawford, eds., *Black Language Reader*. Glencoe, Ill.: Scott, Foresman, 1973. Pp. 96–116.]

Detailed investigation of the Black language and educational implications.

————. *Language in the Inner City: Studies in the Black English Vernacular*. Philadelphia: University of Pennsylvania Press, 1972. 412 pp.

A two-part look at the Black English Vernacular (BEV)—linguistic structure, and social factors relating the vernacular to the culture. Defines BEV as the "consistent grammar of the peer group members that has been analyzed by linguists." Fieldwork—with Paul Cohen, Clarence Robins, and John Lewis—done in New York City. Major focus was preadolescent and adolescent gangs. Uses sociometric and statistical analysis in the integration of language and culture. Four of the nine chapters originally appeared elsewhere but served as building blocks to this study.

————. "The Linguistic Consequences of Being a Lame." *Language in Society*, II (April, 1973), 81–115. [Also in William Labov, *Language in the Inner City: Studies in the Black English Vernacular*. Philadelphia: University of Pennsylvania Press, 1972. Pp. 255–92.]

Defines a "lame" as a person, usually isolated, who is less familiar with the Black vernacular language and norms. Notes that the most uniform Black English is that which is spoken in preadolescent and adolescent peer groups. Uses sociometric and statistical analysis within his sociolinguistic description of the language of Black youths.

———. "Linguistic Research on the Non-Standard English of Negro Children," in Anita Dorr, ed., *Problems and Practices in the New York City Schools*. New York: The New York Society for the Experimental Study of Education, 1965. Pp. 110–17.

Preliminary proposal.

———. "The Linguistic Variable as a Structural Unit." *Washington Linguistic Review*, III (1966), 4–22.

Part of the New York City study.

———. "The Logic of Nonstandard English," in James E. Alatis, ed., *Report of the Twentieth Annual Roundtable Meeting on Linguistics and Language Studies: Linguistics and the Teaching of Standard English to Speakers of Other Languages or Dialects*. Monograph Series on Languages and Linguistics. Washington, D.C.: Georgetown University Press, 1970. Pp. 1–44. [Also in Frederick Williams, ed., *Language and Poverty: Perspectives on a Theme*. Chicago: Markham, 1970. Pp. 153–89; Alfred C. Aarons, Barbara Y. Gordon, and William A. Stewart, eds., *Linguistic-Cultural Differences and American Education*, special issue of the *Florida FL Reporter*, VII (Spring/Summer, 1969). Pp. 60–74, 169 (abridged); William Labov, *Language in the Inner City: Studies in the Black English Vernacular*. Philadelphia: University of Pennsylvania Press, 1972. Pp. 201–40; Pier Paolo Giglioli, ed., *Language and Social Context*. Harmondsworth, England: Penguin Books, 1972. Pp. 179–215; Richard W. Bailey and Jay L. Robinson, eds., *Varieties of Present-Day English*. New York: Macmillan, 1973. Pp. 319–55. Johanna S. DeStefano, ed., *Language, Society, and Education: A Profile of Black English*. Worthington, Ohio: Charles A. Jones, 1973. Pp. 10–44.]

Opposition to views of Basil Bernstein. Defends the "logic" of nonstandard English, stating that dialectal differences are the result of social convention established by historical shifts in social prestige of variations in dialect. Argues that several programs which teach standard English to Black English speakers are based on a misunderstanding of linguistic data.

———. "Modes of Mitigation and Politeness," in Johanna S. DeStefano, ed., *Language, Society, and Education: A Profile of Black English*. Worthington, Ohio: Charles A. Jones, 1973. Pp. 97–106.

Abridged from *The Study of Nonstandard English*.

———. "Negative Attraction and Negative Concord in English Grammar." *Language*, XLVIII (December, 1972), 773–818.

Describes the rules for the attraction of the negative to the indeterminates *any, either,* and *ever,* with respect to both standard and Black English.

———. "The Non-Standard Negro Vernacular: Some Practical Suggestions," in *Position Papers from Language Education for the Disadvantaged.* NDEA Institute for Advanced Study in Teaching Disadvantaged Youth, June, 1968. Pp. 4–7.

Explores conflict between standard and nonstandard dialects of the urban ghetto. Presents brief descriptions of the differences between Black and nonstandard English.

———. "Nonstandard Rules in the Grammar of Negro Speakers." *Project Literacy Reports,* No. 8 (1967).

———. "The Non-Standard Vernacular of the Negro Community: Some Practical Suggestions." Seminar in English and Language Arts, Temple University, Philadelphia, 1967.

Claims that teen-age Black students have little motivation for learning standard English without stimulation through skillful techniques.

———. "The Notion of 'System' in Creole Studies," in Dell H. Hymes, ed., *Pidginization and Creolization of Language: Proceedings of a Conference Held at the University of the West Indies, Mona, Jamaica, April, 1968.* Cambridge, England: Cambridge University Press, 1971. Pp. 447–72.

Implications for study of American Black English.

———. "Phonological Correlates of Social Stratification," in John J. Gumperz and Dell H. Hymes, *The Ethnography of Communication,* special issue of *American Anthropologist,* LXVI (1964). Pp. 164–76.

———. "Psychological Conflict in Negro-American Language Behavior: An Invited Commentary." *American Journal of Orthopsychiatry,* XLI (July, 1971). Pp. 636–37.

Additional comments to John J. Hartman, "Psychological Conflict in Negro-American Language Behavior: A Case Study," in the same issue, pp. 627–35.

———. "The Reading of the -ed Suffix," in Harry Levin and Joanna P. Levin, *Basic Studies in Reading.* New York: Basic Books, 1970. Pp. 222–45.

Discusses dialect interference in beginning reading, with focus upon the /-ed/. Expansion of his New York City study.

———. "The Reflection of Social Processes in Social Structures," in Joshua

A. Fishman, ed., *Readings in the Sociology of Language*. The Hague: Mouton, 1968.

Discusses use of language as a sensitive index to social change, noting that it reflects speaker's social position. Lists benefits of introducing both sociological and linguistic investigation to language and culture dialect study.

————. "Rules for Ritual Insults," in Thomas Kochman, ed., *Rappin' and Stylin' Out: Communication in Urban Black America*. Champaign: University of Illinois Press, 1972. Pp. 265–314. [Also in William Labov, *Language in the Inner City: Studies in the Black English Vernacular*. Philadelphia: University of Pennsylvania Press, 1972. Pp. 297–353.]

Focuses on sounding and playing the dozens within a teenage Harlem gang. Includes several rhymes and insults. Identifies cultural backgrounds which determine verbal and action behavior.

————. *The Social Stratification of English in New York City*. Washington, D.C.: Center for Applied Linguistics, 1966. 655 pp.

Major study of New York City as a separate speech community. Uses sociolinguistic methods. Notes that sound change can be observed directly and that language feelings can be monitored. Several interesting methodological techniques and conclusions. Involves Black and Puerto Rican speakers.

————. "Some Features of the English of Black Americans," in Richard W. Bailey and Jay L. Robinson, eds., *Varieties of Present-Day English*. New York: Macmillan, 1973. Pp. 236–57.

Discusses selected features observed in New York City, relevant patterns postulated, and the effect these features and patterns have on the teaching of reading. Portions of the selection appeared previously in "Some Sources of Reading Problems for Negro Speakers of Nonstandard English."

————. "Some Principles of Linguistic Methodology." *Language in Society*, I (April, 1972), 97–120.

Discusses techniques for solving problems of obtaining data on vernacular and dialectal speech.

————. "Some Sources of Reading Problems for Negro Speakers of Nonstandard English," in Alexander Frazier, ed., *New Directions in Elementary English: Papers Collected from the 1966 Spring Institute on the Elementary Language Arts of the National Council of Teachers of English*. Champaign, Ill.: National Council of Teachers of English, 1967. Pp. 140–67. [Also in Joan C. Baratz and Roger W. Shuy, eds., *Teaching Black Children to Read*. Washington, D.C.: Center for Applied Linguistics, 1969. Pp. 29–67; William Labov, *Language in the Inner City: Studies in the Black English Vernacular*. Philadelphia: University of Pennsylvania Press, 1972. Pp. 3–35; Roger D. Abrahams and Rudolph C. Troike, eds., *Language and Cultural Diversity in American Education*. Englewood Cliffs, N.J.: Prentice-Hall, 1969. Pp. 29–67.]

Notes that there exist two major sources of education problems— ignorance of standard English rules by speakers of nonstandard dialects, and ignorance of nonstandard English rules by teachers and text-writers. Outlines basic differences between standard and nonstandard English.

———. "Stages in the Aquisition of Standard English," in Roger W. Shuy, ed., *Social Dialects and Language Learning: Proceedings of the Bloomington, Indiana, Conference, 1964*. Champaign, Ill.: National Council of Teachers of English, 1965. Pp. 77–104. [Also in Harold B. Allen and Gary N. Underwood, eds., *Readings in American Dialectology*. New York: Appleton-Century-Crofts, 1971. Pp. 473–99.]

Expansion of New York City study.

———. *The Study of Black English*. Champaign, Ill.: National Council of Teachers of English, and Washington, D.C.: Center for Applied Linguistics, 1969. 73 pp.

Originally prepared as a "state of the arts" review for the U.S. Office of Education. Now being used as a text in education colleges. Discusses many of the aspects of Black English research, as well as distinguishing features.

———. "The Study of Language in Its Social Context." *Studium Generale: Journal for Interdisciplinary Studies*, XXIII (February 10, 1970), 30–87. [Also in Pier Paolo Giglioli, ed., *Language and Social Context*. Harmondsworth, England: Penguin Books, 1972. Pp. 283–307 (abridged).]

Studies the language structure and evaluation within social context of the speech community. Also discusses linguistic rules, their system combinations, and the evolution of these rules. Implications for study of Black English development.

———. "The Study of Nonstandard English," in Virginia P. Clark, Paul A. Eschholz, and Alfred A. Rosa, eds., *Language: Introductory Readings*. New York: St. Martin's Press, 1972. Pp. 393–400.

———. *The Study of Non-Standard English*. Champaign, Ill.: National

Council of Teachers of English, 1970. 73 pp. [See Labov, William. *The Study of Black English.*]

———. "Variation in Language," in Carroll E. Reed, ed., *The Learning of Language.* New York: Appleton-Century-Crofts, 1971. Pp. 187–222.

Discusses regional differences in language, urban language differences, language differences by age, the structure of linguistic differences, and how language differences are learned.

———. "Where Do We Go from Here?" in Roger W. Shuy, ed., *Report of the Twenty-Third Annual Round Table—Sociolinguistics: Current Trends and Prospects.* Washington, D.C.: Georgetown University Press, Monograph Series on Languages and Linguistics, 1973. Pp. 43–88.

Discusses the setting of limits on grammar—where and how to allow for dialect interference.

Labov, William, and Paul Cohen. *Some Suggestions for Teaching Standard English to Speakers of Nonstandard Dialects.* ERIC document ED 016 948. Washington, D.C., July, 1967. 34 pp. [Also in Johanna S. DeStefano, ed., *Language, Society, and Education: A Profile of Black English.* Worthington, Ohio: Charles A. Jones, 1973. Pp. 218–37.]

Research paper directed to the Bureau of Curriculum Research of the New York City Board of Education for use in preparing a manual to distinguish between "rules" for standard and nonstandard English. Attempts to present basics of phonology and grammar of Black English in a method useful to teachers of grammar-school children.

———. "Systematic Relations of Standard and Nonstandard Rules in the Grammars of Negro Speakers." *Project Literacy Reports,* No. 8 (May 25, 1967). [Also in Johanna S. DeStefano, ed., *Language, Society, and Education: A Profile of Black English.* Worthington, Ohio: Charles A. Jones, 1973. Pp. 149–60.]

Discussion of dialect interference. Asserts that differences exist in the low-level rules.

Labov, William, Paul Cohen, and Clarence Robins. *A Preliminary Study of the Structure of English Used by Negro and Puerto Rican Speakers in New York City. Final Report.* Cooperative Research Project No. 3091, Office of Education, Department of Health, Education, and Welfare, Washington, D.C., 1965.

Initial findings of major New York City study.

Labov, William, Paul Cohen, Clarence Robins, and John Lewis. "Classroom Correction Tests," in J. L. Dillard, ed., *Perspectives on Black English.* The Hague: Mouton, forthcoming.

————. *A Study of the Non-Standard English of Negro and Puerto Rican Speakers in New York City.* New York: Columbia University Press, 1968. 2 vols. 704 pp.

Volume 1 is a "Phonological and Grammatical Analysis" of the structural and functional differences between the Black English of central Harlem and standard English. Shows difference by low-level rules, and specifies rules for many surface differences. Volume 2, "The Use of Language in the Speech Community," focuses on differences in usage of Black, standard, and Puerto Rican nonstandard English.

Describes social background of nonstandard English speakers of New York. Concludes that Black English is a dialect of English, but with certain extensions and modification of rules found in other dialects. Says that functional conflict is a greater problem than structural conflict. Major linguistic study.

Labov, William, and Clarence Robins. "A Note on the Relation of Reading Failure to Peer-Group Status in Urban Ghettos." *Teachers College Record,* LXX (February, 1969), 395–405. [Also in Alfred C. Aarons, Barbara Y. Gordon, and William A. Stewart, eds., *Linguistic-Cultural Differences and American Education,* special issue of the *Florida FL Reporter,* VII (Spring/Summer, 1969). Pp. 54–57, 167; Johanna S. DeStefano, ed., *Language, Society, and Education: A Profile of Black English.* Worthington, Ohio: Charles A. Jones, 1973. Pp. 312–23.]

Discussion of patterns of language and communication in an urban street gang in Harlem. Draws correlations between reading failure and membership in street gangs.

Labov, William, and Joshua Waletzky. "Narrative Analysis," in June Helm, ed., *Essays on the Verbal and Visual Arts: Proceedings of the 1966 Annual Spring Meeting of the American Ethnological Society.* Seattle: University of Washington Press, 1967. Pp. 12–14.

Urges that study of simple narratives (folklore, etc.) be made prior to study of more complex written forms.

LaBute, Mary T. "The Dialects Course," in Robert H. Bentley and Samuel D. Crawford, eds., *Black Language Reader.* Glencoe, Ill.: Scott, Foresman, 1973. Pp. 128–29.

Laderson, Mose. "Drama and the Black Idiom." Paper presented at the

Conference on English—Black and White, March 4–6, 1971, at Purdue University, West Lafayette, Ind.

A dramatist discusses use of Black syntactical construction.

Laffey, James L., and Roger W. Shuy, eds. *Language Differences—Do They Interfere?* Newark, Del.: International Reading Association, 1973.

Laird, Charlton, and Robert M. Gorrell. *Readings about Language.* New York: Harcourt Brace Jovanovich, 1971. 494 pp.

Laird, Roland. Letter to the editor. *Commonweal,* XCV (January 14, 1972), 359.

Rebuttal to article by Dorothy Seymour [*Commonweal,* XCV (November 19, 1971), 175–78]. Argues against forced standard English teaching, but states that Black English is not a language.

Lambert, Wallace E. "A Social Psychology of Bilingualism." *Journal of Social Issues,* XXIII (April, 1967), 91–108.

A study of relationship of culture to nonstandard English.

————. See Tucker, G. Richard, and Wallace E. Lambert.

Landrum, Roger, ed. *A Day Dream I Had at Night, and Other Stories: Teaching Children How to Make Their Own Readers.* New York: Teachers and Writers Collaborative, 1971. 124 pp.

Description of the development of dialect readers, based on the oral-language stories of Blacks, Chinese, Puerto Ricans, and Mexican-American grade-school students from PS 1 and PS 42 in New York City. Numerous examples of the students' stories and language.

Lane, George S. "The Negro-French Dialect." *Language,* X (December, 1934), 323–33; XI (March, 1935), 5–16.

Technical analysis of the creole of St. Martinville, La.

Lane, Harlan, Lawrence Caroline, and Charles Curran. *The Perception of General American English by Speakers of Southern Dialects.* Center for Research on Language and Language Behavior, University of Michigan, Ann Arbor, n.d. 11 pp.

"Language of Ghetto Hampers Learning Potential, Reading Specialist Finds." Philadelphia *Inquirer,* June 15, 1969, p. 7, northwest section.

Interview with Joseph C. Hall who indicates that Blacks who speak a nonstandard dialect should be taught in that dialect before learning standard English.

Lanier, Cliff. See Lanier, Sidney, and Cliff Lanier. "The Power of Prayer."

———. See Lanier, Sidney, and Cliff Lanier. "Uncle Jim's Baptist Revival Hymn."

Lanier, Sidney, and Cliff Lanier. "The Power of Prayer." *Scribner's Magazine*, X (June, 1875), 239–40.

Black verse poem.

———. "Uncle Jim's Baptist Revival Hymn." *Scribner's Magazine*, XII (May, 1876), 142.

Black verse poem.

Larsen, Carolyn S. See Larsen, Vernon, and Carolyn S. Larsen.

Larsen, Mogens B. *Regional Variations among Negro Dialects in Selected Eastern Cities.* Washington, D.C.: Center for Applied Linguistics, 1967.

Larsen, Vernon, and Carolyn S. Larsen. "Reactions to Pronunciations," in Raven I. McDavid, Jr., and William M. Austin, eds., *Communication Barriers to the Culturally Deprived.* Chicago: University of Chicago and Illinois Institute of Technology, 1966.

Listener ratings of speakers who read words in isolation.

Lavatelli, Celia B. *Problems of Dialect.* ERIC document ED 025 300. Washington, D.C., 1967. 7 pp.

Notes controversy surrounding the question of whether or not nonstandard dialects are a hindrance to the thinking process.

Lawton, D. L. "The Implication of Tone for Jamaican Creole." *Anthropological Linguistics*, X (June, 1968), 22–26.

Notes that one of the significant differences between Creole and English is in tone.

Lawton, David. Review of Walter A. Wolfram and Nona H. Clarke, *Black-White Speech Relationships. Revista Interamericana Review*, II (Winter, 1973).

Lawton, Denis. "Social Class Differences in Language Development: A Study of Some Samples of Written Work." *Language and Speech*, VI (April–June, 1963), 120–42.

Test of a hypothesis that restricted and elaborate codes would be associated with social class and written materials produced by those codes.

Leacock, John. *The Fall of British Tyranny.* Philadelphia: John Gill, and Powers and Willis, 1776.

Drama which includes dialect speech.

Leaverton, Lloyd. "Dialect Readers—Rationale, Use, and Value." Paper presented at the Pre-Convention Institute on Language Development and Reading, 1971. [Also in James L. Laffey and Roger Shuy, eds., *Language Differences—Do They Interfere?* Newark, Del.: International Reading Association, 1973. Pp. 114–26.]

————. "Language Teaching: A Bi-dialectal Approach." Paper presented at the Conference on English—Black and White, March 4–6, 1971, at Purdue University, West Lafayette, Ind.

————. "Should Nonstandard Speech Patterns Be Used in the Urban Language Arts Curriculum?" Paper presented at the Conference on English—Black and White, March 4–6, 1971, at Purdue University, West Lafayette, Ind. 12 pp.

————. See Davis, Olga, Mildred R. Gladney, Melvin J. Hoffman, Lloyd Leaverton, and Zorenda P. Patterson.

————. See Davis, Olga, Mildred R. Gladney, and Lloyd Leaverton.

————. See Gladney, Mildred R., and Lloyd Leaverton.

Leblanc, Jerry. "Blacks Run Off at Jibs for White Scholar: A Short Version in Ghetto Language." Cleveland *Plain-Dealer*, October 7, 1973, section AA, p. 1.

Full-page feature-interview with linguist Edith A. Folb who discusses the use of Black jargon in an urban setting. Includes thirty-word lexicon.

LeCompte, Nolan Philip, Jr. "A Word Atlas of Lafourche Parish and Grand Isle, Louisiana." Doctoral dissertation, Louisiana State University, Baton Rouge, 1967. 438 pp.

Twenty-one informants. Concludes that there is a definite French background in the language; that it is in a state of transition; that the area studied is a dialect island; that a number of inflectional morphemes are not used by the lesser educated; and that a number of the slang terms are being absorbed into the language. Implications for Black English study.

Ledvinka, James David. "Race of Employment Interviewer and the Language Elaboration of Black Job-Seekers." Doctoral dissertation, University of Michigan, Ann Arbor, 1969. 145 pp.

Raises the question of whether White interviewers exert a deleterious influence on Black language performance.

Lee, J. Murray. *Studies of Economically Deprived Elementary Education Children in Southern Illinois: A Summary of Four Doctoral Disserta-*

tions. College of Education, Southern Illinois University, Carbondale, October, 1966. 21 pp.

Concludes that poverty, not race, contributes to several language difficulty factors.

Lee, Maureen T. See Legum, Stanley E., Clyde E. Williams, and Maureen T. Lee.

Lee, Richard R. "Dialect Perception: A Critical Review and Reevaluation." *Quarterly Journal of Speech,* LVII (December, 1971), 410–17.

Review and analysis of literature as an aspect of perception of people as reflected by the language. Indicates that pauses and false starts, when edited from tapes, result in greater reliability perception by listener.

———. "The Sociological Evaluation of Speech: Implications from the Laboratory to the Classroom." Paper presented at the annual TESOL convention, March 5, 1971, at New Orleans. 10 pp.

Author rejects the theory that it is proper procedure to teach dialect modification because speaking and writing standard English can lead to upward mobility.

Leechman, Douglas, and Robert A. Hall. "American Indian Pidgin English: Attestations and Grammatical Peculiarities." *American Speech,* XXX (October, 1955), 163–71.

Thirty-two examples of American Indian Pidgin English, with partial linguistic analysis. Notes that the language is American-originated and substandard, going back to baby talk.

Lefevre, Carl A. *Linguistics and the Teaching of Reading.* New York: McGraw-Hill, 1964. 252 pp.

Background information. Some mention of the nonstandard dialects.

Lefevre, Carl A., Carol Pfaff, Gene Tinnie, and Michael Nicholas. *The Speech of Young Black Children in Los Angeles.* Southwest Regional Laboratory, Inglewood, Calif., September, 1971. 172 pp.

Linguistic description of casual speech of Los Angeles children in kindergarten through third grade. Analyses of phonological, syntactical, and lexical characteristics disclose significant variations in speech. Initial studies suggest Black English has at least a minimal correlation with speech patterns throughout the county.

Legum, Stanley E., Dale Elliot, and Sandra A. Thompson. "Considerations in the Analysis of Syntactic Variation." Paper presented at the annual meeting of the Linguistic Society of America, December 28–30, 1973, at San Diego.

Legum, Stanley E., Clyde E. Williams, and Maureen T. Lee *Social Dialects and Their Implications for Beginning Reading Instruction.* Southwest Regional Laboratory, Inglewood, Calif., 1969.
Teacher-oriented.

Legum, Stanley E., Carol Pfaff, Gene Tinnie, and Michael Nichols. *The Speech of Young Black Children in Los Angeles.* Southwest Regional Laboratory, Inglewood, Calif., September, 1971. 172 pp.
Linguistic description of casual speech of Los Angeles children in kindergarten through third grade. Analysis of phonological, syntactical, and lexical characteristics discloses significant variations in speech. Initial studies suggest Black English has at least a minimal correlation within speech patterns throughout the country.

Legum, Stanley E., and Walter S. Stoltz. *The Role of Dialect in the School Socialization of the Lower Class Children.* Child Development and Research Center, University of Texas, Austin, August, 1967. 96 pp.

Lehmann-Haupt, Christopher. Review of J. L. Dillard, *Black English.* New York *Times*, August 29, 1972, p. 31.

LeJune, Emile. "Creole Folksongs." *Louisiana Historical Quarterly,* II (October, 1919), 454–62.
Lyrics of several Creole folksongs.

Lenneberg, Eric H. "On Explaining Language." *Science,* CLXIV (May, 1969), 635–43.
Presents language and biological concepts. Concludes that language capacity "follows its own natural history."

LePage, Robert B., ed. *Creole Language Studies I.* London: Macmillan, 1960. 182 pp.
Includes social and historical studies of Jamaican Creole. Also includes phonemic transcriptions of Jamaican English by David De-Camp.

————, ed. *Creole Language Studies II.* London: Macmillan, 1961. 130 pp.
Includes "Lexical Problems of the Dictionary of Jamaican English" by Frederic Cassidy and Robert B. LePage; "A Project for the Study of Creole Language History in Surinam" by Jan Voorhoeve; and "A Note on Some Possible Affinities between Creole Dialects of the Old World and Those of the New" by R. W. Thompson.

————. "General Outlines of Creole English Dialects in the British Caribbean." *Orbis,* VI (1957), 373–91; VII (1958), 54–64.

Overview of the language. Includes charts.

―――. "The Language Problem of the British Caribbean." *Caribbean Quarterly*, IV (January, 1955), 40–49.

Discusses problems of "White Talk" and "Creolese English" in one society. Many implications for American problems with standard and Black English in classroom situations.

―――. Review of Robert A. Hall, Jr., *Pidgin and Creole Languages*. *Journal of African Languages*, VI (1967), 83–86.

Lerman, P. "Argot, Symbolic Deviance and Subcultural Delinquency." *American Sociological Review*, XXXII (April, 1969), 209–24.

Identifies four patterns of argot deviation. Presents evidence that argot knowledge is related to shared deviant values.

Lester, Julius. *Black Folktales*. New York: Richard W. Baron, 1969. 159 pp.

Updating of stories told in Africa and America. Modern vernacular and Black English used as mode of communication.

Levin, Harry, and Joanna P. Levin. *Basic Studies in Reading*. New York: Basic Books, 1970. 283 pp.

Anthology of articles directed at teachers.

Levin, Joanna. See Levin, Harry, and Joanna P. Levin.

Levine, Lewis, and Harry J. Crockett, Jr. "Speech Variation in a Piedmont Community: Postvocalic r." *Sociological Inquiry*, XXXVI (1966), 204–26.

Levy, Beatrice K. "Comparison of Black Children's Language and the Language of Selected Reading Materials," in Bernice E. Cullinan, ed., *Black Dialects and Reading*. Urbana, Ill.: ERIC, 1974.

―――. "Teaching Reading Skills to Dialect Speakers," in Bernice E. Cullinan, ed., *Black Dialects and Reading*. Urbana, Ill.: ERIC, 1974.

Levy, Betty E. "Dialect Proficiency and Auditory Comprehension in Standard and Nonstandard English." Paper presented at the annual meeting of the American Educational Research Association, April, 1972, at Chicago.

Examines both oral and auditory dialect comprehension on stories presented in both Black and standard English. Concludes that Black second-graders scored higher on auditory comprehension questions in standard English than in Black English.

Lewis, John. See Labov, William, Paul Cohen, Clarence Robins, and John Lewis. "Classroom Correction Tests."

————. See Labov, William, Paul Cohen, Clarence Robins, and John Lewis. *A Study of the Non-Standard English of Negro and Puerto Rican Speakers in New York City.*

Lewis, Vernon E. "Speech Therapy and Dialect Patterns of Black Students." *Academic Therapy Quarterly,* VI (Spring, 1971), 257–61.

Claims that the child must be taught to identify his own speech patterns and the speech patterns of standard English if he intends to replace Black English with standard English. Says that it is important to determine when a child is linguistically ready to begin language work.

Liebergott, Jacqueline. See Groper, George, Jerry G. Short, Audrey Holland, and Jacqueline Liebergott.

Lieberson, Stanley, ed. *Explorations in Sociolinguistics.* Bloomington: Indiana University Research Center in Anthropology, Folklore, and Linguistics, 1969.

Lieblich, Malcolm. "The High Cost of Speech Change." *Today's Speech,* XIX (Spring, 1971), 47–51.

Study of consequences of forced dialect-change to encourage social mobility. Focuses on Black English. Discusses the insecurity which results from such a forced change, or disappointment from not achieving standard English patterns in place of Black English.

Liebow, Elliot. "Lovers and Exploiters," in Thomas Kochman, ed., *Rappin' and Stylin' Out: Communication in Urban Black America.* Champaign: University of Illinois Press, 1972. Pp. 399–409.

Character sketches of lovers and exploiters of women. Includes street corner language of Blacks.

————. *Tally's Corner: A Study of Negro Street Corner Men.* London: Routledge & Kegan Paul, 1967. 260 pp.

Expansion of a Ph.D. study in anthropology. Includes names and several Black vocabulary words. Focus is on a Black street corner, its sights, sounds, smells, and language.

Light, Richard L. "On Language Arts and Minority-Group Children." *Florida FL Reporter,* VII (Fall, 1969), 5–7, 20. [Also in Roger D. Abrahams and Rudolph C. Troike, eds., *Language and Cultural Diversity in America.* Englewood Cliffs, N.J.: Prentice-Hall, 1972. Pp. 9–15.]

Says that conditions in schools at present limit the effectiveness of language-arts programs for minority group children.

————. "Some Observations Concerning Black Childrens' Conversations." *English Record*, XXI (April, 1971), 155–67.

Study of four nonstandard linguistic features in five Black children. Includes references to the effect of the interviewer on the children.

Lin, San-Su C. "A Developmental English Program for the Culturally Disadvantaged." *College Composition and Communication*, XVI (December, 1965), 273–76.

Three-year research project involving audiolingual methods in teaching English to Black freshmen at Claflin University, Orangeburg, S.C.

————. "Disadvantaged Student? Or Disadvantaged Teacher?" *English Journal*, LVI (May, 1967), 55–61. [Also in William W. Joyce and James A. Banks, eds. *Teaching the Language Arts to Culturally Different Children*. Reading, Mass.: Addison-Wesley, 1971. Pp. 309–15.]

A few observations about Black English. Urges retention of Black English if the student wishes it. Urges teachers to explore how language works.

————. *Pattern Practice in the Teaching of Standard English to Students with a Non-Standard Dialect*. Teacher's College Press, Columbia University, New York, 1965. 220 pp.

Final report of project at Claflin University, Orangeburg, S.C.

"Lingo of Negroes in Literature." *Lippincott's Monthly*, LV (1895), 286.

Several observations about Black speech by literary characters.

Linguistic Atlas of the Middle and South Atlantic States. Fascicle 1. University of Chicago Press, forthcoming.

This is the first of a series of books summarizing the results of one million responses to the *Atlas* survey. The materials for this atlas are stored at the University of Chicago and the Illinois Institute of Technology at Chicago. The *Linguistic Atlas of the Middle and South Atlantic States* is the second regional linguistic atlas to be published. Fieldwork and preparation are continuing in other regions of the United States and Canada for similar atlases. As a group, these atlases are known as *The Linguistic Atlas of the United States and Canada*.

Linguistic Society of America. *LSA Bulletin*, No. 52 (March, 1972), 17–18.

Untitled position statement by the Linguistic Society of America in opposition to statements made by Arthur Jensen regarding reading and nonstandard language in the *Harvard Educational Review*. LSA affirms opposition of deficit theory.

Linn, Michael D. "Urban Black Speech as the Voice of Masculinity." Paper presented at the Southeastern Conference on Linguistics, April 20–21, 1973, at Blacksburg, Va.

Study of stereotypes based upon responses of two tape scripts, one of which incorporates Black nonstandard variations. Student response in urban areas describe the nonstandard speakers as uneducated, but perceives those speakers to be braver, more athletic, and better fighters than standard speakers.

Little, Malcom [Malcolm X]. *Malcolm X Speaks.* New York: Merit, 1965. 242 pp.

Autobiography. Includes some dialogue, but mostly edited into standard English.

Living Webster Encyclopedic Dictionary of the English Language. Chicago: English Language Institute of America, 1971. 1,158 pp.

Includes glossary of one thousand Black terms compiled by Hermese Roberts.

Llorens, David. "What Good the Word without the Wisdom? or, 'English Ain't Relevant'." *College Composition and Communication,* XXII (October, 1971), 209–14.

Expresses the belief that although Whites may have the language, Blacks have the wisdom. The problem is how the Blacks can acquire the language (referred to as the "Word") without losing their wisdom.

Lloyd, John Uri. "The Language of the Kentucky Negro." *Dialect Notes,* II (1901), 179–84.

Presents a word list and discusses methods used by writers of dialect stories. Also discusses the influence of Black speech on White speech.

Loban, Walter. *Problems in Oral English: Kindergarten through Grade 9.* Champaign, Ill.: National Council of Teachers of English, 1966. 79 pp.

A ten-year study of language development of 338 pupils in kindergarten through ninth grade. Concludes that the most difficult usage is the verb *be.* Also discusses age-grading.

————. "A Sustained Program of Language Learning," in *Language Programs of the Disadvantaged: Report of the NCTE Task Force on Teaching English to the Disadvantaged.* Champaign, Ill.: National Council of Teachers of English, 1965. Pp. 221–31.

A recommended program of dialect change is a necessary evil, in the opinion of the author, since teachers cannot be expected to develop teaching programs from theory. Some guidance on a practical level must be given.

———. "Teaching Children Who Speak Social Class Dialects." *Elementary English*, XLV (May, 1968), 592–99, 618.

Locke, Alain LeRoy. *The Negro in America.* Chicago, Ill.: American Library Association, 1933. 64 pp.
Sociological background.

Lockwood, John Palmer. *Darkey Sermons from Charleston County: Composed and Delivered by John Palmer Lockwood (alias Rebrin Isrel Manigo).* Columbia, S.C.: State, 1925. 45 pp.
Three sermons in a form of Black English, written around the turn of the twentieth century.

Löffler, Heinrich. "Mundart als Sprachbarriere." *Wirkendes Wort,* XXII (1972), 23–39.
Examines concept that dialects hinder the learning of standard language. Proposes that bidialectal instructors teach dialect-speaking students the standard language.

Loflin, Marvin D. "Black American English and Syntactic Dialectology," in J. L. Dillard, ed., *Perspectives on Black English.* The Hague: Mouton, forthcoming.

———. "Competing Transformational Generalizations in the Auxiliary Structure of Afro-American English." Paper presented at the annual meeting of the National Council of Teachers of English, November 29, 1968, at Milwaukee.

———. "Negro Non-Standard and Standard English: Same or Different Deep Structure?" *Orbis,* XVIII: 1 (1969), 74–91.
Overview of deep-structure argument. Concludes that the two languages probably have different deep structures. Also suggests what is needed to complete a syntactic comparison.

———. "A Note on the Deep Structure of Nonstandard English in Washington, D.C." *Glossa,* I (1967), 26–32.
Technical syntactic analysis involving certain copulative sentences.

———. "On the Passive in Nonstandard Negro English." *Journal of English as a Second Language,* IV (Spring, 1969), 19–23.
Discussion of Black English from the assumption that its deep structure is different from that of standard English. Defends theory that there are two different, unrelated, deep structures.

————. "On the Structure of the Verb in a Dialect of American Negro English." *Linguistics*, LIX (July, 1970), 14–28. [Also in Harold B. Allen and Gary N. Underwood, eds., *Readings in American Dialectology*. New York: Appleton-Century-Crofts, 1971. Pp. 428–43.]

Linguistic analysis of the verb in Black English. Attempts to construct a set of rules to explain auxiliary structure of the verb in nonstandard Black English.

Loflin, Marvin, T. Guzette, and B. Biddle. "Implications of the Linguistic Differences between Black-Ghetto and White-Suburban Classrooms." Paper presented at the annual meeting of the American Educational Research Association, February, 1971, at New York City. 19 pp.

Discusses language variation.

Logan, Rayford W. *The Negro in the United States: A Brief History*. Princeton, N.J.: D. Van Nostrand Reinhold, 1957. 191 pp.

Logan, Rayford W., and Irving S. Cohen. *The American Negro: Old World Background and New World Experience*. Boston: Houghton Mifflin, 1970. 325 pp.

Loman, Bengt, trans. and ed. *Conversations in a Negro American Dialect*. Washington, D.C.: Center for Applied Linguistics, 1967. 164 pp.

Analysis of fourteen prearranged recordings of urban Black school-age children. Includes transcription in a modified standard orthography. Aim of study is to improve teaching programs. This study is part of the Urban Language Series, a program investigating the position and role of language in large metropolitan areas.

Loman, Bengt. See Hannerz, Ulf, Bengt Loman, and Carolyn Herndon, "Extracts from Free Conversation: I."

————. See Hannerz, Ulf, Bengt Loman, and Carolyn Herndon. "Intonation Patterns in a Negro American Dialect."

Lomangino, Louis. See Walsh, John F., Rita D'Angelo, and Louis Lomangino.

Lomax, Alan. *Negro Prison Songs*. Tradition Records, TLP 1020.

————. See Lomax, John, and Alan Lomax.

Lomax, Alan, and Raoul Abdul, eds. *3,000 Years of Black Poetry*. New York: Dodd, Mead, 1969. 269 pp.

Black poetry, from fourth-century Egyptian to contemporary American. Discussion of poetry, customs, and language.

Lomax, Alan, John Lomax, and Ruby T. Lomax. *Afro-American Spirituals, Work Songs, and Ballads.* Folkway Records, FA 2650–59.

Several songs with emphasis on the Black struggle, recorded in approximation of the Black language.

Lomax, John. See Lomax, Alan, John Lomax, and Ruby T. Lomax.

Lomax, John, and Alan Lomax. *Negro Folk Songs as Sung by Lead Belly.* New York: Macmillan, 1936. 242 pp.

Study of the music and lyrics of Huddie Ledbetter, one of the outstanding Black folksingers.

Lomax, Louis. *To Kill a Black Man.* Los Angeles: Holloway House, 1968. 256 pp.

Lomax, Ruby T. "Negro Nicknames." *Texas Folklore Society Bulletin,* XVIII (1943), 163–71.

————. See Lomax, Alan, John Lomax, and Ruby T. Lomax.

Lombard, Avima. See Stern, Carolyn, and Avima Lombard.

Long, Barbara. See Henderson, Edmund H., and Barbara Long.

————. See Hess, Karen, Barbara Long, and John C. Maxwell.

Long, Richard A. " 'Man' and 'Evil' in American Negro Speech." *American Speech,* XXXIV (December, 1959), 305–306.

————. "The Uncle Remus Dialect: A Preliminary Linguistic Review." Paper presented at the Southwestern Conference on Linguistics, March 28–30, 1969, at Florida State University, Tallahassee. 7 pp.

Concludes that Uncle Remus dialect is primarily of Black middle Georgia, but suggests that Joel Chandler Harris' recording of Black English was far superior to that of Ambrose Gonzales. Also discusses several aspects of Black English.

————. "A Weapon of My Song: The Poetry of James Weldon Johnson." *Phylon,* XXXII (Winter, 1971), 374–82.

Includes discussion of Johnson's dialect poetry.

Lopez, Thomas R., Jr. "Black English." Letter to the editor, *New Republic,* CLXIV (January 16, 1971), 35.

Argues for inclusion of standard English as a second language to aid students professionally and socially.

Loughlin, Richard L. "Giving the Disadvantaged a Boost in English." *College English,* XXVII (November, 1965), 157.

Discusses twelve separate points to aid disadvantaged in language skills.

Love, Theresa R. "Needs and Approaches for Developing Linguistic Abilities." *Journal of Negro Education,* XXXV (Fall, 1966), 400–408.

Emphasizes teaching standard English as a second language to nonstandard English speakers. Opposed to eradicationist theory. Calls for change of attitudes by English teachers to allow full acceptance of Black English as a language. Discusses some of the English language problems in college.

Lueders-Salmon, Erika. See Fishman, Joshua A., and Erika Lueders-Salmon.

Luelsdorff, Philip A. "Dialectology in Generative Grammar," in J. L. Dillard, ed., *Perspectives on Black English.* The Hague: Mouton, forthcoming.

———. "A Segmental Phonology of Black English." Doctoral dissertation, Georgetown University, Washington, D.C.,1970. [Also published by Mouton Publishers, The Hague, the Netherlands, 1973.]

Analysis and description of Black English phonology in urban areas. Several conclusions.

———. "Toward Standard English for Urban Blacks." Paper presented at annual meeting of the National Association of Foreign Student Advisors of Wisconsin, April, 1970, at Milwaukee.

Lyell, Charles. *A Second Visit to the United States of America.* London: J. Murray, 1849. 2 vols.

Suggests that Whites learned "broken English" from Blacks.

M

Macauley, R. K. S. Review of Walter A. Wolfram, *A Sociolinguistic Description of Detroit Negro Speech. Language,* XLVI (September, 1970), 764–73.

Unfavorable review. Charges that the analysis of variables only serves to emphasize the inadequacy of data provided by the Detroit study.

McBride, J. M. "Br'er Rabbit in the Folktales of the Negro and Other Races." *Sewannee Review,* XIX (April, 1911), 185–206.

Comparative analysis and general discussion.

McCarthy, Janet Lee Gorrell. "Changing Parent Attitudes and Improving Language and Intellectual Abilities of Culturally Disadvantaged Four-Year-Old Children through Parent Involvement." Doctoral dissertation, Indiana University, Bloomington, 1968. 115 pp.

McCune, Ben C. III. "A Contrastive Study of the Phonologic and Syntactic Behavior in the Spontaneous Speech of a Select Group of Black and White Children." Doctoral dissertation, Florida State University, Tallahassee, 1972. 133 pp.

Describes differences on a number of measurements.

McDavid, Raven I., Jr. "American Social Dialects." *College English*, XXVI (January, 1965), 254–60. [Also in Raven I. McDavid, Jr., and William M. Austin, eds., *Communication Barriers to the Culturally Deprived*. Chicago: University of Chicago and Illinois Institute of Technology, 1966.]

Summary of history of dialectology in United States, with emphasis on how dialect work is changing its emphasis to bidialectism.

―――. "A Checklist of Significant Features for Discriminating Social Dialects," in Eldonna L. Evertts, ed., *Dimensions of Dialect*. Champaign, Ill.: National Council of Teachers of English, 1967. Pp. 7–10. [Also in Harold B. Allen and Gary N. Underwood, eds., *Readings in American Dialectology*. New York: Appleton-Century-Crofts, 1971. Pp. 468–72; A. L. Davis, William M. Austin, William Card, Raven I. McDavid, Jr., and Virginia Glenn McDavid, eds., *Culture, Class, and Language Variety: A Resource Book for Teachers*. Urbana, Ill.: National Council of Teachers of English, 1972. Pp. 133–39.]

Cites twenty-six of the most common features of nonstandard English which may be encountered in a classroom situation.

―――. "Dialect Differences and Social Differences in an Urban Society," in William Bright, ed., *Sociolinguistics: Proceedings of the UCLA Sociolinguistics Conference, 1964*. The Hague: Mouton, 1966. Pp. 72–83.

―――."Dialectology and the Integration of the Schools." *Transactions of the Yorkshire Dialect Society*, XI, Part 4 (1965), 18–25.

Discusses the necessity of programs serving individuals with several dialect backgrounds in schools.

―――. "Dialectology and the Teaching of Reading." *The Reading Teacher*, XVIII (December, 1964), 206–13. [Also in Joan C. Baratz and Roger W. Shuy, eds., *Teaching Black Children to Read*. Washington, D.C.: Center for Applied Linguistics, 1969. Pp. 1–13.]

Discusses the extent to which dialect differences in American English complicate the teaching of reading. Directed to teachers of reading, this article also discusses how the teacher can overcome fears and hang-ups about language.

————. "The Dialects of American English," in W. Nelson Francis, ed., *The Structure of American English*. New York: Ronald Press, 1958. Pp. 480–543.

Includes a brief background on Gullah.

————. "Go Slow in Ethnic Attributions: Geographic Mobility and Dialect Prejudice," in Richard W. Bailey and Jay L. Robinson, eds., *Varieties of Present-Day English*. New York: Macmillan, 1973. Pp. 258–73.

Dialect variations are recognized by speakers of various regional dialects who may base stereotype attitudes on those variations. Urges respect for "every mode of speaking."

————. "The Grunt of Negation." *American Speech*, XXX (February, 1965), 56.

Letter to the editor in which the author denies theory on origins presented by Elizabeth Uldall, *American Speech*, XXIX (October, 1964), 232.

————. "Historical, Regional, and Social Variation." *Journal of English Linguistics*, I (March, 1967), 25–40. [Also in Leonard F. Dean, Walker Gibson, and Kenneth G. Wilson, eds., *The Play of Language*. 3rd ed. New York: Oxford University Press, 1971. Pp. 203–18; A. L. Davis, William M. Austin, William Card, Raven I. McDavid, Jr., and Virginia Glenn McDavid, eds., *Culture, Class, and Language Variety: A Resource Book for Teachers*. Urbana, Ill.: National Council of Teachers of English, 1972. Pp. 1–20.]

A thorough discussion of historical, regional, and social variation of language dialects and how these factors interact. Presents a set of nine "scales" on which a given detail of usage may be measured to determine its "standardness" of usage.

————. "Language Characteristics of Specific Groups: Native Whites," in Thomas D. Horn, ed., *Readings for the Disadvantaged: Problems of Linguistically Different Learners*. New York: Harcourt, Brace & World, 1970. Pp. 135–39.

Includes reference to nonstandard English speech as a comparison to the speech of the disadvantaged White.

―――――. "The Language of the City." *Midcontinent American Studies Journal*, X (Spring, 1969), 48–59. [Also in Robert H. Bentley and Samuel D. Crawford, eds., *Black Language Reader*, Glencoe, Ill.: Scott, Foresman, 1973. Pp. 22–35.]

Describes the origins of dialects found in urban centers in the United States. Discusses personal attitudes toward dialect differences, and trends likely to develop in the future. Advises caution in imposing "standard" language patterns on various populations.

―――――. "Needed Research in Southern Dialects" in Edgar T. Thompson, ed., *Perspectives on the South: Agenda for Research*. Durham, N.C.: Duke University Press, 1967. Pp. 113–24.

Suggests areas where Black dialect studies are needed. Also discusses mixtures of Southern and Black English.

―――――. "North Central Grammatical Differences." *American Speech*, XXXV (February, 1960), 5–19.

Includes some discussion of Black English speech.

―――――. "The Position of the Charleston Dialect." *Publications of the American Dialect Society*, No. 23 (April, 1955), 35–49. [Also in Juanita V. Williamson and Virginia M. Burke, eds., *A Various Language: Perspectives on American Dialects*. New York: Holt, Rinehart, & Winston, 1971. Pp. 596–609.]

Description of distinctive phonological, grammatical, and lexical features of the "Charleston Dialect." Information gathered in interviews with nine White and two Black informants.

―――――. "Postvocalic /-r/ in South Carolina: A Social Analysis," *American Speech*, XXIII (October–December, 1948), 194–203.

Notes three variables which affect the postvocalic /r/—less constriction within an urban setting, less constriction among the young, less constriction among the better educated. Cites need for correlating linguistic and cultural phenomena.

―――――. Review of Lorenzo Dow Turner, *Africanisms in the Gullah Dialect. Language*, XXVI (1950), 323–33.

Supports Turner's research on African-based Gullah, which is considered revolutionary in the field of Black English.

―――――. Review of William Labov, *The Social Stratification of English in*

New York City. American Anthropologist, LXX (April, 1968), 425–26.

———. "Sense and Nonsense about American Dialects." *PMLA,* LXXXI (May, 1966), 7–17. [Also in William W. Joyce and James A. Banks, *Teaching the Language Arts to Culturally Different Children.* Reading, Mass.: Addison-Wesley, 1971. Pp. 78–95; Juanita V. Williamson and Virginia M. Burke, eds., *A Various Language: Perspectives on American Dialects.* New York: Holt, Rinehart, & Winston, 1971. Pp. 48–65; David L. Shores, ed., *Contemporary English: Change and Variation.* Philadelphia: J. B. Lippincott, 1972. Pp. 134–52; Virginia P. Clark, Paul A. Eschholz, and Alfred A. Rosa, eds., *Language: Introductory Readings.* New York: St. Martin's Press, 1972. Pp. 352–70.]

Dialect study and attitudes, procedures, conclusions, needed research, and implications are discussed in this article.

———. "Social Dialects in America." Paper presented at the Conference on English—Black and White, March 4–6, 1971, at Purdue University, West Lafayette, Ind.

———. "The Sociology of Language," in Albert H. Marckwardt, ed., *Yearbook of the National Society for the Study of Education.* English Language Institute, University of Michigan, Ann Arbor, 1964.

———. "Some Social Differences in Pronunciation," in David L. Shores, ed., *Contemporary English: Change and Variation.* Philadelphia: J. B. Lippincott, 1972. Pp. 42–52.

———. "Teaching Standard English to Non-Standard Speakers." Paper presented at National Council of Teachers of English Pre-Convention Workshop, November 26, 1963, at San Francisco.

Argues that more research into dialectal variations is needed before standard dialect can be effectively taught.

———. "A Theory of Dialect," in James E. Alatis, ed., *Report of the Twentieth Annual Roundtable Meeting on Linguistics and Language Studies: Linguistics and the Teaching of Standard English to Speakers of Other Languages or Dialects.* Monograph Series on Languages and Linguistics. Washington, D.C.: Georgetown University Press, 1970. Pp. 45–62.

Discusses regional and social dialects and the relationship between them. Advocates use of term "variation" to replace "dialect."

———. "Variations in Standard American English." *Elementary English,* XLV (May, 1968), 561–64, 608. [Also in A. L. Davis, ed., *On the*

Dialects of Children. Champaign, Ill.: National Council of Teachers of English, 1968. Pp. 5–9.]

Discussion of general dialect studies. Not directed specifically at Black English.

———. See Davis, A. L., William M. Austin, William Card, Raven I. McDavid Jr., and Virginia Glenn McDavid, eds.

———, ed. See Mencken, H. L.

McDavid, Raven I., Jr., and William M. Austin, eds. *Communication Barriers to the Culturally Deprived.* Chicago: University of Chicago and Illinois Institute of Technology, 1966. 179 pp.

McDavid, Raven I., Jr., and Virginia Glenn McDavid. "The Relationship of the Speech of American Negroes to the Speech of Whites." *American Speech,* XXVI (February, 1951), 3–17. [Also in Walt Wolfram and Nona H. Clarke, eds., *Black-White Speech Relationships.* Washington, D.C.: Center for Applied Linguistics, 1971. Pp. 16–37; with special addendum to the original article, pp. 38–40.]

Discusses numerous myths and misconceptions about Black speech and language characteristics still existing in Black English.

McDavid, Raven I., Jr., and Lee A. Pederson. *A Social Dialect Survey of Chicago.* Chicago: Science Research Associates, 1963.

McDavid, Virginia Glenn. See Davis, A. L., William M. Austin, William Card, Raven I. McDavid, Jr., and Virginia Glenn McDavid, eds.

———. See McDavid, Raven I., Jr., and Virginia Glenn McDavid.

McDavid, Virginia Glenn, and William Card. "Problem Areas in Grammar," in A. L. Davis, William M. Austin, William Card, Raven I. McDavid, Jr., and Virginia Glenn McDavid, eds., *Culture, Class, and Language Variety: A Resource Book for Teachers.* Urbana, Ill.: National Council of Teachers of English, 1972. Pp. 89–132.

Lists important ways in which most dialects differ from standard English. Not geared solely to Black English.

McDowell, Katherine Sherwood Bonner. *Dialect Tales.* New York: Harper & Bros., 1883. 187 pp.

Eleven tales in Black dialect.

———. *Suwanee Tales.* Boston: Roberts Brothers, 1884. 303 pp.

Folklore.

McDowell, Tremaine. "The Negro in the Southern Novel Prior to 1850."

Journal of English and Germanic Philology, XXV (October, 1926), 455–73.

Account of the "awakening" of American writers to the literary value of the Blacks and their language.

————. "Notes on Negro Dialect in the American Novel to 1821." *American Speech*, V (April, 1930), 291–96.

Discussion of Black language in several novels. Includes several quotations. Concludes that most literary dialect was poor representation of accurate Black speech. Says that what was presented was probably Maryland and Virginia speech.

————. "The Use of Negro Dialect by Harriet Beecher Stowe." *American Speech*, VI (June, 1931), 322–26.

Concludes that, for its time, the Black language illustrated in Stowe's works was inferior to that recorded by other writers of that time.

McFarlane, Paul T. See Garvey, Catherine, and Paul T. McFarlane. "A Measurement of Standard English Proficiency of Inner-City Children."

————. See Garvey, Catherine, and Paul T. McFarlane. *A Preliminary Study of Standard English Speech Patterns in Baltimore City Public Schools.*

MacGinitre, Walter H. "Testing Reading Achievement in Urban Schools." *Reading Teacher*, XXVII (October, 1973), 13–21.

Pedagogical implications for nonstandard dialect readers.

McIlwaine, Shields. *The Southern Poor White, from Lubberland to Tobacco Road.* Norman: University of Oklahoma Press, 1939. 269 pp.

Primary focus is on social environment of the poor Whites and their treatment in literature. Includes study of names, with implications for Black English naming studies.

McKay, Claude. *Home to Harlem.* New York: Harper & Bros., 1928. 340 pp.

McKay, June Rumery. "A Partial Analysis of a Variety of Nonstandard Negro English." Doctoral dissertation, University of California, Berkeley, 1969. 484 pp.

One-subject analysis of an elderly Black woman from Louisiana. Comparison of her language to that of standard English.

Mackler, Bernard. See Dentler, Robert A., Bernard Mackler, and Mary Ellen Warshauer, eds.

McLennan, Marcia. "Origin of the Cat: A Negro Tale." *Journal of American Folk-Lore*, IX (January–March, 1896), 71.

McNamara, J. Regis. *Evaluation of the Effects of Head Start Experience in the Area of Self-Concept, Social Skills, and Language Skills.* Dade County Board of Education, Miami, July, 1968. 54 pp.

Experimental research involving 180 Black Head Start pupils in Dade County, Florida.

McNeill, David. "How to Learn a First Language." Paper presented at the Research Planning Conference on Language Development in Disadvantaged Children, June 7–8, 1966, at the Graduate College of Education, Yeshiva University, New York.

Discussion of language acquisition, describing how that of a disadvantaged child differs from that of an advantaged child.

Macon, J. A. *Uncle Gabe Tucker: Or, Reflection, Song, and Sentiment in the Quarters.* Philadelphia: J. B. Lippincott, 1883. 181 pp.

Rhymes, songs, and some folklore. Description of Black English.

Maddox, Marilyn Price. "The Life and Works of Julia Mood Peterkin." Master's thesis, University of Georgia, Athens, 1956.

Largely biographical, but includes several observations about the writings of Mrs. Peterkin.

Major, Clarence, ed. *A Dictionary of Afro-American Slang.* New York: International Publishers, 1970. 127 pp.

Major premise is that Black English colloquialisms result from a painful struggle by Blacks for human freedom, and stem directly from a rejection of the life-styles, social patterns, and thinking of Euro-American sensibilities. Says that American White slang is largely Black in origin. Extensive listing of Black slang.

————, ed. *The New Black Poetry.* New York: International Publishers, 1969. 156 pp.

Poems of seventy-six Black poets.

Malcolm, Andrew. "Reading Assists Youths' Speech." New York *Times*, May 9, 1971, p. 51.

News feature discussing the research under the direction of Bernice Cullinan of the New York University College of Education. Research indicated that use of literature aided in expansion of language skills among Blacks.

Malcolm X. See Little, Malcolm [Malcolm X].

Malkoc, Anna Maria, and A. Hood Roberts. "Bidialectism: A Special Report from CAL/ERIC." *Elementary English*, XLVIII (January, 1971), 125–36. [Also in *English Journal*, LX (February, 1971), 279–88.]

Short annotated bibliography of ERIC documents on dialects. Not restricted to Black language.

Malmstrom, Jean. "Dialects." *Florida FL Reporter*, I (Winter, 1966), 5, 8–9. [Also in David L. Shores, ed., *Contemporary English: Change and Variation*. Philadelphia: J. B. Lippincott, 1972. Pp. 17–25.]

Basic discussion of dialects.

————. "Dialects—Updated," in Alfred C. Aarons, Barbara Y. Gordon, and William A. Stewart, eds., *Linguistic-Cultural Differences and American Education*, special issue of the *Florida FL Reporter*, VII (Spring/Summer, 1969). Pp. 47–49, 168. [Also in Robert H. Bentley and Samuel D. Crawford, eds., *Black Language Reader*. Glencoe, Ill.: Scott, Foresman, 1973. Pp. 13–22.]

Updated version of her "Dialects," *Florida FL Reporter*, I (Winter, 1966), 5, 8–9.

————. "Teaching Linguistically in Elementary School." *Florida FL Reporter*, VIII (Spring/Fall, 1970), 31, 48.

Notes that there are no right answers in a linguistic approach.

————. "Webster's Third on Nonstandard Usage." *Publication of the American Dialect Society*, No. 41 (April, 1964), 1–6.

A few observations on how *Webster's Third New International Dictionary* handles nonstandard English words.

Malmstrom, Jean, and Constance Weaver. *Transgrammar: English Structure, Style, and Dialects*. Glenview, Ill.: Scott, Foresman, 1973. 400 pp.

Includes general discussion (pp. 360–84) of Black English.

Malone, Kemp. "Negro Proverbs from Maryland." *American Speech*, IV (April, 1929), 285.

Three short proverbs.

Mannix, Donrel P. *Black Cargoes: A History of the African Slave Trade (1518–1865)*. London: Longmans, 1962. 306 pp.

A study of the slave trade. Implications for American Black English origins.

Mantell, Arlene Lois. "An Assessment of Two Curricular Strategies for Increasing Bidialectal Proficiency of Speakers of Non-Standard Dialect in the Fifth Grade in the New York Metropolitan Area." Doctoral dissertation, New York University, 1972. 157 pp.

Experimental test on curricular strategies. Uses Education Study Center Bidialectal Task for Determining Language in Economically Disadvantaged Children. Pre- and post-testing reveal no significant differences on use of curricular programs designed to modify language development. Author contends that the social significance of language might be stressed beginning at the fifth grade.

————. "Strategies for Language Programs in the Intermediate Grades," in Bernice E. Cullinan, ed., *Black Dialects and Reading.* Urbana, Ill.: ERIC, 1974.

Marcel. See Allen, William Francis [Marcel].

Marckwardt, Albert H., ed. *Studies in Language and Linguistics in Honor of Charles C. Fries.* English Language Institute, University of Michigan, Ann Arbor, 1964.

————, ed. *Yearbook of the National Society for the Study of Education.* English Language Institute, University of Michigan, Ann Arbor, 1964. 371 pp.

Marckwardt, Albert H., and Fred Walcott. *Facts about Current English Usage.* New York: Appleton-Century-Crofts, 1938. 144 pp.

Analysis of more than two hundred controversial usage items. Not restricted to Black English patterns.

Marquardt, William F. "Creating Empathy through Literature between the Members of the Mainstream Culture and the Disadvantaged Learners of the Minority Cultures," in Alfred C. Aarons, Barbara Y. Gordon, and William A. Stewart, eds., *Linguistic-Cultural Differences and American Education,* special issue of *Florida FL Reporter,* VII (Spring/Summer, 1969), 133–41, 157.

Discusses use of literature to foster empathy to the culturally different person, and to motivate those with negative attitudes toward learning. Says that literature should not be geared to minority culture exclusively, thus placing it in isolation.

Marshall, M. S., and P. M. Bentler. "IQ Increases of Disadvantaged Minority-Group Children Following Innovative Enrichment Program." *Psychological Reports,* XXIX (June, 1971), 805–806.

Nine-month test period resulted in mean average gain of 23.5 points on Peabody Picture Vocabulary Test, Form A. Subjects were eleven four-year-old Blacks.

Martellock, Helen A. See Golden, Ruth I., and Helen A. Martellock.

Martin, John Henry. *Technology and the Education of the Disadvantaged.* ERIC document ED 031 293. Washington, D.C., November, 1968. 23 pp.
Suggestions for improving standard English teaching in classrooms of disadvantaged or nonstandard English speakers.

Martin, S. Rudolph, Jr. "Four Undescribed Verb Forms in American Negro English." *American Speech,* XXXV (October, 1960), 238–39.
Discusses the verbs *josh, toch, jonah,* and *slow around.*

Marwitt, Karen L. See Marwitt, Samuel J., Karen L. Marwitt, and John J. Boswell.

Marwitt, Samuel J. *Nonstandard American English of Socially Disadvantaged Negro Children. Final Report.* University of Missouri, St. Louis, n.d. 27 pp.
Concludes that Black students perform educational tasks within framework of own language.

Marwitt, Samuel J., Karen L. Marwitt, and John J. Boswell. "Negro Childrens' Use of Nonstandard Grammar." *Journal of Educational Psychology,* LXIII (June, 1972), 218–24.
Test of hypothesis that Whites on a grammatical fill-in test would give more standard English forms than would Blacks; that Blacks on the same test would give more nonstandard forms than Whites. Data supports hypothesis.

Maryland, James. "Shoe-shine on 63rd," in Thomas Kochman, ed., *Rappin' and Stylin' Out: Communication in Urban Black America.* Champaign: University of Illinois Press, 1972. Pp. 209–14.
Hypothetical story describing a verbal game played in seriousness by Blacks in a Black section of town. Characters are a pimp, a shoeshine boy, and a Black-power advocate. Strong emphasis on language.

Masling, Joseph, and Richard J. Palmer. "Vocabulary for Skin Color in Negro and White Children." *Developmental Psychology,* I (July, 1969), 396–401.
Found that Black children use more words to describe color than do White children.

Mason, Julian. "The Etymology of 'Buckaroo'." *American Speech,* XXXV (February, 1960), 51–55.
Suggests that the origin of the word *buckaroo* was not a corruption

of the Spanish *vaquero* (cowboy), but of the Gullah *buckra* (White man).

Massad, Carolyn Emrick. "Language-Thought Processes in Children from Differing Socioeconomic Levels." Paper presented at the International Reading Association Conference, April 24–27, 1968, at Boston. 11 pp.

Major focus is to define "creativity" and "language aptitude" and their relationships, assuming that, once defined, they would help clarify the role of socioeconomic level in language instruction.

Matthews, Mitford McLeod. *Some Sources of Southernisms.* University, Ala.: University of Alabama Press, 1948. 154 pp.

Includes lengthy discussion of Africanisms in Southern language.

Mattleman, Marcene S., and Robert L. Emans. "The Language of the Inner City Child: A Comparison of Puerto Rican and Negro Third Grade Girls." *Journal of Negro Education*, XXXVIII (Spring, 1969), 173–76.

Study of five Black and six Puerto Rican girls in the third grade. Noted variations between the two groups.

Maxwell, John C. Letter to the editor. *English Journal*, LIX (November, 1970), 1,158–59.

Argument in favor of bidialectism. Opposition to article by James Sledd in the December, 1969, issue.

———. See Hess, Karen, Barbara Long, and John C. Maxwell.

Mazrui, Ali A. "The English Language and the Origins of African Nationalism." *Mawazo*, I (1967). [Also in Richard W. Bailey and Jay L. Robinson, eds., *Varieties of Present-Day English*. New York: Macmillan, 1973. Pp. 56–76.]

Discusses the spread of the English language throughout African countries and its function in the development of African consciousness and nationalism.

Meade, Edward J. Letter to the editor. *Crisis*, LXXVIII (August, 1971), 174.

Strong opposition to *Crisis* editorial (April–May, 1971) which attacked Brooklyn College and Black English class.

Mellan, Olivia. "Black English, Why Try to Eradicate It?" *New Republic*, CLXIII (November 28, 1970), 15–17.

Argument against eradication of Black English. Underscores controversies between eradicationists and bidialectists.

Melmud, Paul Jay. "Black English Phonology: The Question of Reading Interference." Doctoral dissertation, University of California, Berkeley, 1970. 91 pp. [Also published as Monograph No. 1, Language Behavior Research Laboratory, University of California, Berkeley, 1971; James L. Laffey and Roger Shuy, eds., *Language Differences— Do They Interfere?* Newark, Del.: International Reading Association, 1973. Pp. 70–85 (abridged).]

Experimental investigation into the assumption that Black English interferes with reading. Concludes that pronunciation of standard English forms is not significantly correlated to comprehension of forms.

Mencken, H. L. *The American Language: An Inquiry into the Development of English in the United States.* Edited by Raven I. McDavid, Jr. 4th ed. New York: Alfred A. Knopf, 1936; two supplements, 1948.

Major study and analysis of American English, written by one of the nation's outstanding journalists. Includes study and description of dialects. Supplement 1 includes a few brief observations on Black English word origins. Supplement 2 includes a section on Gullah and a forty-word glossary. Discusses the investigations of Lorenzo Dow Turner.

Mentz, Sidney W. "Comments on the Socio-Historical Background to Pidginization and Creolization." Paper presented at the Mona Conference, April, 1968, at the University of the West Indies, Mona, Jamaica. [Revised as ERIC document ED 071 471. Washington, D.C., May, 1973. 32 pp.]

Study of the Caribbean region. Discusses conditions that might have led to ways in which Creole languages are developed.

Mercer, Jane R. "Sociocultural Factors in the Educational Evaluation of Black and Chicano Children." Paper presented at the Tenth Annual Conference on Civil and Human Rights of Educators and Students, February 18–20, 1972, at Washington, D.C. 16 pp.

Discusses problems of classification in respect of mental retardation based on verbal culture-bound IQ tests, rather than socio-medical analysis.

Mercer, Walter. "When School Children Talk Black . . . at the Teacher." St. Petersburg *Times, Floridian Magazine*, November 5, 1972, pp. 12, 30.

Acknowledges existence of Black English as a separate, viable language, but notes that it is "illogical, nonsensical, and harmful to teach an innocent black child" Black English. Identifies Black English as substandard. Argues that, although teachers should understand reasons for the use of Black English, they should teach standard English.

Mercier, Alfred. "Etude sur la Langue Créole en Louisiane." *Comptes Rendus*, July, 1880, 378.

One of the first articles on Creole grammar.

Meredith, Mamie. "Longfellow's 'Excelsior' Done into Pidgin English." *American Speech*, V (December, 1929), 148–51.

Chinese Pidgin English translation, with discussion. Of comparative value.

————. "Negro Patois and Its Humor." *American Speech*, VI (June, 1931), 317–21.

Humor and retorts of Blacks. Recorded in Black English.

Mersand, Joseph. See Jewett, Arno, Joseph Mersand, and Doris V. Gunderson.

Metcalf, Allan A. *Riverside English: The Spoken Language of a Southern California Community*. University of California at Riverside, 1971. 40 pp.

General dialect study using procedures of the *Linguistic Atlas*. Brief overview of Black English. Notes that it includes features of standard English regional speech, but differs in phonology, syntax, and lexicon.

Metz, Elizabeth F. "Poverty, Early Language Deprivation, and Learning Ability." *Elementary English*, XLIII (February, 1966), 129–33. [Also in Eldonna L. Evertts, ed., *Dimensions of Dialect*. Champaign, Ill.: National Council of Teachers of English, 1967. Pp. 14–18.]

Discussion of limitations in lexical, phonetic, and syntactic aspects of language.

Mey, Jacob L. "Linguistic Performance and Minority Groups." *Today's Speech*, XX (Spring, 1972), 45–56.

Concludes that the linguistic concept of "performance" is not significant when applied to communication, which he defines as an art.

Michener, Charles. "Talking Black." *Newsweek*, LXXX (August 14, 1972), 81.

Review and discussion of J. L. Dillard's book, *Black English*.

Michigan State Department of Public Instruction. *The Disadvantaged*

Child and the Language Arts. Michigan State University, East Lansing, 1964. 33 pp.

Identification of language difficulties of the culturally disadvantaged child. Describes methods of evaluation.

Middleton, Russell, and John Moland. "Humor in Negro and White Sub-Cultures: A Study of Jokes among University Students." *American Sociological Review*, XXIV (February, 1959), 61–69.

Midkiff, Don R., and Ronald Midkiff. *Using Transformations Grammar Theory to Rebuild Language Confidence in Slow Learners in the Junior High School.* Rome, Ga.: Rome City School System, n.d. 79 pp.

Seventeen-lesson text, based on Transformational Grammar theory.

Midkiff, Ronald. See Midkiff, Don R., and Ronald Midkiff.

Miller, Daisy. "Negro Dialects in American Literature." *Opportunity*, II (November, 1924), 327–29.

Discussion of Black English. States that it is a separate and distinct language from White English.

Miller, Elizabeth W., comp. *The Negro in America: A Bibliography.* Cambridge, Mass.: Harvard University Press, 1966. 190 pp.

Bibliography of literature related to the Black.

Miller, Joy L. "Be, Finite and Absence: Features of Speech—Black and White." *Orbis*, XXIII (1972), 22–27.

Cites examples of *be* finite and absence of *be* found in article written by a southern Ku Klux Klansman. Points out that absence of *be* underlies the auxiliaries *is* and *are* in the klansman's article. Concludes that the "*be* rule" is present in both Black and White speech.

Miller, Kent, and Ralph Dreger, eds. *Comparative Studies of Negroes and Whites in the United States.* New York: Basic Books, 1972. 572 pp.

Anthology of articles, including some relating to Black English.

Miller, Leslie M. See Williams, Frederick, Jack L. Whitehead, and Leslie M. Miller.

Miller, Warren. *The Cool World.* Boston: Little, Brown, 1959. 241 pp.

Novel. Use of Black language.

Miller, Wick R. See Ervin-Tripp, Susan M., and Wick R. Miller.

Millstein, Gilbert. "A Negro Says It with Jokes." *New York Times Magazine*, April 30, 1961, pp. 34–35.

Milwaukee Public Schools. *Program for Developing Speech and Language Skills in the Educationally Deprived Child through the Utilization of the Specialized Training of Speech Therapists, September 6, 1966– June 16, 1967.* 1967. 66 pp.

Minderhout, David. "Final Consonant Cluster Reduction," in William K. Riley and David M. Smith, eds., *Languages and Linguistics: Working Papers, Number 5: Sociolinguistics.* Washington, D.C.: Georgetown University Press, 1972. Pp. 8–16.

Points out that consonant cluster reduction is a common feature of English. Examines the hypothesis that a liquid or glide sound has a different effect on a preceding consonant cluster than another vowel or consonant.

Miner, Lynn. See Griffith, Jerry, and Lynn E. Miner, eds.

———. See Shriner, Thomas, and Lynn Miner. *The Culturally Disadvantaged Child's Learning of English Morphology.*

———. See Shriner, Thomas, and Lynn Miner. "Morphological Structures in the Language of Disadvantaged and Advantaged Children."

Minor, Mary Willis. "How to Keep Off Witches (as Related by a Negro)." *Journal of American Folk-Lore,* XI (January–March, 1898), 76.

Minor, Murray S. Review of Joan C. Baratz and Roger W. Shuy, *Teaching Black Children to Read. Linguistics,* No. 86 (1972), 94–98.

Mitchell, Ethel Strothers. "Negro Speech in Drinkwater's 'Abraham Lincoln'." *American Speech,* VII (October, 1931), 76–78.

Points out that Drinkwater was an Englishman; his portrayal of Black dialect was thus inconsistent throughout the play.

Mitchell, Henry M. *Black Preaching.* Philadelphia: J. B. Lippincott, 1970. ["Black English" section reprinted in Arthur L. Smith, ed., *Language, Communication, and Rhetoric in Black America.* New York: Harper & Row, 1972. Pp. 87–97.]

A study of the Black preacher, his sermons and language. Includes sections on "The Black Bible," "Black English," "The Black Style," and "The Black Sermon." Includes discussion about teaching Black English to standard English-speaking Black ministers to enable them to communicate more readily with their congregations.

Mitchell, Margaret. *Gone with the Wind.* New York: Macmillan, 1936. 1,037 pp.

Winner of the Pulitzer Prize in Letters (Fiction) for 1937, the novel describes the South during and after the Civil War. Of especial interest is the characterization and language of Mammy.

Mitchell-Kernan, Claudia "Language Behavior in a Black Urban Community." Doctoral dissertation, University of California, Berkeley, 1969. 171 pp. [Reprinted as Monograph No. 2 from Language and Behavior Research Laboratory, University of California, Berkeley, 1971; a portion reprinted as "Signifying, Loud-Talking, and Marking," in Thomas Kochman, ed., *Rappin' and Stylin' Out: Communication in Urban Black America.* Champaign: University of Illinois Press, 1972. Pp. 315–35.]

Research on language behavior in a Black section of Oakland, Calif. Includes discussion of the dozens, signifying, and nonverbal communication.

————. "On the Status of Black English for Native Speakers: An Assessment of Attitudes and Values," in Courtney B. Cazden, Vera P. John, and Dell H. Hymes, eds., *Functions of Language in the Classroom.* New York: Teacher's College Press, Columbia University, 1972. Pp. 195–210.

Discussion of Black English as it is perceived by Blacks. Research of 1965–1969 points to cultural sensitivity by Blacks. Notes that her subjects thought of themselves as linguistically insecure.

Modiano, Nancy. "Juanito's Reading Problems: Foreign Language Interference and Reading Skill Acquisition," in James L. Laffey and Roger Shuy, eds., *Language Differences—Do They Interfere?* Newark, Del.: International Reading Association, 1973. Pp. 29–39.

————. "Where Are the Children?" in Alfred C. Aarons, Barbara Y. Gordon, and William A. Stewart, eds., *Linguistic-Cultural Differences and American Education,* special issue of the *Florida FL Reporter,* VII (Spring/Summer, 1969). Pp. 93–94, 179.

Discusses Black children's language development from a "start where the child is in intellectual and emotional development" point of view. Claims that advocates of Black dialect should be Black themselves in order to effectively introduce Black English as a medium of instruction. Suggests that cognitive skills must be identified and those needed in the larger society must be taught.

Moland, John. See Middleton, Russell, and John Moland.

Moon, Henry Lee. Letter to the editor. *Crisis,* LXXVIII (August, 1971), 174–75.

Letter favoring Black English eradication.

Moore, Rayburn S. "Thomas Dunn English: A Forgotten Contributor to the Development of Negro Dialect Verse in the 1870's." *American Literature*, XXXIII (March, 1961), 72–75.

Brief biographical sketch of one of the unrecognized pioneers of Black dialect poetry in the post–Civil War era.

Moore, Ruby Andrews. "Superstitions of Georgia." *Journal of American Folk-Lore*, IX (July–September, 1896), 226–28.

Morgan, Kathryn. "Jokes among Urban Blacks: An Analysis and Interpretation." Master's thesis, University of Pennsylvania, Philadelphia, 1968.

Morris, Emily Pettigrew. See Simpson, Dagna, Emily Pettigrew Morris, and N. Louanna Furbee.

Morris, J. Allen. "Gullah in the Stories and Novels of William Gilmore Simms." *American Speech*, XXII (February, 1947), 46–53.

Claims Simms was the first major American author to use Gullah as a dialect/language for a major character in a novel.

Morse, J. Mitchell. *The Irrelevant English Teacher*. Philadelphia: Temple University Press, 1972. 142 pp.

Discusses language, dialect, and the English teacher. Chapter 7, "The Shuffling Speech of Slavery: Black English" (pp. 81–95), is strongly eradicationist in outlook, claiming that the language is a "demoralizing language, an idiom of fettered minds." Strongly prescriptivist.

——. "The Shuffling Speech of Slavery: Black English." *College English*, XXXIV (March, 1973), 834–43.

Chapter from his book, *The Irrelevant English Teacher*.

Mueser, Anne Marie. "A Mini-Course in Black English: Implications for Reading and Language Arts Instruction." *Education for the Disadvantaged Child*, I (Summer, 1973), 24–28.

Proposed program.

Mukerji, Rose. See Robison, Helen F., and Rose Mukerji.

Munford, Robert. *The Candidates*, in *A Collection of Plays and Poems by the Late Col. Robert Munford*. Petersburg, Va: William Prentiss, 1798. Pp. 9–51.

Drama. The character Ralpho, who speaks in dialect, is believed to be the first Negro character introduced into American colonial drama.

Murphy, John. See Drzick, Kathleen, John Murphy, and Constance Weaver.

Murphy, John, and Harry Goff, comps. *Bibliography of African Languages and Linguistics.* Washington, D.C.: Catholic University of America Press, 1969. 147 pp.

Includes some Creole studies and an index to languages.

Muskgrave, Marian E. "Failing Minority Students: Class, Caste, and Racial Bias in American Colleges." *College Composition and Communication,* XXII (February, 1971), 24–29.

Discussion of class attitudes and dialect snobbery among teachers and students—also, the lack of linguistic or language knowledge among teachers.

N

Nagara, Susumi. *Japanese Pidgin English in Hawaii: A Bilingual Description.* Honolulu: University of Hawaii Press, 1972. 322 pp.

Naremore, Rita C. See Williams, Frederick, and Rita C. Naremore. *Language and Poverty: An Annotated Bibliography.*

————. See Williams, Frederick, and Rita C. Naremore. "On the Functional Analysis of Social Class Differences in Modes of Speech."

Nash, J. V. "Joel Chandler Harris: Interpretations of the Negro Soul." *Open Court,* I (February, 1927), 103–10.

Nash, Rosa Lee. *Nonstandard Dialect.* Champaign, Ill.: National Council of Teachers of English, 1968. 38 pp.

Describes a model for teaching: defines the problems and outlines ways to deal with them.

————. "Toward a Philosophy of Speech Communication Education for the Black Child." *Speech Teacher,* XIX (March, 1970), 88–97.

Sees a need for a speech philosophy to meet the educational needs of Black children.

Natalicio, Diana S., and Frederick Williams. "What Characteristics Can 'Experts' Reliably Evaluate in the Speech of Black and Mexican-American Children?" *TESOL Quarterly,* VI (June, 1972), 121–27.

Presents results of a study to determine reliability and accuracy of evaluation by dialect experts of speech characteristics of Black and Mexican-Americans. High reliability determined.

National Council of Teachers of English. See Corbin, Richard, and Muriel Crosby, eds.

"Negro Dialect." *Opportunity,* II (September, 1924), 259–60.

Editorial discussing misuse of Black dialect in literature of the early 1920s.

Negro Newspapers on Microfilm. Committee on Negro Studies, American Council of Learned Societies, Washington, D.C., 1947. (Photographed by the Library of Congress. 101 reels in main series. 12 reels in miscellaneous series.)

One of the richest sources of primary information about Black language is newspapers. This series contains about two hundred newspapers—each with several issues—edited by or for Blacks. Some of the newspapers were published for only a few weeks, others for several years. Both standard and Black English syntax are present. Although the series covers the years 1829–1945, most of the newspapers are from the 1880s and 1890s. Among the newspapers are the *American Citizen* (February 23, 1888–August 2, 1907); the *Appeal* (January 27, 1905–November 24, 1923); the *Broad Ax* (August 31, 1895–April 11, 1903); the Cleveland *Gazette* (August 25, 1883–May 20, 1945); the *Colored American* (March 12, 1898–November 12, 1904); the *Elevator* (irregular, 1865–1893); the *Freeman* (December 2, 1886–December 30, 1916); the *Louisianan* (December 18, 1870–June 17, 1882); the *New Age* (January 6, 1883–April 20, 1907); the St. Louis *Palladium* (January 10, 1903–October 5, 1907); the Washington *Bee* (June 10, 1882–January 21, 1922); the Wichita *Searchlight* (June 2, 1900–October 26, 1912); and the *Wisconsin Weekly Advocate* (May 7, 1898–September 19, 1907). Some of the earlier publications in the series are the *Black Republic* (6 issues, 1865); the *Colored Tennessean* (6 issues, 1865–1866); *Freedman Press* (6 issues, 1868); *L'Union* (10 issues, 1862–1864); the New Orleans *Tribune* (several issues, 1864–1869); the *North Star and Freeman Advocate* (1842); the *Rights of All* (2 issues, 1829); the *South Carolina Lender* (7 issues, 1865–1866); the *Virginia Star* (9 issues, 1829–1897); the *Weekly Anglo African* (1859–1860).

"Negro Patois and Its Humor." *Appleton's Journal of Popular Literature, Science, and Art,* V (February, 1870), 161–62.

The Negro Singer's Own Book: Containing Every Negro Song That Has

Ever Been Sung or Printed. Philadelphia: Turner & Fisher, 1846? 448 pp.

Comprehensive anthology.

Neilson, Peter, ed. *The Life and Adventures of Zamba, an African King, and His Experience in Slavery in South Carolina.* London: Smith, Elder, 1847. 258 pp.

Slave narrative. References to language.

Neithamer, Gayle. "Black English." Ohio University *Post,* LXI (February 15, 1972), 2.

Letter to the editor suggesting that Black English is part of a cultural identity as well as a separate and viable language.

Newman, Stanley M., and Herbert G. Ellis. "The Greaser Is a 'Bad Ass'; the Gouster Is a 'Muthah': An Analysis of Two Urban Youth Roles," in Thomas Kochman, ed., *Rappin' and Stylin' Out: Communication in Urban Black America.* Champaign: University of Illinois Press, 1972. Pp. 369–80.

Discussion of "the presentation of self," including appearance, movement, and language in respect to Gousters (Blacks) and Greasers (Whites). Includes tables showing similarities and contrasts between the two types of "alienated" youth.

Newmeyer, John Anthony. "Creativity and Non-Verbal Communication in the Pre-Adolescent White and Black Children." Doctoral dissertation, Harvard University, Cambridge, Mass., 1970.

Psychological study, by use of films, of Black kinesics and interpretation by Blacks and Whites.

Newton, Eunice Shaed. "The Culturally Deprived Child in Our Verbal Schools." *Journal of Negro Education,* XXXI (Spring, 1962), 184–87.

————. "Planning for the Language Development of Disadvantaged Children and Youth." *Journal of Negro Education,* XXXIII (Summer, 1964), 264–74.

Proposal for a language-arts program.

New York Public Library, Office of Adult Services. *The Negro in the United States: A List of Significant Books.* 9th ed. New York: New York Public Library, 1965. 24 pp.

Nicholas, J. Karl. "Teaching Black Students to Write Standard English." Paper presented at the Southeastern Conference on Linguistics, April 20–21, 1973, at Blacksburg, Va. 13 pp.

Discusses ways to aid the Black student in college composition. Suggests that students be allowed to write in the dialect they speak, then modify it into standard English.

Nichols, Charles H. *Many Thousand Gone: The Ex-Slaves' Account of Their Bondage and Their Freedom.* Leiden, the Netherlands: Brill, 1963. 224 pp. [Also published by Indiana University Press, Bloomington, 1969.]

Discussion of slavery. Original writings by slaves.

————. "Who Read the Slave Narratives?" *Phylon Quarterly*, XX (Summer, 1959), 149–62.

Study of the many published slave narratives of the first half of the nineteenth century. Points to narratives that led to *Uncle Tom's Cabin.*

Nichols, Michael. See Legum, Stanley E., Carol Pfaff, Gene Tinnie, and Michael Nichols.

Nichols, Patricia. "*To* and *From* in Gullah: An Evolutionary View." Paper presented at the annual meeting of the Linguistic Society of America, December 28–30, 1973, at San Diego.

"Nichols Raps Memo Approving 'Black English'." Philadelphia *Bulletin*, August 12, 1969.

News summary of counterargument by two leading Black educators who called for retraction of memorandum explaining arguments in favor of use of dialect readers.

Nida, Eugene A., and Harold U. Fehderau. "Indigenous Pidgins and Koines." *International Journal of American Linguistics*, XXXVI (April, 1970), 146–55.

Discusses misconceptions about Pidgins and Koines.

Nilon, Charles H. *Faulkner and the Negro.* Boulder: University of Colorado Press, 1965. 111 pp.

Study of Faulkner's use of the Black and his language in novels.

Nixon, Cynthia Delmar. "Negro Speech in Haynesville, Ruston, and Baton Rouge, Louisiana." Master's thesis, Louisiana State University, Baton Rouge, 1945. 92 pp.

Study of speech of eight Black women. Classifies deviations ("errors") as substitutions, omissions, insertions, and errors induced by contact with general American speech.

Nixon, Nell Marie. *Gullah and Backwoods Dialect in Selected Works by*

William Gilmore Simms. Chapel Hill: University of North Carolina Press, 1971. 290 pp.

Examination of all nonstandard linguistic forms in Simms's writings. Concludes that Simms's representation of Gullah was historically accurate, but also concludes that the dialogue gives evidence that Gullah is almost entirely derived from the speech of White illiterates of the seventeenth and eighteenth centuries.

Nolan, Patricia S. "Reading Nonstandard Dialect Materials: A Study at Grades Two and Four." *Child Development,* XLIII (September, 1972), 1,092–97.

Experimental study determines that there is no significant difference in Black English–standard English interference at the second-grade level, but the situation changes at fourth grade. Uses stories in both standard and Black English as part of methodology.

Nonstandard Dialect. Champaign, Ill.: National Council of Teachers of English, 1967. 38 pp.

Listing of many grammatical and phonological features of nonstandard languages. Primarily for teachers.

Noreen, Robert S. "Ghetto Worship: A Study of the Names of Chicago Storefront Churches." *Names,* XIII (March, 1965), 19–38.

Includes list of 381 church names in Black Chicago ghetto.

North, George E., and O. Lee Buchanan. "Maternal Attitudes in a Poverty Area." *Journal of Negro Education,* XXXVII (Fall, 1968), 418–25.

Norton, Arthur A. "Linguistic Persistence." *American Speech,* VI (December, 1930), 149.

Unusual and brief look at Gullah as being descended from French Canada.

O

Oakland, Thomas. "Relationships between Social Class and Phonemic and Nonphonemic Auditory Discrimination Ability." Paper presented at the American Educational Research Association conference, February 5–8, 1969, at Los Angeles. 20 pp.

Examination of relationship between social class and race, and performance on phonemic and nonphonemic auditory discrimination tests.

"Objections to the Negro Dialect." *Literary Digest,* LIII (1916), 1,253.

The question of the "inferior language."

O'Donnell, E. P. "Canker." *Yale Review,* XXV (June, 1936), 794–809.

Dialogue-narrative set in the Louisiana Delta. One of the major characters is a Black boy who influences the speech of a White playmate.

O'Donnell, Holly Smith. See Smith, Holly.

Odum, Anna Kranz. *Relationship of Mothers' Language Styles to the Cognitive Styles of Urban Pre-School Children.* ERIC document ED 019 633. Washington, D.C., 1965. 22 pp.

Preliminary findings.

————. "Some Negro Folk-Songs from Tennessee." *Journal of American Folk-Lore,* XXVII (July, 1914), 255–65.

Odum, Howard W. *Negro Workaday Songs.* Chapel Hill: University of North Carolina Press, 1926. 278 pp.

Odum, Howard W., and Guy B. Johnson. *The Negro and His Songs: A Study of Typical Negro Songs in the South.* Hatboro, Pa.: Folklore Associates, 1964. 306 pp.

O'Hern, Edna M. See Putnam, George N. and Edna M. O'Hern.

Olim, Ellis G. "Maternal Language Styles and Children's Cognitive Behavior." *Journal of Special Education,* IV (Winter, 1970), 53–68.

Part of his major study.

————. *Maternal Language Styles and Their Implications for Children's Cognitive Development.* ERIC document ED 012 282. Washington, D.C., 1966. 39 pp. [Also in Frederick Williams, ed., *Language and Poverty: Perspectives on a Theme.* Chicago: Markham, 1970. Pp. 212–28.]

Examines relationships between mothers' language and the concept of attainment of their preschool children. Subjects were 160 urban Blacks from four socioeconomic groups.

Olim, Ellis G., Robert D. Hess, and Virginia C. Shipman. "Role of Mothers' Language Styles in Mediating Their Preschool Childrens' Cognitive Development." *School Review,* LXXV (Winter, 1967), 414–24.

Expansion of Olim's ERIC report *Maternal Language Styles and Their Implications for Childrens' Cognitive Development.*

Oliver, Paul. *Blues Fell This Morning: The Meaning of the Blues.* London: Cassell, 1960. 355 pp.

Claims that Blues lyrics had origins in Gullah or Gombo languages.

"One for the Wastebasket." Philadelphia *Daily News,* August 13, 1969, p. 29.

Editorial statement opposing use of dialect readers for Blacks.

O'Neil, Wayne. "The Politics of Bidialectism." *College English,* XXXIII (January, 1972), 433–38. [Also in Louis Kampf and Paul Lauter, eds., *The Politics of Literature.* New York: Pantheon Books, 1972; Robert H. Bentley and Samuel D. Crawford, eds., *Black Language Reader.* Glencoe, Ill.: Scott, Foresman, 1973. Pp. 184–91.]

Opposition to theories of bidialectism.

————. "A Theory of Linguistic Performance," in *Research Planning Conference on Language Development in Disadvantaged Children.* College of Education, Yeshiva University, New York. Pp. 41–47.

Describes Harvard project involving study of the language of the disadvantaged. Presents possible methods of potential development; discovering what a child *can* do linguistically as opposed to what he *does* do.

O'Neill, George Joseph. "Negro Nonstandard Grammatical Items in the Speech of Negro Elementary School Children as Correlates of Age, Grade, and Social Status." Doctoral dissertation, University of Southern California, Los Angeles, 1972. 185 pp.

Use of nine nonlinguistic variables and their relationships to nonstandard forms. Notes that school experience tends "to reduce the amount of Negro nonstandard English interference."

Onozawa, Yukiko. "The Features of the Copula 'be' in Black English." Unpublished paper, University of Northern Iowa, Cedar Falls, 1971. 11 pp.

Discusses function and behavior of the copula *be* in Black English. Draws conclusions on deep structure–surface structure theories.

O'Piela, Joan M. *Pilot Study of Five Methods of Presenting the Summer Head Start Curricular Program.* Detroit Public Schools, 1968. 20 pp.

"Order to OK 'Black English' in Schools Comes under Fire." Philadelphia *Daily News,* August 11, 1969, p. 5.

News summary of events generating from a memorandum suggesting that teachers look at theories of Black dialect readers.

Orsini, Bette. "New Road for Young Migrants." *Southern Education Reports,* III (March, 1968), 19–23.

Study of program at University of South Florida, Tampa, to aid school dropouts of migrant families—White and Black. Emphasis of program is on teaching standard English as a second language.

Osborn, Jean. *Teaching a Language to Disadvantaged Children.* Institute for Research of Exceptional Children, University of Illinois, Urbana, 1968. 23 pp.

Theory of direct language preparation.

——. See Bereiter, Carl, Siegfried Engelman, Jean Osborn, and Philip A. Reidford.

Osofsky, Gilbert, ed. *Puttin' On Ole Massa: The Slave Narratives of Henry Bibb, William Wells Brown, and Solomon Northup.* New York: Harper & Row, 1969. 404 pp.

Osser, Harry. "Biological and Social Factors in Language Development," in Frederick Williams, ed., *Language and Poverty: Perspectives on a Theme.* Chicago: Markham, 1970. Pp. 248–64.

Reviews various theories of language development, including the nativist position, linguistic viewpoint, environmentalist theory, and sociolinguistic position. Implied references to nonstandard dialect study within sociolinguistic framework.

——. "The Syntactic Structures of Five-Year-Old Culturally Deprived Children." Paper presented at the annual meeting of the Eastern Psychological Association, April, 1966, at New York.

Discusses how much environmental stimulation is necessary for normal language development. Sociolinguistic Black English implications.

Ott, Elizabeth. *Instructional Improvement Program in Language and Reading for Selected Subculture Groups in the Southwest.* ERIC document ED 026 228. Washington, D.C., 1968. 22 pp.

Describes program for education in English as well as native language or dialect. Emphasis is on communication expression in standard English with simultaneous training in the native language/dialect.

Otto, John Solomon, and Augustus M. Burns. "The Use of Race and Hillbilly Recordings as Sources for Historical Research." *Journal of American Folklore,* LXXXV (October–December, 1972), 344–55.

Discusses the phonograph record as one source of primary evidence in understanding the social history of the Black. Also discusses the value of the record in language study.

Owen, Mary Alicia. *Voodoo Tales, as Told among the Negroes of the South-west.* New York: G. P. Putnam's Sons, 1893. 310 pp. [Reprinted by Negro Universities Press, Westport, Conn., 1969.]

Several folk tales told in Southwestern Black English of the late nineteenth century.

P

Page, Thomas Nelson. *In Ole Virginia.* New York: Charles Scribner's Sons, 1896. 275 pp.

Novel. Includes Black language and characterization.

————. "Marse Chan: A Tale of Old Virginia." *Century,* XXVII (April, 1884), 932–42.

Short story that includes Black language and characteristics. Preceded the novel by eight years.

————. *Marse Chan: A Tale of Old Virginia.* New York: Charles Scribner's Sons, 1892. 53 pp.

Novel. Includes Black language and characterizations.

————. "Meh Lady: A Story of the War." *Century,* XXXII (June, 1886), 187–205.

Dialect tale with brief note on dialect variation.

————. *The Novels, Stories, Sketches, and Poems of Thomas Nelson Page.* 18 vols. New York: Charles Scribner's Sons, 1906–18.

Full series of the writings of Page.

————. *The Old Gentlemen of the Black Stock.* New York: Charles Scribner's Sons, 1897. 137 pp.

Novel. Includes Black language and characterizations.

————. "Unc Edinburg's Drowndin'." *Harper's Monthly,* LXXII (January, 1886), 304–15.

Short story that includes much Black English.

————. "Uncle Gabe's White Folks." *Scribner's Magazine,* XIII (April, 1877), 882.

Black dialect verse.

————. See Gordon, A. C., and Thomas Nelson Page.

Palermo, David S. Review of Frederick Williams, ed., *Language and Poverty: Perspectives on a Theme. Science,* CLXXVI (April 21, 1972), 270–71.

Palmer, Richard J., and Joseph Masling. "Vocabulary for Skin Color in Negro and White Children." *Developmental Psychology,* I (July, 1969), 393–401.

Found that Black children use more words to describe color than do White children.

Pardoe, T. Earl. "A Historical and Phonetic Study of Negro Dialect." Doctoral dissertation, Louisiana State University, Baton Rouge, 1937. 395 pp.

Extensive list of Black words with both orthographic and phonetic transcriptions. Records history of the Black language since 1776. Although stating the British-English influence, notes that Black speech still contains phonetic elements of the African languages. Attempt to prove hypothesis that American Black English is a combination of the teachings and influence of English-speaking masters, with modification by African phonetic patterns. Data collected 1934–1937.

Parrish, Lydia. *Slave Songs of the Georgia Sea Islands.* New York: Creative Age Press, 1942. 256 pp. [Reprinted by Folklore Associates, Hatboro, Pa., 1965.]

Parsons, Elsie Clews. *Folk-Lore of the Sea Islands, South Carolina.* Cambridge, Mass.: American Folk-Lore Society, 1923. 216 pp.

Includes 178 folktales and 12 toasts, as well as riddles, gamesongs, and folkways recorded from the Gullah language. Discusses Gullah. Data collected from ninety informants in 1919.

Parsons, Mildred. "Negro Folklore from Fayette County." *Tennessee Folklore Society Bulletin,* XXIX (1963), 67–70.

Pasamanick, Benjamin, and Hilda Knobloch. "Early Language Behavior in Negro Children and the Testing of Intelligence." *Journal of Abnormal and Social Psychology,* L (March 5, 1955), 401–402.

Cites results of lower language scores by test group of Blacks. Reveals that lower verbal scores were probably result of lack of verbal response rather than poor comprehension of the language.

Patrick, Thomas W. "Black English: Road to Failure." Letter to the editor, New York *Times,* July 7, 1971, p. 36.

Strong opposition to Black English teaching. Author is a physician.

————. Letter to the editor. *Crisis,* LXXVIII (August, 1971), 175.
Similar to his letter to New York *Times.*

Paulston, Christina Bratt. "On the Moral Dilemma of the Sociolinguist."
Language Learning, XXI (December, 1971), 175–82.
Discusses conflict between biases and contextual realities of socio-
economic-cultural factors.

Payne, Leonida W. "A Word List from East Alabama." *Dialect Notes,* III,
Part 4 (1908), 279–328; III, Part 5 (1909), 343–91. [Also in J. L.
Dillard, ed., *Perspectives on Black English.* The Hague: Mouton,
forthcoming.]
Careful linguistic analysis, with extensive word list. Notes influence
of Black words on White speech.

Peabody, Ephraim. "Narratives of Fugitive Slaves." *Christian Examiner,*
XLVII (July, 1849), 60–64.
First-person narratives of runaway slaves. Language modified.

Pederson, Lee A. *An Annotated Bibliography of Southern Speech.* Atlanta:
Southeastern Education Laboratory, 1968. 47 pp.
Primary focus is on Southern White speech.

————. "Black Speech–White Speech and the Al Smith Syndrome," in
Lawrence Davis, ed., *Studies in Linguistics in Honor of Raven I.
McDavid, Jr.* University, Ala.: University of Alabama Press, 1972.
Pp. 123–34.
Discussion of some of the aspects of his study of speech of rural
northern Georgia. Notes no linguistic features to distinguish Black
English as a separate language.

————. "Dialect Patterns in Rural Northern Georgia." *Zeitschrift für
Mundartforschung,* in press.

————. "An Introductory Field Procedure in a Current Urban Survey."
Orbis, XI (1962), 465–69.
Brief text on his Chicago dialect survey.

————. "Mark Twain's Missouri Dialects: Marion County Phonemics."
American Speech, XLII (December, 1967), 261–78.
Includes much original research of Missouri dialect by the author
during the late summer of 1964. Some discussion of Twain's Black
dialogue.

————. "Middle Class Negro Speech in Minneapolis." *Orbis*, XVI (December, 1967), 347–53.

Distinguishing features in speech—both standard and Black English.

————. "Negro Speech in *The Adventures of Huckleberry Finn*." *Mark Twain Journal*, XIII (Winter, 1965–66), 1–4.

Preliminary report on projected study of all the literary dialects in Twain's novel. Notes that the Black dialect in *The Adventures of Huckleberry Finn* closely parallels speech of Hannibal County, Mo., as tested by the author in 1964.

————. "Non-Standard Negro Speech in Chicago," in William A. Stewart, ed., *Non-standard Speech and the Teaching of English*. Washington, D.C.: Center for Applied Linguistics. 1964. Pp. 16–20. [Also in *NAFSA Studies and Papers, English Language Series*, No. 10, 1965. Pp. 36–42.]

Says that de facto segregation is linguistically crippling the Black child in urban areas. Advises concentrated "doses" of language study involving the mother and child.

————. "The Pronunciation of English in Metropolitan Chicago." Doctoral dissertation, University of Chicago, 1964. [Also published as *Publications of the American Dialect Society*, No. 44 (November, 1965). 87 pp.]

Survey of speech in Chicago metropolitan area. Notes that difference between Black and White speech is separate patterns of distribution and in frequency of recurring features.

————. "Social Dialects and the Disadvantaged," in Richard Corbin and Muriel Crosby, eds., *Language Programs for the Disadvantaged: The Report of the NCTE Task Force on Teaching English to the Disadvantaged*. Champaign, Ill.: National Council of Teachers of English, 1965. Pp. 236–49.

Review of research. Discusses problems of language underdevelopment, social dialectology studies, and dialect investigation.

————. "Some Structural Differences in the Speech of Chicago Negroes," in Roger W. Shuy, ed., *Social Dialects and Language Learning: Proceedings of the Bloomington, Indiana, Conference, 1964*. Champaign, Ill.: National Council of Teachers of English, 1965. Pp. 28–51. [Also in Harold B. Allen and Gary N. Underwood, eds., *Readings in American Dialectology*. New York: Appleton-Century-Crofts, 1971. Pp. 401–20.]

Contrastive analysis of speech of Blacks who lived in Chicago for more than twenty years and those who are recent arrivals.

―――. "Southern Speech and the LAGS Project." *Orbis*, XX (1971), 79–89.

Background of the *Linguistic Atlas of the Gulf States* (LAGS) which separates Black and White speech. Also discusses empirical methods developed by Hans Kurath.

―――. "Terms of Abuse for Some Chicago Social Groups." *Publications of the American Dialect Society*, No. 42 (1968), 26–48.

Discusses pejorative terms and vocabulary used by Blacks and Whites.

―――. See McDavid, Raven I., Jr., and Lee A. Pederson.

Pée, Willem, W. Gs. Hellinga, and A. Donicie. *Het Neger-Engels van Suriname*. Liege, Belgium: University of Liege Press, 1953. 80 pp.

Study of Negro-English of Surinam. Includes separate chapters by Pée ("Bijdragen en Beschouwingen," "Vragenlijst Nederlands en Surinaams van Paramaribo," and "De Klanken van het Neger-Engels"); Hellinga ("De Waarde van de zg. Mengtalen in de West"); and Donicie ("Anansi Nanga Tiegri," "Overzicht van de Spellinggeschiedenis van het Surinaams"). The final chapter, by all three authors, is "Voorstellen tot een Nieuwe Systematische Spelling van het Surinaams (Neger-Engels) op Linguistische Grondslag."

Peisach, Estelle Cherry. "Children's Comprehension of Teacher and Peer Speech." *Child Development*, XXXVI (1965), 467–80.

Experimental language study involving Black-White language differences.

Perdreau, Connie. "Black Kinesics." *Grosbeak*, I (March, 1972), 9.

Brief overview of some of the features of Black nonverbal language.

Perez, Carlos V. "Bilingualism and Bidialectalism in the Elementary School." Paper presented at the annual meeting of the National Council of Teachers of English, November, 1973.

Perret, Michael Johann. "A Study of the Syntax and Morphology of the Verbs of the Creole Dialect of Louisiana." Master's thesis, Louisiana State University, Baton Rouge, 1933.

Peterkin, Julia M. *Black April*. New York: Grosset & Dunlap, 1927. 315 pp.

Novel about Blacks. Written in standard English, but with extensive Gullah in the dialogue.

———. *Bright Skin.* Indianapolis: Bobbs-Merrill, 1932. 348 pp.

Novel. Includes Black language and characterization.

———. *Collected Short Stories of Julia Peterkin.* Edited by Frank Durham. Chapel Hill: University of North Carolina Press, 1970. 384 pp.

Thirty-three of the author's better short stories about Blacks and plantation life. Mostly written in the 1920s. Includes seven of her sixteen Gullah sketches, as well as a fifty-seven-page introduction by the editor about the life and writings of Mrs. Peterkin. All typographical errors and problems with paragraphing and orthography in the original short stories have been "corrected" in this book.

———. "Daddy Harry." *Reviewer,* IV (October, 1924), 382–83.

Short sketch of a Gullah man, his language and customs.

———. *Green Thursday.* New York: A. A. Knopf, 1924. 188 pp.

Several sketches and short stories about Blacks.

———. "Imports from Africa." *Reviewer,* II (January, 1922), 197–200.

Five short Gullah sketches—"Betsy," "Catfish," "Cooch's Premium," "The Ortymobile," and "The Plat-Eye."

———. "Imports from Africa." *Reviewer,* II (February, 1922), 253–59.

Five short Gullah sketches—"Cato," "Cholera," "Finding Peace," "A Sketch," and "Uncle Bill."

———. *A Plantation Christmas.* Boston: Houghton Mifflin, 1934.

Novel. Includes Black language and characterization.

———. *Roll, Jordan, Roll.* New York: R. O. Ballou, 1933. 251 pp. Photographs by Boris Ulmann.

In-depth study of social and plantation life, language and customs of Blacks.

———. "Silhouettes." *Reviewer,* II (June, 1922), 500–503.

Two short Gullah sketches—"A Crutch" and "A Wife."

———. "Studies in Charcoal." *Reviewer,* II (March, 1922), 319–27.

Two short Gullah sketches—"Green Walnuts" and "Root Work."

Peterson, Sue Ann Woestehoff. "Attitudes of Children toward Literary Characters Who Speak Regional Dialects of American English." Doctoral dissertation, University of Minnesota, Minneapolis, 1969. 179 pp.

Attitudinal survey of sixth-graders. Students were neutral to mildly positive if main character spoke in a dialect. However, students reading rewritten Black passages gave more positive statements regarding the character of the individual.

Petrella, Beatrice. "Verbs without Color." Letter to the editor, New York *Times*, June 28, 1972, p. 44.

A teacher in a ghetto junior high school argues against Black English teaching.

Pfaff, Carol W. *A Coding System for the Study of Linguistic Variation in Black English*. Southwest Regional Laboratory, Inglewood, Calif., December, 1971. 51 pp.

Documents coding system designed for use to describe Black English. Includes codes for forty-one phonological and syntactic variables in speech of children in kindergarten through first grade.

————. *Historical and Structural Aspects of Sociolinguistic Variation: The Copula in Black English*. Southwest Regional Laboratory, Inglewood, Calif., August, 1971. 41 pp.

Study refutes Creolist hypothesis that the underlying structure of Black English differs from that of Anglo-American. Includes analysis of phonology, syntax, semantic environments of the full, contracted, and deleted forms of "is." Concludes that only the full and contracted forms are conditioned by stress.

————. See Berdan, Robert, and Carol W. Pfaff.

————. See Legum, Stanley E., Carol Pfaff, Gene Tinnie, and Michael Nichols.

Pfaff, Carol W., and Gene Tinnie. *Spelling-to-Sound Correspondences in Black English*. Southwest Regional Laboratory, Inglewood, Calif., January 21, 1970.

Phillips, Judith. *The Effects of the Examiner and Testing Situation upon the Performance of Culturally Deprived Children. Phase 1—Intelligence and Language Ability Test Scores as a Function of the Race of the Examiner*. Nashville, Tenn.: George Peabody College for Teachers, 1966. 18 pp.

Results of a six-month language development program.

Pickford, Glenna Ruth. "American Linguistic Geography: A Sociolinguistic Appraisal," in J. L. Dillard, ed., *Perspectives on Black English*. The Hague: Mouton, forthcoming.

"Pidgin English." *Nation*, XI (August 25, 1870), 118–19.

Argument for acceptance of Chinese Pidgin English as a potentially viable dialect, with same acceptance of Lingua Franca. Earlier base for arguments of creolization stage for American Black English.

Pierce, B. E. "Negro and Akan Anansi Stories in Surinam: Some Comparisons." Paper presented at the annual meeting of the African Studies Association, October 31–November 3, 1973, at Syracuse, N.Y.

Pierce-Jones, John, and Ira Iscoe. "Divergent Thinking, Age, and Intelligence in White and Negro Children." *Child Development*, XXXV (September, 1964), 785–97.

Pierson, Laura S., and Ralph Vanderslice. "Prosodic Features of Hawaiian English." *Quarterly Journal of Speech*, LIII (April, 1967), 156–66.

Internal implications for Black English scholars.

Pilon, A. Barbara. "Culturally Divergent Children and Creative Language Activities," in James L. Laffey and Roger Shuy, eds., *Language Differences—Do They Interfere?* Newark, Del.: International Reading Association, 1973. Pp. 127 ff.

Pittsburgh Public Schools. *Standard Speech Development Program*. Pittsburgh, 1968. 40 pp.

Discusses development of pattern drills, with aim of eliminating nonstandard speech.

Pixton, William H. "Response to CCCC Executive Committee's Resolution 'The Student's Right to His Own Language'." *College Composition and Communication*, XXIII (October, 1972), 298–300.

Opposition to the sociolinguistic statement on Black English presented in 1972 by the executive committee of the Conference on College Composition and Communication. Author claims that Black English is a deficit.

Plaister, Ted. "Audio-Lingual Methods in the Language Arts Program." Paper presented at annual convention of the National Association of Teachers of English, November 21–25, 1967, at Honolulu. 9 pp.

Discusses methods for teachers to stress change to standard English, but emphasizes that the teacher must recognize the fact that students do not speak incorrectly, only differently. Primary aim is for Blacks.

Platt, J. "Negro Element in the English Language." *Atheneum* (London), 1900, p. 283.

Poe, Edgar Allan. "The Gold Bug." *Dollar Newspaper*, June 21, 28, 1843.

Mystery involving a formerly rich southern gentleman and his slave. The language of Jupiter, the slave, is of especial importance.

Polite, Dennis. "Black, Standard English Be 2 Kinds." *Dayton* (Ohio) *Daily News*, February 12, 1973, p. 30.

Discusses Black English workshop for teachers in Dayton, Ohio.

Politzer, Robert L. "Problems in Applying Foreign Language Teaching Methods to the Teaching of Standard English as a Second Dialect," in Johanna S. DeStefano, ed., *Language, Society, and Education: A Profile of Black English*. Worthington, Ohio: Charles A. Jones, 1973. Pp. 238–50.

Politzer, Robert L., and Diane E. Bartley. *Standard English and Nonstandard Dialects: Phonology and Morphology*. Center for Research and Development in Teaching, Stanford University, Stanford, Calif., June, 1969. 47 pp.

Systematic listing and description of the salient features of English phonology and morphology, accompanied by parallel listing of features of the nonstandard languages (Black and Mexican-American).

Politzer, Robert L., and Mary Rhodes Hoover. *The Development of Awareness of the Black Standard/Black Nonstandard Dialect Contrast among Primary School Children: A Pilot Study*. Center for Research and Development in Teaching, Stanford University, Stanford, Calif., 1972.

————. *The Effect of Pattern Practice and Standard/Nonstandard Dialect Contrast on Language Achievement among Black Children*. Center for Research and Development in Teaching, Stanford University, Stanford, Calif., March, 1972. 53 pp.

Experimental data suggests that pattern practices are not advantageous.

————. *Teaching Standard English as a Second Dialect: Suggested Teaching Procedures and Sample Microlessons*. Center for Research and Development in Teaching, Stanford University, Stanford, Calif., 1970.

Politzer, Robert L., Mary Rhodes Hoover, and Dwight Brown. *An Experiment in Teaching Reading to Bidialectal Children*. Center for Research and Development in Teaching, Stanford University, Stanford, Calif., February, 1973. 33 pp.

————. *A Test of Proficiency in Black Speech and Nonstandard Speech*. Center for Research and Development in Teaching, Stanford University, Stanford, Calif., February, 1973. 12 pp.

Polk, William T. "Uncle Remus Spake Queen's English," in *Southern Ac-*

cent: From Uncle Remus to Oak Ridge. New York: William Morrow, 1953. Pp. 57–71.

Ponder, Eddie G. "Understanding the Language of the Culturally Disadvantaged Child." *Elementary English,* XLII (November, 1965), 769–74, 797. [Also in Eldonna L. Evertts, ed., *Dimensions of Dialect.* Champaign, Ill.: National Council of Teachers of English, 1967. Pp. 23–29; William W. Joyce and James A. Banks, eds., *Teaching the Language Arts to Culturally Different Children.* Reading, Mass.: Addison-Wesley, 1971. Pp. 59–67.]

Discussion of phenomena regarding oral language of disadvantaged and Black children. Discusses necessity of teachers to recognize the spoken and written languages of the child.

Pope, Michael. "The Syntax of Speech of Urban (Tallahassee) Negro and White Fourth Graders." Doctoral dissertation, Florida State University, Tallahassee, 1969. 137 pp.

Porter, Dorothy B., comp. "Early American Negro Writings: A Bibliographic Study." *Bibliographic Society of America: Papers,* XXXIX (January, 1945), 192–268.

Discussion and listing of several early journals, letters, newspapers, hymnbooks, minutes of meetings, and sermons edited or written by Blacks during the eighteenth and nineteenth centuries.

————, comp. *Negro American Poets: A Bibliographic Checklist of Their Writings, 1760–1944.* Hattiesburg, Miss.: Book, 1945. 90 pp. [Reprinted by Burt Franklin, Philadelphia, 1963.]

Postman, Neil, Charles Weingartner, and Terrence Moran, eds. *Language in America.* New York: Pegasus, 1969. 240 pp.

Potter, Thomas C. *Reading Comprehension among Minority Groups: Child Generated Instructioned Materials.* ERIC document ED 031 546. Washington, D.C., 1968. 7 pp.

Experimental data suggests that studies written in dialect may be more meaningful to Black English speakers than studies written in standard English.

Pound, Glenn. "Social Shibboleths: Dialect Interference in Educational and Social Mobility." *Contemporary English,* XLIII (February, 1971), 101–105.

Discusses the problems of nonacceptance of Blacks and Indians because of language differences.

Povich, Edna A. See Baratz, Joan C., and Edna A. Povich. *A Discussion of the Language Studies of the Economically Disadvantaged Child.*

————. See Baratz, Joan C., and Edna A. Povich. *Grammatical Constructions in the Language of the Negro Preschool Child.*

Powell, Evan R. See Hooper, Peggy R., and Evan R. Powell.

Powell, Samuel. "Layin' Down a Rap." *Journal of Reading,* XVII (December, 1973), 184–85.

Text in a modified Black English.

Preston, Dennis R. "Dialect Expansion: The College Level." Paper presented at annual TESOL convention, March 5–8, 1969, at Chicago.
10 pp.

Proposal for development of a basic college course to teach about
dialects, as well as to teach a dialect. Two-track approach would
be adaptable for Black English, as well as White regional variation.

————. "Social Dialects and College English." *Speech Teacher,* XX (November, 1971), 237–46.

Discusses attitudes of many Black English speakers toward forced
instruction of standard English.

————. "Social Dialectology in America: A Critical Rejoinder." *Florida
FL Reporter,* X (Spring/Fall, 1972), 13–16, 57.

Reaction to article by Lawrence Davis, *Journal of English Linguistics,* IV, 46–56. In-depth discussion of cultural history of dialect
studies and problems of dialect research in general.

Price, Richard, and Sally Price. "Saramakra Onamastics: An Afro-American Naming Practice." *Ethnology,* XI (October, 1972), 341–67.

Discusses personal naming practices among the Saramakra Maroons
of Surinam, and relationships to Black American naming systems
and practices. Questions whether the amount of African lexical items
in a naming system is indicative of that culture's relationship to
Africa.

Price, Sally. See Price, Richard, and Sally Price.

Prince, John Dyneley. "Surinam Negro-English." *American Speech,* IX
(October, 1934), 181–86.

General description. Includes transcriptions.

Puckett, Newbell Niles. *Folk Beliefs of the Southern Negro.* Chapel Hill:
University of North Carolina Press, 1926. 644 pp.

Background on origins of about 3,500 beliefs. Primarily from Alabama, Mississippi, and Georgia.

————. "Names of American Negro Slaves," in *Studies in the Science of Society, Presented to Albert Gallaway Keller in Celebration of His Completion of Thirty Years as Professor of the Science of Society in Yale University.* New Haven: Yale University Press, 1937. 555 pp.

Sociolinguistic analysis of more than twelve thousand slave names from the South, about seven thousand of them from Mississippi. The names are mostly of the period 1803–1865, but there are sixty-five pre-1700 names. Notes possible African origins. Includes tables of the hundred most common names of both male and female slaves. Comparison to modern Black names. General discussion of the more unusual Black names.

Pugh, Griffith T. "George Washington Cable's Theory and the Use of Folk Speech." *Southern Folklore Quarterly,* XXIV (December, 1960), 287.

A few comments on Cable's use of the Creole language.

Purcell, J. M. "Mrs. Stowe's Vocabulary." *American Speech,* XIII (October, 1938), 230–31.

Glossary of twenty-two items from *Uncle Tom's Cabin.* Slant is on Black word identification.

Putnam, George N., and Edna M. O'Hern. "The Status Significance of an Isolated Urban Dialect." *Language,* XXXI: 4, Part 2 (October–December, 1955). 32 pp. supplement.

Experimental findings on Washington, D.C., Black speech. Claims one difference between standard and Black English is "confined rather strikingly to a limited range of phenomena." Includes analysis of objective versus perceived status of Black speakers as viewed by "neutral" listeners.

Q

Quay, Lorene C. "Language Dialect Reinforcement, and the Intelligence Test Performance of Negro Children." *Child Development,* XLII (March, 1971), 5–15.

Concludes that there were no reliable IQ differences among one hundred four-year-old Blacks who were divided into Black-English and standard-English education groups and given two types of "plus-minus" reinforcement. Noted that neither positive reinforcement (candy) nor placement into a group using Black English instruction improved IQ scores to any significant degree.

————. "Negro Dialect and Binet Performance in Severely Disadvantaged Black Four-Year-Olds." *Child Development*, XLIII (March, 1972), 245–50.

Isolation of students by language (Black or standard English). Administration of Stanford-Binet IQ test to fifty four-year-olds revealed no reliable IQ differences.

Quigg, H. D. "Black Slang Called Shield for Oppression." Milwaukee *Journal*, December 1, 1970.

Opinion-review of Clarence Major's *Dictionary of Afro-American Slang*.

R

Radloff, Barbara. "From Nonstandard to Standard English: Exploring How Black Children Cope." *Carnegie Quarterly*, XXI (Fall, 1973), 7–8.

Brief summary of experimental research of psychologist William Hall whose studies of Black-White speech and I.Q. differences suggest that Blacks are not racially inferior.

Rafferty, Max. "Rafferty Slaps Any Use of Dialects in Schools: 'Only One Correct Grammar'." San Diego *Union*, September 9, 1967. [See Shearer, Lloyd. "Americans Who Can't Speak Their Own Language."]

The California Superintendent of Public Instruction lashes out against statements by Charles G. Hurst, Jr. Says that public schools must teach standard English.

Ramchand, Kenneth. "The Language of the Master?" in Kenneth Ramchand, *The West Indian Novel and Its Background*. New York: Barnes & Noble, 1970. Pp. 77–114. [Also in Richard W. Bailey and Jay L. Robinson, eds., *Varieties of Present-Day English*. New York: Macmillan, 1973. Pp. 115–49.]

Discussion of the language used in literature—the language of the dominant political unit and culture or that of the people.

————. *The West Indian Novel and Its Background*. New York: Barnes & Noble, 1970. 295 pp.

Ramos, Arthur. *The Negro in Brazil*. Translated by Richard Pattee. Washington, D.C.: Associate Publishing, 1939. 203 pp.

Discusses traces of Black African language in Brazil. Part of base of American Black English studies on African linguistic survivals.

Ramsey, Catherine Imogene. "A Comparison of First Grade Negro Dialect Speakers' Comprehension of Material Presented in Standard English and in Negro Dialect." Doctoral dissertation, Indiana University, Bloomington, 1970. 112 pp. [Also in *Elementary English*, XLIX (May, 1972), 688–96 (abridged).]

Experimental data suggests little value in use of Black language dialect readers for beginning readers. Sixty-subject sample.

Raph, Jane Beasley. "Language and Speech Deficits in Culturally Disadvantaged Children: Implications for Speech Clinicians." *Journal of Speech and Hearing Disabilities*, XXXII (August, 1967), 203–14.

Proposals for "improvement" of language.

———. "Language Characteristics of Culturally Disadvantaged Children: Review and Implications," in Milly Cowles, ed., *Perspectives in the Education of Disadvantaged Children: A Multi-Disciplinary Approach*. Cleveland: World Publishing, 1967. Pp. 183–208.

Discusses problems of language and speech deficiency in children from impoverished families. Also discusses social context of language, with implications for race.

Raphael, Lawrence J. See Bronstein, Arthur J., Lawrence J. Raphael, and Elsa M. Bronstein.

Raspberry, William. "Should Ghettoese Be Accepted?" *Today's Education*, LIX (April, 1970), 30–31, 61–62. [Also in Virginia P. Clark, Paul A. Eschholz, and Alfred A. Rosa, eds., *Language: Introductory Readings*. New York: St. Martin's Press, 1972. Pp. 412–17.]

Brief overview of Black English as an acceptable language.

Ravenal, Henry W. "Recollections of Southern Plantation Life." *Yale Review*, XXV (June, 1936), 748–77.

Reminiscences written in 1876. Includes a brief sketch of a "Fancy Talk" Black.

Read, Allen Walker. "Eighteenth Century Slaves as Advertised by Their Masters." *Journal of Negro History*, I (April, 1916), 163–216.

Presentation of several newspaper advertisements advising the public of runaway slaves. Most advertisements are of the late eighteenth and early nineteenth centuries, and most contain references to speech and language abilities of the runaways.

————. "The Speech of Negroes in Colonial America." *Journal of Negro History*, XXIV (July, 1939), 247–58.

Cites some inconsistencies between Black speech in writings of the seventeenth through nineteenth centuries, and what truly was Black speech. Uses newspaper ads for runaways as primary historical-linguistic evidence.

Read, William A. *Louisiana-French*. Baton Rouge: Louisiana State University Press, 1931. 253 pp.

Interesting for historical comparative purposes. Discusses varieties of Creole words, as well as fifteen words of African origins.

Redding, J. Saunders. "The Problems of the Negro Writer." *Massachusetts Review*, VI (Autumn–Winter, 1964–65), 57–70.

A look at a few of the problems with language and publishers, as faced by Black writers.

————. *To Make a Poet Black*. Chapel Hill: University of North Carolina Press, 1939. 142 pp.

A study of Black literature, with particular reference to Black poets in history—their lives, culture, and language. Includes several poems.

Redfearn, Susan Fort. "Songs from Georgia." *Journal of American Folk-Lore*, XXXIV (January, 1921), 121–24.

Redpath, James. *The Roving Editor: Or, Talks with Slaves in the Southern States*. New York: A. B. Burdick, 1859. 349 pp.

Interview-narrative with about one hundred slaves. Includes numerous direct quotes.

Reeback, Robert T. *The Extension of Control in Verbal Behavior*. Verbal Behavior Laboratory, University of Rochester, Rochester, N.Y., 1968. 21 pp.

Indirect references to nonstandard language teaching.

Reed, Carroll E. "Adapting TESL Approaches to the Teaching of Written Standard English as a Second Dialect to Speakers of American Black English Vernacular." *TESOL Quarterly*, VII (September, 1973), 289–308.

Describes the use of contrastive analysis and various TESL (Teaching English as a Second Language) approaches to effect bidialectism in the schools.

————, ed. *The Learning of Language*. New York: Appleton-Century-Crofts, 1971. 430 pp.

Anthology of articles dealing with all phases of language learning. Includes article by William Labov, "Variation in Language" (pp. 187–222).

Reed, David. "Linguistics and Literacy," in James E. Alatis, ed., *Report of the Twentieth Annual Roundtable Meeting on Linguistics and Language Studies: Linguistics and the Teaching of Standard English to Speakers of Other Languages or Dialects.* Monograph Series in Languages and Linguistics. Washington, D.C.: Georgetown University Press, 1970. Pp. 93–103.

States that the linguistic discipline can contribute to active research on learning to read and write by specifying the relationships between the grammatical system of a language and the phonological and orthographic systems.

Regan, John. "Co-lingualism, Anthropological Linguistics and Compensatory Education." Paper presented at the Language Seminar, Claremont Graduate School, Claremont, Calif., January, 1967. 29 pp. [Also published as ERIC document ED 074 832. Washington, D.C., August, 1973.]

Urges that teachers accept the dialect of their students.

Reidy, John. See Scholler, Harold, and John Reidy, eds.

Reinecke, John Ernest. "Marginal Languages: A Sociological Survey of the Creole Languages and Trade Jargons." Doctoral dissertation, Yale University, New Haven, Conn., 1937. 893 pp.

Reviews Creoles from a historical-sociological point of view, then describes several of the languages. Large sections on languages developed by the slaves. Comprehensive and thorough analysis.

————. " 'Pidgin English' in Hawaii: A Local Study in the Sociology of Language." *American Journal of Sociology*, XLIII (March, 1938), 778–89.

Many implications for Black English research.

————. "Trade Jargon and Creole Dialects as Marginal Languages." *Social Forces*, XIII (October, 1938), 107–18.

Includes slave language and discussion of development of Creoles. Notes that language of slaves was primarily a communication between masters and slaves.

Reinstein, Steven. See Cohen, S. Alan, and Steven Reinstein.

Reinstein, Steven, and Judy Hoffman. "Dialect Interaction between Black and Puerto Rican Children in New York City: Implications for the

Language Arts." *Elementary English*, XLIX (February, 1972), 190–96.

Discusses relationships between dialect, auditory discrimination, and reading comprehension of Blacks and Puerto Ricans in order to determine similarities. Notes that Puerto Ricans who interact with Blacks have a different dialect than Puerto Ricans in isolation.

Reisman, Karl. "Cultural and Linguistic Ambiguity in a West Indian Village," in Norman E. Whitten, Jr., and John F. Szwed, eds., *Afro-American Anthropology: Contemporary Perspectives*. New York: The Free Press, 1970. Pp. 129–44.

Long passages dealing with meaning and status of Creole, and of Creole as a symbol. Not oriented toward American Black English, but has many implications which can be applied to the study of Black English.

Rens, L. L. E. *The Historical and Social Background of Surinam Negro-English*. Amsterdam: North Holland Publishing, 1953. 155 pp.

Thorough analysis and discussion.

Rensink, Ken. "On Teaching Standard English to Speakers of Non-Standard Dialects—with Special Attention to Black English." Unpublished paper, University of Northern Iowa, Cedar Falls, 1971. 13 pp.

Conclusions based on evaluation of presently accepted methods of teaching standard English as a second dialect.

Rhodes, Odis O. "Some Implications for Teaching Reading to Speakers of Black Dialect." *Viewpoints*, XLVI (May, 1970), 117–47.

Reviews Black English problems, and discusses some of the features that distinguish it from standard English.

Rice, Frank A., ed. *Study of the Role of Second Languages in Asia, Africa, and Latin America*. Washington, D.C.: Center for Applied Linguistics, 1962. 123 pp.

Richards, Jack. "Social Factors, Interlanguage, and Language Learning." *Language Learning*, XXII (December, 1972), 159–88.

Describes five contexts for language learning and relates each to the social context for learning through the concept of interlanguage. Implications for Black English pedagogy.

Richey, Herman G., ed. *Early Childhood Education: The Seventy-first Yearbook of the National Society for the Study of Education, Part 2*. Chicago: National Society for the Study of Education, 1972.

Rideout, Ransom. *Hallelujah!* Metro-Goldwyn-Mayer, Culver City, Calif., 1929.

MGM film with all-Black cast. Filmed in the South, with focus on Black religion—the preachers, their sermons, and their audiences. Directed by King Vidor in semidocumentary style.

Riesman, Frank, and Frank Alberts. "Diggin' the Man's Language." *Saturday Review*, XLIX (September 17, 1966), 80–81, 98.

Study of second dialects, with discussion of benefits of Black English.

Riley, James Whitcomb. "Dialect in Literature." *Forum*, XIV (December, 1893), 465–73.

Pleads for literary dialectal equality for all dialects. Touches briefly on the Black language in the stories of Joel Chandler Harris.

Riley, William K. See Shuy, Roger W., Walter A. Wolfram, and William K. Riley. *Field Techniques in an Urban Language Study.*

———. See Shuy, Roger W., Walter A. Wolfram, and William K. Riley. *Linguistic Correlates of Social Stratification in Detroit Speech.*

Riley, William K., and David M. Smith, eds. *Languages and Linguistics: Working Papers, Number 5: Sociolinguistics.* Washington, D.C.: Georgetown University Press, 1972. 101 pp.

Among the nine articles are "Final Consonant Cluster Reduction" by David Minderhout; "The Black Preaching Style: Historical Development and Characteristics" by Anna Fay Vaughn-Cooke; "Dialect Differences in Testing the Language of Children: A Review of the California Language Tests" by Marcia Whiteman; "Toward an Ethnography of Contemporary African-American Oral Poetry" by Carolyn Fitchett Bins; and "A Look at the Form *be* in Standard English" by Ralph Fasold.

Rist, Ray C. "Black Studies and Paraprofessionals: A Prescription for Ailing Reading Programs in Urban Black Schools." *Journal of Reading*, XIV (May, 1971), 525–30, 583.

Notes that Black studies material and paraprofessionals may enhance basic reading programs for Blacks.

Roberts, A. Hood. See Malkoc, Anna Maria, and A. Hood Roberts.

Roberts, Hermese. "Don't Teach Them to Read." *Elementary English*, XLVII (May, 1970), 638–40.

Proposes a program for encouraging standard English reading for Black students at an early age, with emphasis on building dialect acquisition during the ages of four through six "when the child is ready."

———, comp. "Glossary." *Living Webster Encyclopedic Dictionary of the English Language*, 1971.

Glossary of about one thousand Black words, terms, and phrases.

Roberts, Margaret Mills. "The Pronunciation of Vowels in Negro Speech." Doctoral dissertation, Ohio State University, Columbus, 1966. 107 pp.

Speech pathology study. Determined that there were a lot of vowels "mispronounced" by the Black subjects. Conclusions suggest that Black and White speech can be distinguished, but that the principle differences are in pronunciation of vowels and diphthongs (Blacks "mispronounce" more) and in the fact that Whites have greater amplitude in the language spectra than Blacks.

Roberts, Paul. "Speech Communities," in Virginia P. Clark, Paul A. Eschholz, and Alfred A. Rosa, eds., *Language: Introductory Readings*. New York: St. Martin's Press, 1972. Pp. 335–43.

Robin, C. C. *Voyages dans l'Interview de la Louisiane (1802–1806)*. Paris: F. Buisson, 1807. 3 vols.

Vol. 3 (pp. 185–89) includes one of first major discussions of Creole languages in Louisiana.

Robinett, Betty W. "Teacher Training for English as a Second Dialect and English as a Second Language: The Same or Different?" in James E. Alatis, ed., *Report of the Twentieth Annual Roundtable Meeting on Linguistics and Language Studies; Linguistics and the Teaching of Standard English to Speakers of Other Languages or Dialects*. Monograph Series on Languages and Linguistics. Washington, D.C.: Georgetown University Press, 1970. Pp. 121–32.

Discusses areas in which there is an overlap between English as a second language and English as a second dialect, but also points out areas where different approaches are necessary.

Robinett, Ralph F. "Reading and the Oral Approach at the Secondary Level." Paper presented at the annual TESOL convention, March, 1968, at San Antonio, Tex. 6 pp. [Also in *TESOL Quarterly*, II (December, 1968), 274–79.]

Points out that nonstandard (Black) English represents its own language and not a lot of mistakes.

Robins, Clarence. See Labov, William, Paul Cohen, and Clarence Robins.

———. See Labov, William, Paul Cohen, Clarence Robins, and John Lewis. "Classroom Correction Tests."

———. See Labov, William, Paul Cohen, Clarence Robins, and John Lewis. *A Study of the Non-Standard English of Negro and Puerto Rican Speakers in New York City.*

———. See Labov, William, and Clarence Robins.

Robinson, Jay L. "The Wall of Babel; Or, Up Against the Language Barrier," in Richard W. Bailey and Jay L. Robinson, eds., *Varieties of Present-Day English.* New York: Macmillan, 1973. Pp. 413–50.

Discusses the necessity for English teachers to respond to the real needs of society. Indicates that teachers should help their students become linguistically confident in whatever dialect or language they speak.

———. See Bailey, Richard W., and Jay L. Robinson, eds.

Robinson, Virginia Hope. "Comparison of Standard English Patterns Produced by Head Start Participants and Comparable Children with No Head Start Experience." Doctoral dissertation, Arizona State University, Tempe, 1972. 168 pp.

Study of oral language shows no measurable increase in use of standard English forms by preschool Black or Chicano children participating in a Head Start program.

Robinson, W. F. "Cloze Procedure as a Technique for the Investigation of Social Class Differences in Language Usage." *Language and Speech,* VIII (January–March, 1965), 42–55.

Concludes that structural elements of working-class language and lower-class language are more predictable than that of the middle class in relation to writing. Indirect references to Blacks.

Robison, Helen F., and Rose Mukerji. *Concept and Language Development in a Kindergarten of Disadvantaged Children.* ERIC document ED 027 967. Washington, D.C., May, 1966. 228 pp.

Proposes a special kindergarten curriculum for the disadvantaged. Advises selection of specific language goals.

Rodgers, Carolyn. "Black Poetry—Where It's At." *Negro Digest,* XVIII (September, 1969), 7–16. [Also in Thomas Kochman, ed., *Rappin' and Stylin' Out: Communication in Urban Black America.* Champaign: University of Illinois Press, 1972. Pp. 336–45.]

Classification of Black poetry. Gives examples for each of ten classes.

Rogge, Heinz. "Das Erbe Afrikas in Sprache und Kultur der Nordameri-kanischen Gullahs." *Zeitschrift für Volkskunde,* LXI (1965), 30–37.

Rohwer, William D., Jr. *Learning Efficiency as a Function of Depiction, Verbalization, Grade, and Social Class.* ERIC document ED 013 854. Washington, D.C., 1967. 12 pp.

Experimental study involving students in kindergarten through third and sixth grades. Data suggests that lower-class (Black) students can learn as efficiently as middle-class (White) students in language arts.

Romeo, A. "The Language of Gangs." Unpublished paper, Mobilization for Youth, New York, n.d.

Emphasis on New York street gangs—Black and White.

Romero, C. Gilbert. Letter to the editor. *Commonweal,* XCV (January 14, 1972), 339, 359.

A few additional comments to an article by Dorothy Z. Seymour [*Commonweal,* XCV (November 19, 1971), 175–78]. Discusses Black English education.

Rosa, Alfred F. See Clark, Virginia P., Paul A. Eschholz, and Alfred F. Rosa, eds.

Rosenbaum, Peter S. "Prerequisites for Linguistic Studies on the Effects of Dialect Differences on Learning to Read." *Project Literacy Reports,* No. 2 (1964).

Notes that Black English and standard English have the same deep structure.

Ross, Stephen B. "On the Syntax of Written Black English." *TESOL Quarterly,* V (June, 1971), 115–22.

Analysis of the writing of Black students in five predominantly Black elementary schools in the Watts district of Los Angeles. Determined that rule-governed patterns exist in writing, as in speech.

———. "A Syntactic Analysis of the Written Language of Selected Black Elementary School Children with Reference to Social Variables." Doctoral dissertation, University of Southern California, Los Angeles, 1973. 195 pp.

Field study in the Watts section of Los Angeles. Concludes that Black English is a separate dialect from standard English. Data does not support Creolist theory.

Rounds, Stephen R. Review of J. L. Dillard, *Black English: Its History and Usage in the United States. Library Journal*, XCVII (September 1, 1972), 2,709.

Brief review.

Rubin, Louis D. *George Washington Cable: The Life and Times of a Southern Heretic.* New York: Pegasus, 1969. 304 pp.

Biographical study of the outstanding writer about New Orleans, its people, and their languages. Includes Black language dialogues.

Ruddell, Robert B., and Barbara W. Graves. "Socio-Ethnic Status and the Language Achievement of First-Grade Children." *Elementary English*, XLV (May, 1968), 635–42.

Rulon, Curt M. "Geographical Delimitation of the Dialect Areas in *The Adventures of Huckleberry Finn.*" *Mark Twain Journal*, XIV (Winter, 1967), 9–12. [Also in Juanita V. Williamson and Virginia M. Burke, eds., *A Various Language: Perspectives on American Dialects.* New York: Holt, Rinehart, & Winston, 1971. Pp. 215–21.]

Discusses various dialect areas from a geographical viewpoint. Challenges Twain's statements that he used three to seven separate dialects (including Black). Rulon claims to find no more than three.

Rundell, Edward E. See Williams, Frederick, and Edward E. Rundell.

Russell, Irwin. "Mahsr John." *Scribner's Magazine*, XIV (May, 1877), 127.

Dialect verse.

———. "Uncle Cap Interviewed." *Scribner's Magazine*, XI (January, 1876), 454–55.

Black verse poem.

Rustin, Bayard. "Won't They Ever Learn?" New York *Times*, August 1, 1971, Section 4, p. 7.

Brief debunking of the concepts of Black English being a separate language or dialect. Claims that Black English study is a "cult."

Rutherford, Philip K., comp. *Bibliography of American Doctoral Dissertations in Linguistics, 1900–1964.* Washington, D.C.: Center for Applied Linguistics, 1968. 139 pp.

Bibliography of a significant majority of doctoral dissertations in all areas of linguistics, including sociolinguistics, psycholinguistics, and dialectology.

Rutherford, William. "Teaching Reading to Children with Dialect Differences," in J. Allen Figurel, ed., *Reading Goals for the Disadvantaged.* Newark, Del.: International Reading Association, 1970, Pp. 114–23.

A few observations on theories of linguists working with Black English. Included are theories of William A. Stewart, Kenneth S. Goodman, and Walter Loban, as well as a countertheory by psychologist Allison Davis.

Ryan, Joseph S. "Black Is White on the Bay Islands." University of Michigan Papers in Linguistics, I (November, 1973), 128–39.

Ryckman, David B. *A Comparison of Information Processing Abilities of Middle and Lower Class Negro Kindergarten Boys.* Center for Research on Language and Language Behavior, University of Michigan, Ann Arbor, 1967. 16 pp.

Comparative study of social and racial class distinctions and cognitive abilities.

Rystrom, Richard. "Caveat Qui Credit (Let the Believer Beware)." *Journal of Reading*, XVI (December, 1972), 236–40.

Basic overview of the deficit-difference theories, with strong support of the difference theory. Notes that Black English is a constantly changing language and warns against overgeneralization.

———. "Dialect Training and Reading: A Further Look." *Reading Research Quarterly*, V (Summer, 1970), 581–99.

Results of a dialect training project in a rural Georgia Black school. Concludes that it was impossible to determine if dialect differences cause reading achievement problems.

———. "The Effects of Standard Dialect Training on Negro First-Graders Learning to Read." Doctoral dissertation, University of California, Berkeley, 1968. 149 pp.

Probes relationships between first graders' Black English and problems in beginning reading.

———. "The Effects of Standard Dialect Training on Negro First-Graders Learning to Read." Paper presented at annual meeting of the American Educational Research Association, February, 1969, at Los Angeles.

Revision and updating of doctoral dissertation.

———. "Negro Speech and Others: A Reply." *Reading Research Quarterly*, VI (Fall, 1970), 123–25.

Rejoinder to criticism by Kenneth Goodman in Vol. 5, pp. 600–603.

———. "Reading, Language, and Nonstandard Dialects: A Research Report," in James L. Laffey and Roger Shuy, eds., *Language Differences*

—Do They Interfere? Newark, Del.: International Reading Association, 1973. Pp. 86–90.

————. "Testing Negro-Caucasian Dialect Differences." Unpublished paper, Research and Development Center in Educational Stimulation, University of Georgia, Athens, January, 1969.

Experimental test methodology.

Rystrom, Richard, and Harry Cowart. "Black Reading Errors or White Teachers' Bias?" *Journal of Reading*, XV (January, 1972), 273–76.

Argues that teachers must listen to and understand the dialects of their students.

S

Sale, John B. *A Tree Named John.* Chapel Hill: University of North Carolina Press, 1929. 151 pp.

Includes Black English in dialogue.

Salzer, Richard T. See Woodworth, William D., and Richard T. Salzer.

Savage, A. Delorise. See Savage, John A., and A. Delorise Savage.

Savage, John A., and A. Delorise Savage. "Taped Studies of Black English Stress Peer Attitudes as a Factor in Inducing Language Change." *California English Journal*, IX (February, 1973), 30–39.

Analysis of speech of a Black male from Louisiana, and a female from Hong Kong, now students in a Los Angeles high school. Notes that peer motivation is the primary force in dialect change.

Saville, Muriel R. "Interference Phenomena in Language Teaching: Their Nature, Extent, and Significance in the Acquisition of Standard English." *Elementary English*, XLVIII (March, 1971), 396–405. [Also in Thomas D. Horn, ed., *Research Bases for Oral Language Instruction.* Urbana, Ill.: National Council of Teachers of English, 1970. Pp. 11–20.]

Discusses four main factors which act as possible barriers to a person's acquisition of standard English.

————. "Language and the Disadvantaged," in Thomas D. Horn, ed., *Reading for the Disadvantaged: Problems of Linguistically Different Learners.* New York: Harcourt, Brace, & World, 1970. Pp. 115–34.

General discussion of dialect, with emphasis on applied techniques. Includes discussion of Spanish-American, Acadian French, and Navajo, as well as Black English.

Sawyer, Granville M. See Dickens, Milton, and Granville M. Sawyer.

Sawyer, Janet B. "Dialects, Education, and the Contribution of Linguistics," in Richard Corbin and Muriel Crosby, eds., *Language Programs for the Disadvantaged: The Report of the NCTE Task Force on Teaching English to the Disadvantaged.* Champaign, Ill.: National Council of Teachers of English, 1965. Pp. 216–20.

Defines *dialect* and *language,* noting that there is a need for more information on linguistic differences between the nonstandard English languages and standard English.

————. "Some Aspects of Bilingualism in San Antonio, Texas." *Publications of the American Dialect Society,* No. 41 (1964), 7–15. [Also in Virginia P. Clark, Paul A. Eschholz, and Alfred A. Rosa, eds., *Language: Introductory Readings.* New York: St. Martin's Press, 1972. Pp. 430–37; Richard W. Bailey and Jay L. Robinson, eds., *Varieties of Present-Day English.* New York: Macmillan, 1973. Pp. 226–33.]

Saxon, Lyle, comp. *Gumbo Ya-Ya: A Collection of Folktales.* Boston: Houghton Mifflin, 1945. 581 pp.

Several Black folktales collected and recorded by the Writers' Program of Louisiana, a group of professional writers.

Scarborough, Dorothy. *On the Trail of Negro Folk-Songs.* Cambridge: Harvard University Press, 1925. 289 pp.

Includes lyrics and music to nine Black Creole songs. Discussion of Black folk music.

Scarborough, W. S. "The Negro Element in Fiction." *Proceedings of the American Philological Association,* XXI (1890), xlii–xliv.

Discussion and examination of Black English, noting that the language is subject to regional variations. Uses literature about Blacks for his primary emphasis.

————. "Negro Folk-Lore and Dialect." *Arena,* XVII (January, 1897), 186–92.

Cites importance of Black folklore and language to the study of language evaluation.

————. "Notes on the Function of Modern Languages in Africa." *Proceedings of the American Philological Association,* XXVII (1896), xlvi–xliii.

A few observations about sounds in African languages. Some implications for American Black English historians.

Scarr-Salapatek, Sandra. "Race, Social Class, and IQ." *Science*, CLXXVI (December 24, 1971), 1,285–95.

Discussion of environment vs. heredity involving intelligence and language. Environmental orientation.

Schneider, Gilbert D. "Black English and the Mass Media—Primary Sources." Paper presented at the Midwestern Regional Meeting of the American Dialect Society, August 2, 1973, at Ann Arbor, Mich.

Discussion of the use of the mass media for primary source data in Black English studies. Points out that contemporary dialect researchers have overlooked a wealth of data by not utilizing appropriate literature of the nineteenth century.

———. *Cameroons Creole Dictionary*. Bamenda, Southern Cameroons: Cameroon Baptist Mission, 1960. 258 pp.

Includes words likely to have been used by captured slaves.

———. *First Steps in Wes-Kos*. Hartford, Conn.: Hartford Seminary Foundation, 1963. 81 pp.

———. *Pidgin-English Proverbs*. African Studies Center, Michigan State University, East Lansing, 1965. 46 pp.

Presentation of African Pidgin proverbs, with annotations. Useful for comparative studies.

———. *A Preliminary Glossary: English* ≅ *Pidgin-English (Wes-Kos)*. Athens, Ohio: Ohio University Center for International Studies, 1965. 73 pp.

———. "The Uncle Remus Dialect and Its Value to the Serious Scholar." Paper presented at the Linguistics Colloquium on Black English, February 20, 1973, at Ohio University, Athens.

Discussion of primary source data in American literature. Includes discussion of the "backwash" of American Black language to Africa. Extensive comparisons of American Black English and African languages.

———. "West African Pidgin-English: A Descriptive Analysis with Texts and Glossary from the Cameroon Area." Doctoral dissertation, Hartford Seminary Foundation, Hartford, Conn., 1966. 242 pp. [Reprinted by the Center for International Studies, Ohio University, Athens, 1967.]

Extensive analysis of the West African (Wes-Kos) Pidgin English, the result of more than fifteen years of field research. Includes several passages in Wes-Kos, with translations. Excellent for comparative purposes to American Black English, as well as for its methodology.

————. *West-African Pidgin-English: An Historical Overview.* Athens, Ohio: Ohio University Center for International Studies, 1967. 24 pp.

————. "West African Pidgin-English—An Overview: Phonology-Morphology." *Journal of English Linguistics,* I (March, 1967), 49–56. [Also in Robert H. Bentley and Samuel D. Crawford, eds., *Black Language Reader.* Glencoe, Ill.: Scott, Foresman, 1973. Pp. 37–45.]

Brief linguistic analysis, with methodological implications for study of American Black English.

————. See Brasch, Walter Milton, and Gilbert D. Schneider.

Schneider, Mary. "Black Dialect: The Basis for an Approach to Reading Instruction?" *Educational Leadership,* XXVIII (February, 1971), 543–49.

Survey of research. Does not see value in use of dialect readers for Blacks.

Schneider, Murray. "Use Dialect Readers? The Middle Class Black Establishment Will Damn You If You Do. The Black Children Will Damn You If You Don't." *Florida FL Reporter,* IX (Spring/Fall, 1971), 45–46, 56.

Description of the Developmedial Reading Kit, developed by the author. Kit includes numerous passages in Black English.

Scholler, Harold, and John Reidy, eds. *Lexicography and Linguistic Geography: Festschrift for Hans Kurath.* Wiesbaden, Germany: Steinder-Verlag, 1973.

Schomberg, Arthur A. *A Bibliographic Checklist of American Negro Poetry.* New York: Charles F. Heartman, 1916.

First major bibliography of works of Black poets.

Schotta, S. G. "Differentiation of Dialects by Black Children in the Rural South." Paper presented at the Southeastern Conference on Linguistics, October 16–17, 1970, at Atlanta. 24 pp.

Schwartz, William Leonard. "American Speech and Haitian Creole." *American Speech,* XXIV (December, 1949), 282–85.

Schubert, Molly G. "The Use of Non-Standard Negro Dialect in the Written English of College Students." Seminar paper. Georgetown University, Washington, D.C., 1967.

Schwartz, William Leonard. "American Speech and Haitian French." *American Speech*, XXIV (December, 1949), 282–85.

Discusses influence of American Black English upon Haitian Creole.

Searle, Chris. *The Forsaken Lover: White Words and Black People.* Boston: Routledge & Kegan Paul, 1972. 108 pp.

A teacher claims that Blacks better identify with their "own language" and are forced to use the White man's language.

Sebastian, Hugh. "Negro Slang in Lincoln University." *American Speech*, IX (December, 1934), 287–90.

General word list from students at Lincoln University.

Sébillot, Paul. See Gaidoz, H., and Paul Sébillot.

Seidleman, Morris. "Survivals in Negro Vocabulary." *American Speech*, XII (October, 1937), 231–32.

Observations on a few archaic English words preserved in Black English.

Seidman, Dolores M. *The Influence of Disability Labels and Dialect Differences on the Semantic Differential Response of College Students.* Center for Research on Language and Language Behavior, University of Michigan, Ann Arbor, 1968. 12 pp.

Experimental test involving college students in education suggests future teacher-bias toward Black speech variables, /-ai/, /-ing/, /r/, and consonant cluster simplification. Data suggests that Puerto Ricans with Black contacts show Black English assimilation. Notes that the /r/ variable shows nearly complete Puerto Rican assimilation to some Black English patterns, but notes that Puerto Rican identity is maintained.

———. *Standard Oral English, Tenth Grade: Instructional Guide D.* Los Angeles Public Schools, 1967. 161 pp.

Bidialectal approach for Mexican-Americans attending Los Angeles schools. Pedagogical approaches for Blacks.

Sellers, T. J. "English Not Dialect." New York *Times*, June 9, 1972, p. 37.

A special assistant in the office of the superintendent of the New York school system calls Black English teaching "a cruel hoax."

Semmel, Melvyn I. *The Influence of Disability Labels and Dialect Differ-*

ences on the Semantic Differential Response of College Students. Center for Research on Language and Language Behavior, University of Michigan, Ann Arbor, 1968. 12 pp.

Experimental test involving college students in education suggests future teacher bias toward Black speech.

————. See Barritt, Loren S., Melvyn I. Semmel, and Paul D. Weener.

Serwer, Blanche L. "Linguistic Support for a Method of Teaching Beginning Reading to Black Children." *Reading Research Quarterly,* IV (Summer, 1969), 449–67.

Discusses the value of dialect readers.

Severson, Roger A., and Kristin E. Guest. "Toward the Standardized Assessment of the Language of Disadvantaged Children," in Frederick Williams, ed., *Language and Poverty: Perspectives on a Theme.* Chicago: Markham, 1970. Pp. 309–34.

Survey of literature of standardized tests available for use with disadvantaged and minority-group children.

Seymour, Dorothy Z. "Black Children, Black Speech." *Commonweal,* XCV (November 19, 1971), 175–78.

Basic discussion of Black English, intended for general audience. Points out several characteristics that distinguish Black English from standard English. Urges acceptance of Black English as a viable language. [See also Laird, Roland.]

————. "Black English in the Classroom." *Today's Education,* LXII (February, 1973), 63–64.

Basic overview of Black English. Includes chart to show the basic linguistic differences between standard English and Black English. Presents a few ideas on how teachers can handle the problems of Black English in the classroom.

————. "Neutralizing the Effect of the Nonstandard Dialect," in James L. Laffey and Roger Shuy, eds., *Language Differences—Do They Interfere?* Newark, Del.: International Reading Association, 1973. Pp. 149–62.

Shaffer, Stuart M. "The Measurement and Evaluation of Language Instruction." Paper presented at annual TESOL convention, March 5–8, 1969, at Chicago. 13 pp.

Discusses bidialectism studies in the Pittsburgh, Pa., public schools.

Shamo, G. Wayne. See Williams, Frederick, and G. Wayne Shamo.

Shapiro, Howard. See Sigel, Irving E., Larry M. Anderson, and Howard Shapiro.

Sharpe, Johnnie M. "The Disadvantaged Trapped Behind the Verb 'to Teach'." *College Composition and Communication*, XXIII (October, 1972), 271–76.

Briefly discusses nonstandard English from the cultural bias of the teacher.

Shaw, Cecil Taylor. "Developmental Aspects of Auditory Discrimination in Black English." Doctoral dissertation, Stanford University, Stanford, Calif., 1972. 96 pp.

Notes that dialect affects auditory discrimination, but that older children are better able to discriminate among spoken words than are younger children.

Shayer, Howard B. *The Stressed Vowels of Negro and White Speech of the Southern States: A Comparison.* ERIC document ED 057 640. Washington, D.C., April, 1972. 61 pp.

Uses the chorophone forms to analyze differences in Black and White Southern speech. Draws comparisons with Gullah, noting that the vowels of Southern Black English are closer to Gullah vowels than are the vowels in Southern White English.

Shearer, Lloyd. "Americans Who Can't Speak Their Own Language." *Parade*, June 11, 1967, 4–5.

Views of Black English education. Points to need for dialect differentiation by students and teachers. Extensively quotes views of Charles G. Hurst, Jr., and Kenneth S. Johnson. Includes thirteen-phrase vocabulary of Black English.

Shelby, Gertrude Matthews. See Stoney, Samuel Gaillard, and Gertrude Matthews Shelby.

Sheppard, Lila. "Talk Written Down." *Elementary English*, XLI (January, 1964), 40–43, 61. [Also in Eldonna L. Evertts, ed., *Dimensions of Dialect*. Champaign, Ill.: National Council of Teachers of English, 1967. Pp. 52–56.]

Describes her program of teaching reading and writing simultaneously in classrooms where there are nonstandard English speakers.

Shiels, Marie Eileen, "Dialects in Contact: A Sociolinguistic Analysis of Four Phonological Variables of Puerto Rican English and Black English in Harlem." Doctoral dissertation, Washington, D.C.: Georgetown University, 1972. 270 pp.

Study of language contact between Blacks and second-generation Puerto Ricans in Harlem. Analysis of the four phonological variables, /ai/, /-ing/, /r/, and consonant cluster simplification. Data suggests that Puerto Ricans with Black contacts show Black English assimilation. Notes that the /r/ variable shows nearly complete Puerto Rican assimilation to some Black English patterns, but notes that Puerto Rican identity is maintained.

Shipman, Virginia C. See Olim, Ellis G., Robert D. Hess, and Virginia C. Shipman.

Shores, David L., ed. *Contemporary English: Change and Variation.* Philadelphia: J. B. Lippincott, 1972. 380 pp.

Anthology of articles on American dialects. Introductions to various sections by Irwin Feigenbaum, Philip B. Gove, and Roger W. Shuy. Sections (and authors) are "Standard and Nonstandard English: Temporal, Regional, and Social Variation" (Morton W. Bloomfield, Jean Malmstrom, Raven I. McDavid, Jr., Ralph W. Fasold and Walter A. Wolfram, William A. Stewart, A. L. Davis); "Standard English: The Problem of Definition" (Thomas Pyles, John S. Kenyon, Patrick E. Kilburn, Martin Joos, and David DeCamp); "Standard and Nonstandard English: Learning and Teaching Problems" (Morton W. Bloomfield, Archibald A. Hill, Virginia F. Allen, Irwin Feigenbaum, Roger W. Shuy, J. L. Dillard, Kenneth S. Goodman, Rudolph C. Troike, and James Sledd).

Short, Jerry G. See Groper, George, Jerry G. Short, Audrey Holland, and Jacqueline Liebergott.

Shrigley, Robert L. "Learning African English." *Elementary English,* XLIX (January, 1972), 62–63.

Brief review for elementary education teachers.

Shriner, Thomas, and Lynn Miner. *The Culturally Disadvantaged Child's Learning of English Morphology.* Children's Research Center, University of Illinois, Urbana, n.d.

Several applications to Black English studies and pedagogy.

———. "Morphological Structures in the Language of Disadvantaged and Advantaged Children." *Journal of Speech and Hearing Research,* XI (September, 1968), 605–10.

Found no measurable differences in abilities of twenty-five disadvantaged children and twenty-five advantaged children to apply standard morphological rules to unfamiliar situations.

Shulman, David. "Words from the Southern Negro." *American Speech,* XII (October, 1937), 243.

Presents questions of *copesetic* and *cuffy* as being "colored" words.

Shuy, Roger W. "Bonnie and Clyde Tactics in English Teaching." Paper presented at annual convention of the National Council of Teachers of English, November 29, 1968, at Milwaukee. [Also in Alfred C. Aarons, Barbara Y. Gordon, and William A. Stewart, eds., *Linguistic-Cultural Differences and American Education,* special issue of the *Florida FL Reporter,* VII (Spring/Summer, 1969). Pp. 81–84, 160–61; David L. Shores, ed., *Contemporary English: Change and Variation.* Philadelphia: J. B. Lippincott, 1972. Pp. 278–88.]

Discusses current approaches to the problems of nonstandard and Black English, including eradication, biloquialism, nonstandard English for standard English speakers. Also discusses motivation for change and current literature.

————. "Current Theory and Knowledge for the Teaching of English." *English in Australia,* No. 22 (October, 1972), 25–45.

Discussion of bidialectal methodologies used in the United States for the language teaching of Blacks.

————. "Detroit Speech: Careless, Awkward, and Inconsistent, or Systematic, Graceful, and Regular?" *Elementary English,* XLV (May, 1968), 565–69. [Also in A. L. Davis, ed., *On the Dialects of Children.* Champaign, Ill.: National Council of Teachers of English, 1968. Pp. 10–14; William W. Joyce and James A. Banks, eds., *Teaching the Language Arts to Culturally Different Children.* Reading, Mass.: Addison-Wesley, 1971. Pp. 107–15.]

Strong plea that Black English not be considered to be "slovenly or non-verbal or inexact or lazy." Based upon extensive field study in Detroit. Argues that the Black English speaker must retain his own language for appropriate social situations.

————. *Discovering American Dialects.* Champaign, Ill.: National Council of Teachers of English, 1967. 68 pp.

General discussion of dialects. Brief mention of Black sociolinguistic history.

————. "Introduction" to "Standard and Nonstandard English: Temporal, Regional, and Social Variations," in David L. Shores, ed., *Contemporary English: Change and Variation.* Philadelphia: J. B. Lippincott, 1972. Pp. 3–6.

234

————. "Language and Success: Who Are the Judges?" in Richard W. Bailey and Jay L. Robinson, eds., *Varieties of Present-Day English*. New York: Macmillan, 1973. Pp. 303–18.

Discusses attitudes of sixteen interviewers for major Washington, D.C., companies in response to taped dialect selections. The results indicate that language is correlated with intelligence and ability in the minds of personnel interviewers.

————. "Language Problems of Disadvantaged Children" in John Irwin and Michael Marge, eds., *Principles of Childhood Language Disabilities*. New York: Appleton, 1972.

————. "Language Variation and Literacy," in J. Allen Figurel, ed., *Reading Goals for the Disadvantaged*. Newark, Del.: International Reading Association, 1970. Pp. 11–22.

Includes discussion and rationale of Black English as a separate language and not just poor grammar.

————. "Language Variation in the Training of Teachers." *Viewpoints*, XLVII (March, 1971), 6–13, 21–24. [Also in Johanna S. DeStefano, ed., *Language, Society, and Education: A Profile of Black English*. Worthington, Ohio: Charles A. Jones, 1973. Pp. 201–208.]

Discusses weaknesses of teacher training programs, arguing that a major deficiency is that such programs fail to include study of the role of Black English in society and education. Presents some suggestions for strengthening the curriculum.

————. "A Linguistic Background for Developing Beginning Reading Materials for Black Children," in Joan C. Baratz and Roger W. Shuy, eds., *Teaching Black Children to Read*. Washington, D.C.: Center for Applied Linguistics, 1969. Pp. 117–37.

Examination and analysis of reading and reading difficulty, with attention to four assumptions formulated by Morton Wiener and Ward Cromer. Argues that beginning reading materials should reflect the underlying language structure of the reader, rather than attempting to change that structure before the child can read well.

————. "The Linguistic Problems of Teachers," in Johanna S. DeStefano, ed., *Language, Society, and Education: A Profile of Black English*. Worthington, Ohio. Charles A. Jones, 1973. Pp. 196–200.

From "Language Problems of Disadvantaged Children." Discusses misconceptions held by teachers regarding Black English and makes several recommendations for better understanding of dialect by teachers.

———. "Locating the Switching Devices of Oral Language," in James Walden, ed., *Oral Language and Reading*. Champaign, Ill.: National Council of Teachers of English, 1969. Pp. 89–99.

Discusses the rules that allow a speaker to switch from one dialect to another in order to attain the goal of "functional bi-dialectism."

———. "Nonstandard Dialect Problems: An Overview," in James L. Laffey and Roger Shuy, eds., *Language Differences—Do They Interfere?* Newark, Del.: International Reading Association, 1973. Pp. 3–16.

———. "The Reasons for Dialect Differences," in Virginia P. Clark, Paul A. Eschholz, and Alfred A. Rosa, eds., *Language: Introductory Readings*. New York: St. Martin's Press, 1972. Pp. 344–49.

———. "The Relevance of Sociolinguistics for Language Teaching." Paper presented at annual TESOL convention, March 5–8, 1969, at Chicago. [Also in *TESOL Quarterly*, III (March, 1969), 13–22.]

———, ed. *Report of the Twenty-Third Annual Round Table—Sociolinguistics: Current Trends and Prospects*. Monograph Series on Languages and Linguistics. Washington, D.C. Georgetown University Press, 1973. 351 pp.

Collection of the papers presented at the 1972 Round Table at Georgetown University. Among the fourteen sociolinguistics papers is "Where Do Grammars Stop?" by William Labov.

———. "A Selective Bibliography on Social Dialects." *Linguistic Reporter*, X (June, 1968), 1–5. [Reprinted by Center for Applied Linguistics, Washington, D.C., 1968.]

Forty-six-entry listing of significant studies in the field of sociolinguistics.

———. "Sex as a Factor in Sociolinguistic Research." Paper presented at annual meeting of the Anthropological Society of Washington, February 18, 1969, at Washington, D.C. 15 pp.

Outgrowth of the Detroit study.

———. "Social Dialect and Interdisciplinary Conflict." *Journal of the Reading Specialist*, VII (October, 1967), 41–44.

———. *Social Dialects and Language Learning: Proceedings of the Bloomington, Indiana, Conference, 1964*. Champaign, Ill.: National Council of Teachers of English, 1965. 157 pp.

Proceedings of the "invitation only" conference of twenty-four of the nation's leading sociolinguists. Several articles of interest to students of Black English.

———. "Social Dialects and Second Language Learning: A Case of Territorial Overlap." Paper presented at annual TESOL convention, March, 1971, at New Orleans. [Also in *TESOL Quarterly*, V (September/December, 1971), 5, 19–21.]

Describes problems of territorial overlap in the study of social dialect. Calls for mutual assistance of researchers, rather than operation in isolation.

———. "Social Dialects: Teaching vs. Learning." Paper presented at annual convention of the National Council of Teachers of English, November 28, 1970, at Atlanta. [Also in *Florida FL Reporter*, IX (Spring/Fall, 1971), 28–33, 55.]

Outlines a few popular misconceptions about dialects and nonstandard English teaching. Urges that educators and linguists give "reasonable proof" that a second dialect can be consciously taught in schools.

———. "Sociolinguistic Strategies for Studying Urban Speech," in Maurice Imhoof, ed., *Social and Educational Insights into Teaching Standard English to Speakers of Other Dialects*, special issue of *Viewpoints*, XLVII (March, 1971), 1–25.

———. "The Sociolinguists and Urban Language Problems," in Frederick Williams, ed., *Language and Poverty: Perspectives on a Theme*. Chicago: Markham, 1970. Pp. 335–50.

Describes a sociolinguistic approach to urban (Black) language study.

———. "Some Considerations for Developing Beginning Reading Materials for Ghetto Children." *Journal of Reading Behavior*, I (Spring, 1969), 33–43.

Discusses development of reading materials. Uses three levels of data—lexical, phonological, and grammatical.

———. "Some Language and Cultural Differences in a Theory of Reading," in Kenneth S. Goodman and James T. Flemming, eds., *Psycholinguistics and the Teaching of Reading: Selected Papers of the IRA Pre-Convention Institute Held in Boston, 1968*. Newark, Del.: International Reading Association, 1969, pp. 34–47.

Outlines processive and positional methods of learning language symbolism, with emphasis on aiding children with reading disabilities as the result of minority-group status.

———. "Some Problems in Studying Negro/White Speech Differences." *English Record*, XXI (April, 1971), 179–85.

Discusses problems of the researcher versus the respondent. Also discusses aspects of developing relationship of linguistics to social concern.

———. "Speech Differences and Teaching Strategies: How Different Is Enough?" in David L. Shores, ed., *Contemporary English: Change and Variation*. Philadelphia: J. B. Lippincott, 1972. Pp. 331–45.

Brief overview of teaching problems and nonstandard language.

———. "Teacher Training and Urban Language Problems," in Ralph W. Fasold and Roger W. Shuy, *Teaching Standard English in the Inner City*. Washington, D.C.: Center for Applied Linguistics, 1970. Pp. 120–41.

Practical, applied approaches to assist teachers who have had little background in dialects and linguistics.

———. "Whatever Happened to the Way Kids Talk?" Paper presented at the National Conference of Language Arts, April, 1967, at Philadelphia. 19 pp.

A few "do's" and "don'ts" of language instruction, with applicability in Black English situations.

———. See Bailey, Charles-James N., and Roger W. Shuy, eds.

———. See Baratz, Joan C., and Roger W. Shuy, eds.

———. See Baratz, Joan C., Roger W. Shuy, and Walter A. Wolfram.

———. See Fasold, Ralph W., and Roger W. Shuy, eds.

Shuy, Roger W., and Ralph W. Fasold, eds. *Language Attitudes: Current Trends and Prospects*. Washington, D.C.: Georgetown University Press, 1973. 201 pp.

Collection of twelve papers presented to the special-interest group in language attitudes at the Twenty-third Georgetown Round Table, 1972. Among the articles are "Some 'Unexpected' Reactions to Various American-English Dialects" by Bruce Fraser; "Stereotyped Attitudes of Selected English Dialect Communities" by Roger W. Shuy and Frederick Williams; "Some Research Notes on Dialect Attitudes and Stereotypes" by Frederick Williams; "Objective and Subjective Parameters of Language Assimilation Among Second-Generation Puerto Ricans in East Harlem" by Walter A. Wolfram; and "Teachers' Attitudes toward Black and Nonstandard English as Measured by the Language Attitude Scale" by Orlando L. Taylor.

Shuy, Roger W., and Frederick Williams. "Stereotyped Attitudes of Selected English Dialect Communities," in Roger W. Shuy and Ralph W. Fasold, eds., *Language Attitudes: Current Trends and Prospects.* Washington, D.C.: Georgetown University Press, 1973. Pp. 85–96.

Study of social stratification of attitudes regarding speakers. Uses Detroit study by Walter Wolfram as its base.

Shuy, Roger W., Walter A. Wolfram, and William K. Riley. *Field Techniques in an Urban Language Study.* Washington, D.C.: Center for Applied Linguistics, 1968. 128 pp.

A report of the methodology of the Detroit Dialect Study (1966–1967). Includes procedures, fieldwork design and evaluation, and field-worker orientations. Discusses the questionnaire.

———. *Linguistic Correlates of Social Stratification in Detroit Speech.* United States Office of Education, Washington, D.C., April, 1967.

Report on goals of Detroit field survey; its field methods, analytical procedures, structural frequencies, and results from the seven-hundred-respondent survey. Major study involving inner-city Blacks.

Sigel, Irving E., Larry M. Anderson, and Howard Shapiro. "Categorization Behavior of Lower and Middle-Class Negro Preschool Children: Differences in Dealing With Representation of Familiar Objects." *Journal of Negro Education,* XXXV (Summer, 1966), 218–29.

Sigelman, C. K. See Von Raffler Engel, Walburga, and C. K. Sigelman.

Silverman, Stuart Harold. "The Effects of Peer Group Membership on Puerto Rican English." Doctoral dissertation, Yeshiva University, New York City, 1971. 113 pp.

Comparative analysis, with implications for Black English study.

———. "The Learning of Black English by Puerto Ricans in New York City," in J. L. Dillard, ed., *Perspectives on Black English.* The Hague: Mouton, forthcoming.

Simmons, Donald C. "Possible West African Sources for the American Negro Dozens." *Journal of American Folklore,* LXXVI (October–December, 1963), 339–40.

Brief discussion, with examples, of possible origins of the dozens.

Simms, William Gilmore. *Eutaw.* New York: Redfield, 1856. 562 pp.

Novel. Includes Gullah.

———. *Guy Rivers, the Outlaw: A Tale of Georgia.* London: J. Clements, 1841. 213 pp.

Novel. Includes Gullah.

———. *Guy Rivers: A Tale of Georgia.* New York: Redfield, 1856. 503 pp. Rev. ed.

———. *Mellichampe.* New York: Harper & Bros., 1836. 2 vols.

Novel. Includes Gullah.

———. *The Sword and the Distaff, or, 'Fair, Fat, and Forty': A Story of the South, at the Close of the Revolution.* Philadelphia: Lippincott, Grambo, 1853. 591 pp.

Novel. Includes Gullah.

———. *The Wigwam and the Cabin.* New York: Wiley & Putnam, 1845. 2 vols.

Collection of stories. Includes Gullah.

———. *The Yemassee.* New York: Harper & Bros., 1835. 2 vols.

Novel. Includes Gullah.

Simons, Herbert D. See Johnson, Kenneth R., and Herbert D. Simons.

Simpson, Dagna, Emily Pettigrew Morris, and N. Louanna Furbee. "Transcriptions," in A. L. Davis, William M. Austin, William Card, Raven I. McDavid, Jr., and Virginia Glenn McDavid, eds., *Culture, Class, and Language Variety: A Resource Book for Teachers.* Urbana, Ill.: National Council of Teachers of English, 1972. Pp. 202–13. (Includes audio casette of transcriptions.)

Transcriptions of the speech of a thirteen-year-old Puerto Rican girl in Chicago (recorded and transcribed by Simpson); a fourteen-year-old Black girl in Memphis (recorded and transcribed by Morris); and a ten-year-old Appalachian boy, born in Kentucky, in Chicago (recorded and transcribed by Furbee). Orthographic transcription of each subject is followed by phonetic transcription of a selected passage.

Sims, Rudine. "A Psycholinguistic Description of Miscues Generated by Selected Young Readers During the Oral Reading of Text Material in Black Dialect and Standard English." Doctoral dissertation, Wayne State University, Detroit, Mich., 1972. 195 pp.

Experimental study. Argues against dialectal readers on basis of her research with ten second-graders. Notes that dialect miscues cause no change in meaning and usually no change in deep structure interpretation.

Sithole, Elkin T. "Black Folk Music," in Thomas Kochman, ed., *Rappin'* *and Stylin' Out: Communication in Urban Black America.* Champaign: University of Illinois Press, 1972. Pp. 65–82.

Discussion of Black folk music and its dependence upon gestures and other nonverbal language to convey meaning. Uses Zulu lyrics for emphasis, but also notes similarities in American Black folk music.

Skinner, Vincent P. *Mountaineers Aren't Really Illiterate.* ERIC document ED 020 236. Washington, D.C., 1967. 3 pp.

Mostly oriented to "WASP" lower-class, but has implications and parallels for study of American Black English.

Slager, William R. "Effecting Dialect Change through Oral Drill." *English Journal,* LVI (November, 1967), 1,166–75.

A few applied practical suggestions for teachers involved with teaching English to nonstandard English speakers.

Slave Narratives: A Folk History of Slavery in the United States, from Interviews with Former Slaves. See Federal Writer's Project.

Sledd, James. "Bi-Dialectism: The Linguistics of White Supremacy." *English Journal,* LVIII (December, 1969), 1,307–15. [Also in Leonard F. Dean, Walker Gibson, and Kenneth G. Wilson, eds., *The Play of Language.* 3rd ed. New York: Oxford University Press, 1971. Pp. 19–26; Charlton G. Laird and Robert M. Gorrell, eds., *Reading about Language.* New York: Harcourt Brace Jovanovich, 1971; David L. Shores, ed., *Contemporary English: Change and Variation.* Philadelphia: J. B. Lippincott, 1972. Pp. 319–30; Virginia P. Clark, Paul A. Eschholz, and Alfred A. Rosa, eds., *Language: Introductory Readings.* New York: St. Martin's Press, 1972. Pp. 418–419; edited.]

Claims that the "basic assumption of bidialectism is that the prejudices of Middle-Class Whites can not be changed but must be accepted and enforced on lesser breeds." Suggests that bidialectism is based on concept of White chauvinism.

———. "Black English to World English: Or, Linguistics and Literature Again." Paper presented at the annual meeting of the South Central Region, American Dialect Society, November 1, 1973, at Fort Worth, Texas.

Reemphasizes his opposition to biloquialism. Suggests that studying language in terms of literature is less productive than examining the causes and effects of standard English in view of the emergence of national and regional English in other parts of the world.

————. "Doublespeak: Dialectology in the Service of Big Brother." *College English*, XXXIII (January, 1972), 439–56. [Also in Robert H. Bentley and Samuel D. Crawford, eds., *Black Language Reader.* Glencoe, Ill.: Scott, Foresman, 1973. Pp. 191–214; Richard W. Bailey and Jay L. Robinson, eds., *Varieties of Present-Day English.* New York: Macmillan, 1973. Pp. 360–80.]

Throws a few barbs at Roger Shuy and the biloquialists.

————. "On Not Teaching English Usage." *English Journal*, LIV (November, 1965), 698–703.

Urges that teachers disregard teaching standard English and replace it with teaching a respect for whatever dialect is being spoken.

Smith, Arthur L., ed. *Language, Communication, and Rhetoric in Black America.* New York: Harper & Row, 1972. 388 pp.

General reader. Includes "Should Black Children Learn White Dialect?" by Joan C. Baratz; "Negro Dialect: The Last Barrier to Integration" by Gordon C. Green; " 'F'Get You Honky!': A New Look at Black Dialect and the Schools" by Frederick David Erickson; "Sociolinguistic Premises and the Nature of Nonstandard Dialects" by Walter A. Wolfram; "The Ethno-Linguistic Application to Speech-Language Learning" by Grace Sims Holt; "The English Language Is My Enemy" by Ossie Davis; "Toward an Ethnography of Black American Speech Behavior" by Thomas Kochman; "Black English" by Henry H. Mitchell; "African Survivals in American Culture" by Romeo B. Garrett; and "The Rhetoric of Soul: Identification in Negro Society" by Ulf Hannerz.

————. Review of Clarence Major, ed., *A Dictionary of Afro-American Slang. Quarterly Journal of Speech*, LVII (April, 1971), 231–32.

Cites weaknesses as well as strengths of the dictionary.

————. *Transracial Communication.* Englewood Cliffs, N.J.: Prentice-Hall, 1973. 152 pp.

Smith, Arthur L., Deluvina Hernandez, and Anne Allen. *How to Talk with People of Other Races, Ethnic Groups and Cultures.* Monograph No. 1 of the Trans-Ethnic Education/Communication Foundation, Los Angeles, 1971.

Smith, Bertha Rowena. "Oral Communication Skills and the Black Urban Child in the Seventies." *Language, Speech, and Hearing Services in Schools,* III (1972), 68–72.

Smith, C. Alphonso. "Dialect Writers," in W. P. Trent, ed., *Cambridge History of American Literature, 1917–1921.* Vol. 2. New York: Macmillan, 1943. Pp. 347–66.

Smith, David. See Dwyer, David, and David Smith.

———. See Riley, William K., and David M. Smith, eds.

Smith, Donald H. "Imperative Issues in Urban Education," in *Teacher Education: Issues and Innovations,* 1968. Pp. 49–62.

Discusses problems of nonstandard language as an educational handicap, noting that as long as society perceives the language of Blacks as inferior, it will also perceive Blacks as inferior.

Smith, Ernie. See Key, Mary Ritchie, Laila Fiege-Kollman, and Ernie Smith.

Smith, Harley. "A Recording of English Sounds at Three Age Levels in Ville Platte, Louisiana." Doctoral dissertation, Louisiana State University, Baton Rouge, 1936. 182 pp.

A study of spoken English, both standard and nonstandard.

Smith, Holly. "Bidialectalism: A Review of Recent Literature." Paper presented at the annual conference of the National Council of Teachers of English, November, 1973.

———. "Black Culture in the Classroom." *Elementary English,* XLIX (February, 1972).

———. "Dialect Interference and Reading." ERIC document, in press.

———. "Standard or Nonstandard: Is There an Answer?" *Elementary English,* L (February, 1973), 225–33, 241.

Smith, Kenneth J., and Henry M. Truby. "Dialectal Variance Interferes with Reading Instruction." Paper presented at the International Reading Association Conference, April 24–27, 1968, at Boston. 11 pp.

Study of language gap between teacher and pupil, with focus on nonstandard and Black languages.

Smith, Reed. *Gullah.* Bureau of Publications, University of South Carolina, Columbia, 1926. 45 pp.

Recognizes Gullah as a legitimate dialect, based upon both vocabulary and phonetics. Also discusses historical and literary background and cites numerous examples of proverbs, spirituals, and sayings. Provides some transcriptions. Adheres to non-African–origins theory.

Smith, Riley B. "Hyperformation and Basilect Reconstruction." Paper presented at the annual meeting of the Linguistic Society of America, December 28–30, 1973, at San Diego.

————. "Interrelatedness of Certain Deviant Grammatical Structures in Negro Nonstandard Dialect." *Journal of English Linguistics,* III (March, 1969), 82–88. [Also in Robert H. Bentley and Samuel D. Crawford, eds., *Black Language Reader.* Glencoe, Ill.: Scott, Foresman, 1973. Pp. 90–96; Roger D. Abrahams and Rudolph C. Troike, eds., *Language and Cultural Diversity in American Education.* Englewood Cliffs, N.J.: Prentice-Hall, 1972.]
Discussion of cross-code ambiguity.

Smith, Veta. See Isenbarger, Joan, and Veta Smith.

Smitherman, Geneva. "Black Idiom." *Negro American Literature Forum for School and University Teachers,* V (February, 1971), 89–91, 115–17.
Briefly discusses eradicationist, bi-dialectalist, and legitimization views of Black English. Makes a strong argument for legitimization, using contemporary literature as a force toward the recognition of Black English as a real and legitimate language in American society.

————. "A Comparison of the Oral and Written Styles of a Group of Inner-City Black Students." Doctoral dissertation, University of Michigan, Ann Arbor, 1969. 157 pp.
Study which finds significant differences between speech and writing.

————. "English Teacher, Why You Be Doing the Thangs You Don't Do?" *English Journal,* LXI (January, 1972), 59–65.
Discusses the role of the English teacher in inner-city Black schools who are trying to eradicate Black English. Presents some ideas on dual dialect studies.

————. "God Don't Never Change: Black English from a Black Perspective." *College English,* XXXIV (March, 1973), 828–33.
Sharp, often emotional slap at scholarly linguistic research. Claims that the differences between Black and standard English are "style, not language." Attempts to write in affected Black English format.

————. "The Legitimacy of the Black Idiom." Paper presented at the

Conference on College Composition and Communication March, 1972, at Boston.

Review and discussion of the linguistic research being done on Black language and culture. Includes comparisons and contrasts between Black and standard English.

————. "White English in Blackface: Who Do I Be?" *Black Scholar*, IV (May–June, 1973), 32–39.

Sobin, Linda Lee Andrews. "Noun Plural Marker Deletion in the Speech of Black Children." Master's thesis, University of Texas, Austin, 1970. 59 pp. [Reprinted by Center for Communication Research, University of Texas, Austin, December, 1971. 59 pp.]

Concludes that there is no relationship between frequency of noun plural marker deletion and the presence of quantifier expression.

Solkoff, Norman. "Race of Experimenter as a Variable in Research with Children." *Developmental Psychology*, VII (July, 1972), 70–75.

Study determines significant differences in intelligence and verbal testing between Blacks and Whites in relation to race of examiner.

Solomon, Denis. "The System of Prediction in the Speech of Trinidad: A Quantitative Study of Decreolization." Master's thesis, Columbia University, New York, 1966.

"Some Negro Slang," in Nancy Cunard, ed., *Negro Anthology*. London: privately published, 1934. Pp. 75–78.

More than a hundred slang words in Black English. Includes words and phrases for skin-color differences.

Somervill, M. A., and J. F. Jacobs. "Use of Dialect Reading Materials for Black Inner-City Children." *Negro Education Review*, XXIII (January, 1972), 13–23.

Sorrells, Mary Suzanne Kirkman. "Black Dialect: Current Linguistic Studies and Black American Novels." Doctoral dissertation, East Texas State University, Commerce, 1971. 151 pp.

Determined that early Black writers often used dialogue-dialect consistent with the stereotypes of the times, while later writers were able to free themselves of social pressure and present a rather accurate portrayal of dialect.

Spaulding, Henry George. "Under the Palmetto." *Continental Monthly*, IV (August, 1863), 188–202.

Includes discussion of "Negro shouts" and "shout songs."

Spears, M. K. "You Makin' Sense." *New York Review of Books*, November 16, 1972, pp. 32–35.

Review of David Claerbant's *Black Jargon in White America*, and J. L. Dillard's *Black English: Its History and Usage in the United States*. Most of the review deals with Dillard.

Speers, Mary Walker Finley. "Negro Songs and Folk-Lore." *Journal of American Folk-Lore*, XXIII (October–December, 1910), 435–39.

Mostly from Virginia and Maryland.

Spencer, John, ed. *The English Language in West Africa*. New York: Humanities Press, 1971. 190 pp.

Introduction traces development of English into West Africa, from Pidgin to official British or American English. Many of the essays trace linguistic features of West African English and provide a base for research on American Black English.

Stafford, Jean. "Enriching the Idiom." Washington *Post, Book World*, September 17, 1972, pp. 8, 10.

Review of J. L. Dillard's *Black English*.

Stamps, Edith P. "An Investigation of Phonological Variations among Fourth Grade Black Children." *Ohio Journal of Speech and Hearing*, VII (March, 1972), 43–53.

Phonological investigation of the phonemes /l/, /r/, and /ð/.

Stanley, Oma. "Negro Speech in East Texas." *American Speech*, XVI (February, 1941), 3–16.

Argues that the speech of Blacks in East Texas is of the "plantation type" which was learned from slave ancestors who learned it from their masters.

Staples, I. Ezra. See Horowitz, David A., I. Ezra Staples, and Marjorie Farmer.

Starling, Marion Wilson. "The Slave Narrative: Its Place in American Literary History." Doctoral dissertation, New York University, 1946.

Discussion and analysis of slave narratives, including social and linguistic value as well as literary importance.

Stearns, Jean. See Stearns, Marshall, and Jean Stearns. "Frontiers of Humor: American Vernacular Dance."

———. See Stearns, Marshall, and Jean Stearns. "Vernacular Dance in Musical Comedy: Harlem Takes the Lead."

Stearns, Marshall, and Jean Stearns. "Frontiers of Humor: American Vernacular Dance." *Southern Folklore Quarterly*, XXX (September, 1966), 227–35.

Vaudeville humor by Blacks. Cites some examples of the language of the Black vaudevillians.

———. "Vernacular Dance in Musical Comedy: Harlem Takes the Lead." *New York Folklore Quarterly*, XXII (December, 1966), 251–61.

Stein, Annette S. *Analysis of Word Frequencies in the Spoken Language of Adult Black Illiterates*. Department of Elementary and Remedial Education, State University of New York, Buffalo, September 1972. 78 pp.

Includes discussion of development of vocabulary list for purposes of reducing Black illiteracy.

Steinig, Wolfgang. See Hess-Lüttich, Ernest W. B., and Wolfgang Steinig.

Stephens, Mary Irene Cattran. "Elicited Imitation of Selected Features in Black English and Standard English in Head Start Children." Doctoral dissertation, Purdue University, West Lafayette, Ind., 1972. 46 pp.

Concludes that, of sample group of one hundred, Blacks are better in Black English than in standard English.

Stephenson, Bobby L. "An Investigation of the Linguistic Abilities of Negro and White Children from Four Socioeconomic Status Levels." N.p., May, 1970. 92 pp.

Stephenson, Bobby L., and William O. Gay. "Psycholinguistic Abilities of Black and White Children from Four SES Levels." *Exceptional Children*, XXXVIII (June, 1972), 705–709.

Study indicates that socioeconomic status has little influence on psycholinguistic abilities of Blacks, but that it does influence psycholinguistic abilities of Whites.

Stern, Carolyn. *Preschool Language Project*. ERIC document ED 015 055. Washington, D.C., June, 1967. 4 pp.

Brief discussion of project involving language abilities of the disadvantaged.

———. See Gupta, Willa, and Carolyn Stern.

———. See Keislar, Evan, and Carolyn Stern.

Stern, Carolyn, and Willa Gupta. "Echoic Responding of Disadvantaged

Preschool Children as a Function of the Type of Speech Modeled."
Journal of School Psychology, VIII (March, 1970), 24–27.

Findings question the validity of the assumption that children can
learn more readily in a familiar dialect than in an unfamiliar dialect.

Stern, Carolyn, and Evan Keislar. "Comparative Effectiveness of Echoic and
Modeling Procedures in Language Instruction with Culturally Disadvantaged Children." Paper presented at annual meeting of the
American Psychological Association, August, 1968, at San Francisco.
14 pp.

Data suggests that modeling procedures rather than echoic prompt-
ing will produce better-structured sentences.

———. *An Experimental Investigation of the Use of Dialect vs. Standard
English as a Language of Instruction.* Washington, D.C.: United
States Government Printing Office, Project No. IED 55–1–12.

Stern, Carolyn, and Avima Lombard. *Head Start Research and Evaluation.*
University of California at Los Angeles, November, 1967. 134 pp.

Stewart, Barbara H. " 'Sesame Street': A Linguistic Detour for Black Language Speakers." *Black World,* XXII (August, 1973), 12–20.

Opposition to what she defines as the "verbal deprivation" concepts of
the television show "Sesame Street."

Stewart, Robert David. "The Oral Language of the Inner City Black Child:
Syntactic Maturity and Vocabulary Diversity." Doctoral dissertation,
Indiana University, Bloomington, 1972.

Study of the developmental patterns of syntactic maturity. Data
suggests that Black inner-city children are similar to White middle-
class children in pattern development.

Stewart, Sadie E. "Seven Folk-Tales from the Sea Islands, South Carolina." *Journal of American Folk-Lore,* XXXII (July–September, 1919),
394–96.

Stewart, William A. "Continuity and Change in American Negro Dialects."
Florida FL Reporter, VI (Spring, 1968), 3. [Also in Frederick Wil-
liams, ed., *Language and Poverty: Perspectives on a Theme.* Chi-
cago: Markham, 1970. Pp. 362–76; Walt Wolfram and Nona H.
Clarke, eds., *Black-White Speech Relationships.* Washington, D.C.:
Center for Applied Linguistics, 1971. Pp. 51–73; David L. Shores,
ed., *Contemporary English: Change and Variation.* Philadelphia:
J. B. Lippincott, 1972. Pp. 96–106; Harold B. Allen and Gary N.
Underwood, eds., *Readings in American Dialectology.* New York:

Appleton-Century-Crofts, 1971. Pp. 454–65; Robert H. Bentley and Samuel D. Crawford, eds., *Black Language Reader*. Glencoe, Ill.: Scott, Foresman, 1973. Pp. 55–69; J. L. Dillard, ed., *Perspectives on Black English*. The Hague: Mouton, forthcoming.]

Cites evidence of African influence in the structure of American Black English, and notes creolization. Compares grammatical patterns of Black English, White standard and nonstandard English, Gullah, English-based Creoles, and West African Pidgin English. Includes history of Black English since the Civil War.

———. "Creolization in the Carribbean," in Frank A. Rice, ed., *Study of the Role of Second Languages in Asia, Africa, and Latin America*. Washington, D.C.: Center for Applied Linguistics, 1962. Pp. 34–53.

Historical developments and consequences of Creole languages in the Caribbean area and Louisiana. Cites five main Creoles and discusses the geographical areas of each.

———. "Current Issues in the Use of Negro Dialect in Beginning Reading Texts." Paper presented at the Southern Conference on Language Teaching, February 20, 1970, at Jacksonville, Fla.

Discusses relationships between dialect interference hypothesis and the use of dialect readers. Also examines some of the reasons why the Black dialect readers are opposed by some linguists, educators, and the lay public. Suggests that dialect interference in beginning reading can be alleviated through the use of Black dialect readers.

———. "Current Issues in the Use of Negro Dialect in Beginning Reading Texts." *Florida FL Reporter*, VIII (Spring/Fall, 1970), 3–7.

Expansion and revision of paper presented at Southern Conference on Language Teaching, February 20, 1970, at Jacksonville, Fla.

———. "Facts and Issues Concerning Black Dialect." *English Record*, XXI (April, 1971), 121–35.

Text of an essay, "The Dialect of the Black American," produced by the Community Relations Division of Western Electric of New York. General discussion of Black English; outlines several features.

———. "Foreign Language Teaching Methods in Quasi-Foreign Language Situations," in Ralph W. Fasold and Roger W. Shuy, eds., *Teaching Standard English in the Inner City*. Washington, D.C.: Center for Applied Linguistics, 1970. Pp. 1–19.

Urges further development of foreign language teaching methods in the teaching of standard English to Black English speakers. Also discusses some of the features of Black English.

249

—————. "Historical and Structural Bases for the Recognition of Negro Dialect," in James E. Alatis, ed., *Report of the Twentieth Annual Roundtable Meeting on Linguistics and Language Studies: Linguistics and the Teaching of Standard English to Speakers of Other Languages or Dialects*. Monograph Series on Languages and Linguistics. Washington, D.C.: Georgetown University Press, 1970. Pp. 239–47.

Discusses bases for challenge of European-derived concept of Black English. Sees three bases—historical, comparative, synchronic.

—————. *Language and Communication Problems in Southern Appalachia*. Washington, D.C.: Center for Applied Linguistics, 1967. 43 pp.

Identification of the Appalachian dialects of Mountain Speech and Black English, including comparisons and contrasts with standard English. Includes suggestions for effective teaching of standard English to nonstandard English speakers. Advises use of dialect readers, development of pronunciation guides, specialized teaching programs, and further research into the languages of Appalachia.

—————. "Language Learning and Teaching in Appalachia." *Appalachia*, IV (July, 1971), 27–34.

Discusses Black English languages of Appalachia, with primary focus being directed to teachers. Includes table of basic differences among Mountain, Black, and standard English.

—————. "Negro and White Speech: Continuities and Discontinuities." *Acta Symbolica*, II (Spring, 1971), 42–43.

Brief historical look at contact of Europeans with African languages.

—————, ed. *Non-Standard Speech and the Teaching of English*. Washington, D.C.: Center for Applied Linguistics, 1964. 32 pp.

Discusses need for teaching standard English to Black English speakers, but in a foreign-language situation.

—————. "Non-Standard Speech Patterns." *Baltimore Bulletin of Education*, XLIII (1966–67), 52–65.

Detailed account of origins and development of Black English from slavery to the present. Traces development of Pidgin English. Several insights into sociocultural background.

—————. "Observations on the Problems of Defining Negro Dialect." Paper presented at Conference on the Language Component in the Training of Teachers of English and Reading, April, 1966, at Washington, D.C.

First public recognition of the uninflected *be* in Black English. Defines the distinctions between Black English and White standard English, and discusses the problems which accompany such a definition.

———. "Observations (1966) on the Problems of Defining Negro Dialect." *Florida FL Reporter*, IX (Spring/Fall, 1971), 47–49, 57. [Also in J. L. Dillard, ed., *Perspectives on Black English*. The Hague: Mouton, forthcoming.]

Edited and modified version of an April, 1966, conference paper.

———. "On the Use of Negro Dialect in the Teaching of Reading," in Joan C. Baratz and Roger W. Shuy, eds., *Teaching Black Children to Read*. Washington, D.C.: Center for Applied Linguistics, 1969. Pp. 156–219. [Also in Johanna S. DeStefano, ed., *Language, Society, and Education: A Profile of Black English*. Worthington, Ohio: Charles A. Jones, 1973, Pp. 276–90.]

Overview of problems encountered in teaching reading in a foreign language. Draws comparisons to teaching reading in a second dialect. Discusses three theories of reading instruction and presents a three-step process of moving from written dialect to written standard English.

———. "An Outline of Linguistic Typology for Describing Multi-Lingualism," in Frank A. Rice, ed., *The Study of the Role of Second Languages in Asia, Africa, and Latin America*. Washington, D.C.: Center for Applied Linguistics, 1962. Pp. 15–25.

Describes a sociolinguistic typology developed especially for use in describing a national language, with references to pidginization and creolization of language.

———. "Partial Nonstandard Verbal Paradigm." Unpublished paper. Center for Applied Linguistics, Washington, D.C., 1966.

———. *Research in Progress—Social Dialects of English*. Washington, D.C.: Center for Applied Linguistics, September, 1967. 44 pp.

Report on thirty-six sociolinguistic studies. Not confined to Black English dialectology.

———. Review of Walt Wolfram and Nona H. Clarke, eds., *Black-White Speech Relationships*. *Florida FL Reporter*, X (Spring/Fall, 1972), 25–26, 55–56.

Unfavorable review of the Wolfram-Clarke book. Stewart charges that the editors had sociopolitical motivations for inclusion of certain material. Also charges that the dialect-geographer position (identified as Anglicist) is not properly represented, and that the editors failed to include nonacademic opinion on the nature of Black English.

———. "Social Dialect." Paper presented at Research and Planning Conference on Language Development in Disadvantaged Children, June 7–8, 1966, at the Graduate College of Education, Yeshiva University, New York.

Discusses problems in studying social dialects. Takes a look at problem of standard English speakers' analysis of nonstandard dialects.

———. "Sociolinguistic Factors in the History of American Negro Dialects." *Florida FL Reporter*, V (Spring, 1967), 11. [Also in Frederick Williams, ed., *Language and Poverty: Perspectives on a Theme.* Chicago: Markham, 1970. Pp. 353–62; Walt Wolfram and Nona H. Clarke, eds., *Black-White Speech Relationships.* Washington, D.C.: Center for Applied Linguistics, 1971. Pp. 74–89; Harold B. Allen and Gary N. Underwood, eds., *Readings in American Dialectology.* New York: Appleton-Century-Crofts, 1971. Pp. 444–53; David L. Shores, ed., *Contemporary English: Change and Variation.* Philadelphia: J. B. Lippincott, 1972. Pp. 86–95; Virginia P. Clark, Paul A. Eschholz, and Alfred A. Rosa, eds., *Language: Introductory Readings.* New York: St. Martin's Press, 1972. Pp. 401–11; Robert H. Bentley and Samuel D. Crawford, eds., *Black Language Reader.* Glencoe, Ill.: Scott, Foresman, 1973. Pp. 45–55.]

Strong argument for the acceptance of pidginization and creolization stages in American Black English. Uses literature of the antebellum era for emphasis. Points to internal conflicts between Creolists and dialect geographers. Discusses history of Black English language, claiming that Black field slaves spoke a true Creole, and suggests that traces of that Creole are present in modern Black English. Cites kinds of literary and comparative evidence which exist for determining the earlier stages of Black English. Also points out that the disadvantaged don't use verbal communication as much as the middle class.

———. "Sociopolitical Issues in the Treatment of Negro Dialect," in James E. Alatis, ed., *Report of the Twentieth Annual Roundtable Meeting on Linguistics and Language Studies: Linguistics and the Teaching of Standard English to Speakers of Other Languages or Dialects.* Monograph Series on Languages and Linguistics. Washington, D.C.: Georgetown University Press, 1970. Pp. 215–23.

Discusses the social and political views that shape and distort theoretical descriptions of Black English.

———. "Toward a History of American Negro Dialect," in Frederick

Williams, ed., *Language and Poverty: Perspectives on a Theme*. Chicago: Markham, 1970. Pp. 351–79.

Discussion of Black English history.

———. "Urban Negro Speech: Sociolinguistic Factors Affecting English Teaching," in Roger W. Shuy, ed., *Social Dialects and Language Learning: Proceedings of the Bloomington, Indiana, Conference, 1964*. Champaign, Ill.: National Council of Teachers of English, 1965. Pp. 10–19. [Also in Alfred C. Aarons, Barbara Y. Gordon, and William A. Stewart, eds., *Linguistic-Cultural Differences and American Education*, special issue of the *Florida FL Reporter*, VII (Spring/Summer, 1969). Pp. 50–53, 166; Johanna S. DeStefano, ed., *Language, Society, and Education: A Profile of Black English*. Worthington, Ohio: Charles A. Jones, 1973. Pp. 161–65.]

Urges that teachers develop linguistic competence in the basics of Black English. Presents concepts of basilect-acrolect.

———. See Aarons, Alfred C., Barbara Y. Gordon, and William A. Stewart, eds.

———. See Strickland, Dorothy S., and William A. Stewart.

Stewart, William A., and Joan C. Baratz. *Friends. Old Tales. Ollie*. Washington, D.C.: Education Study Center, 1970. Illustrated by Julie Shapiro.

Three dialect readers. Two books for each title—one in standard English, one in Black English with standard English orthography and Black English syntax. *Friends* (62 pp.) is a story about young boys. *Ollie* (54 pp.) is a story of a young boy and the people he meets. *Old Tales* (30 pp.) is a retelling of the tales of "Goldilocks and the Three Bears," and "Icarus and Daedelus."

Stockton, Eric. "Poe's Use of Negro Dialect in 'The Gold Bug'," in Albert H. Marckwardt, ed., *Studies in Language and Linguistics in Honor of Charles C. Fries*. English Language Institute, University of Michigan, Ann Arbor, 1964. Pp. 249–70. [Also in Juanita V. Williamson and Virginia M. Burke, eds., *A Various Language: Perspectives on American Dialects*. New York: Holt, Rinehart, & Winston, 1971. Pp. 193–214.]

Examines the dialect of Jupiter, Poe's only Black character. Bases conclusions on 1,031 words. Concludes this is a poor representation of Black speech by Poe.

Stoddard, Albert H. "Animal Tales Told in the Gullah Dialect." *Archives of Folk Songs* I, Library of Congress, Washington, D.C., 1949.

————. "Origin, Dialect, Beliefs, and Characteristics of the Negroes of South Carolina and Georgia Coasts." *Georgia Historical Quarterly*, XXVIII (September, 1944), 186–95.

Cites origins of Black speech. Notes that most Black speech is a matter of syntax, rather than phonetics or words developed from African languages. Claims that Gullah is becoming obsolete.

Stoltz, Walter S. See Bills, Garland, and Walter S. Stoltz.

Stoltz, Walter S., and Stanley E. Legum. *The Role of Dialect in the School —Socialization of the Lower Class Children*. Child Development and Research Center, University of Texas, Austin, August, 1967. 96 pp.

Data suggests that assimilation into a different subculture is not based upon the assimilation of the language, and that assimilation of language does not lead to assimilation into the culture.

Stoney, Samuel Gaillard, and Gertrude Matthews Shelby. *Black Genesis*. New York: Macmillan, 1930. 192 pp. Illustrated by Martha Bensley Bruère.

Traces the background of Gullah to England, but notes presence of a few African words. Most of book, however, is transcriptions of Gullah folk beliefs from the Bible, including views on "Creation," "Adam an' Ebe," "Abel an' de Guinea-Fowl," "How Come de Hump on Br' Frog Back," "De Secon' Sin," and "Cain an' de Goin's-On."

Stowe, Harriet Beecher. *Uncle Tom's Cabin: Or, Life among the Lowly*. Cleveland, Ohio: J. P. Jewett, 1852. 2 vols.

Classic tale about the hardships of a slave. Much dialect.

Strickland, Dorothy S. "Black Is Beautiful vs. White Is Right." Paper presented at annual meeting of the National Council of Teachers of English, November, 1970, at Atlanta. [Also in *Elementary English*, XLIX (February, 1972), 220–23.]

Presents seven instruction guidelines. Argues that Black English should be accepted by teachers as a legitimate, viable language.

————. "The Effects of a Special Literature Program on the Oral Language Expansion of Linguistically-Different Negro, Kindergarten Children." Doctoral dissertation, New York University, 1971. 127 pp.

Notes that it is possible to expand language abilities of nonstandard English speakers to include standard English without negating their own language.

————. "A Program for Linguistically Different Black Children." Paper presented at the annual convention of the International Reading Association, April 22, 1971, at Atlantic City. 13 pp. [Also in *Research in the Teaching of English*, VII (Spring, 1973), 79–86.]

Describes language program to add standard English to child's language abilities.

———. See Cullinan, Bernice E., Angela M. Jaggar, and Dorothy Strickland. "Expanding Children's Language in the Primary Grades."

———. See Cullinan, Bernice E., Angela M. Jaggar, and Dorothy Strickland. "A Language Expansion Program for Primary Grades: A Research Report."

Strickland, Dorothy S., and William A. Stewart. "Issues and Debate: The Use of Dialect Readers." *Reading Instruction Journal*, XVI (1973).

Argument by Strickland against use of dialect readers, with point-by-point rebuttal by Stewart.

Stronks, James B. "Chicago Store-Front Churches: 1964." *Names*, XII (June, 1964), 127–28.

Brief discussion of Black store-front churches of the south and west sides of Chicago.

———. "Names of Store-Front Churches in Chicago." *Names*, X (September, 1962), 203–204.

Listing of names of Black churches in Chicago.

———. "New Store-Front Churches in Chicago." *Names*, XI (June, 1963), 136.

Additional list of names of Black store-front churches.

Stroud, R. Vernon. "About Black People." *Hearing & Speech News*, XXXVIII (March–April, 1970), 6–9.

Includes brief description of the language.

Sullivan, Jane Ellen. "The Effect of Dialect Interference and Response on the Assessment of Auditory Discrimination." Doctoral dissertation, State University of New York, Buffalo, 1972. 156 pp.

Summerlin, NanJo Corbitt. "A Dialect Study: Affective Parameters in the Deletion and Substitution of Consonants in the Deep South." Doctoral dissertation, Florida State University, Tallahassee, 1972. 156 pp.

Study of lower-class students—ages seven to nine and fifteen to twenty—in second grade and in tenth through twelfth grades. Compares to college graduates. Phonological investigation notes differences in (1) simplification of alpha-voiced consonant clusters ending in /-d/ or /-t/; (2) loss of the postvocalic /-r/; (3) substitution of the stop /d/ for the fricative /f/; (4) substitution of the stops /d/ and /t/ and the fricative /f/, for the fricative /θ/. Uses statistical analysis to determine phonological differences.

————. "Linguistic Heterogeneity within Sociologically Determined 'Homogeneous' Groups." Paper presented at the annual meeting of the American Dialect Society, December 26–27, 1973, at Chicago.

————. "The Regional Standard/Standards: Variation from It/Them in the Oral Language of Lower Socio-Economic Black and White Students in a Rural Deep South County." Paper presented at the annual meeting of the South Central Region American Dialect Society, October, 1972, at Tulsa, Okla.

A portion of her dissertation.

————. *Some Systematic Phonological Variations from the Regional Standard in the Oral Language of Lower Socio-Economic White and Negro Students in a Rural Deep South County.* Office of Education, United States Department of Health, Education, and Welfare, Washington, D.C., January, 1973. Project 1–D–066.

Study of the pronunciation of certain consonants in rural Deep South areas. Developed out of her dissertation.

Surlin, Stuart H. "Projective Response to Racially Identifiable Speech by Racially Prejudiced and Non-Prejudiced Individuals." Paper presented to conference of the International Communication Association, April 22–24, 1971, at Phoenix, Ariz. 35 pp.

Exploratory study. Several initial findings support hypothesis that language determines one's perception of the socioeconomic status of another—that Whites tend to judge Blacks by speech as well as other stereotypes.

Swennes, Robert H. "Can White Liberals Teach Black English in Negro Colleges in the South?" *College Composition and Communication,* XX (December, 1969), 333–38.

Discusses the problems confronting white educators at Black colleges, including problems of language.

Szilak, Dennis. "Afro-Americanisms: Renaissance in the Revolution." *College English,* XXXI (April, 1970), 685–94.

Sees vital need to recognize Africanisms in American Black English. Points out some of the African-originated words. Attacks teachers determined to maintain English "purity" at the expense of Blacks.

Szwed, John F. "Musical Adaptation among Afro-Americans." *Journal of American Folklore*, LXXXII (April–June, 1969), 112–21.

———. "Music Style and Racial Conflict." *Phylon*, XXVII (Winter, 1966), 358–66.

The language of the "soul" and the language of music.

———. See Abrahams, Roger D., and John F. Szwed.

———. See Whitten, Norman E., Jr., and John F. Szwed, eds.

T

Taba, Hilda, and Deborah Elkins. *Teaching Strategies for the Culturally Disadvantaged*. Chicago: Rand, McNally, 1966. 295 pp.

Taber, Charles Russell. "The Structure of Sango Narrative." Doctoral dissertation, Hartford Seminary Foundation, Hartford, Conn., 1966. 248 pp. [Reprinted by Hartford Studies in Linguistics, Hartford Seminary Foundation, May, 1966. 2 vols.]

Linguistic analysis.

Taft, Jerome, and Melvin Tennis. *The Development of a Test to Assess the Occurrence of Selected Features of Non-Standard English in the Speech of Disadvantaged Primary Children*. Dade County Public Schools, Miami, Fla., 1968. 22 pp.

Study of special teacher language project in Dade County in the early part of 1967.

Tallant, Robert. *Voodoo in New Orleans*. New York: Macmillan, 1946. 247 pp.

Talley, Thomas W. *Negro Folk Rhymes*. New York: Macmillan, 1922. 347 pp.

Tarone, Elaine E. "Aspects of Intonation in Vernacular White and Black Speech." Doctoral dissertation, University of Washington, Pullman, 1972. 267 pp.

Study of the intonation patterns of Black and White speech, noting that Black English includes a higher pitch range and more rising and level final contours than standard English. Also notes that Black English speakers use a falsetto register with far greater frequency than do speakers of standard English.

————. *A Selected Annotated Bibliography on Social Dialects for Teachers of Speech and English.* Seattle: University of Washington, 1970. 41 pp.

Prepared for teachers needing a background in social dialectology. Not confined to Black English studies.

Taylor, Douglas. "Language Shift or Changing Relationships?" *International Journal of American Linguistics*, XXVI (April, 1960), 155–61.

A few observations about Creoles.

————. "New Language for Old." *Comparative Studies in Society and History*, III (1961), 277–88.

Discussion of origin and evolution of Creoles.

Taylor, Orlando. "The Black Student and His Language." Paper presented at the Conference on English—Black and White, March 4–6, 1971, at Purdue University, West Lafayette, Ind.

————. "Historical Development of Black English and Implications for American Education." Paper presented at Institute on Speech and Language of the Rural and Urban Poor, July 15, 1969, at Ohio University, Athens.

————. *An Introduction to the Historical Development of Black English: Some Implications for American Education.* Washington, D.C.: Center for Applied Linguistics, July 15, 1969.

Parallels paper presented at Ohio University conference.

————. "Should Black Children Be Taught White Dialect?" Tape recording of panel discussion at annual convention of the American Speech and Hearing Association, November 14, 1969, at Chicago.

Says that increased Black pride will help eliminate feelings by Blacks that they should talk the way Whites talk.

————. "Some Sociolinguistic Concepts of Black Language." *Today's Speech*, XIX (Spring, 1971), 19–26.

Discusses importance of studying Black English and the current dilemmas facing American Black English scholars in urban areas.

————. "Teachers' Attitudes toward Black and Nonstandard English as Measured by the Language Attitude Scale," in Roger W. Shuy and Ralph W. Fasold, eds., *Language Attitudes: Current Trends and Prospects.* Washington, D.C.: Georgetown University Press, 1973. Pp. 174–201.

Discusses development of the Language Attitude Scale (LAS), a Lickert-type test. Results of an LAS survey suggest that there are more positive attitudes toward Black English and language variation than is commonly believed. Notes more positive attitudes by elementary school teachers than by high school teachers.

Temple, Truman R. "A Program for Overcoming the Handicap of Dialect." *New Republic,* CLVI (March 25, 1967), 11–12.

Brief description of programs designed to add standard English as a second dialect for Black English speakers.

Tennis, Melvin. See Taft, Jerome, and Melvin Tennis.

Thomas, Dominic R. "Oral Sentence Structure and Vocabulary of Kindergarten Children Living in Low Socio-Economic Urban Areas." Doctoral dissertation, Wayne State University, Detroit, 1962. 267 pp.

Analysis of structure, grammatical errors, parts of speech, and vocabulary.

Thomas, J[ohn] J[acob]. *The Theory and Practice of Creole Grammar.* Port of Spain, Haiti: Chronicle Publishing Office, 1869. 135 pp.

Primarily Black-French. Written by the son of a freed slave. Original hypothesis is that Black Creole is a dialect developed by Africans from European languages. Study includes orthography, etymology, syntax, and interpretation idioms.

Thomas, William J. "Black English." Unpublished paper, Department of English, Wichita State University, Wichita, Kans., June, 1972. 4 pp.

A few comments on the failure of American society to recognize Black English as a language. Points to differences and similarities between Black English, standard English, and other American dialects.

————. "History and Structure of Black English." Unpublished paper, Department of English, Wichita State University, Wichita, Kans., June, 1972. 5 pp.

Discusses Blacks' first contacts with White Americans. Also discusses American Black Creoles, both history and features, as well as the "decreolization" of the Black language.

Thompson, Donald Eugene. "An In-Service Program Designed to Change Elementary Teacher Attitudes toward Black Speakers." Doctoral dissertation, Western Michigan University, Kalamazoo, 1973. 155 pp.

Thompson, Edgar T. *Perspectives for Research on the South: Agenda for*

259

Research. Durham, N.C.: Duke University Press, 1967. 231 pp. [See McDavid, Raven I., Jr., "Needed Research in Southern Dialects."]

Thompson, Peggie Bebie. "Language of the Negro Child." *Progressive,* XXXII (February, 1968), 36–38.

Reviews progress of the Urban Language Study, noting favorable teacher reaction. Presents a nontechnical explanation of Black English features.

Thompson, Sandra A. See Legum, Stanley E., Dale Elliot, and Sandra A. Thompson.

Thomson, Peggy. "Washington's Second Language." Washington *Post,* June 11, 1967, Potomac section, pp. 24–26, 28–30.

Discussion of Black English and Black English educational programs in the nation's capital. Interviews and quotes William S. Carroll, J. L. Dillard, Irwin Feigenbaum, and William A. Stewart.

Thornton, Barbara L. *Bibliography for a Research of the Literature in Non-Verbal Communication and Its Application, as Related to the Study of Black American Non-Verbal Communication.* ERIC document ED 070 108. Washington, D.C., May, 1973. 16 pp.

General bibliography of nonverbal language articles, but includes only a handful of articles pertaining to Black nonverbal language. Most of the 230 articles and books do include passing references or sections on Black nonverbal language, as part of its treatment of nonverbal language in general.

Thorpe, Virginia, ed. *Drums and Shadows: Survival Studies among the Georgia Coastal Negroes.* Athens: University of Georgia Press, 1940. 274 pp.

Study undertaken by the Savannah unit of the Georgia Writers Project. Describes customs and beliefs of the Georgia coastal Blacks, with a nonlinguistic transcription of the speech of Black residents. Includes a short glossary.

Tidwell, James Nathan. "Mark Twain's Representation of Negro Speech." *American Speech,* XVII (October, 1942), 174–76.

Argues that Jim's speech in *The Adventures of Huckleberry Finn* is an accurate portrayal of Black speech at that time.

Tinker, Edward Laroque. "Cable and the Creoles." *American Literature,* V (January, 1934), 311–26.

Biographical sketch of George Washington Cable. Includes discussion of Black language.

—————. *Creole City: Its Past and Its People*. New York: Longmans, Green, 1953. 359 pp.

Includes section on French Cajun and Gombo.

—————. "Gombo, the Creole Dialect of Louisiana." *Proceedings, American Antiquarian Society*, XLV (1935), 101–42.

General discussion of history and grammar of Gombo. Also discusses Gombo fables, proverbs, and sayings. Includes much transcription and translation from and into Gombo, Old French, and standard English.

—————. *Lafcadio Hearn's American Days*. New York: Dodd, Mead, 1924. 382 pp.

Includes brief passages relating to Hearn's research into Gombo.

—————. "Louisiana Gombo." *Yale Review*, n.s., XXI (March, 1932), 566–79.

This article contains a few misconceptions about the origins of Creole, but gives a description of the dialect.

Tinnie, Gene. See Legum, Stanley E., Carol Pfaff, Gene Tinnie, and Michael Nichols.

Tinnie, Gene, and Carol Pfaff. *Spelling-to-Sound Correspondences in Black English*. Southwest Regional Laboratory, Inglewood, Calif., January 21, 1970.

Todd, Hollis Bailey. "An Analysis of the Literary Dialect of Irwin Russell and a Comparison with the Spoken Dialect of Certain Native Informants of West Central Mississippi." Doctoral dissertation, Louisiana State University, Baton Rouge, 1965. 292 pp.

Concludes that the dialect of Blacks in Russell's poetry was an accurate representation.

Tomlinson, Loren R. "Accepting Regional Language Differences in School." *Elementary English*, XXX (November, 1953), 420–23.

General plea for acceptance of language variation.

Torrey, Jane W. "Illiteracy in the Ghetto." *Harvard Educational Review*, XL (May, 1970), 253–59.

Notes that although Black English has rules and is a language, it is regarded by the public as having low status and is therefore rejected. Points to negative attitudes of teachers.

—————. *The Language of Black Children in the Early Grades*. Department of Psychology, Connecticut College, New London, 1972.

————. "Teaching Standard English to Speakers of Other Dialects," in *Applications of Linguistics: Selected Papers of the Second International Congress of Applied Linguistics.* Cambridge, England, 1969. Pp. 423–28.

Preliminary report of larger study.

————. *Understanding the Grammar of Standard English: A Study of Children Who Speak a Different Dialect.* Washington, D.C.: National Institute of Child Health and Development, 1969. 155 pp.

Study of the spontaneous speech of twenty-seven Harlem Black children. Discusses effects of nonstandard speech upon learning another dialect.

Torrey, Jane W., and Linda Silverman. "Teaching Standard English Grammatical Morphemes to Speakers of Another Dialect," in *Proceedings of the 79th Annual Convention of the American Psychological Association.* Washington, D.C.: American Psychological Association, 1971. Pp. 531–32.

Trappey, Adams Shelby Holmes. "Creole Folklore in Phonetic Transcription." Master's thesis, Louisiana State University, Baton Rouge, 1916.

Traugott, Elizabeth C. "Principles in the History of American English—a Reply." *Florida FL Reporter,* X (Spring/Fall, 1972), 5–6, 56.

Reply to J. L. Dillard, "Principles in the History of American English—Paradox, Virginity, and Cafeteria," *Florida FL Reporter,* VIII (Spring/Fall, 1970), 32–33. Suggests that the answer to Black English historical factors is far more complex than either the Creolists or the advocates of British origins have recognized; that a synthesis of the two forces is the most likely answer.

————. "Why Black English Retains So Many Creole Forms." Paper presented at the annual meeting of the American Dialect Society, November 24, 1972, at San Francisco. 8 pp.

Basic overview of Black English history. Discusses the concepts of acrolect-basilect briefly. Oriented to Creolist-origins theory.

Traupmann, Jane. See Williams, Frederick, Jack L. Whitehead, and Jane Traupmann.

Troike, Rudolph C. "Receptive Competence, Productive Competence, and Performance," in James E. Alatis, ed., *Report of the Twentieth Annual Roundtable Meeting on Linguistics and Language Studies: Linguistics and the Teaching of Standard English to Speakers of Other Languages or Dialects.* Monograph Series on Languages and Linguistics. Washington, D.C.: Georgetown University Press, 1970. Pp. 63–73.

Urges that second-dialect methods recognize the differences between receptive competence and productive competence, as well as the relationships between them which allow teachers to build on receptive competence to develop productive competence.

―――. "Social Dialects and Language Learning: Implications for TESOL." Paper presented at annual TESOL convention, March, 1968, at San Antonio, Texas. [Also in *TESOL Quarterly*, II (September, 1968), 176–80; Alfred C. Aarons, Barbara Y. Gordon, and William A. Stewart, eds., *Linguistic-Cultural Differences and American Education*, special issue of the *Florida FL Reporter*, VII (Spring/Summer, 1969). Pp. 98–99, 165.]

Discussion of dialectology research studies with implications for development of action programs in the schools. Urges development of positive rather than negative stimuli in dialect teaching.

―――. See Abrahams, Roger D., and Rudolph C. Troike, eds.

Trout, Lawana. "Not Unteachable—Just Unteached." *NEA Journal*, LVI (April, 1967), 26–29. [Also in William W. Joyce and James A. Banks, eds., *Teaching the Language Arts to Culturally Different Children*. Reading, Mass.: Addison-Wesley, 1971. Pp. 281–85.]

Study of the manipulation of standard English words to reflect pejoratively against Blacks.

Truby, Henry M. See Smith, Kenneth J., and Henry M. Truby.

Tucker, G. Richard, and Wallace E. Lambert. "White and Negro Listeners' Reactions to Various American-English Dialects." *Social Forces*, XLVII (June, 1969), 462–68. [Also in Richard W. Bailey and Jay L. Robinson, eds., *Varieties of Present-Day English*. New York: Macmillan, 1973. Pp. 293–302; J. L. Dillard, ed., *Perspectives on Black English*. The Hague: Mouton, forthcoming.]

Listener identification test to measure social acceptability ratings of dialects. All groups—Blacks and Whites of various classes and regions—rated network standard English as being the most preferred dialect/language.

Tucker, Joseph C. "A Comparison of the Spoken Vocabulary of Low Socio-Economic Black Kindergarten Children, to the Written Vocabulary Found in Three Multiethnic Pre-Primer and Primer Basal Reading Series." Doctoral dissertation, Hofstra University, New York, 1972. 106 pp.

Notes that there is a high correlation between the words found in the language of Black and White kindergarten children. Methodology included use of Weppman and Hass word list, as well as Criterion word list. Points to a core vocabulary.

Tucker, Nathan Beverly. *The Partisan Leader: A Tale of the Future*. Washington, D.C.: D. Green, 1836.

Novel. Includes lengthy Black dialogue.

Tulane University Head Start Evaluation and Research Center. *Annual Report*. Tulane University, New Orleans, August 31, 1968. 83 pp.

Outlines Head Start research program involving letter recognition and identification. Study involves Blacks and Whites.

Turner, Darwin T., ed. *Black American Literature: Poetry*. Columbus, Ohio: Charles E. Merrill, 1969. 132 pp.

Brief anthology of Black poetry. Includes the works of Phyllis Wheatley, George Moses Horton, Paul Laurence Dunbar, W. S. Braithwaite, Georgia Douglas Johnson, Claude McKay, Jean Toomer, Countee Cullen, Langston Hughes, Arna Bontemps, Sterling Brown, Melvin B. Tolson, Robert E. Hayden, Owen Dodson, Margaret Walker Alexander, Gwendolyn Brooks, Dudley Randall, Naomi Long Madgett, LeRoi Jones, Don L. Lee, and Darwin T. Turner.

Turner, Lorenzo Dow. *Africanisms in the Gullah Dialect*. Chicago: University of Chicago Press, 1949. 317 pp. [Reprinted by Arno Press and the New York *Times*, New York, 1969; University of Michigan Press, Ann Arbor, 1973.]

Major research study of Gullah developed over a period of fifteen years. Turner's research findings reject earlier assumptions that Gullah was based almost entirely on English forms and structure. First large body of conclusive evidence of Africanisms in Gullah. Extensive word list, with significant notations on individual words. Includes complete linguistic analysis.

————. *An Anthology of Krio Folklore and Literature*. Department of English, Roosevelt University, Chicago, n.d.

Folklore from the Sierra Leone region of West Africa, believed to be where most of the American Black slaves originally lived.

————. "Linguistic Research and African Survivals." *American Council of Learned Societies Devoted to Humanistic Studies. Bulletin*, XXXII (1941), 68–89.

Strongly attacks theory of Gullah being poor English with few African survivals. Discusses problems of performing linguistic research, including problems of gaining confidence of the subjects. Points to academic problems in attempting to refute almost universally accepted authority of George Philip Krapp, Ambrose Gonzales, and Reed Smith. Points to over five thousand Gullah words he has traced to their African origins.

————. "Notes on the Sound and Vocabulary of Gullah." *Publications of the American Dialect Society*, No. 3 (May, 1945), 13–28. [Also in Juanita V. Williamson and Virginia M. Burke, eds., *A Various Language: Perspectives on American Dialects*. New York: Holt, Rinehart, & Winston, 1971. Pp. 121–35.]

General linguistic analysis of Gullah. Points out similarities between Gullah and African languages.

————. "Problems Confronting the Investigator of Gullah." *Publications of the American Dialect Society*, No. 9 (April, 1948), 74–84. [Also in Walt Wolfram and Nona H. Clarke, eds., *Black-White Speech Relationships*. Washington, D.C.: Center for Applied Linguistics, 1971. Pp. 1–15.]

Strong argument on the Black English theory of African influence as opposed to American-developed.

————. "Some Contacts of Brazilian Ex-Slaves with Nigeria, West Africa." *Journal of Negro History*, XXVII (January, 1927), 55–67.

————. "West African Survivals in the Vocabulary of Gullah." Paper presented at the annual meeting of the Modern Language Association, December, 1938, in New York.

Discussion of the African influence on Gullah.

Turner, Ralph R. See Hall, Vernon C., and Ralph R. Turner.

Twain, Mark. See Clemens, Samuel Langhorne [Mark Twain].

Twiggs, Robert D. *Pan-African Language in the Western Hemisphere*. North Quincy, Mass.: Christopher Publishing House, 1973. 282 pp.

Description of Black English, with emphasis upon its integration within the Black culture. Approaches the study of Black English— which he identifies as Pan-African Language in the Western Hemisphere (PALWH)—from a number of perspectives, but focuses upon pedagogical implications. Includes glossary.

Tyler, Ralph W. See Eells, Kenneth, Allison Davis, Robert J. Havinghurst, Vergil E. Herrick, and Ralph W. Tyler.

U

Udell, Gerald. "Concerning Black McGuffey Readers." *Acta Symbolica,* III (Spring, 1972), 63–64.

Suggests that Blacks consider limited use of Black McGuffey readers.

———. "The Speech of Akron, Ohio: The Segmental Phonology; A Study of the Effects of Rapid Industrialization on the Speech of a Community." Doctoral dissertation, University of Chicago, 1966. 355 pp.

Study of the speech of Akron, Ohio, including both a description of current speech (segmental phonology) and the effects on a speech community with a large influx of speakers from other regions (1920–1960). Includes investigation of Black speech, parallel to that of White standard English. Concludes that large increase in "other-dialect" population had great importance and effect on the speech of the native speakers.

Uldall, Elizabeth T. "[m?m], ETC." *American Speech,* XXIX (October, 1964), 232.

Brief notes about the "grunt of negation" in Black language.

Underwood, Gary N. "Problems in the Study of Arkansas Dialects." Paper presented at the South Central meeting of the Modern Language Association, October 30, 1970, at Memphis. 12 pp.

Puts more emphasis on regional White dialect than on Black English.

———. See Allen, Harold B., and Gary N. Underwood, eds.

The Use of Vernacular Languages in Education. Paris: UNESCO, 1953. 154 pp.

Dialect policy statement for acceptance of the student's first language or dialect, no matter what it is. Includes language atlas of the world.

V

Vance, Barbara J. *The Effect of Preschool Group Experience on Various Language and Social Skills in Disadvantaged Children.* ERIC document ED 019 989. Washington, D.C., August, 1967. 217 pp.

Intensive language-development program involving fifty students, thirty-three to fifty-six months of age.

Vanderslice, Ralph. See Pierson, Laura S., and Ralph Vanderslice.

Van Dijk, Pieter. *Nieuwe en Nooit Bevoorens Onderwijzinge in het Bastert Engels, of Neger Engels.* Amsterdam: n.p., n.d.

Language course text to teach Creole to Dutch immigrants to Surinam.

Van Hoffman, Nicholas. "The Acid Affair." Washington *Post*, October 26, 1967, pp. E1–E2.

Brief news feature. Notes that the language of the Haight-Ashbury section of San Francisco is primarily derived from the Black ghetto.

Van Patten, Nathan. "The Vocabulary of the American Negro as Set Forth in Contemporary Literature." *American Speech*, VII (October, 1931), 24–31.

Study of Black vocabulary in four books published in 1926–1927. Two of the books were written by Blacks and about Blacks; two were written by Whites, but with Blacks as central characters.

Vaughn-Cooke, Anna Fay. "The Black Preaching Style: Historical Development and Characteristics," in William K. Riley and David M. Smith, eds., *Language and Linguistics: Working Papers, Number 5: Sociolinguistics.* Washington, D.C.: Georgetown University Press, 1972. Pp. 28–39.

Discusses features of traditional styles of Black preachers.

Veith, Donald P. "Dialect and Linguistic Change." *California English Journal*, IV (Fall, 1968), 52–55.

Basic discussion about language and the nature of dialects.

Venezky, Richard L. "Nonstandard Language and Reading." *Elementary English*, XLVII (March, 1970), 334–45. [Also in Thomas D. Horn, ed., *Research Bases for Oral Language Instruction.* Urbana, Ill.: National Council of Teachers of English, 1971. Pp. 102–13.]

Advocates the "common core" approach—teaching materials which minimize dialect and cultural differences, noting that in extreme cases, standard English should be taught as a second dialect before reading instruction is begun.

Venezky, Richard L., and Robin S. Chapman. "Is Learning to Read Dialect Bound?" in James L. Laffey and Roger Shuy, eds., *Language Differences—Do They Interfere?* Newark, Del.: International Reading Association, 1973. Pp. 62–69.

Verna, Gary B. See Kligman, Donna Schwab, Bruce A. Cronnell, and Gary B. Verna.

Vick, Marian Lee, and Joseph Carlton Johnson II. *A Study of the Relationships between Primary Grade Pupils Labeled as Either Culturally Disadvantaged or Culturally Advantaged and Their Development of Certain Language Skills.* ERIC document ED 028 038. Washington, D.C., February 8, 1969. 16 pp.

Discusses interrelationships among the language-skill complex—grade and intelligence level and numerous sociological factors.

Von Raffler Engel, Walburga. "Black English, Topi e Bilinguisimo." *Rassegna Italiana di Linguistica Applicata*, III (1971), 111–13.

Brief study of the problems faced by English teachers in a Black English classroom situation.

———. "Language in Context: Situationally Conditioned Style Change in Black Speakers." Paper presented at the International Congress of Linguistics, 1972, at Bologna, Italy.

———. "Some Phono-Stylistic Features of Black English." *Phonetica*, XXV: 1 (1972), 53–54.

Notes that verbalization follows conceptualization, and that syntactic component is likely to follow phonetic component.

———. See French, Patrice, and Walburga von Raffler Engel.

Von Raffler Engel, Walburga, and C. K. Sigelman. "Rhythm, Narration, Description in the Speech of Black and White School Children." *Language Science*, No. 18 (December, 1971), 9–14.

Study in Nashville, Tenn. Notes that Blacks tend to use shorter communication units than Whites. Focuses on subcultural differences in style and content of oral language.

Voorhoeve, Jan. *Voorstudies tot een Beschrijving van het Sranan Tongo (Negerengels van Suriname).* Amsterdam: North Holland Publishing, 1953. 108 pp.

Study of Negro-English of Surinam.

Vukelich, Carol. *The Language of the Disadvantaged Child: A Deficient Language?* ERIC document ED 075 097. Washington, D.C., August, 1973. 13 pp.

Argues that Black English is not a deficit language, that Black English–speakers have linguistic competence.

W

Wakefield, Edward. "Wisdom of Gombo." *Nineteenth Century*, XXX (October, 1891), 575–82.

A number of Creole proverbs from Louisiana.

Walcott, Fred. See Marckwardt, Albert H., and Fred Walcott.

Walden, James, ed. *Oral Language and Reading*. Champaign, Ill.: National Council of Teachers of English, 1969. 112 pp.

Waletzky, Joshua. See Labov, William, and Joshua Waletzky.

Walker, Karen Van Beyer. "Black Language: A Study of the Linguistic Environments of the Black Preschool Children in New Orleans." Doctoral dissertation, Tulane University, New Orleans, 1972. 115 pp.

Notes significant syntactical differences from home and school environments. Calls for further research.

Walker, Kenneth. "Inner City Slang! You Have to Dig It to Know What's Being Said in Ghetto." *Milwaukee Journal*, January 9, 1969, Accent section, pp. 1, 2.

A Black teenager discusses use of slang among Blacks. Includes forty-six-word glossary.

Walker, Saunders. "A Dictionary of Folk Speech of the East Alabama Negro." Doctoral dissertation, Western Reserve University, Cleveland, 1956.

Study of folk speech of twelve east Alabama counties.

Walker, Sheila. "Black English: Expression of the Afro-American Experience." *Black World*, XX (June, 1971), 4–16.

Walker, Ursula Genung. "Structural Features of Negro English in Natchitoches Parish (Louisiana)." Master's thesis, Northwestern State College, Natchitoches, La., 1968. 112 pp.

Experimental research to test whether West African characteristics are present in written Black English of a Black-dominated section of Louisiana. Also urges linguistic training for teachers.

Walser, Richard. "Negro Dialect in Eighteenth Century Drama." *American Speech*, XXX (December, 1955), 269–76.

Brief historical-linguistic analysis of Black English as represented by playwrights of ten dramas of 1767–1798. Suggests that the Black English dialogue was not systematic and was probably created by the individual writers. Notes a dialect progression, however.

Walsh, John F., Rita D'Angelo, and Louis Lomangino. "Performance of Negro and Puerto Rican Head Start Children in the Vane Kindergarten Test." *Psychology in the Schools*, VIII (January, 1971), 357–58.

Data suggests higher vocabulary ability in Blacks than in Puerto Ricans, but lower abilities in other language traits.

Ward, Henry W. See Cronise, Florence M., and Henry W. Ward.

Wardhaugh, Ronald. "The Implications of Linguistics for Reading." *Florida FL Reporter*, VII (Fall, 1969), 3–4, 23.

Links recent research to the teaching of reading, finding a few implications of linguistics for reading achievement. Of comparative interest.

———. *Teaching English to Speakers of Other Languages: The State of the Art*. ERIC document ED 030 119. Washington, D.C., August, 1969. 26 pp.

Overview of resources, methodologies, and activities in TESOL.

Ware, Charles Pickard. See Allen, William Francis, Charles Pickard Ware, and Lucy McKim Garrison.

Warner, Don. *Reading Games and Activities for Disadvantaged Youth*. Omaha, Neb.: Omaha Public Schools, 1967. 27 pp.

Includes specific directions for conducting numerous reading game-like activities for both Black and White.

Warren, Maxine A. "The Relative Effectiveness of Three Approaches to Teaching Reading to Third Grade Negro Children." Doctoral dissertation, North Texas State University, Denton, 1968. 101 pp.

Study of the effectiveness of individualized approaches, basal-SRA approach, and basal approach.

Warshauer, Mary Ellen. See Dentler, Robert A., Bernard Mackler, and Mary Ellen Warshauer, eds.

Washburn, David E. "A Conceptual Framework for Multi-Cultural Education." *Florida FL Reporter*, X (Spring/Fall, 1972), 27–28.

Discusses the danger of social, as well as educational, assimilation. Urges schools to adopt curricula which include cultural pluralism in all facets, including language.

Waterhouse, Lynn. "The Acquisition of Code Switching." Paper presented at the annual meeting of the Linguistic Society of America, December 28–30, 1973, at San Diego.

Watkins, Floyd C. "De Dry Bones in de Valley." *Southern Folklore Quarterly*, XX (June, 1956), 136–49.

Watts Writers' Workshop. *From the Ashes: Voices of Watts.* Edited by Budd Schulberg. New York: New American Library, 1967. 277 pp.
Modern fiction written by Blacks.

Wax, Murray. "Cultural Deprivation as an Educational Ideology," in Robert H. Bentley and Samuel D. Crawford, eds., *Black Language Reader*. Glencoe, Ill.: Scott, Foresman, 1973. Pp. 215–20.

Wayne, Mary C. "Black English Features in the Writing Samples of Five College Freshmen: A Linguistic Analysis." Unpublished paper, n.d.

Weaver, Constance Waltz. "Analyzing Literary Representation of Recent Northern Urban Negro Speech: A Technique with Application to Three Books." Doctoral dissertation, Michigan State University, East Lansing, 1970. 245 pp.
Analysis of Black English in three books, with focus on concepts developed by William Labov and Walter A. Wolfram.

————. See Drzick, Kathleen, John Murphy, and Constance Weaver.

————. See Malmstrom, Jean, and Constance Weaver.

Webb, Patricia Kimberley. "A Comparison of the Psycholinguistic Abilities of Anglo-American, Negro, and Latin-American Lower-Class Preschool Children." Doctoral dissertation, North Texas State University, Denton, 1968. 108 pp.
Test of sixty children on Illinois Test of Psycholinguistic Abilities—Auditory Discrimination Test.

Weber, David. "The Influence of Dialect Differences on Immediate Recall of Verbal Messages." Doctoral dissertation, University of Michigan, Ann Arbor, 1967. 98 pp. [Reprinted by Center for Research on Language and Language Behavior, University of Michigan, Ann Arbor, 1967.]
Investigation of communication noise as related to syntactic, semantic, and phonetic variables in dialects.

————. "A Note on the Language of White Racism." *College English*, XXXI (May, 1970), 863–65.

Suggests that White standard English strongly reflects White racist attitudes and beliefs.

————. "Social Dialect Differences and the Recall of Verbal Messages." *Journal of Educational Psychology*, LX (June, 1969), 194–99.

Weber, Rose-Marie. "Dialect Differences in Oral Reading: An Analysis of Errors," in James L. Laffey and Roger Shuy, eds., *Language Differences—Do They Interfere?* Newark, Del.: International Reading Association, 1973. Pp. 47–61.

Weener, Paul D. "The Influence of Dialect Differences on the Immediate Recall of Verbal Messages." Doctoral dissertation, University of Michigan, Ann Arbor, 1967. 98 pp. [Reprinted by Center for Research on Language and Language Behavior, University of Michigan, Ann Arbor, 1967.]

Investigation of communication noise as related to syntactic, semantic, and phonetic variables in dialects.

————. "Social Dialect Differences and the Recall of Verbal Messages." *Journal of Educational Psychology*, LX (June, 1969), 194–99.

Data suggests that children should be required to develop standard English facility at an early age.

————. See Barritt, Loren S., Melvyn I. Semmel, and Paul D. Weener.

Welty, S. L. "Reading and Black English." *International Reading Association Conference Papers: Language, Reading, and the Communication Process*, XV (1971), 71–93.

Werner, Roland John, Jr. "Morphological Inflections of Black and White Children by Age, Achievement and Socio-Economic Levels." Doctoral dissertation, University of Missouri, Columbia, 1971. 126 pp.

Investigation of acquisition patterns of certain morphological inflections exhibited by Black and White children of different classes. Also investigates inflectional patterns used by mothers.

West, Earl H., comp. *A Bibliography of Doctoral Research on the Negro, 1933–1966*. Washington, D.C.: Xerox, 1969. 134 pp.

Includes all aspects of Black culture.

West, William W. "On Being Bi-Dialectal." *Commonweal*, XCV (February 11, 1972), 454–55.

Comments on the advantages of teaching standard English to speakers of Black English. Includes results of a questionnaire-mailer sent to socioeconomically successful Blacks for purpose of determining their opinions of the value of Black English studies or teaching standard English to Black English speakers.

W[eygandt], G. C. *Gemeenzaame Leerwijze om het Bastard of Neger-Englisch op een Gemakkelijke Wijze te Leeren Verstaan en Sprachen.* Paramaribo, Surinam: G. C. W., 1798.

Language course text to teach Creole to Dutch immigrants to Surinam.

Whaley, Marcellus S. *The Old Types Pass: Gullah Sketches of the Carolina Sea Islands.* Boston: Christopher, 1925. 192 pp. Illustrated by Edna Reed Whaley.

Presentation of the language of several Blacks living on the Carolina Sea Islands. Includes glossary, chronology, and vocabulary of about one thousand Gullah words.

Whitacre, Robert. See Jaffee, Cabot L., and Robert Whitacre.

White, Doris, comp. *Multi-Ethnic Books for Head Start Children: Part I: Black and Integrated Literature.* ERIC document ED 031 312. Washington, D.C., 1969. 38 pp.

Annotated bibliography of Black awareness literature for children in kindergarten through second grade.

Whitehead, Henry S. "Negro Dialect of the Virgin Islands." *American Speech*, VII (February, 1932), 175–79.

A character sketch, "Zachary and His Number Eleven Boots," is used to illustrate Black English on the American Virgin Islands.

Whitehead, Jack L. See Williams, Frederick, Jack L. Whitehead, and Leslie M. Miller.

———. See Williams, Frederick, Jack L. Whitehead, and Jane Traupmann.

Whiteman, Marcia. "Dialect Differences in Testing the Language of Children: A Review of the California Language Tests," in William K. Riley and David M. Smith, eds., *Languages and Linguistics: Working Papers, Number 5: Sociolinguistics.* Washington, D.C.: Georgetown University Press, 1972. Pp. 48–60.

Suggests that these tests be revised so that they will be dialect-free, or that one specific section would test standard English usage to measure improvement in learning it as a second dialect.

———. See Wolfram, Walter A., and Marcia Whiteman.

Whiteman, Martin, and Martin Deutsch. "Social Disadvantages as Related to Intellective and Language Development," in Martin Deutsch, Irwin Katz, and Arthur R. Jensen, eds., *Social Class, Race, and Psychological Development*. New York: Holt, Rinehart, & Winston, 1968. Pp. 86–114.

Study of verbal performance of first- and fifth-grade children to identify some of the specific background variables which are related to the development of linguistic skills.

Whiteman, Maxwell. *A Century of Fiction by American Negroes, 1853–1952*. Philadelphia: Maurice Jacobs, 1955. 64 pp.

A bibliography of works by Black authors.

Whitney, Anne Weston. "De Los' Ell an' Yard." *Journal of American Folk-Lore*, X (October–December, 1897), 293–98.

Title refers to Black English version of sword and belt of Orion. Discusses the need for knowledge of Black English studies.

————. "Negro American Dialects: I and II." *The Independent*, LIII (August 22, 1901), 1979–81; (August 29, 1901), 2,039–42.

Urges in-depth study of Negro dialects and their importance socially, historically, and politically. Also discusses why "Uncle Remus" stories are not accepted as Black dialect in many parts of the country, although the dialect is accurately portrayed.

Whitten, Norman E., Jr., and John F. Szwed, eds. *Afro-American Anthropology: Contemporary Perspectives*. New York: The Free Press, 1970. 468 pp.

Includes sections on cultural patterning, socioeconomic adaptations, Black culture, and ghetto ethnography, with separate chapters by J. L. Dillard, Thomas Kochman, and Karl Reisman.

Wiener, Morton, and Ward Cromer. "Reading and Reading Difficulty: A Conceptual Analysis." *Harvard Educational Review*, XXXVII (1967), 620–43.

Some directed implications in Black English teaching, but not specifically concerned with Black English.

Wiggam, Albert E. "Let's Explore Your Mind." Cleveland *Plain-Dealer*, July 3, 1949.

Briefly discusses the postvocalic /-r/, noting that anatomical features discriminate against the Black's ability to pronounce the standard English forms.

Wiggins, Antoinette Violet. "A Study of Dialect Differences in the Speech of First Grade Negro Children in the Inner City Schools of Cleveland, Ohio." Doctoral dissertation, Indiana University, Bloomington, 1970. 154 pp.

Concludes that variations exist in individual use of Black English verb forms, and that there are separate dialects of Black English in two groups of Black students.

Wiggins, Rudolf Valentino. "A Comparison of Children's Interest in and Attitude towards Reading Materials Written in Standard and Black English Forms." Doctoral dissertation, Ohio State University, Columbus, 1971. 135 pp.

Concludes that third- and fourth-grade Blacks are more interested in standard English reading material than Black English materials and are more positive toward standard English.

Wilcox, Roger. "Racial Differences in Associative Style." *Language and Speech*, XIV (July–September, 1971), 251–55.

Suggests that application of developmental word association model as expanded by Doris Entwisle may be useful in study of racial differences. Suggests that Blacks show developmental lag or deficiency in comparison to Whites. Urges remedial programs.

Wilkerson, Doxey A., comp. "Bibliography on Education of Socially Disadvantaged Children and Youth." *Journal of Negro Education*, XXXIII (Summer, 1964), 358–66.

Wilkins, Roy. Letter to the editor, *Crisis*, LXXVIII (August, 1971), 175.

Reprinted letter favoring Black English study.

Williams, Annette Powell. "Dynamics of a Black Audience," in Thomas Kochman, ed., *Rappin' and Stylin' Out: Communication in Urban Black America*. Champaign: University of Illinois Press, 1972. Pp. 101–106.

Williams, Clyde E. See Legum, Stanley E., Clyde E. Williams, and Maureen T. Lee.

Williams, Darnell. "Teaching Standard English as a Second Dialect." Paper presented at the Conference on English—Black and White, March 4–6, 1971, at Purdue University, West Lafayette, Ind.

Williams, Frederick, ed. *Language and Poverty: Perspectives on a Theme*. Chicago: Markham, 1970. 459 pp.

Anthology of twenty articles with the focus on language and the lower class. Authors are Joan C. Baratz, Basil Bernstein, Marion Blank, Courtney B. Cazden, Siegfried Engelman, Doris R. Entwisle, Vera P. John and Vivian M. Horner, William Labov, Paula Menyuk, Ellis G. Olim, Lynn R. Osborn, Harry Osser, Davenport Plumer, Roger A. Severson and Kristin E. Guest, Roger W. Shuy, William A. Stewart, David E. Yoder, Rita C. Naremore, and Frederick Williams.

―――. *Language and Speech: Introductory Perspectives.* Englewood Cliffs, N.J.: Prentice-Hall, 1972. 139 pp.

Discusses social aspects of language study, urban language research, attitudinal correlates of language, sociolinguistic development, and mode of concept.

―――. "Language, Attitude, and Social Change," in Frederick Williams, ed., *Language and Poverty: Perspectives on a Theme.* Chicago: Markham, 1970. Pp. 380–99.

Discusses stereotypes, speech attitudes, social status attitudes, attitudes of teachers toward nonstandard languages, and other factors that foster social change.

―――. *Psychological Correlates of Speech Characteristics: On Sounding Disadvantaged.* Institute for Research on Poverty, University of Wisconsin, Madison, March, 1969.

―――. "Social Class Differences in How Children Talk about Television." *Journal of Broadcasting,* XIV (Fall, 1969), 345–57.

―――. "Some Preliminaries and Prospects," in Frederick Williams, ed., *Language and Poverty: Perspectives on a Theme.* Chicago: Markham, 1970. Pp. 1–10.

Introductory discussion of poverty and theories of language differences between the disadvantaged and the advantaged child. Also discusses theories for enriching the child's language development.

―――. "Some Research Notes on Dialect Attitudes and Stereotypes," in Roger W. Shuy and Ralph W. Fasold, eds., *Language Attitudes: Current Trends and Prospects.* Washington, D.C.: Georgetown University Press, 1973. Pp. 113–28.

Examines the method for determining and measuring teacher attitudes about dialects and nonstandard English. Speculates on how dialect stereotypes appear to enter into the process of speech evaluation.

―――. See Natalicio, Diana S., and Frederick Williams.

―――. See Shuy, Roger W., and Frederick Williams.

Williams, Frederick, Charles E. Cairns, and Helen S. Cairns. *An Analysis*

*of the Variation from Standard English Pronunciation in the Pho-
netic Performance of Two Groups of Nonstandard-English-Speaking
Children.* Center for Communication Research, University of Texas,
Austin, July, 1971. 206 pp.

Attributes phonetic variation to phonetic interference between a
foreign primary language and English. Notes reduction in complexity of segments, decreasing with age. Points to differing phonological rules between Black English and standard English. Extensive statistical analysis of speech of 192 Mexican-Americans in San
Antonio, Tex., and 192 Blacks in Niagara Falls, N.Y.

Williams, Frederick, and Rita C. Naremore. *Language and Poverty: An
Annotated Bibliography.* Institute for Research on Poverty, University of Wisconsin, Madison, 1967.

————. "On the Functional Analysis of Social Class Differences in Modes
of Speech." *Speech Monographs,* XXXVI (June, 1969), 77–102.

A study of whether modes of speech can be differentiated in terms
of the functions of language usage when observed within well-
defined speech situations, with samples obtained from the tapes of
the Detroit Dialect Study. Includes analysis of mode of speech characteristics and their correlations with social class differences.

Williams, Frederick, and Edward E. Rundell. "Teaching Teachers to Com-
prehend Negro Nonstandard English." *Speech Teacher,* XX (September, 1971), 174–77.

Describes how teachers can be helped to understand Black English
in the classroom. Also discusses prerequisites to understanding and
communicating effectively with Black English–speaking children.

Williams, Frederick, and G. Wayne Shamo. "Regional Variations in
Teacher Attitudes toward Children's Language." *Central States
Speech Journal,* XXIII (Summer, 1972), 73–77.

Notes significant cultural stereotyping of nonstandard English–
speaking students by both Black and White teachers. Indicates that
even after a very short exposure to the child's language, teachers
will classify Black English speakers as "culturally disadvantaged."

Williams, Frederick, and Jack L. Whitehead. "Language in the Class-
room: Studies of the Pygmalion Effect." *The English Record,* XXI
(April, 1971), 108–13. [Also in Johanna S. DeStefano, ed., *Language,
Society, and Education: A Profile of Black English.* Worthington,
Ohio: Charles A. Jones, 1973. Pp. 169–76.]

Report of study of teachers' attitudes. Finds that some teachers judge speech on the basis of confidence-eagerness and ethnicity-nonstandardness. Also discusses implications of stereotypic rating.

Williams, Frederick, Jack L. Whitehead, and Leslie M. Miller. "Ethnic Stereotyping and Judgements in Children's Speech." *Speech Monographs*, XXXVIII (August, 1971), 166–70.

Speech tapes with film of a child, in profile, assembling a model car. Was tested on forty-four undergraduate education majors to determine the effect of ethnic stereotyping. Included two tapes of White children, one tape of a Black child, one tape of a Mexican-American child. Bias directed toward Black child tended to make him sound more nonstandard than his White peer.

Williams, Frederick, Jack L. Whitehead, and Jane Traupmann. "Teachers' Evaluations of Children's Speech." *Speech Teacher*, XX (November, 1971), 247–54.

Data suggests that teachers stereotype students' abilities by their phonetic speech rather than by content and quality of work presented. Evidence points to racial prejudice by White teachers.

Williams, Frederick, and Barbara Sundene Wood. "Negro Children's Speech: Some Social Class Differences in Word Predictability." *Language and Speech*, XIII (July–September, 1970), 141–50.

Teenage Black girls from a poverty-area school were found to be less able to imitate language samples from girls of a middle-class-area school than the language samples of their peers. By contrast, the middle-class Black girls were able to imitate language samples of both their middle-class peers and lower-class peers.

Williams, Hazel Browne. "A Semantic Study of Some Current, Pejoratively Regarded Language Symbols Involving Negroes in the United States." Doctoral dissertation, New York University, 1953. 350 pp.

Investigation of the role of language in racial conflict.

Williams, John A., Langston Hughes, and LeRoi Jones. "Problems of the Negro Writer." *Saturday Review*, XLVI (April 20, 1963), 19–21, 40.

Three short essays.

Williams, John G. "*De Ole Plantation*": *Elder Coteney's Sermons*. Charleston, S.C.: Evans and Cogswell, 1895. 67 pp.

Fifteen of Brudder Coteney's sermons and two portraits of plantation life. Written in Gullah and originally printed in the Charleston *Weekly News and Courier* and the *Sunday News* in South Carolina. In seven-page preface, author discusses the Gullah language, noting that it is the purest form and most genuine of all "nigger talk."

Williams, Nancy Gilmore. "The Acquisition of Syntax by Middle-Class and Culturally Different Black Children in Grades One, Two, Three, Five, Six, and Eight." Doctoral dissertation, University of Alabama, University, Ala., 1972. 145 pp.

Concludes that grade level and maturity lead to an ability to determine ambiguity in language. Notes correlation with socioeconomic factors.

Williams, Ronald. "Black English, Society, and Education." *Acta Symbolica*, II (Spring, 1971), 8–13.

Urges teacher-recognition of Black English, but notes that it is not the single cause for Black problems in education.

———. "Race and the Word." *Today's Speech*, XIX (Spring, 1971), 27–33.

Notes that problems arise from dialectal differences of Black English and standard English and the failure of educators to recognize Black English as a linguistic system. Suggests that the question really becomes a racial one—many educators feel Black children cannot learn.

Williams, Stephanie A. "Black Talk: Creative Communication." UFAHAMU—*Journal of the African Activist Association*, II (Spring, 1971), 61–67.

Williams, Warren S. "A Study of the Use of the Semantic Differential by Fifth Grade Children from Different Socioeconomic Groups." *Journal of Psychology*, LXXXI (July, 1972), 343–50.

Statistical analysis to investigate a number of assumptions internal to the semantic differential, as applied to Blacks and Whites.

Williamson, Juanita V. "A Look at Black English." *Crisis*, LXXVIII (August, 1971), 169–73, 185.

Discusses the new emphasis on Black English in schools and describes features of Black English and standard English.

———. "A Look at the Direct Question," in Lawrence Davis, ed., *Studies in Linguistics in Honor of Raven I. McDavid, Jr.* University, Ala.: University of Alabama Press, 1972. Pp. 207–14.

Analysis of wh-questions and yes/no questions in Black English, with comparison to literary dialect. Concludes that the features that distinguish Black English are also present in White English in literary novels.

———. "A Note on It Is/There Is," in Juanita V. Williamson and Virginia

M. Burke, eds., *A Various Language: Perspectives on a Theme.* New York: Holt, Rinehart, & Winston, 1971. Pp. 434–36.

———. "On the Subdued Question," in Harold Scholler and John Reidy, eds., *Lexicography and Linguistic Geography: Festschrift for Hans Kurath.* Wiesbaden, Germany: Steinder-Verlag, 1973.

———. "A Phonological and Morphological Study of the Speech of the Negro of Memphis, Tennessee." Doctoral dissertation, University of Michigan, Ann Arbor, 1961. 139 pp. [Also in *Publications of the American Dialect Society,* No. 50 (November, 1968), 1–53 (rev. ed.); Juanita V. Williamson and Virginia M. Burke, eds., *A Various Language: Perspectives on American Dialects.* New York: Holt, Rinehart, & Winston, 1971. Pp. 583–95 (reprint of chapter on morphology).]

A major study of Black speech. Phonemic system found to be similar to other dialects in the South. Morphological differences are primarily due to educational differences, according to the author's conclusions.

———. "Report on a Proposed Study of the Speech of Negro High School Students in Memphis," in Roger W. Shuy, ed., *Social Dialects and Language Learning: Proceedings of the Bloomington, Indiana, Conference, 1964.* Champaign, Ill.: National Council of Teachers of English, 1965. Pp. 23–27.

Brief background of the proposal, including some of the methodology, preliminary data, and linguistic findings.

———. "Selected Features of Speech: Black and White." *CLA Journal,* XIII (June, 1970), 420–23. [Also in Juanita V. Williamson and Virginia M. Burke, eds., *A Various Language: Perspectives on American Dialects.* New York: Holt, Rinehart, & Winston, 1971. Pp. 496–507.]

Comparison of selected features in White and Black languages. Concludes that the features are representative of general southern dialect, rather than racial. Examples are from literature, rather than field interview.

———. *A Study of the Speech of Negro High School Students in Memphis, Tennessee.* Bureau of Research, United States Office of Education, Washington, D.C., 1968. 99 pp.

Phonological and grammatical description of speech of Black high school students in Memphis. Phonological analysis is limited to description of the segmental phonemes, their allophones and incidence. Grammatical analysis is limited to description of parts of speech, the function of words, the major sentence patterns, and the major patterns of modification and coordination.

Williamson, Juanita V., and Virginia M. Burke, eds. *A Various Language: Perspectives on a Theme.* New York: Holt, Rinehart, & Winston, 1971. 706 pp.

Includes five main sections dealing with an overview and introduction to American Black English, historical perspective, literary representation, linguistic analysis, and urban speech studies. Authors for Part 1 ("A Various Language," pp. 3–64) are Fred Newton Scott, Hans Kurath, George Philip Krapp, John S. Kenyon, Haver C. Currie, and Raven I. McDavid, Jr. Authors for Part 2 ("Inherited Features," pp. 69–142) are Thomas Pyles, Archibald A. Hill, Hans Kurath, W. Nelson Francis, Lorenzo D. Turner, and Cleanth Brooks. Authors for Part 3 ("Literary Representations of American English Dialects," pp. 145–241) are Sumner Ives, Paul Hull Bowdre, Jr., W. Edward Farrison, Eric Stockton, Curt M. Rulon, and Ruth M. Blackburn. Authors for Part 4 ("Aspects of Regional and Social Dialects," pp. 245–386) are Hans Kurath, E. Bagby Atwood, Lucia C. Morgan, Robert Howren, Charles C. Thomas, Frank L. La Ban, Arthur Norman, Carmelita Klipple, Lawrence M. Davis, Raven I. McDavid, Jr., and Virginia G. McDavid, Alva L. Davis, Harold B. Allen, and Carroll E. Reed. Authors for Part 5 ("Selected Sounds and Forms," pp. 389–507) are Walter S. Avis, Thomas H. Wetmore, Hans Kurath, E. Bagby Atwood, Juanita V. Williamson, Lewis Levine and Harry J. Crockett, Jr., James H. Sledd, and James B. McMillan. Authors for Part 6 ("Studies of Urban Dialects," pp. 511–659) are Raven I. McDavid, Jr., Lee A. Pederson, David DeCamp, Janet B. Sawyer, Juanita V. Williamson, Robert L. Parslow, Arthur J. Bronstein, and William Labov. Most of the articles are reprints from magazines.

Williamson, Kay. "The Nigerian River Readers Project." *Linguistic Reporter*, XIV (December, 1972), 1–2.

Study of bidialectal program in Nigeria.

Wilson, Kenneth G. See Dean, Leonard F., Walker Gibson, and Kenneth G. Wilson, eds.

Wilson, Marilyn. *Standard Oral English, Seventh Grade: Instructional Guide A.* Los Angeles, Calif.: Los Angeles City Schools, 1967. 135 pp.

Includes tapes and a filmstrip.

Wilson, Robert M. See Grant, Walter N., and Robert M. Wilson.

Wise, C. M. *Applied Phonetics.* New York: Prentice-Hall, 1957. 546 pp.

See especially Chapter 15, "Substandard Southern Negro Speech," pp. 293–302. Recognizes dialects within the broad area of "Black Dialect." Structuralist approach; sees differences as pronunciation, vocabulary, declension, intonation, and voice-quality differences.

————. "Negro Dialect." *Quarterly Journal of Speech*, XIX (November, 1933), 522–28. [Also in J. L. Dillard, ed., *Perspectives on Black English*. The Hague: Mouton, forthcoming.]

Prescribes a sound system for reproducing dialect differences; claims Black and White English have little effect on each other.

Wissot, Jay. "Manipulating Ethnic Pride in an English as a Second Language Class," in Alfred C. Aarons, Barbara Y. Gordon, and William A. Stewart, eds., *Linguistic-Cultural Differences and American Education*, special issue of the *Florida FL Reporter*, VII (Spring/Summer, 1969). Pp. 130, 163.

Recognition of ethnic pride and individual differences is a positive force in teaching English as a second language.

Wolf, Abraham. See Clark, Dennis, Abraham Wolf, Henry Goehl, and Donald Ecroyd.

Wolf-Dietrich, Bald. "The Scope of Negation and Copula Sentences in English." *Journal of English Linguistics*, V (March, 1971), 1–28.

Technical analysis of negation and copula sentences.

Wolfe, Virginia Smith. "The Social Significance of Negro Speech." Doctoral dissertation, Ohio State University, Columbus, 1968. 121 pp.

Presents several conclusions about the social and occupational acceptability of southern Blacks and Whites compared to northern Blacks and Whites.

Wolfram, Walter A. *An Appraisal of ERIC Documents on the Manner and Extent of Nonstandard Dialect Divergence*. ERIC document 034 991. Washington, D.C., December, 1969. 23 pp.

Evaluation of eleven ERIC documents on nonstandard dialects.

————. "Black-White Speech Differences Revisited." *Viewpoints*, XLVII (March, 1971), 27–50. [Also in Walt Wolfram and Nona H. Clarke, *Black-White Speech Relationships*. Washington, D.C.: Center for Applied Linguistics, 1971. Pp. 139–61.]

Concludes there are definite differences between Black speech and White speech of individuals of comparable socioeconomic levels.

————. "Hidden Agendas and Witch Hunts: Which is Witch? A Reply to Bill Stewart." *Florida FL Reporter*, XI (1973).

A stinging rebuttal to William A. Stewart's review of the Wolfram-Clarke book, *Black-White Speech Relationships*, in *Florida FL Reporter*, X (Spring/Fall, 1972), 25. Wolfram points out that Stewart's criticism is, itself, based on sociopolitical motives rather than being a disagreement based on the linguistic evidence. Stewart had charged that the Wolfram-Clarke book was sociopolitically motivated.

———. *Linguistic Assimilation: A Study of Puerto Rican English in New York City.* Arlington, Va.: Center for Applied Linguistics, 1973.

———. "Linguistic Assimilation in the Children of Immigrants." *The Linguistic Reporter*, XIV (February, 1972), 1–3.

Projects findings in Black English studies toward a theory about Puerto Rican English speech.

———. "Linguistic Correlates of Social Differences in the Negro Community," in James E. Alatis, ed., *Report of the Twentieth Annual Roundtable Meeting on Linguistics and Language Studies: Linguistics and the Teaching of Standard English to Speakers of Other Languages or Dialects.* Monograph Series on Languages and Linguistics. Washington, D.C.: Georgetown University Press, 1970. Pp. 249–57.

Discusses need to recognize the wide range of Black English dialects, rather than assuming all are the same.

———. "Linguistic Correlates of Social Stratification in the Speech of Detroit Negroes." Doctoral dissertation, Hartford Seminary Foundation, Hartford, Conn., 1969. 324 pp.

Linguistic analysis of speech of forty-eight Black informants living in Detroit. Includes comparison with speech of twelve upper-class White informants. Describes sociocultural history of the Detroit Black population. Analyzes phonological variables of the postvocalic /-r/, morpheme-medial and final /o/, syllable final /-d/, and the word-final clusters. Includes detailed discussion of the copula in both Black and White speech.

———. "The Nature of Non-Standard Dialect Divergence." *Elementary English*, XLVII (May, 1970), 739–48. [Also in Thomas D. Horn, ed., *Research Bases for Oral Language Instruction.* Urbana, Ill.: National Council of Teachers of English, 1971. Pp. 1–10.]

Evaluates ERIC documents regarding deficiency vs. difference theories.

———. "Objective and Subjective Parameters of Language Assimilation among Second-Generation Puerto Ricans in East Harlem," in Roger

W. Shuy and Ralph W. Fasold, eds., *Language Attitudes: Current Trends and Prospects.* Washington, D.C.: Georgetown University Press, 1973. Pp. 148–73.

Study of cross-cultural assimilation of Black English by Puerto Rican children living in East Harlem, N.Y. Includes descriptive linguistic analysis. Notes hostile attitude toward Black English speech by older generation Puerto Ricans. Includes discussion of sounding.

———. *Overlapping Influence in the English of Second Generation Puerto Rican Teenagers in Harlem. Final Report.* U.S. Office of Education, and ERIC document ED 060 159. Washington, D.C., June, 1972. 460 pp.

Analysis of contiguity of Puerto Rican population within Harlem, N.Y. Includes analysis of assimilation of linguistic features from Black English.

———. "The Relationship of White Southern Speech to Vernacular Black English: Copula Deletion and Invariant *Be.*" Paper presented at the Linguistic Institute, Linguistic Society of America, August, 1973, at the University of Michigan, Ann Arbor. 43 pp.

Report of a study of White speech in Franklin County, Miss., using taped interviews of one hundred informants. Focus of the study is on the zero copula and invariant forms of *be.* Includes discussion of historical development, process of deletion of the copula, and rule ordering. Suggests that White speakers' use of these features is a result of assimilated forms originally found in decreolized Black speech.

———. Review of J. L. Dillard, *Black English: Its History and Usage in the United States. Language,* XLIX (September, 1973), 670–79.

Critical review. Suggests that although Dillard presents an "honest, forthright treatment" of Black English, there is a lack of linguistic evidence to adequately support the basic theory presented. Suggests that Dillard uses a very free latitude in interpretation of primary data.

———. "Social Stigmatizing and the Linguistic Variable in a Negro Speech Community." Paper presented at the annual meeting of the Speech Association of America, December, 1968, at Chicago. 8 pp.

Sociolinguistic analysis and discussion of the linguistic variable.

———. "Sociolinguistic Alternatives in Teaching Reading to Nonstandard Speakers." *Reading Research Quarterly,* VI (Fall, 1970), 9–33. [Also in Johanna S. DeStefano, ed., *Language, Society, and Education: A*

Profile of Black English. Worthington, Ohio: Charles A. Jones, 1973. Pp. 291–311.]

Discusses two major concepts in the teaching of reading. Recommends experimentation with dialect readers.

————. *A Sociolinguistic Description of Detroit Negro Speech.* Washington, D.C.: Center for Applied Linguistics, 1969. 237 pp.

Concludes high correlation of phonological and grammatical variables with social variables of syntax, sex, age, racial isolation, and style in the speech of Detroit Black speakers.

————. *Sociolinguistic Implications for Educational Sequencing.* ERIC document ED 029 281. Washington, D.C., February 28, 1969. 17 pp. [Also in Ralph W. Fasold and Roger W. Shuy, eds., *Teaching Standard English in the Inner City.* Washington, D.C.: Center for Applied Linguistics, 1970. Pp. 105–19; Johanna S. DeStefano, ed., *Language, Society, and Education: A Profile of Black English.* Worthington, Ohio: Charles A. Jones, 1973. Pp. 251–62.]

Suggests five factors that should determine relevancy and order of presentation of standard English dialect to Black English speakers, and presents a sociolinguistic matrix.

————. "Sociolinguistic Perspectives on the Speech of the 'Disadvantaged'." Paper presented at the annual meeting of Speech Association of the Eastern States, April 19, 1969, at New York. 12 pp.

Theoretical examination of basic premises on the nature of language.

————. "Sociolinguistic Premises and the Nature of Nonstandard Dialects." *Speech Teacher,* XIX (September, 1970), 176–84. [Also in Arthur L. Smith, ed., *Language, Communication, and Rhetoric in Black America.* New York: Harper & Row, 1972. Pp. 28–40.]

Overview of Black English in Black society. Discussion of nonstandard dialects and some basic assumptions of sociolinguists.

————. "Some Illustrative Features of Black English." Paper presented at Workshop on Language Differences, February, 1970, at Coral Gables, Fla. 14 pp.

Defines several principles of Black English, including an attempt to "exemplify some general principles concerning the nature of nonstandard dialects" with the chief goal of demonstrating the legitimacy of such dialects and fostering an attitude of respect toward them.

————. "Underlying Representations in Black English Phonology." *Language Sciences,* X (April, 1970), 7–12.

Presents theories of relationship between standard English and Black English, and concludes that the underlying phonological correspondences between Black English and standard English are identical.

————. See Fasold, Ralph W., and Walter A. Wolfram.

————. See Baratz, Joan C., Roger W. Shuy, and Walter A. Wolfram.

————. See Shuy, Roger W., Walter A. Wolfram, and William K. Riley. *Field Techniques in an Urban Language Study.*

————. See Shuy, Roger W., Walter A. Wolfram, and William K. Riley. *Linguistic Correlates of Social Stratification in Detroit Speech.*

Wolfram, Walt and Nona H. Clarke, eds. *Black-White Speech Relationships.* Washington, D.C.: Center for Applied Linguistics, 1971. 161 pp.

Eight papers focusing on dialect research from eight separate time-periods. Includes articles by Lorenzo Dow Turner; Raven I. McDavid, Jr., and Virginia Glenn McDavid; Beryl Bailey; William A. Stewart (two articles); Lawrence M. Davis; David Dalby; and Walter Wolfram.

Wolfram, Walt and Nona H. Clarke, eds. *Black-White Speech Relationships.* Washington, D.C.: Center for Applied Linguistics, 1971. 161 pp.

Discusses obstacles to gaining acceptance for a translation in a dialect which many feel is substandard English. Includes annotations for the passage.

————. *Social Dialects in the United States.* Englewood Cliffs, N.J.: Prentice-Hall, 1974.

Thorough and comprehensive look at American dialects, including Black English. Chapters are "Foundation of Sociolinguistics," "Social Dialects as a Field of Inquiry," "Field Methods—Studies of Social Dialects," "The Social Variable," "The Linguistic Variable," "Social Diagnosis of Phonological Procedures," "Social Diagnosis of Grammatical Features," and "Social Dialects in Education."

————. "Toward Reading Materials for Speakers of Black English: Three Linguistically Appropriate Passages," in Joan C. Baratz and Roger W. Shuy, eds., *Teaching Black Children to Read.* Washington, D.C.: Center for Applied Linguistics, 1969. Pp. 138–55. [Also in Robert H. Bentley and Samuel D. Crawford, eds., *Black Language Reader.* Glencoe, Ill.: Scott, Foresman, 1973. Pp. 172–84.]

Presents three passages which could be used to add a new dialect to the child's linguistic ability while assuring the child that nonstandard speech is appropriate in some situations. Suggests that four factors must be considered in formulating reading materials for speakers of Black English, including recognition of the mismatching of orthography and phonology, language applicability in specific situations, acceptability of the materials to Black people, and acceptability of the materials to educators.

Wolfram, Walter A., and Marcia Whiteman. *The Role of Dialect Interference in Composition.* Washington, D.C.: Center for Applied Linguistics, January, 1971. 27 pp. [Also in *Florida FL Reporter*, IX (Spring/Fall, 1971), 34–38, 59.]

Concludes dialect interference plays an important role in the writing of Black English. Sees a clear distinction between speech and writing and notes that each demands an individual technique.

Wood, Barbara Sundene. "Implications of Psycholinguistics for Elementary Speech Programs." *Speech Teacher*, XVII (September, 1968), 183–92.

Discusses social class differences which affect the language acquisition process in children. Outlines implications for speech education in the early elementary grades and evaluates some of the texts available.

———. See Williams, Frederick, and Barbara Sundene Wood.

Wood, Barbara Sundene, and Julia Curry. "Everyday Talk and School Talk of the City Black Child." *Speech Teacher*, XVIII (November, 1969), 282–96.

Interview conditions found to influence variations in speech related to home environment and demands and to school environment and demands.

Wood, Gordon Reid. "Questionable White Dialects: If Questionable, What Then?" Paper presented to the 60th annual meeting of the National Council of Teachers of English, October 8, 1970, at Atlanta. 21 pp.

Opposes strict use of "standard English" in the classroom. Paper deals primarily with regional dialects.

———. *Sub-Regional Speech Variations in Vocabulary, Grammar, and Pronunciation.* ERIC document ED 019 263. Washington, D.C., 1967. 148 pp.

Discussion of computer analysis of dialect, methodology, and possibilities.

————. *Vocabulary Change: A Study of Variation in Regional Words in Eight of the Southern States.* Carbondale: Southern Illinois University Press, 1970. 392 pp.

Woodward, C. M. "A Word List from Virginia and North Carolina." *Publications of the American Dialect Society*, No. 6 (December, 1946), 1–43.

Includes some Black informants, but most information was collected from White informants.

Woodworth, William D. "Speech Styles as a Factor in Teachers' Evaluation of the Oral Reports of Urban Negro and White Sixth-Grade Children." Doctoral dissertation, State University of New York, Buffalo, 1971. 99 pp.

Statistical analysis reveals high correlation between speech of students and teacher evaluation, with White students receiving higher ratings than Blacks on all variables, although both Black and White students gave identically written reports.

Woodworth, William D., and Richard T. Salzer. "Black Children's Speech and Teachers' Evaluations." *Urban Education*, VI (July/October, 1971), 167–73.

Experimental test data suggests that teachers react negatively toward Black English speech, disregarding both content and quality.

Woofter, T. J., Jr. *Black Yeomanry: Life on St. Helena Island.* New York: H. Holt, 1930. 291 pp.

Description of life in and development of the St. Helena community. Includes comments on dialect of Old England.

Word Lists from the South. Publications of the American Dialect Society, No. 2 (1944). 72 pp.

Eight separate word lists.

Work, John Wesley. *Folk Songs of the American Negro.* Nashville, Tenn.: Press of Fisk University, 1915. 131 pp.

Discusses African origins of Black folk music, and the development of Black folk music within the United States.

Work, Monroe N. *A Bibliography of the Negro in Africa and America.* New York: Octagon Books, 1928. 698 pp.

————. "Geechee Folk-Lore." *Southern Workman*, XXXIV (November–December, 1905), 633, 695.

Wullschlägel, H. R. *Deutsch-Negerenglisches Worterbüch.* Lobau, Germany: J. V. Duroldt, 1856. 339 pp.

    Lexicon of German-to-Surinam Negro-English words, phrases, idioms, and proverbial statements.

————. "Iets Over de Neger-Englische Taal en de Bydragen Tot Hare Ontwikkeling en Literatuur." *West-Indië,* I (1856), 286–95.

————. *Kurzgefasste Neger-Englische Grammatik.* Bautzen, Germany: Ernst Moritz Monse, 1854. 68 pp.

    Description and linguistic analysis of Negro-English of Surinam.

X

X, Malcolm. See Little, Malcolm [Malcolm X].

Y

Yancey, William, and Boone Hammond. *Glossary of Negro Jive.* Social Science Institute, Washington University, St. Louis, Mo., 1965.

Yarborough, Ralph W. "Bilingual Education as a Social Force." *Foreign Language Annual,* II (March, 1969), 325–27.

    Discussion of Bilingual Education Act of 1967, including funding problems, possible amendments.

Yeshiva University Graduate School of Education. *Research Planning Conference on Language Development in Disadvantaged Children, June 7–8, 1966.* Graduate School of Education, Yeshiva University, New York, 1966. 147 pp.

Yetman, Norman R. "The Background of the Slave Narrative Collection." *American Quarterly,* XIX (Fall, 1967), 534–53.

    Review of and analysis of the Slave Narrative Collection developed as a federal writers project.

Z

Zach, Lillian. "The IQ Test: Does It Make Black Children Unequal?" *School Review*, LXXVIII (February, 1970), 249–58.

Zale, Eric M. "The Case Against Bidialectism." Paper presented at the annual TESOL conference, February 28, 1972, at Washington, D.C. 13 pp.

Sharp attack against bidialectism in the schools. Argues that any linguistic description, developed on a basis of social class, is racist. Strongly advocates standard English teaching.

Zarate, Leonore T. See Hubbard, James L., and Leonore T. Zarate.

Zarco, Mariano de. *Dialecto Inglés-Africano: O, Broken-English de la Colonia Española del Golfo de Guinea.* Turnhout, Belgium: H. Proost, 1918? 473 pp.

Study of the syntax and vocabulary of Negro English near Spain.

Zengel, Marjorie Smith. "Literacy as a Factor in Language Change." *American Anthropologist*, LXIV (February, 1962), 132–39.

Suggests that a literate society is more conservative in language than an illiterate society.

Zimmermann, G. P. H. "Het Neger-Englisch in Suriname." *Vragen van den Hag*, XXXVI (1921), 940–45.

Zuck, Louis V., and Yetta M. Goodman. "On Dialects and Reading." *Journal of Reading*, XV (April, 1972), 500–503.

Brief overview of dialect, with pedagogical implications. Lists nine articles of importance to teachers.

————, comps. *Social Class and Regional Dialects: Their Relationship to Reading—an Annotated Bibliography.* Newark, Del.: International Reading Association, 1971.